T0207351

Lecture Notes in Computer Science 13445

More information about this series at https://link.springer.com/bookseries/558

Lucio Tommaso De Paolis · Pasquale Arpaia ·
Marco Sacco (Eds.)

Extended Reality

First International Conference, XR Salento 2022
Lecce, Italy, July 6–8, 2022
Proceedings, Part I

 Springer

Editors
Lucio Tommaso De Paolis 🆔
University of Salento
Lecce, Italy

Pasquale Arpaia 🆔
Università di Napoli Federico II
Naples, Italy

Marco Sacco 🆔
CNR-STIIMA
Lecco, Italy

ISSN 0302-9743 ISSN 1611-3349 (electronic)
Lecture Notes in Computer Science
ISBN 978-3-031-15545-1 ISBN 978-3-031-15546-8 (eBook)
https://doi.org/10.1007/978-3-031-15546-8

This Springer imprint is published by the registered company Springer Nature Switzerland AG
The registered company address is: Gewerbestrasse 11, 6330 Cham, Switzerland

Preface

In recent years, there has been a huge research interest in virtual reality (VR), augmented reality (AR), and mixed reality (MR) technologies that now play a very important role in various fields of application such as medicine, industry, cultural heritage, and education. The boundary between the virtual and real worlds continues to blur, and the constant and rapid spread of applications of these technologies makes it possible to create shortcuts that facilitate the interaction between humans and their environment and to encourage and facilitate the process of recognition and learning.

Virtual reality technology enables the creation of realistic looking worlds and enables users to completely isolate themselves from the reality around them, entering a new digitally created world. User inputs are used to modify the digital environment in real time and this interactivity contributes to the feeling of being part of the virtual world.

Augmented reality and mixed reality technologies, on the other hand, allow the real-time fusion of digital content into the real world to enhance perception by visualizing information that users cannot directly detect with their senses. AR and MR complement reality rather than replacing it completely and the user has the impression that virtual and real objects coexist in the same space.

Extended reality (XR) is an umbrella term encapsulating virtual reality, augmented reality, and mixed reality technologies.

Thanks to the increase in features that allow us to extend our real world and combine it with virtual elements, extended reality is progressively expanding the boundaries of how we live, work, and relate.

The potential of XR technology is amazing and can transform consumers' everyday experiences and generate benefits in many market sectors, from industrial manufacturing to healthcare, education, and retail.

This book contains the contributions to the 1st International Conference on eXtended Reality (XR SALENTO 2022) held during July 6–8, 2022, in Lecce (Italy) and organized by the Augmented and Virtual Reality Laboratory (AVR Lab) at the University of Salento (Italy). To accommodate many situations, XR SALENTO 2022 was scheduled as a hybrid conference, giving participants the opportunity to attend in person or remotely.

The goal of XR SALENTO 2022 was to create a friendly environment leading to the creation or strengthening of scientific collaborations and exchanges between participants and, therefore, to solicit the submission of high-quality original research papers on any aspect and application of virtual reality, augmented reality, or mixed reality.

We received 84 submissions, out of which 58 papers were accepted for publication, 16 of which are short papers. Each submission was reviewed by at least two reviewers. We used the OCS-Unisalento Conferences system for managing the submission and review process. The Scientific Program Committee, with the help of external reviewers, carefully evaluated the contributions considering originality, significance, technical soundness, and clarity of exposition.

We are very grateful to the members of the Scientific Program Committee for their support and time spent in reviewing and discussing the submitted papers and doing so in a timely and professional manner.

We would like to sincerely thank the keynote speakers who gladly accepted our invitation and shared their expertise through enlightening speeches, helping us to fully meet the conference objectives. We were honored to have the following invited speakers:

- Vincenzo Ferrari – University of di Pisa, Italy
- Nicola Masini – CNR, Institute of Cultural Heritage Sciences, Italy
- Christian Sandor – Paris-Saclay University, France

We cordially invite you to visit the XR SALENTO 2022 website (www.xrsalento.it) where you can find all relevant information about this event.

We hope the readers will find in these pages interesting material and fruitful ideas for their future work.

July 2022

Lucio Tommaso De Paolis
Pasquale Arpaia
Marco Sacco

Organization

Conference Chair

Lucio Tommaso De Paolis   University of Salento, Italy

Program Chairs

Pasquale Arpaia   University of Naples Federico II, Italy
Marco Sacco   STIIMA-CNR, Italy

Scientific Program Committee

Andrea Abate	University of Salerno, Italy
Sara Arlati	STIIMA-CNR, Italy
Selim Balcisoy	Sabanci University, Turkey
Sergi Bermúdez i Badia	University of Madeira, Portugal
Monica Bordegoni	Polytechnic University of Milan, Italy
Andrea Bottino	Polytechnic University of Turin, Italy
Pierre Boulanger	University of Alberta, Canada
Andres Bustillo	University of Burgos, Spain
Silvia Mabel Castro	Universidad Nacional del Sur, Argentina
David Checa Cruz	University of Burgos, Spain
Rita Cucchiara	University of Modena, Italy
Yevgeniya Daineko	International Information Technology University, Kazakhstan
Egidio De Benedetto	University of Naples Federico II, Italy
Mariolino De Cecco	University of Trento, Italy
Valerio De Luca	University of Salento, Italy
Giovanni D'Errico	Polytechnic University of Turin, Italy
Giuseppe Di Gironimo	University of Naples Federico II, Italy
Tania Di Mascio	University of L'Aquila, Italy
Aldo Franco Dragoni	Polytechnic University of Marche, Italy
Ugo Erra	University of Basilicata, Italy
Ben Falchuk	Peraton Labs, USA
Vincenzo Ferrari	University of Pisa, Italy
Emanuele Frontoni	Polytechnic University of Marche, Italy
Luigi Gallo	ICAR-CNR, Italy
Carola Gatto	University of Salento, Italy

Fabrizio Lamberti	Polytechnic University of Turin, Italy
Mariangela Lazoi	University of Salento, Italy
Leo Joskowicz	Hebrew University of Jerusalem, Israel
Tomas Krilavičius	Vytautas Magnus University, Lithuania
Vladimir Kuts	Tallinn University of Technology, Estonia
Salvatore Livatino	University of Hertfordshire, UK
Luca Mainetti	University of Salento, Italy
Eva Savina Malinverni	Polytechnic University of Marche, Italy
Matija Marolt	University of Ljubljana, Slovenia
Nicola Masini	CNR, Institute of Cultural Heritage Sciences, Italy
Fabrizio Nunnari	German Research Center for Artificial Intelligence (DFKI), Germany
Tauno Otto	Tallinn University of Technology, Estonia
Üyesi Yasin Ortakci	Karabük University, Turkey
Miguel A. Padilla Castañeda	Universidad Nacional Autónoma de México, Mexico
Volker Paelke	Bremen University of Applied Sciences, Germany
Roberto Paiano	University of Salento, Italy
Giorgos Papadourakis	Technological Educational Institute of Crete, Greece
Alessandro Pepino	University of Naples Federico II, Italy
Eduard Petlenkov	Tallinn University of Technology, Estonia
Roberto Pierdicca	Polytechnic University of Marche, Italy
Sofia Pescarin	CNR ITABC, Italy
Paolo Proietti	MIMOS, Italy
Arcadio Reyes Lecuona	Universidad de Malaga, Spain
Christian Sandor	Paris-Saclay University, France
Andrea Sanna	Polytechnic University of Turin, Italy
Jaume Segura Garcia	Universitat de València, Spain
Huseyin Seker	Birmingham City University, UK
Franco Tecchia	Scuola Superiore Sant'Anna, Italy
Antonio Emmanuele Uva	Polytechnic University of Bari, Italy
Aleksei Tepljakov	Tallinn University of Technology, Estonia
Kristina Vassiljeva	Tallinn University of Technology, Estonia
Krzysztof Walczak	Poznań University of Economics and Business, Poland

Panel Committee

Alessandro Pepino	University of Naples Federico II, Italy
Paolo Proietti	MIMOS, Italy
Ersilia Vallefuoco	University of Naples Federico II, Italy

Award Committee

Lucio Tommaso De Paolis	University of Salento, Italy
Pasquale Arpaia	University of Naples, Italy

Organizing Committee

Ilenia Paladini	University of Salento, Italy
Silke Miss	XRtechnology, Italy

Local Organizing Committee

Silvia Liaci	University of Basilicata, Italy
Laura Corchia	University of Salento, Italy
Sofia Chiarello	University of Salento, Italy
Federica Faggiano	University of Salento, Italy
B. Luigi Nuzzo	University of Salento, Italy
Giada Sumerano	University of Salento, Italy

Keynote Abstracts

Key Note Abstracts

Extend Human Performances with Augmented Reality

Vincenzo Ferrari

Università di Pisa, Italy

AR allows the integration of spatial relation between visible and invisible information under a natural naked eye view. Furthermore, the augmented information could guide the user's hand during precision tasks improving human efficiency and accuracy. This improvement could bring human performance closer to that of the robot with a higher level of flexibility and humanization of the task. For tasks unfeasible with the sole hands, AR becomes particularly useful in robotics applications where the humans are engaged for remote controlling or cooperative working. In current AR displays, the augmentation lacks geometrical coherence along the three dimensions between real and virtual information that determine perceptual issues as wrong spatial, focus, and depth cues for both eyes. These issues will be detailed during the talk and possible solutions will be explained.

Past and Coming 20 Years with Augmented Reality

Christian Sandor

Paris-Saclay University, France

Augmented Reality embeds spatially-registered computer graphics into a user's view of the real world. During the last 20 years, AR has progressed enormously from a niche technology to a widely investigated one. This keynote consists of two parts. First, I speak about how major challenges for AR have been solved over the last 20 years. Second, I speculate about what the next 20 years are going to bring. The goal is to present a Birdseye view of the AR domain, including the balance of power between the major AR forces US and China. In my view, Europe has a very big, possibly almost impossible, challenge ahead to catch up. I hope that my talk will contribute to laying the seeds of a major European AR initiative.

Remote and Close Range Sensing, Imaging and eXtended Reality for the Interpretation and Conservation of Cultural Heritage

Nicola Masini

CNR, Institute of Cultural Heritage Sciences, Italy

Cultural heritage is not only the legacy of tangible and intangible heritage assets of a community inherited from past generations, to be maintained and transmitted to future generations, but it is also a domain of study and research where multidisciplinary skills compare, combine and contaminate each other, stimulating the development of new technologies and methods of analysis and study that can be re-applied in other domains. The reason is due to the heterogeneity of data to be analysed (from historical sources to imaging), phenomena to be observed (from chemical degradation to structural risks), objectives (from safeguarding to conservation). Effective tools to enrich knowledge of Cultural properties are remote and close range sensing, for diagnostic purposes, which provide a number of data on biophysical parameters without any contact with the object/artefact/site to be investigated. However, the heterogeneity of the data and the difficulty of transforming them into useful information for knowledge and conservation of CH, makes it necessary to use tools aimed at facilitating their interpretation. To this end, a useful tool for this purpose is the creation of combined real and virtual environments, i.e. extended reality capable to cover the entire spectrum from "completely real" to "completely virtual" in the concept of reality-virtuality continuum. This approach allows to interrelate data and results of the different diagnostic imaging techniques (from thermal infrared to high frequency georadar) with the spatial and architectural contexts of reference, in its constructive components and materials, facilitating their interpretation to improve the knowledge and to support decisions for restoration.

Contents – Part I

Augmented Reality

eXtended Reality

Contents – Part II

Artificial Intelligence and Machine Learning for eXtended Reality

eXtended Reality in Geo-information Sciences

Industrial eXtended Reality

eXtended Reality in the Digital Transformation of Museums

eXtended Reality Beyond the Five Senses

Virtual Reality

Rehabilitation of Post-COVID Patients: A Virtual Reality Home-Based Intervention Including Cardio-Respiratory Fitness Training

Vera Colombo[1,2]([⊠]), Marta Mondellini[1], Giovanni Tauro[1], Giovanna Palumbo[4], Mauro Rossini[4], Emilia Biffi[5], Roberta Nossa[5], Alessia Fumagalli[6], Emilia Ambrosini[3], Alessandra Pedrocchi[3], Franco Molteni[4], Daniele Colombo[6], Gianluigi Reni[5], Marco Sacco[1], and Sara Arlati[1]

[1] Institute of Intelligent Industrial Technologies and Systems for Advanced Manufacturing, Italian National Research Council, Lecco, Italy
{vera.colombo,marta.mondellini,giovanni.tauro,marco.sacco, sara.arlati}@stiima.cnr.it

[2] Department of Electronics, Information and Bioengineering, Politecnico di Milano, Milan, Italy
veramaria.colombo@polimi.it

[3] Nearlab and WE-COBOT Lab, Department of Electronics, Information, and Bioengineering, Politecnico di Milano, Milan, Italy
{emilia.ambrosini,alessandra.pedrocchi}@polimi.it

[4] Valduce Hospital –Villa Beretta Rehabilitation Center, Costa Masnaga, LC, Italy
{gpalumbo,mrossini,fmolteni}@valduce.it

[5] Scientific Institute, IRCCS E. Medea, Bioengineering Lab, Bosisio Parini, LC, Italy
{emilia.biffi,roberta.nossa,gianluigi.reni}@lanostrafamiglia.it

[6] Scientific Institute, IRCCS INRCA, Casatenovo, LC, Italy
{a.fumagalli,d.colombo}@inrca.it

Abstract. The post-COVID syndrome is emerging as a new chronic condition, characterized by symptoms of breathlessness, fatigue, and decline of neurocognitive functions. Rehabilitation programs that include physical training seem to be beneficial to reduce such symptoms and improve patients' quality of life. Given this, and considering the limitations imposed by the pandemic on rehabilitation services, it emerged the need to integrate telerehabilitation programs into clinical practice. Some telerehabilitation solutions, also based on virtual reality (VR), are available in the market. Still, they mainly focus on rehabilitation of upper limbs, balance, and cognitive training, while exercises like cycling or walking are usually not considered. The presented work aims to fill this gap by integrating a VR application to provide cardio-respiratory fitness training to post-COVID patients in an existing telerehabilitation platform. The ARTEDIA application allows patients to perform a cycling exercise and a concurrent cognitive task. Patients can cycle in a virtual park while performing a "go/no-go" task by selecting only specific targets appearing along the way. The difficulty of the practice can be adjusted by the therapists, while the physiological response is continuously monitored through wearable sensors to ensure safety. The application has been integrated into the VRRS system by Khymeia. In the next months, a study to assess the feasibility

L. T. De Paolis et al. (Eds.): XR Salento 2022, LNCS 13445, pp. 3–17, 2022.
https://doi.org/10.1007/978-3-031-15546-8_1

of a complete telerehabilitation program based on physical and cognitive training will take place. Such a program will combine the existing VRRS exercises and the cardio-respiratory fitness exercise provided by the ARTEDIA application. Feasibility, acceptance, and usability will be assessed from both the patients' and the therapists' sides.

Keywords: Virtual reality · Post-COVID syndrome · Telerehabilitation · Physical exercise · Chronic diseases

1 Introduction

Italy has been severely affected by the SARS-CoV-2 pandemic, which resulted, in 2020, in a reduction of life expectancy by almost one year [1, 2]. COVID-19 spreading has also caused the interruption or the restriction of several clinical services that were not considered essential for the management of the emergency situation: among these, there were all the rehabilitation-related services [3].

Rehabilitation is crucial for chronic patients, as they need to exercise to avoid the further decline of their physical and cognitive abilities and to exclude the occurrence of secondary pathologies [4–6]. COVID-19 itself has contributed to increasing the number of chronic patients: 87% of people requiring hospitalization because of SARS-CoV-2 infection showed persistence of at least one symptom even at 60 days after discharge, even if tested negative at PCR [7]. Post-COVID (or long-COVID) symptoms entail fatigue, breathlessness, cough, pain, headache, joint pain, myalgia and weakness, insomnia, and neurocognitive issues, including memory and concentration problems [8, 9].

First evidence shows that rehabilitation in COVID-19 patients is effective in restoring pulmonary functions, reducing fatigue, and improving quality of life [10]. In particular, pulmonary rehabilitation usually addressed to patients with chronic respiratory diseases, turned out to be potentially beneficial in this new population of patients. Due to the variety of symptoms, rehabilitation in post-COVID patients must be customized and defined by a multidisciplinary team of specialists [11, 12].

Given this, the interruption of rehabilitation services during COVID-19 peaks has thus raised a question about how National Health Systems can invest in new strategies to support rehabilitation and continuity of care [13]. IT technologies may represent a quick and valuable solution, being flexible and available to most of the population worldwide (e.g., smartphones, tablets, and computers). Moreover, they allow administering treatments that are controllable also from remote locations, thus enabling the clinicians to monitor progress over time. IT technologies have also been tested in physical and cognitive rehabilitation programs and have been demonstrated to be well-accepted and motivate patients more than standard therapy [14].

Recently, several telerehabilitation systems have been made available on the market. These systems generally exploit a cloud-based architecture to enable data exchange between the patient and the clinicians and contain a series of exercises that the patient can perform at home. In addition, they often integrate different sensors that allow monitoring the physical activity and enable the generation of a performance report for the therapist. These systems have been validated in studies enrolling patients with mainly neurological, cardiological, and musculoskeletal diseases with positive outcomes [15]. However, most of them address cognitive issues, upper limb and trunk rehabilitation, and balance training. For reasons of safety, training programs aimed at retraining walking, strengthening lower limbs, or improving cardio-respiratory fitness are generally excluded. Nonetheless, the importance of endurance training (walking or cycling) is instead crucial for regaining autonomy in daily life for several groups of chronic patients, especially for post-COVID patients.

To fill this gap, this work presents a solution combining the current state-of-the-art with an innovative VR-based solution allowing for the training of lower limbs and aerobic capacity in a safe way. In detail, we designed and developed a system integrating a cycle-ergometer and a virtual environment allowing for the combined training of physical and cognitive abilities. The use of the cycle-ergometer excludes the risk of tripping and falling that could instead be present when using other devices like treadmills and force boards. Moreover, previous studies have demonstrated this device to be safe even in the case of frail older adults [16].

Such an application has been integrated into a commercial telerehabilitation platform, namely Virtual Reality Rehabilitation System (VRRS) by Khymeia, already including exercises dedicated to cognitive abilities, upper limb, and respiratory functions. In such a way, we obtained several advantages: (i) clinicians will have the chance to adapt the training program according to each specific patients' needs – also including an aerobic and lower limb exercise; (ii) patients can train at home, avoiding the risk of a (re)infection, and more continuously; (iii) patients can be monitored by the therapists, who can also revise the training program.

The remainder of this paper is structured as follow: Sect. 2 presents related works; Sect. 3 presents the rationale and the architecture of the application, together with the devices needed for its functioning; Sect. 4 presents the protocol we design to assess the feasibility of an intervention combining VRRS cognitive and upper limb-dedicated exercises and our virtual environment; Sect. 5 outlines future works and draws the conclusions.

2 Related Work

In recent years, several telerehabilitation platforms, also including VR scenarios, have been presented both in the literature and on the market. In our project, we focused on commercial solutions, already certified as medical devices, that guarantee a high degree of robustness and security, needed to ensure patients' safety and privacy. A first example is represented by MindMotion GO and MindMotion PRO, developed by Mindmaze[1]. These two telehealth solutions, CE-certified and FDA-approved, are designed for patients with mild/moderate to severe neurological diseases. Thanks to the integration with motion tracking devices (Microsoft Kinect and Leap Motion), they allow performing neurorehabilitation exercises for the upper and lower body in the form of serious games. The patients who tried the solutions at home showed clinical outcomes comparable with the standard treatment and a higher awareness of their capabilities. Another

---

[1] Digital therapies for neurorehabilitation: MindMotion, available at: https://mindmaze.com/hea lthcare/mindmotion.

example is the BTS Telerehab[2], a medical platform by BTS Bioengineering, based on a wearable sensor that can be placed on different body districts and allows performing both motor/cognitive rehabilitation exercises and functional evaluation tests connecting to a digital application. The application shows the video image of the patient and overlaps some graphical elements that guide him/her towards a correct execution. It also allows the therapist to connect remotely and access a detailed report on the patient's progress.

A third example is RIABLO[3] system by CoRehab, a medical device composed of wearable sensors and a stabilometric platform that can be adapted to different users, including orthopedic and neurologic patients and individuals with spinal injuries. The system includes a library of serious games for balance training, upper and lower limbs rehabilitation, back pain, and total joints rehabilitation. Finally, the VRRS system[4] by Khymeia, which will be further described in the following section, is a medical device certified Class I, that provides comprehensive rehabilitation and telerehabilitation based on virtual reality.

All of these commercial solutions undergo clinical trials to test their efficacy with different groups of patients, mainly with neurologic, cardiac, orthopedic, and muscle-skeletal disorders. The results of these studies are promising in terms of acceptability, feasibility, and cost-effectiveness and show that telerehabilitation programs are comparable to the standard ones. However, even if some important steps have been done with respect to the past, there is still a need for well-structured procedures to integrate them into the clinical practice.

From the early stages of the COVID-19 pandemic, clinical experts have suggested that exercise may be beneficial for the most frequent clinical manifestations of post-COVID syndrome. Pulmonary rehabilitation protocols, specifically, can be personalized for post-COVID-19 patients, given the similarities in terms of symptoms and possible pathogenic mechanisms with patients with chronic respiratory diseases [17, 18]. The World Health Organization (WHO) stated that both aerobic and strengthening exercises might help patients in increasing fitness, muscle strength, balance, and coordination, reducing breathlessness, and improving confidence and mood. Exercise intensity should be adequate for the specific patient and, therefore, should be carefully defined based on clinical evaluations [19]. Although the scientific evidence is still limited, the literature presents some studies and case reports confirming such assumptions. One of the first studies showed how a structured exercise intervention improved physical function in a group of 33 post-COVID elderly patients. The intervention consisted of 30-min daily multicomponent therapy, including upper and lower limb resistance exercises, endurance training (step, cycle ergometer, or walking), balance exercises, and breathing therapy [20]. Another study presented four cases with different degrees of severity, showing that a physical exercise program based on cardiovascular and pulmonary rehabilitation improved functional capacity in all patients, disregarding the severity of their health

---

[2] BTS Telerehab – Telerehabilitation – Rehabilitation at home as in the clinic, available at: https://www.btstelerehab.com/teleriabilitazione/.

[3] RIABLO – Motivate your patients, measure the movement, available at: https://www.corehab.it/en/riablo-bf/.

[4] Khymeia VRRS – Virtual Reality Rehabilitation System, available at: http://khymeia.com/en/products/vrrs/.

condition [21]. Exercise may be relevant not only to recover physical function but also for cognitive and psychological aspects. Recent findings indicate that post-COVID are, indeed, more likely to manifest cognitive impairment 12 or more weeks after the diagnosis [22]. Despite still-limited evidence, the effects seem more significant in attention and executive functions domains [23]. Therefore, including neuropsychological treatment in post-COVID rehabilitation seems relevant for patients' recovery.

Given its relevance, several clinical and scientific communities have already made several efforts to propose engaging and effective training based on cycling. Augmenting cycling with VR has proven feasible and effective in improving patients' motivation, also acting as a distraction from the perceived physical effort [24–26]. Both aspects contribute to improving exercise tolerance and, consequently, the treatment compliance that, especially for chronic patients, is often a critical issue.

Past experiences of our research group, CNR-STIIMA, demonstrate how training on an ergometer with a VR system simulating a ride in a park is a feasible and promising solution for different groups of patients. The first example is a VR-based intervention, including physical training on the cycle-ergometer and cognitive training in a virtual supermarket. The intervention, tested in a group of older adults with Mild Cognitive Impairment, resulted effective in reducing some physiological markers of neural decline and was largely accepted by all the participants in the intervention groups, who reported to have enjoyed this innovative training program and to feel better after its conclusion [27]. A more immersive version, based on a CAVE and integrating a cognitive task, was proposed to a group of frail elderly to assess its usability; such an experience demonstrated acceptable, involving, and free from any side effects [16]. Another study presented an adaptation of the virtual park for endurance training in pulmonary rehabilitation. The usability and acceptability of the system were tested on 8 patients with respiratory diseases, who found the VR motivating and a positive distraction from the feelings of fatigue and breathlessness caused by the exercise [28]. Our system can be interfaced with different VR devices (e.g., HMD, projected screen, CAVE), integrates various sensors (e.g., heart rate bands and pulse-oximeters), and implements different training protocols. These features are adapted depending on the context of use and the target users, thus allowing a high degree of personalization. This modularity opens the possibility to provide a useful tool also for patients recovering from COVID-19.

3   ARTEDIA Application

The application developed within the presented project, namely ARTEDIA, consists of a virtual reality (VR) environment supporting aerobic/lower limb training. Such an application has been integrated in the Khymeia platform to make it available for patients using their VRRS system.

Given the potential offered by the VR technology, we also added a cognitive exercise to perform concurrently. The rationale of this choice is two-fold: (i) to train post-COVID patients' cognitive abilities, which may also be impaired; (ii) to distract – at least partially – the persons from the physical effort they are doing by providing them with an engaging task shifting the attention away from the physical sensations [24, 29]. The application presented in this work is integrated into the VRRS system by Khymeia to allow the delivery of a complete telerehabilitation intervention.

3.1 Equipment

Fig. 1. Diagram of the ARTEDIA system integrated in the VRRS platform.

The equipment of ARTEDIA project comprises a VR-based system for cycling training and the VRRS telerehabilitation system. A diagram of the whole system is represented in Fig. 1.

The VRRS system, developed by Khymeia, offers different rehabilitation modules, each providing specific functionality, e.g., cognitive, speech therapy, neuromotor, respiratory, orthopedic exercises, both in the form of serious games and with a virtual assistant. Some studies demonstrated how rehabilitation with VRRS is equivalent to the standard intervention on different groups of patients, e.g., people with brain injury or patients with aphasia [30, 31]. The system's modularity allows the use in the clinic and at home.

In the case of telerehabilitation, the system is composed of the Telecockpit and the VRRS Home Tablet. The first is a desktop application installed at the hospital that allows the therapist to configure the rehabilitation plan for the specific patient by setting specific parameters for each exercise, e.g., the duration, the number of repetitions, the level of difficulty, etc. It also allows controlling patients' performance remotely, both directly interacting with them and visualizing the report generated by the platform. The VRRS Home Tablet is a Windows-based tablet (i.e., Microsoft Surface laptop) through which the patient follows the prescribed rehabilitation plan. Thanks to the integration with one or more external devices, the patient receives real-time feedback and directly interacts with the virtual contents. The communication between the Telecockpit and the Home Tablet occurs via a web cloud platform.

The main components of the VR cycling system, which has been integrated into the VRRS, are a cycle-ergometer, a button for the execution of the cognitive task, and one or more wearable sensors for measuring the physiological response.

The ergometer is a certified medical device by COSMED[5], which is connected through a serial cable to our application. The ergometer receives signals from two wearable devices: an Ergoline chest band to measure heart rate (HR) and a finger pulse oximeter to detect oxygen saturation level (SpO_2). The latter is required for those patients who suffer from respiratory deficits to control exercise-induced desaturation. The data exchange between the ergometer and the VR environment is handled within Unity

---

[5] COSMED ergometers, available at: https://www.cosmed.com/it/prodotti/ergometri/cicloergo metri-cosmed.

through an ad-hoc communication protocol that allows retrieving the cycling speed, the HR, and the SpO_2 and controlling the workload to adjust the exercise intensity.

The ergometer is connected via cable to a USB port of the tablet. A Puck.js button[6] communicates via Bluetooth with the ARTEDIA application through a library provided by Khymeia. To ensure patient safety and ease the interaction with the button and the VR environment, ad-hoc support has been 3D-printed.

The VR environment application, presented in Sect. 3.2, has been installed on the Home Tablet to be retrievable when launched from the VRSS system.

3.2 Exercise

As mentioned, the VR environment is designed to support both physical and cognitive tasks. It has been developed with Unity exploiting existing assets (i.e., Gaia[7], Curvy Spline[8]) and integrating the functionalities to make it available in the VRRS Khymeia platform.

The environment represents a park in which the patient travels while cycling; the forward velocity in the VR environment is synchronized according to cycle-ergometer currently-measured RPMs. The path to follow in the park is predefined and has been designed placing nodes along the path, which are subsequently interpolated with a spline.

The implemented cognitive exercise foresees the accomplishment of a "go/no-go" task, meaning that the patient has to react when a "go" target appears and do nothing when a "no-go" target does. In our application, go targets are represented by monsters, while no-go targets are animals; both are randomly instanced at runtime on either side of the path. During the exercise, patients have to press the button each time a monster appears alongside their path. To handle the selection of targets, we implemented a trigger collider (i.e., an object able to detect collisions but with no physical properties) that moves along with the virtual bike. Targets are selectable only if they are within the volume of such an object. Each time the patient presses the button, the target disappears, and visual feedback is provided showing if the reaction was due or not (Fig. 2). In case of a missed target, no feedback is provided.

To allow the therapists to customize the task according to the patients' needs, different parameters can be configured within ARTEDIA application; these are:

- Level of difficulty of the cognitive exercise (1–2–3): by adjusting this value, therapists could set how frequently the target is generated and if and how it is highlighted (Fig. 3). In level 1, targets appear every 15 s, go targets are highlighted in red, and no-go targets in green; in level 2, targets appear every 12 s and are all highlighted in the same way; in level 3, targets are generated every 10 s, and no highlight is provided.

---

[6] Puck.js - the JavaScript Bluetooth Beacon, available at: https://www.puck-js.com/.

[7] Gaia Pro 2021 - Terrain & Scene Generator by Procedural Worlds, available at: https://assets tore.unity.com/packages/tools/terrain/gaia-pro-2021-terrain-scene-generator-193476.

[8] Curvy Spline by ToolBuddy, available at: https://assetstore.unity.com/packages/tools/utilities/curvy-splines-8-212532.

Fig. 2. Feedback for the wrong and the correct answers.

Fig. 3. Go target, level 1 (left); go target, level 2 (center); no-go target, level 3 (right).

- Cycle-ergometer workload (30–40–50–60–70 W);
- Maximum heart rate (HR): this represents a safety threshold; if the measured HR overcomes and stays over this value for 10 s, the exercise is automatically interrupted.
- Minimum oxygen saturation (SpO$_2$): this represents a safety threshold; if the measured SpO$_2$ decreases and stays below this value for 10 s, the exercise is automatically interrupted.
- Exercise duration (10–15–20 min).

The velocity to keep during the exercise is fixed and in between 60 and 70 RPM.

A graphical user interface (GUI) is displayed during the exercise to show the patients all the relevant exercise-related variables. Given the context of use, i.e., at home with no supervision of the clinical personnel, this is an important feature to ensure the patients and their caregivers are always aware of the situation and physiological parameters, in particular. The GUI is also used to communicate errors of different types, such as: (i) cycle-ergometer absence or incorrect setup resulting in an impossible communication with the environment; (ii) lack of signals from the HR and/or the SpO$_2$ sensors; (iii) too low velocity during the exercise. To be clear and avoid misunderstandings, all these error messages are given via written text (Fig. 4).

Fig. 4. A screenshot of the ARTEDIA environment. At the top of the screen, written text signals that the current velocity is too slow. Other indicators report (from the top to the bottom): HR and SpO2 values, RPMs, remaining time, and number of correctly-selected targets.

All the configuration parameters are made available to the therapists via the VRRS Khymeia dashboard running on the Telecockpit and are subsequently configured in the ARTEDIA application each time a patient launches it on his/her Home Tablet. Therapists have also access to the performance data that are stored during the course of the exercise. These are correct answers (selected go targets, not selected no-go targets), errors (not selected go target, selected no-go targets), average speed, average HR, and SpO$_2$.

4 Feasibility Study

Given the innovativeness of the proposed intervention, we designed a study to evaluate its feasibility both for patients and for the clinical personnel. In fact, as mentioned before, this approach could positively impact on QoL of patients, who can benefit from continuity of care, and also on therapists who can provide assistance to more patients at the same time.

Indeed, the study aims to assess these two aspects rather than the clinical effectiveness of the intervention. About the study outcomes, we expect that if patients perceive the system as meaningful and usable, their attitude toward new technologies and their willingness to use the system in daily life will improve. The same is worthy for the clinical personnel, who need to comprehend and acquire confidence with the paradigm of home-based rehabilitation prior to implementing it in the standard practice. To verify whether the latter results are generalizable to different contexts, the study we designed is multi-centric and foresees the participation of three clinics in Lombardy: (i) Ospedale Valduce, Clinica di Riabilitazione Villa Beretta, (ii) IRRCS E. Medea – La Nostra Famiglia, and (iii) IRCCS INRCA. The study protocol has obtained clearance by the medical ethical committees of the three involved centers.

4.1 Participants

The feasibility of the rehabilitation intervention will be carried out involving a number of patients between 30 and 35 enrolled among the patients of the involved clinics. Sample size calculation was made considering the Attitude toward Technology Questionnaire developed Huygelier et al. [32] as the main outcome (effect size: 0.69, $\alpha = 0.05$, power $= 0.9$).

The high degree of personalization of the treatment, the continuous monitoring of the patient with the possibility of changes in the rehabilitation protocol, and the opportunity to perform the training at home allowed proposing this telerehabilitation program not only to post-COVID patients but also to other populations of users who may benefit from a home-based program including lower limb and cardio-respiratory training. For example, further users can be: patients with respiratory diseases in which aerobic and muscular exercises are strongly recommended [33], post-stroke patients who need to train the lower limbs and perform cognitive training [34], and young people with neuromotor pathologies for which pedaling can have beneficial effects [35, 36].

Thus, we will include patients over 12 years old who have respiratory issues due to COVID-19 or other pathologies (e.g., COPD), or with either congenital or acquired neuromuscular disorders, and who may benefit – according to their therapist – from a multidisciplinary home-based motor and cognitive intervention. All the enrolled patients have to be settled in the Lombardy region and have at least one caregiver who can provide informal assistance during the home-rehabilitation period. Moreover, all participants or their legal tutors (in case of underage) have to sign an informed consent form.

Exclusion criteria will be: chronic pain, tracheostomy or need of oxygen therapy for more than 18 h a day, severe cognitive, sensory, or motor impairment preventing the person from making use of the provided equipment and/or performing a moderate physical effort; severe communication deficits, dysmetria, renal insufficiency, or hepatic insufficiency; history of epilepsy and contraindication of their therapist.

4.2 Protocol

The telerehabilitation program is made the following phases:

1. **Undertaking the patient.** The telerehabilitation program is offered to patients who meet the inclusion criteria described above and their caregivers during the hospitalization or at its end. Patients sign the informed consent.
2. **The Individual Rehabilitation Program (PRI) is defined**. A personalized training program is proposed after the evaluation of the patient's baseline through ad-hoc clinical scales. The program could include both functional-motor and cognitive exercises available on the Khymeia platform (including ARTEDIA application) such as:

(i) upper or lower limb motor control; (ii) trunk stability and balance, (iii) speech therapy; (iv). training attention and memory.

3. **Patient and caregiver training.** The patient and his/her care-given are invited to the clinic of reference to be informed about the system functionalities. A training session with the VRSS laptop and the cycle-ergometer is performed under the supervision of a therapist. Also, documentation about the telerehabilitation program is provided to users.

4. **Delivery of technological equipment.** The cycle-ergometer is installed at home and the correct functioning of the system is verified.

5. **Execution of the rehabilitation program and monitoring.** The patient is monitored remotely, thus allowing clinicians to manage and eventually modify the exercises. The intervention program lasts 4 weeks: users will exercise 5 days a week for 1 h; training can be divided into 2 sessions of 30 min, both to facilitate compliance and adapt to the patient's lifestyle while maintaining the overall intensity of the treatment. Each session will include a set of – cognitive and/or motor – exercises tailored to the needs of each patient.

A teleconsultation session is scheduled every 8 days with the therapist in charge of the patient's treatment to review his progress and check the performance of exercises; in this way, the therapist could redefine the rehabilitation program if necessary.

6. **Results.** A personal report is created using measurements obtained during the entire duration of the treatment.

7. **Analysis.** Data collected from patients and from the therapists involved in the study are analyzed to identify the strengths and weaknesses of the approach and to design guidelines for future telerehabilitation interventions.

4.3 Measures

As mentioned, the main study outcome is the attitude towards technology and how it will change in the users who will use the telerehabilitation program. For this purpose, users will be asked to fill in the Attitude Questionnaire before and after the intervention (Huygelier et al. 2019).

Some scales will be proposed at the baseline to evaluate if the participants suit the defined inclusion criteria; these are: (i) Visual Analogue Scale for Pain - VAS Pain [37]; (ii) Trunk Control Test [38], to assess trunk stability; and (iii) Mini Mental State Examination [39] to evaluate cognitive function. For patients with respiratory issues, a simple spirometry test will be performed, and the following scales will be administered: (iv) Dyspnea scale (Modified British Medical Research Council questionnaire, mMRC [40]); (v) 6-min walk test (6MWT) [41]; (vi) Short Physical Performance Battery (SPPB) [42]. Lower limb functions will be assessed with sensorized pedals allowing to retrieve the work produced by the two legs, mechanical effectiveness and symmetry indexes [43].

At the end of the training program, in addition to the Attitude Questionnaire, the following outcomes will also be assessed for each patient: (i) the overall workload necessary to complete the rehabilitation program, with NASA Task Load Index (NASA-TLX, [44]), (ii) the usability of the system, with System Usability Scale (SUS, [45]) and (iii) the acceptance of the technological system using a questionnaire based on the Technological Acceptance Model [46].

Finally, after the six months dedicated to the study execution, a semi-structured interview will be proposed to therapists who assisted the patients throughout the telere-habilitation program to evaluate usability, acceptance, and personal opinion about this technical proposal.

5 Conclusions and Future Work

This work presents a virtual reality-based application developed to support physical and cognitive rehabilitation in chronic patients. In particular, the ARTEDIA application has been integrated into an existing telerehabilitation platform to allow the delivery of a customized training program at home. Though it has been conceived to treat post-COVID patients, its use can be extended to other patients who can benefit from continuity of care.

We also present the feasibility study we designed to assess the feasibility of such an intervention, which will foresee the creation of a customized training program including both our applications and the one that Khymeia already provided within their platform (i.e., application for cognitive, upper limb, and respiratory training).

In the next months, the study will start with the enrolment of the patients in the three clinics. If the study has a positive impact both for patients and their therapists, larger trials are recommended to better assess the clinical effectiveness of the proposed interventions. These trials will also pave the way to define a roadmap for the implementation of home-based rehabilitation as part of the standard care recognized by the Regional and the National Health systems.

Acknowledgments. The authors would like to acknowledge the support of Khymeia Group for the integration of the presented virtual reality-based application in their platform. This work has been funded by Fondazione Cariplo within the project "Applicazione della tele-Riabilitazione come sTrumEnto DI continuità di curA (ARTEDIA)".

References

1. Ceylan, Z.: Estimation of COVID-19 prevalence in Italy, Spain, and France. Sci. Total Environ. **729**, 138817 (2020). https://doi.org/10.1016/j.scitotenv.2020.138817
2. Aburto, J.M., et al.: Quantifying impacts of the COVID-19 pandemic through life-expectancy losses: a population-level study of 29 countries. Int. J. Epidemiol. **51**(1), 63–74 (2022). https://doi.org/10.1093/ije/dyab207
3. Lugo-Agudelo, L.H., et al.: Adaptations to rehabilitation services during the COVID-19 pandemic proposed by scientific and professional rehabilitation organizations. J. Rehabil. Med. **53**(9), jrm00228 (2021). https://doi.org/10.2340/16501977-2865
4. Koch, S.J., Arego, D.E., Bowser, B.: Outpatient rehabilitation for chronic neuromuscular diseases. Am. J. Phys. Med. **65**(5), 245–257 (1986)
5. Salman, G.F., Mosier, M.C., Beasley, B.W., Calkins, D.R.: Rehabilitation for patients with chronic obstructive pulmonary disease. J. Gener. Int. Med. **18**(3), 213–221 (2003)
6. Aprile, I., et al.: Effects of rehabilitation on quality of life in patients with chronic stroke. Brain Inj. **22**(6), 451–456 (2008). https://doi.org/10.1080/02699050802060639

7. Carfi, A., Bernabei, R., Landi, F.: Persistent symptoms in patients after acute COVID-19. JAMA - J. Am. Med. Assoc. **324**(6), 602–603 (2020)
8. Raveendran, A.V., Jayadevan, R., Sashidharan, S.: Long COVID: an overview. Diabetes Metab. Syndr. Clin. Res. Rev. **15**(3), 869–875 (2021). https://doi.org/10.1016/j.dsx.2021. 04.007
9. Lopez, S.: More than 50 long-term effects of COVID-19: a systematic review and meta-analysis (1914)
10. Wise, J.: Long covid: WHO calls on countries to offer patients more rehabilitation. BMJ. **372**, n405 (2021). https://doi.org/10.1136/bmj.n405
11. Lemhöfer, C., et al.: Assessment of rehabilitation needs in patients after COVID-19: development of the COVID-19-rehabilitation needs survey. J. Rehabil. Med. **53**(4), jrm00183 (2021). https://doi.org/10.2340/16501977-2818
12. Wang, T.J., Chau, B., Lui, M., Lam, G.T., Lin, N., Humbert, S.: Physical medicine and rehabilitation and pulmonary rehabilitation for COVID-19. Am. J. Phys. Med. Rehabil. **99**(9), 769–774 (2020). https://doi.org/10.1097/PHM.0000000000001505
13. Sheehy, L.M.: Considerations for postacute rehabilitation for survivors of COVID-19. JMIR Public Heal. Surveill. **6**(2), e19462 (2020). https://doi.org/10.2196/19462
14. Tieri, G., Morone, G., Paolucci, S., Iosa, M.: Virtual reality in cognitive and motor rehabilitation: facts, fiction and fallacies. Expert Rev. Med. Devices **15**(2), 107–117 (2018). https://doi.org/10.1080/17434440.2018.1425613
15. Portaro, S., et al.: Telemedicine for Facio-Scapulo-humeral muscular dystrophy: a multidisciplinary approach to improve quality of life and reduce hospitalization rate? Disabil. Health J. **11**(2), 306–309 (2018)
16. Jimeno-Almazán, A., et al.: Post-covid-19 syndrome and the potential benefits of exercise. Int. J. Environ. Res. Public Health. **18**(10), 5329 (2021). https://doi.org/10.3390/ijerph181 05329
17. Demeco, A., et al.: Rehabilitation of patients post-COVID-19 infection: a literature review. J. Int. Med. Res. **48**(8), 1–10 (2022). https://doi.org/10.1177/0300060520948382
18. World Health Organization: Support for Rehabilitation Self-Management after COVID-19-Related Illness (2021)
19. Udina, C., Ars, J., Morandi, A., Vilaró, J., Cáceres, C., Inzitari, M.: Rehabilitation in adult post-COVID-19 patients in post-acute care with therapeutic exercise. J. Frailty Aging **10**(3), 297–300 (2021). https://doi.org/10.14283/jfa.2021.1
20. Tozato, C., Ferreira, B.F.C., Dalavina, J.P., Molinari, C.V., Dos Santos Alves, V.L.: Cardiopulmonary rehabilitation in post-COVID-19 patients: case series. Rev. Bras. Ter. Intensiva. **33**(1), 167–171 (2021). https://doi.org/10.5935/0103-507X.20210018
21. Ceban, F., et al.: Fatigue and cognitive impairment in Post-COVID-19 syndrome: a systematic review and meta-analysis. Brain. Behav. Immun. **101**, 93–135 (2022). https://doi.org/10.1016/ j.bbi.2021.12.020
22. Daroische, R., Hemminghyth, M.S., Eilertsen, T.H., Breitve, M.H., Chwiszczuk, L.J.: Cognitive impairment after COVID-19—a review on objective test data. Front. Neurol. **12**, 699582 (2021). https://doi.org/10.3389/fneur.2021.699582
23. Baños, R.M., et al.: "Using virtual reality to distract overweight children from bodily sensations during exercise. Cyberpsychol. Behav. Soc. Netw. **19**(2), 115–119 (2016). https://doi. org/10.1089/cyber.2015.0283
24. Hoeg, E.R., Bruun-Pedersen, J.R., Serafin, S.: Virtual reality-based high-intensity interval training for pulmonary rehabilitation: a feasibility and acceptability study. In: Proceedings of 2021 IEEE Conference Virtual Reality 3D User Interfaces Abstract Work. VRW 2021, pp. 242–249 (2021). https://doi.org/10.1109/VRW52623.2021.00052
25. Mestre, D.R., Ewald, M., Maiano, C.: Virtual reality and exercise: behavioral and psychological effects of visual feedback. Stud. Health Technol. Inform. **167**, 122–127 (2011)

26. Mrakic-Sposta, S., et al.: Effects of combined physical and cognitive virtual reality-based training on cognitive impairment and oxidative stress in MCI patients: a pilot study. Front. Aging Neurosci. **10**, 282 (2018)
27. Pedroli, E., et al.: Characteristics, usability, and users experience of a system combining cognitive and physical therapy in a virtual environment: positive bike. Sensors (Switzerland) **18**(7), 2343 (2018). https://doi.org/10.3390/s18072343
28. Colombo, V., Mondellini, M., Gandolfo, A., Fumagalli, A., Sacco, M.: Usability and acceptability of a virtual reality-based system for endurance training in elderly with chronic respiratory diseases. In: Bourdot, P., Interrante, V., Nedel, L., Magnenat-Thalmann, N., Zachmann, G. (eds.) Virtual Reality and Augmented Reality. LNCS, vol. 11883, pp. 87–96. Springer, Cham (2019). https://doi.org/10.1007/978-3-030-31908-3_6
29. Secoli, R., Milot, M.H, Rosati, G., Reinkensmeyer, D.J.: Effect of visual distraction and auditory feedback on patient effort during robot-assisted movement training after stroke. J. Neuroeng. Rehabil. **8**(1), 21 (2011). https://doi.org/10.1186/1743-0003-8-21
30. Calabrò, R.S., et al.: Telerehabilitation in individuals with severe acquired brain injury rationale, study design, and methodology. Med. (United States). **97**(50), e13292 (2018). https://doi.org/10.1097/MD.0000000000013292
31. Maresca, G., et al.: Toward improving poststroke aphasia: a pilot study on the growing use of telerehabilitation for the continuity of care. J. Stroke Cerebrovasc. Dis. **28**(10), 104303 (2019). https://doi.org/10.1016/j.jstrokecerebrovasdis.2019.104303
32. Huygelier, H., Schraepen, B., Van Ee, R., Vanden Abeele, V., Gillebert, C.R.: Acceptance of immersive head-mounted virtual reality in older adults. https://doi.org/10.1038/s41598-019-41200-6
33. Zeng, Y., Jiang, F., Chen, Y., Chen, P., Cai, S.: Exercise assessments and trainings of pulmonary rehabilitation in COPD: a literature review. Int. J. COPD **13**, 2013–2023 (2018)
34. Langhorne, P., Bernhardt, J., Kwakkel, G.: Stroke rehabilitation. Lancet **377**(9778), 1693–1702 (2011)
35. Armstrong, E.L., Spencer, S., Kentish, M.J., Horan, S.A., Carty, C.P., Boyd, R.N.: Efficacy of cycling interventions to improve function in children and adolescents with cerebral palsy: a systematic review and meta-analysis. Clin. Rehabil. **33**(7), 1113–1129 (2019). https://doi.org/10.1177/0269215519837582
36. Barclay, A., Paul, L., MacFarlane, N., McFadyen, A.: The effect of cycling using active-passive trainers on spasticity, cardiovascular fitness, function and quality of life in people with moderate to severe Multiple Sclerosis (MS); a feasibility study. Mult. Scler. Relat. Disord. **34**, 128–134 (2019)
37. Manfredini, D., et al.: Measures of adult pain: visual Analog scale for pain (VAS Pain), numeric rating scale for pain (NRS Pain), McGill pain questionnaire (MPQ), Short-Form McGill pain questionnaire (SF-MPQ), Chronic pain grade scale (CPGS), Short Form-36 Bodily Pain Scale (SF). Int. J. Prosthodont. **120**(4), 678–685 (2017)
38. Wade, D.T., Collin, C.: The Barthel ADL index. Int. Disabil. Stud. **10**(2), 1–2 (1988)
39. Folstein, M.F., Folstein, S.E., McHugh, P.R.: Mini-mental state: a practical method for grading the cognitive state of patients for the clinician. J. Psychiatr. Res. **12**(3), 189–198 (1975)
40. Agarwal, R., et al.: Global strategy for the diagnosis, management, and prevention of chronic obstructive pulmonary disease. COPD J. Chronic Obstr. Pulm. Dis. **8**(5), 1463–1474 (2020)
41. Bs. physical therapy Solway Sherra MSc candidate, Ms. Bs. physical therapy Brooks Dina PhD, Ms. Lacasse Yves MD, and Ms. Bs. Thomas Scott Ph.D. A Qualitative Systematic Overview of the Measurement Properties of Functional Walk Tests Used in the Cardiorespiratory Domain. Chest. **119**(1), 256–270 (2001)
42. Volpato, S., et al.: Predictive value of the short physical performance Battery following hospitalization in older patients. J. Gerontol. Ser. Biol. Sci. Med. Sci. **66**(1), 89–96 (2011). https://doi.org/10.1093/gerona/glq167

43. Ambrosini, E., Parati, M., Peri, E., et al.: Changes in leg cycling muscle synergies after training augmented by functional electrical stimulation in subacute stroke survivors: a pilot study. J NeuroEng. Rehabil. **17**, 35 (2020). https://doi.org/10.1186/s12984-020-00662-w
44. Hart, S.G.: NASA-task load index (NASA-TLX); 20 years later. Proc. Hum. Factors Ergon. Soc. **50**, 904–908 (2006). https://doi.org/10.1177/154193120605000909
45. Brooke, J.: SUS: a quick and dirty usability scale (1996)
46. Venkatesh, V., Bala, H.: Technology acceptance model 3 and a research agenda on interventions. Decis. Sci. **39**(2), 273–315 (2008)

Comparison of the Effect of Exposing Users for Height While Being Active Versus Passive in a Virtual Environment - A Pilot Study

Günter Alce[✉] [iD], Felicia Hanserup, and Kornelia Palm

Lund University, Lund, Sweden
Gunter.Alce@design.lth.se

Abstract. Phobias have historically and evolutionary been vital for humans to escape quickly or fight in dangerous situations. The anxieties that phobias evoke have made people live longer. Evolutionarily, anxiety has been good, but fear and anxiety come in unjustified situations for the civilized population in the 21st century. Some people have an extra sensitive reaction system activated too often in irrelevant contexts. More than 10% of Sweden's population has some phobia. However, only a few persons search for help to overcome their phobias, partly because they know they have to be exposed to their phobia to overcome it. An alternative exposure treatment is using virtual reality (VR). Recently, we have seen an intensified development of VR headsets such as HTC Vive and Oculus Quest. These headsets come with relatively high display resolution and great tracking of the hand controllers, which opens up opportunities to develop and evaluate more immersive interactive virtual environments that can be used, e.g., for exposure treatment.

This paper presents two VR prototypes developed and evaluated using the new generation of VR technology. The two VR prototypes were then compared in a user study with 22 participants exposed to height while being active versus being passive.

The main contribution of this paper is to elucidate knowledge about the experiment of comparing AE versus PE of heights.

Keywords: Virtual reality · Exposure treatment · Acrophobia

1 Introduction

Are you or someone close to you afraid of spiders, snakes, darkness, heights, or flying? Then you are not alone because only in Sweden more than 10% of the population suffers, has suffered or will at some point suffer from a specific phobia [8]. Phobias have historically and evolutionary been vital for humans to escape quickly or fight in dangerous situations [14]. The anxieties that phobias

Supported by JayWay Development.

evoke have made people live longer, but fear and anxiety can come in unjustified situations for the civilized population in the 21st century. For these people, fear becomes an obstacle and so excessive that it can lead to avoidance or escape. If this happens, it is said that the person has developed a phobia. Phobias are treated through cognitive-behavioral therapy (CBT) by exposing the patient to anxiety-producing stimuli while allowing anxiety to attenuate [1, 22, 27]. However, very few seek help to overcome their phobias because they are aware that they must be exposed to their fear to overcome their phobias. Using virtual reality (VR), a technology that can create computer-generated environments, is an alternative way to be exposed to your fears. The use of VR has become more and more common in the past few years, thanks to the availability of low-cost head-worn devices, such as the Oculus Quest or HTC Vive [10]. Moreover, VR enables to immerse a user into a virtual environment (VE) and reproduce situations that could be dangerous in reality in a safe way. VR has therefore been used as a tool for a few decades in many different domains, including architecture, city planning, behavior studies, education/training in the industry, and as a therapy to treat other phobias [9, 10]. One major reason why VR is used for exposure treatment is that patients are willing to go into situations that trouble them and try alternative ways of responding because they know it is a simulation [13]. VR simulations are easier to face compared to facing fears in real life, but they still reproduce anxiety upon exposure of, e.g., heights [20]. A common measure of the quality of effectiveness of a VR is the amount of presence it evokes in users [20]. According to Slater [25], presence includes three aspects:

- The sense of "being there" in the environment depicted by the VE.
- The extent to which the VE becomes the dominant one, that is, that the participant will tend to respond to events in the VE rather than in the "real world."
- The extent to which participants after the VE experience remember it as having visited a "place" rather than just having seen images generated by a computer.

According to Meehan et al. [20], a higher sense of presence evokes higher anxiety in a VE. Therefore, an important parameter to consider. The newer VR headsets such as HTC Vive and Oculus Rift come with relatively high display resolution and great tracking of the hand controllers. This opens up opportunities to develop and evaluate more immersive interactive virtual environments, e.g., exposure treatment.

This paper compares active exposure (AE) versus passive exposure (PE) to heights in VR.

The main contribution of this paper is to elucidate knowledge about the experiment of comparing AE versus PE of heights.

The following section presents relevant related work that has previously used VR for exposure treatment. Then the developed VR prototype is then described, followed by the experiment, results, discussion, and conclusion.

2   Related Work

Using VR for exposure treatment is an area that has been well studied in the last decades. This section reviews previous research on VR as an exposure treatment method, including earlier experiments. For example, in healthcare VR has been tested to help women manage childbirth [2], in therapy Maples-Keller [19] list several areas, including relieving post-traumatic stress disorder, schizophrenia, eating disorders, and phobias. Cognitive-behavioral therapy (CBT) is the most common form of therapy when it comes to treating phobias [14]. CBT includes several treatment methods, such as exposure therapy, imaginal exposure therapy, and virtual reality exposure therapy. Exposure therapy is about exposing oneself to what is experienced as unpleasant. According to Hedman and Axelsson [16], imaginal exposure therapy (IET) is used in contexts where fear is difficult to be exposed to in reality. It can be a very complex or very specific fear. Then the patient, together with a therapist, must try to visualize the fear and thus gradually overcome it. According to North et al. [21], using exposure therapy in the virtual environment has been a known phenomenon since 1992 when a research group in interaction design at Atlanta University came up with this method. The method is called virtual reality therapy (VRT) or virtual reality exposure therapy (VRET). It was developed because it turned out that many patients who needed to be treated with CBT had difficulty visualizing what caused anxiety and refused to be exposed to a real situation. Therefore, it was great to use a virtual environment to visualize what is causing the patient anxiety. VRET was shown to be able to produce the same stimuli as those produced by standard exposure therapy. An obvious advantage of VRET is that the therapy can always be practiced in a closed room and thus avoid distractions while being much safer [21].

Several studies have been conducted on height perception in VEs and explored possibilities to use it to treat acrophobia. One of the first VR applications to treat phobias was for treating fear of heights [22]. Cleworth et al. [6] conducted an experiment comparing the effects of real and virtual heights on changes to standing postural control, electrodermal activity, and psycho-social state. Seventeen subjects stood at low and high heights in real and virtual environments matched in scale and visual detail. It appears that anxiety and fear measurements significantly increase with height, but their variations are less important in a virtual exposure compared to an in vivo exposure. Freeman et al. [13] tested to use an automated cognitive intervention for fear of heights guided by an avatar virtual coach (animated using motion and voice capture of an actor) in VR and compared with usual treatment. Compared with participants in the control group, the VR treatment reduced fear of heights at the end of treatment. In this regard, VR has shown to be at least as effective as an in vivo exposure for the treatment of acrophobia [7,12,17].

Zerophobia [11] is an application developed to treat acrophobia in VR. It is developed for mobile phones and is intended for use with solutions such as *Google Cardboard* or similar. The patient is gradually exposed to heights and given tasks, such as counting the number of bicycles on the ground. However, it is not possible to interact with the environment. A study has been done on

Zerophobia [11] with 193 participants to investigate how well the participants could be treated for acrophobia at home. After three months, the treatment showed good effects when a follow-up measurement was made. About 60% of those treated were cured.

Oxford VR has developed the "Now I can do heights" application for HTC Vive where the patient can meet a virtual therapist who guides the patient through a game. The game is not built on exposure therapy but repeated behavioral experiments. They are based on the patient learning that heights are safer than they thought. The patient has to go to different levels to identify their fears. Tasks that can be performed are, for example, rescuing a cat or throwing balls. In 2019, a study was conducted on the Oxford VR application with 100 participants, of which 49 tested the application and 51 acted control group [13]. The test participants were treated using the application for two weeks, and after these two weeks, their fear of heights had been significantly reduced.

In summary, over the past 20 years, researchers have developed a range of different VR simulators for phobia treatments. The studies show the benefits of VR as an exposure treatment tool. However, there has been less research comparing passive versus active height exposure with an avatar guiding through different levels. Next, the VR prototype will be presented.

3   The VR Prototype

Designing the prototype was performed in an iterative approach, starting with interviewing therapists with knowledge about phobias and CBT to understand better how the treatment is performed today.

3.1   Virtual Environment

According to Schuemie et al. [24], it is essential to have nearby reference points that indicate different heights to visualize how high above the ground you are. Therefore, we decided to develop a VE of a city in which it is easy to visualize height differences and levels naturally by using high-rise buildings. New York theme was chosen where you will be in a skyscraper overlooking a park inspired by the Central Park. Being in a high-rise building is also a situation that most people are ever exposed to and was therefore considered essential to overcome fear in such an everyday environment. The VR prototype was developed using the game engine Unity [26].

3.2   Therapist

Early in the project, three therapists were contacted with knowledge of phobias and CBT to gain a deeper understanding and initiate a possible collaboration throughout the work. However, one therapist who works with CBT treatment and currently offers VR treatment for phobias showed interest in a collaboration. Due to the pandemic (COVID-19), we only had a digital meeting. The therapist shared his experiences of treating phobias in VR compared to real life. According to the therapist, offering VR treatment of phobias could help patients seek help.

The most important thing that emerged during the interview with the therapist was that it is important that the patient is relieved at their own pace and have the opportunity to redo different levels and decide for themselves when they are ready to move on to the next level. The idea with this is that the anxiety should be non-existent before the patient goes on to the next level. The therapist also pointed out how important it is for the patient to learn how to deal with the anxiety the patient feels when exposed to heights. Additionally, the patient should be given information about why they feel the way they do. The therapist considered that the optimal VR application for relieving acrophobia should include several levels where the first level can be, for example, standing on a chair to change a light bulb until the last level is to stand on the roof on a skyscraper and lookout. He also considered that each level should contain several sub-tasks of a similar nature so that the patient can be exposed to the same level in different ways.

Based on the therapist's interview, we decided that different levels would be created in the form of different floors in the skyscraper. One would be similar to exposure therapy in that you are exposed to the different levels and get to practice looking and breathing. In the other variant of the VR prototype, the user would have to perform various tasks at different levels. This is to "force" the user to have to experience the height but also to possibly distract the user from the high height by being active.

The VR prototype starts from a gazebo in Central Park before entering a building (Fig. 1). The reason it starts from Central Park is to be close to nature. Nature was chosen because it has been shown to have a positive effect on health, well-being and to have calming impact [3,15,18]. So, starting in a calm environment with no height exposure, close to nature with ambient sound, and the first meeting with the avatar.

3.3 Avatar

The introduction started on the ground, where the user was welcomed by an avatar that accompanied the user throughout the prototype. The avatar's purpose was to provide the user with strategies to manage the anxiety and guide the user through the treatment. One of the authors recorded audio instructions and explanations, explaining why you get anxiety and how to handle it through breathing. Deep breathing suppresses the sympathetic nervous system while at the same time eliciting activity in the parasympathetic nervous system, which in turn lowers the level of stress hormones and raises the "feel-good" hormone oxytocin [4].

We decided to give the avatar a name and called her Jessie. Jessie had a more active role in the passive version of the VR prototype, i.e., she is the one who guides the user through each breathing exercise, and she is the one who decides when everything should happen. In the VR prototype in which the user is active, the user can set the pace of how quickly the tasks are to be performed, and therefore Jessie has a more passive role.

Fig. 1. The gazebo in which the user stands during the introduction.

3.4   Interaction in Each Level

As already mentioned, the VR prototype starts in a gazebo in the park (Fig. 1). The first interaction is with the avatar and a sphere (Fig. 2), which was animated to perform the breathing exercises. The animation of the sphere made it more significant to symbolize that you should fill your lungs with air and then smaller again when you breathe out. So, the user had both visual and audio feedback while doing the breathing exercise. Each inhalation and exhalation takes five seconds for the user to take a deep breath. The sphere was chosen as a green color as green represents peace and security [5].

In order for the user to understand what to do at the different levels, instructions were written for each level. These instructions were adapted in appearance to suit the level of the user. Moreover, the instructions were on a bullet list, which was deleted as soon as it was executed.

In the first level in the building, which corresponds to the second floor, the user must do the following steps to move on to the next level:

- Take a photo through the window, using a virtual camera placed on the table (Fig. 3).
- Nail up a nail by standing on a stool that is both in the virtual environment and physically in reality (Fig. 4)
- Hang up the captured picture.

In the second level, which corresponds to being up on the tenth floor, the user must do the following steps to move on to the next level:

Fig. 2. The sphere used to perform breathing exercises.

- Plant a seed in the flower box at the balcony (Fig. 5).
- Water the seed in the flower box, at the balcony.
- Taste the lemon you sowed (after five seconds a plant grows with lemon fruits).

The third level, which corresponded to the fifteenth floor, the users had to do the following steps to finish the treatment:

- Set up balloons on a pole in the balcony railing (Fig. 6).
- Place bottles that are placed in different places into an ice bucket.
- Go out on a platform to throw down invitations.

In order to challenge the user, it was decided that the user would go out on a narrow platform to take and throw out the invitations. So, when the user finished setting up the balloons and the bottles were set in the ice bucket, the balcony railing "opens" and a platform folds out, which the user can go out on (Fig. 6).

The same environment was used for the prototype with passive exposure (PE) as for the active exposure (AE). However, what distinguishes the two VR prototypes is that there are no tasks to complete in the prototype with PE. Instead, the user must perform the breathing exercise during all levels of the house with Jessie. The purpose of the breathing exercise at all levels was to calm the user and force the user to look out or down from the house since the sphere was placed accordingly. To clarify where the sphere appeared, a marker

Fig. 3. The first level.

was created in the VE. The marker illustrated two footprints with a ring around them. At the same time as the marking is shown, Jessie tells what it is and that you should stand on the marking, look at the sphere and get ready for the breathing exercise.

3.5 Limitations

Initially, it was thought that the prototype would be tested only on people with acrophobia, but this idea was changed early in the process due to the COVID-19 pandemic. Instead, we tested on whoever we "found" and wanted to be tested.

4 Evaluation

A comparative evaluation was conducted in a VR laboratory environment to compare the two VR prototypes. A within-subject study was designed to assess the two VR prototypes. Both quantitative and qualitative data were collected. This test mainly aimed to explore the participants' experience of being exposed to heights while being active and when being passive. At the same time, we wanted to gather valuable information concerning participants' immersion and presence.

Fig. 4. Participant getting up on a stool to nail and hang up a picture.

Fig. 5. The balcony at the second level.

Fig. 6. The platform that folds out for the user to throw out invitations at the third level.

Data were collected using several different methods to have as much material as possible to evaluate the users. The list below describes the different ways and how the data was collected.

- *Observing*, how the participants acted in the virtual environment and recorded any comments they made. This was recorded in a prepared test protocol for each test participant.
- *Igroup presence questionnaire (IPQ)*, after testing each prototype, IPQ was given as well as a separate questionnaire with ratings that studied participants' presence and experience of the two prototypes.
- *Semi-structured interview* was held after both prototypes were tested, where above all comparative questions were asked between the different prototypes.

It was also decided to analyze qualitative data concerning any stated comments about the prototypes.

4.1   Setup

The evaluation was conducted at JayWay's VR lab using an HTC VIVE headset with associated controllers. A desktop computer with Unity [26] was used to run the VR prototype, and questionnaires were completed on laptops. The final interview was also conducted in the VR lab. One session involved one participant and two test leaders, where one was in charge of the HTC Vive equipment, and one guided the participants through the test and performed interviews.

4.2 Participants

Twenty-two participants were recruited, and all of them were asked to fill in a questionnaire about their fear of heights. Seven participants had no fear of heights, while fifteen had respect for heights. Four of the fifteen reported that they have high respect for heights. The participants consisted of twelve males and ten females, between 20 and 52 years old ($M = 28.3$, $SD = 8.86$) and from various backgrounds (although nine of them were students from Lund University). Nine of the participants claimed to have experience with VR, three of them had none, and ten had moderate (tried at least once). All participants were offered coffee and water.

4.3 Procedure

All participants were given a brief introduction to the project and its purpose. Next, all participants filled in a short questionnaire including demographic data and fear of heights together with informed consent regarding their participation and the use of collected data. Thereafter, they were asked to start the test. Beginning at the gazebo allowed the participants to get familiarized with the VE and calm down the participant by doing breathing exercises.

In an attempt to understand and describe the participant's perceived level of presence Igroup presence questionnaire (IPQ) [23] was used as an assessment tool. IPQ is designed as a self-report questionnaire to measure the sense of presence in virtual reality environments. It contains 14 items rated on a seven-point Likert scale ranging from 0 to 6. The IPQ is based on three sub-scales that measure different components of presence; 1) *Spatial presence* (SP), which means how physically present you are in the virtual environment. 2) *Involvement* (INV), which measures the amount of attention paid to the virtual environment and engagement. 3) *Experienced realism* (REAL), which measures the subjective experience of realism in the virtual environment. Additionally, the IPQ contains one general item which assesses the general "the sense of being there" (G) and affects all the previous factors. Five of the questions concern SP, four of the questions concern INV, four of the questions concern REAL, and one question concerns G. An average value is calculated for the questions that concern the same subscale.

To avoid sequential effects, the order of the versions was alternated, half of the participants started the prototype with active exposure and the other half with passive exposure.

After this, the participants filled in a post-questionnaire followed by a semi-structured interview. Each session lasted about 45 min. The whole procedure of the test session is visualized in a block diagram (Fig. 7).

5   Result

The measurements were successful, and all participants performed all moments without incidents or major problems.

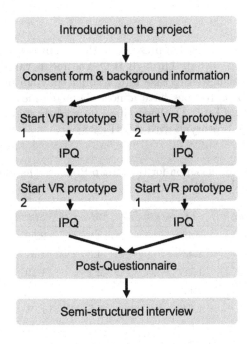

Fig. 7. Test session procedure.

5.1   Observations

During the test, the participants expressed some things spontaneously. Some answered Jessie with different phrases like "Yes" and "Okay" when she explained different things. Others expressed more about the surroundings or how they reacted to the height. For example, one participant commented "Oh My God! I know it is fake!" another participant expressed positive reaction "Hi hi, soo nice!", another participant felt unpleasant with the height "This is actually really unpleasant." Other examples, "This is how I also want to live!" and "Wow, this feels real!"

During the test, different actions were observed that the participants did unconsciously. 18 participants leaned over the balcony railing as if there were one in front of them. Fourteen participants tried to touch the balcony railing or the plank with one foot. It also happened that participants accidentally dropped objects in the virtual environment, and everyone who did this had the reaction to try to capture the objects with their other hand. During the task at the second level, where the participants would eat a lemon, eleven participants gaped when they put the virtual lemon in their mouth. Some participants wavered when standing still and looking down, and four even backed up against the house wall when they were on the balconies. The fact that all of those who reported they have high respect for heights, backed into the wall of the house also indicates that they were really scared and tried to avoid the height, i.e. take on an avoidant behavior that is common in a phobia.

5.2 IPQ

To assess the participants' level of presence in the two prototypes, IPQ was given after each version was tested. Through IPQ, the mean value of four different subscales has been calculated to take into account the high presence of the two prototypes. The two prototypes have almost the same mean value of presence for the four subscales (Table 1). The values are slightly better on all subscales except REAL for the prototype with AE (Fig. 8).

Table 1. Means and std. deviation for the Igroup Presence Questionnaire of the prototype with (a) PE and (b) AE.

	Mean (a)	Std. deviation (a)	Mean (b)	Std. deviation (b)
G1	4.9	2.43	4.9	2.56
SP1	4.8	1.43	4.8	1.31
SP2	2.1	1.18	2.1	1.19
SP3	4.8	1.11	5.0	1.08
SP4	4.8	1.04	4.8	1.01
SP5	5.0	.84	5.1	.82
INV1	3.8	.74	4.6	.64
INV2	4.0	.65	3.8	.55
INV3	1.5	.53	2.0	.48
INV4	4.3	.41	4.5	.41
REAL1	2.4	.31	2.1	.39
REAL2	4.1	.27	4.1	.29
REAL3	3.8	.16	3.7	.26
REAL4	2.9	.12	2.5	.17

Both the "sense of being there" (G) and spatial presence (SP) were just under five for both prototypes. Involvement (INV) was just under four for both prototypes and is also a high value. A subscale with the lowest score was experienced realism (REAL) which was around three, which is neither high nor low.

5.3 Semi-structured Interview

Below is presented based on the semi-structured interviews.

If it is Possible to Treat Acrophobia in VR. When asked if the participants thought it was possible to treat acrophobia with a solution similar to any of the prototypes they tested, twelve of 22 answered "Yes", eight out of 22 "Yes as a first step" and two participants responded that they did not know.

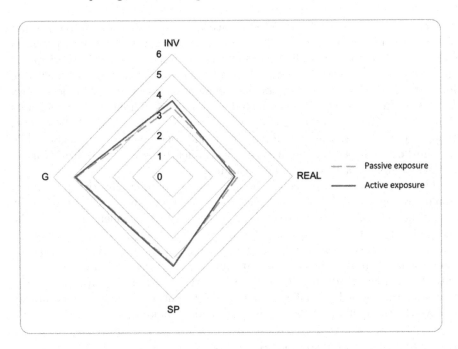

Fig. 8. Perceived discomfort of height at the different levels.

The twelve who thought that it would be possible to treat fear of heights with the help of VR perceived the VR experience as very immersive. They also thought that it could help practice their senses, meaning they thought it was necessary to do this on most occasions. Those who thought being exposed to height in VR could be a first step in treating their acrophobia thought that they needed to be exposed to a height even in reality. But they believed that a VR solution could provide tools to deal with the anxiety that arises. They also thought that it would be easier to then dare to be exposed to the heights in reality. The two who did not know if it would be possible to treat fear of heights with the help of VR were unsure because they did not feel that it was uncomfortable with the height from the prototypes.

Which Prototype Did You Prefer? 16 of 22 participants appreciated the prototype with AE more than the prototype with PE. The 16 people had similar motivations for this and that was because the prototype with AE was more fun as it was more interactive. The remaining six people answered that they had mainly appreciated a combination of the two VR prototypes. This is because they both appreciated the calmness of the prototype with PE and the opportunity to be able to interact in the prototype with AE.

Which Prototype Had the Most Potential to Alleviate Acrophobia?
The answers to which prototype the participants thought had the most potential
to help people with a fear of heights were very scattered. Seven of 22 participants
thought that the prototype with AE would help the most because they were
forced to do things they would not have done otherwise while not reflecting on
being high up until they had completed certain steps. Three of 22 participants
thought that the prototype with PE would help the most. Two of those three
thought this because they felt more secure and focused more on height, while
the third one believed this because they had to learn a strategy to deal with the
feelings of anxiety and feel safe by breathing.

The remaining twelve people thought that combining the two prototypes
would have been the best solution. They expressed themselves slightly differently,
but all had the same basic idea: the prototype with AE challenged more while
the prototype with PE provided tools and aids for dealing with fear. They felt
that it would have been good to first breathe as in the prototype without the
interaction to prepare to face the fear and then face the fear in the prototype
with the interaction added value or was distracting. The participants commented
that the tasks helped to challenge one for the height, could help to temporarily
remove the thoughts from the height, and made it more fun.

**If a VR Solution Can Entice More People to Expose Themselves to
Treat Acrophobia.** All participants answered that a VR solution could entice
them to seek help. The most common reason was that it was an easier step to be
exposed in a virtual environment than in a real environment. Because after all,
you know it's virtual, which makes it easier and more comfortable. Additionally,
the majority of the participants felt that it feels more like a "game" as it is in VR,
which both makes it more fun and removes some of the unpleasant feelings of
being attracted to treat acrophobia. The participants were also asked, assuming
they have all VR equipment at home, whether they would rather have done this
at home or with a therapist, only five had preferred to undergo the treatment
at home. Therefore, it can be assumed that it would not be completely foreign
to test VR in connection with a therapist.

6   Discussion

As a whole, VR could be considered as an interesting and valuable tool for
exposure treatment of acrophobia, mainly due to the immersive user experience
and in particular when the user performs other tasks while being exposed.

6.1   Observations

One thing that indicates that some people had a very high presence is those
who answered Jessie when she explained different things. Also, some comments
such as "This is actually really unpleasant" and "Wow, this feels real!" indicate
high attendance. The fact that as many as 18 of the participants leaned over the

balcony railing to see the ground instead of just taking a step outside the balcony railing or leaning through the balcony railing also indicates a high presence and that they felt that they were high up. As there was technically no physical balcony railing.

6.2 IPQ

Overall, the IPQ values of both prototypes were similar and relatively high.

In order to be able to create emotions virtually, it is important that you feel a presence and experience the virtual environment as if it were real. As G and SP (Fig. 8) are high, it indicates that the participants were both physically and mentally in the VE without being disturbed so much by reality. Additionally, INV was relatively high, which indicates that the participants' commitment and attention were high. On the other hand, REAL was somewhat lower, which indicates that the environment did not look and feel exactly like reality. This is consistent with several of the answers given by the participants when they thought the world looked cartoonish.

6.3 Semi-structured Interview

Based on the results, it seems possible to treat or at least alleviate acrophobia in VR. However, VR has both advantages and disadvantages. A positive aspect of using VR in exposure therapy is that the step of testing a VR game to treat your phobia feels shorter than seeking professional help from a therapist. This is because you know that you have to expose yourself to your worst fears. This was a theory that both the interviewed therapist had but also something the participants expressed when they were asked if they thought they would try to cure their acrophobia if there was a VR solution. It also emerged during the interviews with the participants that it was an easier step to take and that a VR solution feels more like a game, which does not put the same pressure. However, there are still relatively few people who have a VR set at home, which means that it is still not so easily accessible at the moment. Another positive aspect of using VR compared to traditional exposure therapy, especially in connection with heights, is that if the user experiences a height that is too uncomfortable, it is easy to take off the headset and then immediately be on solid ground again. On the other hand, if a person is treated with regular exposure therapy, it is not as easy to come back from the height in reality. A negative aspect of using VR as exposure therapy may be that an agent in a VR game can not read the user's feelings and actions. Therefore, it can be very wrong if the user does not do as the agent says or if the agent says "Good job!" then the participant has a panic attack. To solve this, an idea is to expose yourself to your phobia in VR with a therapist. Then the therapist can handle the person's feelings and support when needed. This would also solve the problem that many do not have VR sets at home. Additionally, results show that the participants would prefer to visit a therapist.

6.4   Virtual Environment Improvements

As previously mentioned, it is important during exposure therapy to increase the difficulty of the tasks in a therapy. However, for this pilot study, only three levels were developed. These levels would represent the easiest and most difficult levels, as well as a level in between. This is to create reference points to start from in the event of further development. But also to see large differences in levels, as two consecutive levels should only have small, barely noticeable differences.

A further improvement discussed during the development of the two VR prototypes was the opportunity to seek comfort and peace with the avatar Jessie if you experience discomfort at the height during the treatment. This would have needed to be developed if the prototype were to be something used by people afraid of heights, especially if the treatment would be conducted at home. If, on the other hand, it had been used by a therapist, this functionality could have been replaced by the therapist's knowledge and human treatment instead, which could also be more adapted to the person and the occasion. Another possible improvement based on the semi-structured interviews could be to merge the two prototypes. A combination of the two prototypes would have been the best solution were expressed from twelve participants. Perhaps a combination of breathing exercise and interaction at each level would be the most effective? It could give the person afraid of heights peace of mind with the breathing exercise, which could also be a tool for the upcoming, more challenging, and interactive tasks at the level. It is difficult to determine whether this would have been a better solution as this was not investigated in the project, but it would have been interesting to study more about it. Another interesting aspect to study would have been to use additional modalities to see how it had affected the user's ability to feel the height. Partly by adding additional physical objects, such as the stool at the second level. Partly by weaving in your senses such as smell and tactile feeling. This could have been done by, for example, starting a fan so that the user feels the wind at the higher levels.

7   Conclusion

Two VR prototypes were compared in a controlled experiment. Based on the results, creating a virtual environment that credibly evokes a feeling of height and relatively high presence seems quite possible. Moreover, the results indicate that it does not make a difference whether the participant performs tasks or not.

Acknowledgments. We thank all the participants who volunteered to test our application, and Pär Sikö from JayWay who allowed us to conduct the study and helped to organize.

References

1. Abelson, J.L., Curtis, G.C.: Cardiac and neuroendocrine responses to exposure therapy in height phobics: desynchrony within the 'physiological response system'. Behav. Res. Therapy **27**(5), 561–567 (1989)

2. Amirtha, T.: Can virtual reality help women cope with childbirth? (2016). https://www.theguardian.com/technology/2016/dec/09/virtual-reality-childbirth-pain-relief

3. Bratman, G.N., Hamilton, J.P., Daily, G.C.: The impacts of nature experience on human cognitive function and mental health. Ann. N.Y. Acad. Sci. **1249**, 118–136 (2012). https://doi.org/10.1111/j.1749-6632.2011.06400.x

4. Brown, R.P., Gerbarg, P.L.: Yoga breathing, meditation, and longevity. Ann. N.Y. Acad. Sci. **1172**(1), 54–62 (2009)

5. Cerrato, H.: The meaning of colors. The graphic designer (2012)

6. Cleworth, T.W., Horslen, B.C., Carpenter, M.G.: Influence of real and virtual heights on standing balance. Gait Posture **36**(2), 172–176 (2012)

7. Coelho, C.M., Santos, J.A., Silva, C., Wallis, G., Tichon, J., Hine, T.J.: The role of self-motion in acrophobia treatment. Cyberpsychol. Behav. **11**(6), 723–725 (2008)

8. Dahlström, C.: Är ångest vanligt? statistik över hur många som drabbas av ångest (2014), https://vadardepression.se/ar-angest-vanligt-statistik-over-hur-manga-som-drabbas-av-angest/

9. Davies, R.C.: Applications of systems design using virtual environments. In: Handbook of Virtual Environments. Erlbaum, Mahwah, pp. 1079–1100 (2002)

10. Di Loreto, C., Chardonnet, J.R., Ryard, J., Rousseau, A.: Woah: A virtual reality work-at-height simulator. In: 2018 IEEE Conference on Virtual Reality and 3D User Interfaces (VR), pp. 281–288. IEEE (2018)

11. Donke, T., et al.: Effectiveness of self-guided app-based virtual reality cognitive behavior therapy for acrophobia: a randomized clinical trial. JAMA Psychiatr. **76**(7), 682–690 (2019)

12. Emmelkamp, P.M., Bruynzeel, M., Drost, L., van der Mast, C.A.G.: Virtual reality treatment in acrophobia: a comparison with exposure in vivo. CyberPsychol. Behav. **4**(3), 335–339 (2001)

13. Freeman, D., et al.: Automated psychological therapy using immersive virtual reality for treatment of fear of heights: a single-blind, parallel-group, randomised controlled trial. Lancet Psychiatr. **5**(8), 625–632 (2018)

14. Furmark, T., Holmstroöm, A., Sparthan, E., Carlbring, P., Andresson, G.: Social fobi - social ångest. Liber AB, Stockholm (2019)

15. Hartig, T., Mitchell, R., de Vries, S., Frumkin, H.: Nature and health. Ann. Rev. Public Health **35**, 207–228 (2014). https://doi.org/10.1146/annurev-publhealth-032013-182443

16. Hedman-Lagerlöf, E., Axelsson, E.: Cognitive behavioral therapy for health anxiety. In: The Clinician's Guide to Treating Health Anxiety, pp. 79–122. Elsevier (2019)

17. Jang, D.P., et al.: The development of virtual reality therapy (VRT) system for the treatment of acrophobia and therapeutic case. IEEE Trans. Inf. Technol. Biomed. **6**(3), 213–217 (2002)

18. Keniger, L.E., Gaston, K.J., Irvine, K.N., Fuller, R.A.: What are the benefits of interacting with nature? Int. J. Environ. Res. Public Health **10**(3), 913–935 (2013)

19. Maples-Keller, J.L., Bunnell, B.E., Kim, S.J., Rothbaum, B.O.: The use of virtual reality technology in the treatment of anxiety and other psychiatric disorders. Harv. Rev. Psychiatr. **25**(3), 103 (2017)

20. Meehan, M., Insko, B., Whitton, M., Brooks, F.P., Jr.: Physiological measures of presence in stressful virtual environments. ACM Trans. Graph. **21**(3), 645–652 (2002)

21. North, M.M., North, S.M., Coble, J.R.: Virtual reality therapy: an effective treatment for psychological disorders. Stud. Health Technol. Inform. **44**, 59–70 (1997)

22. Rothbaum, B.O., Hodges, L.F., Kooper, R., Opdyke, D., Williford, J.S., North, M.: Virtual reality graded exposure in the treatment of acrophobia: a case report. Behav. Therapy **26**(3), 547–554 (1995)

23. Schubert, T., Friedmann, F., Regenbrecht, H.: The experience of presence: factor analytic insights. Presence Teleoperat. Virtual Environ. **10**, 266–281 (2001). https://doi.org/10.1162/105474601300343603

24. Schuemie, M., et al.: Treatment of acrophobia in virtual reality: a pilot study. In: Conference Proceedings Euromedia, pp. 271–275. Citeseer (2000)

25. Slater, M.: Measuring presence: A response to the witmer and singer presence questionnaire. Presence **8**(5), 560–565 (1999)

26. Unity Technologies: Unity - game engine (2017). https://unity.com/

27. Williams, S.L., Dooseman, G., Kleifield, E.: Comparative effectiveness of guided mastery and exposure treatments for intractable phobias. J. Consult. Clin. Psychol. **52**(4), 505 (1984)

A Proposal for a Computational Framework Architecture and Design for Massive Virtual World Generation and Simulation

Zintis Erics[(⊠)] and Arnis Cirulis

Faculty of Engineering, Vidzeme University of Applied Sciences, Valmiera, Latvia
{zintis.erics,arnis.cirulis}@va.lv

Abstract. In recent decades, computer games have become a pervasive form of entertainment leading to dramatic growth in complexity and scale in terms of content and employed technologies. However, several flaws in design methodology complicate the development process of massive and highly interactive virtual worlds. This paper proposes a novel architecture for a computational framework to cope with the growing complexity and scale of computer games. The research done should provide both a conceptual basis for a data driven development methodology and a practical implementation of systems designed for integration of various computation technologies. This paper lays out the proposed architecture, discusses concepts and design considerations involved and notes future research required.

Keywords: Computer simulations · Computer games · Virtual worlds · Level of detail · Algorithmic efficiency

1 Introduction

In the last few decades computer games have gained in popularity as a widely available form of entertainment, even more so in the last few years [3]. This rise can be mostly attributed to computer games being able to offer various challenges and immersion into virtual worlds. These capabilities are further enhanced by the continued rise in computational power and availability of consumer grade hardware furthering the graphics fidelity of virtual worlds. However, these advances are approaching the limits of what is reasonable [25]. The combination of these aspects has put focus on the intelligence, or lack thereof, within virtual worlds. More often than not, this intelligence is painted in a negative light. Classical examples of this include artificial intelligence (AI) driven non-player character (NPC) obliviousness to the changing environment or incapability to choose effective tactics in combat. Equally, if not more, problematic can be the lack of appropriate challenge presented by such NPCs often seen as incapable of exploiting obvious weaknesses in the player's tactics or inability to track line of sight

© Springer Nature Switzerland AG 2022
L. T. De Paolis et al. (Eds.): XR Salento 2022, LNCS 13445, pp. 37–47, 2022.
https://doi.org/10.1007/978-3-031-15546-8_3

exploiting targets. These and many other observations led to the realization that existing methods and techniques for computer game AI development and implementation are incapable to efficiently scale with the growing size and complexity of virtual worlds.

This incapability should be considered alongside the various issues concerning the interactivity of virtual worlds. The most prevalent examples are the various implementations of world borders, an artificial and sometimes blatantly obvious limitation of where the players can go and explore. The inability to interact with seemingly functional objects or the limitation of being able to break down walls, chop trees or dig ground only in very specific, designer approved and specially prepared places. Not to mention the impossibility to climb over various kinds of fallen trees, rocks or mountains that would be perfectly reasonable maneuvers in real life. These issues have been prevalent for decades and are often accepted as design or hardware limitations. While there are games that successfully address select issues [9, 11, 21], these often come with a significant increase in development time and a shift or two in design philosophy often making the solutions one of the selling points and core elements of the game [11, 21].

Both of these limitations, in the realms of intelligence and interactivity, often stem from the practice of faking various real-life systems with minimal effort. The fakes will often look akin to the real-life counterparts when viewed or interacted with from angles or in ways anticipated by the designers. The illusion tends to dissipate rapidly when used in an unusual way, giving rise to various bugs and exploits. Fixing such issues often requires patching each individual location or redesigning the involved systems. While the first fix may be attractive in smaller projects, its efficiency in terms of development time falls short in larger ones. On the other hand, the second fix may be overkill for smaller projects, but the only reasonable option for larger ones. Additionally, system redesign often places requirements on or reveals flaws in other systems resulting in a cascade of redesigns. All of these issues intensify when considering moddable games. In such cases, the original designers do not control all the potential content of the game. This requires robust, expressive, performant and well-documented systems and limits the original designers' capability to redesign existing systems requiring more refined implementation from the start.

This methodology of faking systems and various related techniques comes from a time when visual spectacle was one of the main goals and computational resources were much more limited, especially on consumer grade hardware. In the time since the spectacle has been polished to such a degree that further improvements are marginal at best [25], and as a result, focus is being shifted to game design. In addition, the research and advances in algorithm and simulation design are more accessible than ever before. As such, this paper identifies key requirements and proposes an architecture of a data driven simulation framework for generation and operation of scalable virtual worlds. The rest of this document is laid out as follows: the Sect. 2 offers a brief overview of the most notable problems observed and expands on several requirements for the proposed framework. Section 3 provides overview of the main concepts of the proposed framework and Sect. 4 follows up with a discussion of the more obscure yet fundamental aspects of the architecture. Finally, the Sect. 5 draws conclusions and lays out future work.

2   Problems and Requirements

One of the main reasons for the aforementioned issues is the lack of data; this is an internal consequence especially visible in moddable games. In the intelligence department, this is often seen as NPC unawareness of certain objects, states or entire systems that are represented to the player. A prime example are various animation states or even animation systems in general. Another area to consider is the lack of NPC memory of objects or states, especially in combination with spatial awareness, an example scenario would be tracking or intercepting a target through a complex environment like a city. One final aspect to consider would be awareness of other NPCs, such capabilities would aid in both, strategical analysis for long-term planning and tactical analysis for more complex combat encounters. All of this should be considered in an environment that can present partial or even misleading information, such as limited visibility or use of camouflage, to both players and NPCs.

Meanwhile, in terms of interactivity, one of the hardest problems to solve would be the world borders as these represent the fundamental spatial limitations of the area of content, removing these would require either a planet's worth of content [11,20,30] or procedural generation [11,21]. The problem of both terrain and object destructibility seems simple enough until potential implications on structural stability or object functionality are considered [9,21]. The climbing problem would be simple to solve on its own, albeit it would require redesign of world borders and various other systems to account for the player's location in unusual places [23].

This is only half of the story. One also needs to consider where to acquire the data required and how to use it. In most of the aforementioned problems most of the complexity lies in the use of the data while its acquisition provides only minor to no hindrance. An exception to this rule is the world border problem. Here the complexity shifts almost exclusively to data acquisition. In terms of intelligence, the availability of all the aforementioned data would lead to a severe increase in requirements for computational power and AI complexity. These would increase further because of multiplying possibilities to consider in terms of interactivity.

While the computational power necessary for reasonably accurate solutions to aforementioned problems is available on consumer grade hardware, the issues often lie in its inefficient use. For example, several of the most popular game engines offer limited multithreading support, often restricting engine access to a single thread [8,13]. While this simplifies engine design, it complicates, hinders and requires special considerations in the use of multithreading in games [28,33]. Such design decisions may have been reasonable in previous decades, but with the rise and focus on CPU core counts in the recent years [14,19], it is becoming a problem. Another issue is the object-oriented programming paradigm often employed in game design. While it is the bread and butter of modern programming practices [17] and easy to use, it often leaves performance on the table when it comes to systems and algorithms working on large amounts of objects [10].

This leads us to the first major requirement of the proposed framework, the ability to use as much performance as possible while still being approachable by developers used to the old ways. The second requirement is maximal modularity. This should aid in both system development and moddability of the resulting games, as well as portability of designed systems. The third and final major requirement is maximal usability outside the gaming industry. This effectively means that the framework should be generic enough to be usable for simulation and computation in other industries and scientific pursuits. One minor requirement should be addressed: the portability of the framework itself. This means that the framework should be developed to maximize simplicity, and minimize and compartmentalize the reliance on and interaction with the engine. This is of secondary priority though and perfect portability is most likely unachievable, albeit such development practices should aid in porting of both the framework itself and various systems developed within it to other game engines.

3   Framework Architecture

The overall architecture of the proposed framework consists of three main concepts: worlds, simulations and layers (see Fig. 1). Each world encapsulates a system of simulations and functions as an ordered directed acyclic graph. Each simulation is a process that executes some kind of computation receiving inputs and producing outputs. The input and output data of a simulation is partitioned into layers, each layer functions as a container holding data of a similar nature.

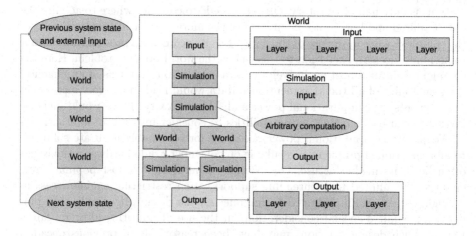

Fig. 1. An overview of the architecture depicting the looping operation of the entire system, nesting of worlds, parallel execution of simulations without interdependencies and linear execution of a distributed simulation.

A world functions similarly to a higher order simulation, it has inputs and outputs, represents an arbitrary computational process and can be executed. This means that a world can be used as a simulation itself allowing for greater flexibility given by a nested approach to the overall system architecture. In this sense, a world represents a higher order process that facilitates access to and orchestration of other processes. To this end, it provides access to the underlying simulations to external processes, executes the simulations when requested and manages the computational graph. In addition, the world is responsible for passing the data, in form of layers, along the computation path while individual simulations are responsible for interpreting and linking of their relevant input and output layers. Such division of responsibility should allow for addition and replacement of individual simulations while still maintaining the possibility to use custom communication formats between knowledgeable simulations.

The simulations themselves can represent any computational process. This includes, but is not limited to, classical simulations using agent, event or stock-based approaches as well as various hybrids. The computation itself can use any means necessary to arrive at the result, for instance, classical algorithms executed on the CPU, parallel algorithms executed on the GPU or special purpose schemes such as ECS. Note that this flexibility extends beyond single processes or even machines, individual simulations could be executed in a distributed fashion with or without knowledge of encompassing worlds. This is aided by the worlds only passing around layers, effectively pointers to arbitrary data collections. Since simulations and layers do data linking and interpretation, this allows for more performant use schemes amongst knowledgeable simulations by exploiting access to the raw data. Additionally, this allows for smart layers hiding the complexities and potentially distributed nature of the underlying data by providing a generic access interface.

The layers provide a data exchange interface that satisfies patterns for generic and more specialized raw access to the underlying data. Moreover, the generic access can hide various peculiarities of the underlying data storage such as distribution over the network or processes and internal data structure complexities as well as the use of various caches to aid efficiency. Meanwhile, the raw access serves as a more direct route to the underlying data storage exposing all the peculiarities and controls of the distribution process. This effectively means that the underlying data storage can use any means, regions or entities from a structural standpoint and RAM, VRAM, HDD, SSD or network resources from a technology standpoint.

Some general notes need to be addressed. First, while this architecture allows mixing of various technologies through generic interfaces, it also emphasizes performance gains by using a single technology throughout facilitated by the raw access interfaces. It is probable that these smart layer interfaces will aid in the use of various linking techniques amongst knowledgeable simulations increasing the overall performance by cutting out unnecessary back and forth transformations. Second, this architecture uses similar principles to already established technologies such as ECS [1,18,32] and GP GPU [31] and can be considered a more generic approach encompassing both. This framework will aid in practical use and combination of various technologies exploiting benefits of each while minimizing drawbacks, as well as providing common terminology and metrics for discussing various technicalities.

4 Design Considerations

In addition to the aforementioned general structure, several other aspects need to be considered, the first of which is the temporal integration methodology. It must be noted that one of the expected main use cases of the proposed framework involves various simulations of drastically different temporal scales. This effectively means that a world may be executing varied simulations concerning everything from cosmological scale mega structure and galaxy formation to the processes of individual cells and tissues. Such a variety of processes has a matching variety of effective temporal resolutions, meaning that a scheduler is required to execute all simulations at the right times to maintain both simulated process integrity and overall system efficiency. Additionally, each world and simulation may have its own scheduler. This is aided by the nested overall structure, but also means that each simulation must use the same generic scheduling interface. This also implies that each individual simulation may use its own internal scheduling methodology as long as it conforms to the external interface. To achieve this at least two scheduling strategies will be provided, a more discrete one using the closest discrete bins based on powers of two [29] and a more arbitrary one using an unbalanced binary tree with a smart iterator. Of course, any other strategy may be implemented and used, as long as it conforms to the external interface.

Similarly, the spatial integration methodology also requires consideration. In this case, the same foreword can be referred to for a visualization of the vast differences in the spatial scale of simulated processes. However, this case is more complicated than temporal integration since various simulations may use vastly different methods for partitioning the simulated region. So far various methods have been observed, chiefly amongst them are the classical grid-based approaches [6], various octree-based implementations [2], use of Voronoi tessellation and Delaunay triangulation [29] and simple collections of discrete entities [29]. It should be noted that the proposed framework needs to be able to support use cases in both two and three-dimensional space as well as different coordinate systems local to larger entities such as planets and moons. Together all of this means that the external interface of layers needs to support generic value lookups based on coordinates and a reference coordinate system while providing some additional information such as coordinate system extents and translation functions between local and global coordinate systems. These considerations raise concerns regarding potential loss of precision across different coordinate system interfaces. As an extreme example, the coordinates necessary for an astrophysical simulation spanning hundreds of parsecs cannot be put on the same 64-bit float as the ones measured in nanometers and used in bacterial simulations, certainly not without loss of precision. Moreover, while indefinite precision numerical schemes that could allow for unified storage exist [26], these are almost exclusively implemented in software and prohibitively expensive in terms of computational power [12]. Additionally, the highest performance hardware available to consumers prioritizes support of 32-bit floats [15, 24] leading to a necessary choice between performance and precision.

So far, we have discussed the proposed framework's support for two types of dynamic resolutions, temporal and spatial. Both of these concepts have for decades been used as ways to improve simulation efficiency by cutting out unnecessary detail [2]. In a sense, this goal is the same as that of level of detail (LOD) systems used in computer games, also, for a considerable amount of time [27]. These LOD systems increase the performance of games mainly by limiting the resolution of graphical assets used for far away objects while maintaining acceptable graphical fidelity. As such we consider the concepts of temporal and spatial resolutions to be just single aspects of larger concepts, temporal level of detail (T-LOD) and spatial level of detail (S-LOD) respectively. This assumption aids in two aspects, firstly it provides umbrella terms to group various not only resolution-based techniques together and, secondly, it provides a flexible terminology to measure and manipulate the fidelity of simulations. The regard of these concepts, alongside the terminology, have paved the way for another: functional level of detail (F-LOD). This is the concept of changing the executed simulation logic based on the required fidelity of the region under consideration. While, at first glance, this may seem similar to S-LOD, F-LOD merely builds on top of it. Where S-LOD partitions space into regions of varying sizes, F-LOD decides what logic should be executed upon them, meanwhile T-LOD determines how often this execution should happen. Note that some games [4, 16, 22] and simulations [34] have used similar techniques, but to our knowledge, there has been no attempt of consolidating these approaches under a single banner.

In the previous discussion, we briefly mentioned fidelity, and while the concept itself is clear, it expresses how close a replica is to the original, the question lays in the measurement of perceived fidelity. Perceived fidelity is of importance since it effectively measures what level of fidelity can be expressed given the observer's interface. The key factors to consider here are the limitations of the observer's interface. These introduce a point beyond which any increase in fidelity does not produce any noticeable effect [7]. In classic LOD systems, this is measured using geometric and pixel errors relative to the highest fidelity assets available. The system tries to minimize these errors while remaining within bounds of its limited resources [5]. This raises an important question: how should the errors be measured in temporal, spatial and functional aspects of various simulations? While the exact measurement unit is unimportant, what is of paramount importance is the relative stability and consistency of the measurements used by various simulations. While the exact considerations and guidelines of this system remain unclear and a subject to further study what is clear is that significant considerations should be directed to the observer attachment to certain aspects of the virtual world. In this sense attachment effectively measures how noticeable would be the loss of the aspect under consideration. Again, this is of paramount importance since the focus of the entire framework is to provide believable and consistent virtual worlds on a massive scale within limited resources. Under such conditions exploration is inevitable, which will lead to the generation of new or LOD increase of the existing regions of the world. This will also lead to pressure on the limited resources and the need to lower the LOD or entirely leave something out. One of the first things to leave would be something of the least consequence for the observers. The currently unresolved question is how to measure this potential consequence, this attachment in a stable and consistent manner. Again, this is a subject for further study.

The preceding outline paints the proposed framework as a system of simulations for partial or complete generation and evolution of interactive environments with potential to use both random and hard-coded initial conditions. This brings up the discussion regarding two of the main algorithm design considerations: evolution and generation. In this sense the evolution is the application of iterative logic to the simulation state advancing it to the next one in time. This methodology can be employed to both create content and provide interactivity. Meanwhile, generation is the application of initialization logic to create a simulation state. This methodology can only be used to create content. The evolution methodology is mostly used for simulations in more scientific endeavors due to its temporal causality and problem domain complexity while the generation methodology is mostly applied to computer games due to the lack of computational resources for complex simulations and necessity for perfect realism. In this context let us recall that the proposed framework may need to increase LOD or generate entirely new regions in response to observer exploration. As such at least parts of the region state, if not the entire region, would need to be created using the generation methodology. This effectively means that to ensure consistency with already existing, potentially evolved regions the generation method used would need to rapidly bring the state of the region to the desired point in time or LOD while still maintaining the desired fidelity. Again, depending on the complexity of the simulations and temporal interdependencies of the region states involved it may not be feasible to evolve the region due to computational resources or temporal logistics. This means that each simulation with multiple LODs or indefinite bounds would need at least two algorithms, one for evolving the regions normally and the other for increasing LOD or generating new regions on the spot. While for simpler simulations with fewer time steps repeated application of evolution logic to generate new regions could be performant enough, that cannot be said for more complex simulations, worlds that are advanced significantly far enough in time or LOD increase. Moreover, it may be difficult to provide matching generation algorithms for more complex simulations, as such this is a subject for further study.

Altogether it can be seen that the proposed framework would specialize in the creation and operation of partial virtual worlds in a sense that these worlds would not be complete due to the constraints of computational resources. As such these worlds would have more realized regions and ones that are more imaginary in the sense of higher and lower simulation LODs respectively. Effectively the created virtual worlds would not be complete realizations, rather they would be more akin to a moving window serving as an interface with everything out of its bounds, potentially blurred. In this regard the key challenges lie in designing a system that could adapt to observer interactions in a performant enough way to keep up with the required fidelity while remaining flexible enough to support moddability and incorporation of both standard and cutting-edge technologies.

5   Conclusion

This paper outlined and exemplified some systematic problems concerning common patterns employed in the design methodology of computer game systems. For brevity, we classified these into two avenues: intelligence and interactivity. We noted several performance, modularity and portability requirements that should be addressed to construct a framework to successfully alleviate these issues. Next, we proposed such a framework employing data driven development methodology that should fulfil the noted requirements and sketched its core architecture in terms of worlds, simulations and layers. We also noted several considerations to take into account during the proposed framework's development phase, namely, temporal, spatial and functional integration, perceived fidelity and observer attachment and the mixed use of both evolution and generation algorithms.

In addition, we noted several areas for further study, specifically, the measurements of error terms in temporal, spatial and functional integration, the evaluation of observer attachment and matching evolution and generation algorithms. Albeit it must be noted that these are largely overarching conceptual directions, as such most of the following research should concern implementation technicalities. In this regard we already foresee a number of potential avenues chiefly concerning massively parallel algorithm design, implementation and notation as well as other, more miscellaneous questions.

References

1. Andrea Catania: Godex, March 2022. https://github.com/GodotECS/godex. Accessed 29 Mar 2022
2. Barnes, J.H., Hut, P.: A hierarchical o(n log n) force-calculation algorithm. Nature **324**, 446–449 (1986)
3. Barr, M., Copeland-Stewart, A.: Playing video games during the Covid-19 pandemic and effects on players' well-being. Games Cult. **17**(1), 122–139 (2022). https://doi.org/10.1177/15554120211017036
4. Bay 12 Games: Slaves to Armok: God of blood Achapter II: Dwarf fortress. https://www.bay12games.com/dwarves. Accessed 1 Mar 2022
5. CesiumGS: 3D Tiles, February 2022. https://github.com/CesiumGS/3d-tiles/blob/main/3d-tiles-reference-card.pdf. Accessed 1 Mar 2022
6. Chan, K.H., Im, S.K.: Fast Grid-Based Fluid Dynamics Simulation with Conservation of Momentum and Kinetic Energy on GPU, pp. 299–310, December 2017. https://doi.org/10.1007/978-3-319-71598-8_27

7. Deering, M.: The Limits Of Human Vision, October 2000
8. Gerke Max Preussner: East coast devcon 2014: Concurrency & parallelism in ue4 - tips for programming with many CPU cores, April 2015. https://www.slideshare.net/GerkeMaxPreussner/concurrency-parallelism-in-ue4-tips-for-programming-with-many-cpu-cores. Accessed 29 Mar 2022
9. Ghost Ship Games: Deep rock galactic. https://store.steampowered.com/app/548430/Deep_Rock_Galactic. Accessed 1 Mar 2022
10. Ali, H.: Why OOP is not performance efficient, May 2020. https://www.linkedin.com/pulse/why-we-need-move-from-oop-hadid-ali. Accessed 29 Mar 2022
11. Hello Games: No Man's Sky. https://www.nomanssky.com. Accessed 1 Mar 2022
12. Turner-Trauring, I.: Massive memory overhead: Numbers in python and how NumPy helps, October 2021. https://pythonspeed.com/articles/python-integers-memory. Accessed 29 Mar 2022
13. Bonastre, J.: Why should I use threads instead of coroutines?, November 2016. https://support.unity.com/hc/en-us/articles/208707516-Why-should-I-use-Threads-instead-of-Coroutines. Accessed 29 Mar 2022
14. Rupp, K.: 42 years of microprocessor trend data, February 2018. https://www.karlrupp.net/2018/02/42-years-of-microprocessor-trend-data. Accessed 29 Mar 2022
15. Carbotte, K.: Nvidia's new Titan v pushes 110 teraflops from a single chip, December 2017. https://www.tomshardware.com/news/nvidia-titan-v-110-teraflops,36085.html. Accessed 29 Mar 2022
16. Ludeon Studios: Rimworld. https://store.steampowered.com/app/294100/RimWorld. Accessed 1 Mar 2022
17. Medi Madelen Gwosdz: If everyone hates it, why is OOP still so widespread?, September 2020. https://stackoverflow.blog/2020/09/02/if-everyone-hates-it-why-is-oop-still-so-widely-spread. Accessed 29 Mar 2022
18. Michele Caini: EnTT, March 2022. https://github.com/skypjack/entt. Accessed 29 Mar 2022
19. Bailey, M.: Parallel programming: Moore's law and multicore, March 2022. https://web.engr.oregonstate.edu/~mjb/cs475/Handouts/moores.law.and.multicore.2pp.pdf.Accessed 29 Mar 2022
20. Mobius Digital: Outer wilds, https://store.steampowered.com/app/753640/Outer_Wilds. Accessed 1 Mar 2022
21. Mojang Studios: Minecraft. https://www.minecraft.net. Accessed 1 Mar 2022
22. Netcore Games: Tales of Maj'eyal, https://te4.org. Accessed 1 Mar 2022
23. Nintendo: The legend of Zelda: Breath of the wild. https://www.zelda.com/breath-of-the-wild. Accessed 1 Mar 2022
24. NVIDIA Corporation & affiliates: CUDA C++ Programming Guide, March 2022. https://docs.nvidia.com/cuda/cuda-c-programming-guide/index.html. Accessed 29 Mar 2022
25. Gallaga, O.L.: Is it really worth upgrading your PC for 'ultra' gaming graphics?, February 2021. https://debugger.medium.com/is-it-really-worth-upgrading-your-pc-for-ultra-gaming-graphics-634c61c6f75f. Accessed 29 Mar 2022
26. Python Software Foundation: Built-in Types, March 2022. https://docs.python.org/3/library/stdtypes.html. Accessed 29 Mar 2022
27. RasterGrid Kft.: GPU based dynamic geometry LOD, October 2010. https://www.rastergrid.com/blog/2010/10/gpu-based-dynamic-geometry-lod. Accessed 29 Mar 2022
28. Meredith, R.: Simple multithreading for unity, July 2017. https://richardmeredith.net/2017/07/simple-multithreading-for-unity. Accessed 29 Mar 2022

29. Springel, V.: E pur si muove:galilean-invariant cosmological hydrodynamical simulations on a moving mesh. **401**(2), 791–851 (2010). https://doi.org/10.1111/j.1365-2966.2009.15715.x
30. System Era Softworks: Astroneer. https://store.steampowered.com/app/361420/ASTRONEER. Accessed 1 Mar 2022
31. Unity Technologies: Compute shaders. March 2022. https://docs.unity3d.com/2022.2/Documentation/Manual/class-ComputeShader.html. Accessed 29 Mar 2022
32. Unity Technologies: Entities overview, March 2022. https://docs.unity3d.com/Packages/com.unity.entities@0.50/manual/index.html. Accessed 29 Mar 2022
33. Blanco, V.: Multithreading overview March 2021. https://vkguide.dev/docs/extra-chapter/multithreading. Accessed 29 Mar 2022
34. Weinberger, R., Springel, V., Pakmor, R.: The Arepo public code release. Astrophys. J. Suppl. Ser. **248**(2), 32 (2020). https://doi.org/10.3847/1538-4365/ab908c

Evaluating Forms of User Interaction with a Virtual Exhibition of Household Appliances

Mikołaj Maik[1]([✉])[iD], Paweł Sobociński[1][iD], Krzysztof Walczak[1][iD],
and Tomasz Jenek[2]

[1] Poznań University of Economics and Business, Poznań, Poland
{maik,sobocinski,walczak}@kti.ue.poznan.pl
[2] Amica S.A., Wronki, Poland
tomasz.jenek@amica.com.pl
http://www.kti.ue.poznan.pl/

Abstract. A promising application area of virtual reality is the marketing of home appliances. A VR exhibition can combine the visual realism close to physical exhibition spaces with remote access, flexibility, interactivity, user-friendliness, and attractiveness, thus bringing advantages for both consumers and manufacturers. In this article, we present a VR system for interactive visualization of household appliances, which can support both individual sales and wholesale of products, allowing customers to visualize different versions of devices before making a purchase decision. The visualization of products takes place in a specially designed virtual kitchen so that the user can examine how the home appliances will present themselves in the context of a typical environment. However, an important open research question is to what extent this kind of interactive product presentation is appropriate for end-users not experienced in VR. In this paper, we describe an experiment aiming at evaluating different forms of users' interaction with a product exhibition in virtual reality. Popular controller-based and natural hand interactions are evaluated in the context of navigation and product operation.

Keywords: Visualization · VR · 3D interfaces · Interaction · Marketing · Household appliances

1 Introduction

In recent years, virtual reality has become one of the quickest developing branches of multimedia technology. New hardware and software solutions are continuously being developed, making this technology more efficient and allowing it to represent the physical world more realistically. Because of the continued introduction of new devices and reduction of their prices, more and more companies have started to introduce VR in their everyday activity to improve their performance and competitiveness in the market. One of the areas that VR can greatly improve is marketing. Because customers are overwhelmed with the traditional advertisement and information about the products, manufacturers are looking for new ways to present their products and gain the interest of buyers.

L. T. De Paolis et al. (Eds.): XR Salento 2022, LNCS 13445, pp. 48–62, 2022.
https://doi.org/10.1007/978-3-031-15546-8_4

One of the elements of the promotion that can greatly benefit from the use of VR is the visualization of products. Compared to the traditional real-life exhibitions, visualization in VR has important advantages, such as remote access to the exhibition spaces, freedom of viewing the exhibited products from any angle and any distance, and the possibility of visualization of their way of operation. Moreover, by using VR, it is possible to save space that is required for displaying physical merchandise while having the ability to show as many products as it is required and gaining the capability for their easy and quick rearrangement. Additionally, no damage to the exhibited goods is possible, which eliminates the eventual expenses.

Another advantage of the use of VR, especially in the case of household appliances, is the possibility of interaction with the products. Customers can test a product and learn how it works before buying, which can influence their final purchase decision. It is also possible to allow a customer to personalize the appliances or the environment in which they are exhibited.

In this paper, we demonstrate how VR technologies can be used for the visualization of household appliances by presenting a VR application that enables users to look and interact with products manufactured by Amica S.A. An essential open research question is, however, to what extent this kind of product presentation is appropriate for end-users who are not experienced with the use of VR systems. In this paper, we describe an experiment aiming at the evaluation of different forms of users' interaction with a product exhibition in virtual reality. Popular controller-based and natural hand interactions are evaluated in the context of the user's navigation and operation of products.

The remainder of this paper is structured as follows. Section 2 presents an overview of the current state of the art. Next, Sect. 3 presents the technical setup and system software used in the application. An experimental evaluation of the forms of user interaction in the application is described in Sect. 4. Section 5 provides a discussion of the findings. Finally, Sect. 6 concludes the paper and describes further development and research directions .

2   Related Works

2.1   VR in Marketing

There is an undeniable need to offer customers remote access to product information. However, the common audience has become increasingly resistant toward traditional visual media as a source of information [6]. It caused both researchers and companies to start searching for new ways to communicate product information, leading to a significant increase in research about the use of virtual reality for marketing purposes [14].

One of the most important research topics is the use of virtual reality to create 3D virtual stores. It is being predicted that such stores can become mainstream and co-exist with the physical ones [1]. In both VR and physical stores, attributes such as the variety of products, quick access, prices, and atmosphere play significant roles in shopping experiences [10]. Furthermore, it is confirmed that VR stores can create compelling virtual sensory affluence, where a customer can engage in active shopping activity [13]. Yet, it is important to remember that the user's experience may differ depending on the level of immersion. For example, there can be an increase in variety seeking and a decrease in price sensitivity in high immersive virtual scenes compared to low immersive ones [15].

Another advantage of virtual stores is their independence from the place where they are used. VR technology generally can be used almost anywhere and by anyone, which is essential in the modern-day market where e-retail revenues grow continuously [19]. It is important to notice, however, that there are still multiple factors that can limit the widespread use of immersive VR technology [11]. Nevertheless, it is possible to create less immersive spaces for marketing purposes than can be used more widely [18].

Another important use of virtual stores is to perform merchandising studies. Such studies verify how different product arrangements in the modeled physical space influence customers' perception of the products. It can increase the store's selling numbers by influencing the customers or promoting a particular product or a group of products. Currently, such merchandising research is typically performed with the use of physical mock-ups of physical stores [3]. However, the use of virtual spaces has significant advantages compared to traditional physical spaces. It enables fast, easy, and well-controlled rearrangement of products. Moreover, there is no need to possess physical versions of all different kinds of products, which may quickly become outdated [21]. In virtual reality, it is also possible to check how the look of the particular product will influence the purchasing process [4].

A different element of marketing that can be highly influenced by virtual reality is promotion. The significant part of promotion is visualizing the product to the customer and passing information about it. VR gives new methods to present the products in a 3D environment [22]. Moreover, in VR, it is easier to influence customers' emotions, which is important in the promotion process and, for example, is used in charity promotion to increase its efficiency [8].

2.2   Interaction in VR

There are many methods of interaction with objects within a virtual scene, so it is essential to match them to the needs of the user in order to prepare an enjoyable experience. This section presents the methods of interaction that can be used in a VR environment.

The first approach is based on the use of specific equipment such as dedicated VR devices (tracked controllers) or gaming devices (pads) for interaction with the 3D objects in the virtual scene. The main advantage is the user's comfort, efficiency, and accurate control in virtual environments that are adequately configured [5,9]. Unfortunately, this kind of equipment usually has higher costs and shorter standard change times, which can limit the practicality of this approach. Nevertheless, the approach based on specialized devices is often the basis for further research [2,20].

The next approach uses a quickly developing approach to interaction, which analyzes natural human behavior. Examples of such techniques are motion capture (e.g., with marker tracking or directly like in the case of the Microsoft Kinect sensor system [17]), gesture recognition [12], eye tracking [16], and verbal/vocal input [23]. This approach provides an intuitive and user-friendly interface even for less experienced users, sometimes at the cost of higher fatigue and loss of privacy.

The context-based approach is an interaction technique popular in computer games, in particular in simulations (e.g., "The Sims" and "SimCity" series by Maxis) and in adventure games. This approach is not based on specific input devices but focuses on the use of commonly available devices to interact with the use of a contextual on-screen menu. The set of operations that can be performed from within the interface depends on the current state of the environment and its objects (e.g., time, position, current object state). The context-based approach is also often used in modern VR environments [7]. However, this approach can be uncomfortable for the user due to the mismatch between classic UI elements (buttons, menus, charts) and the 3D virtual environment.

3   Technical Setup and System Software

To support immersive product visualization, we developed a system that allows users to experience product models in a virtual exhibition space. For this purpose, we used the HTC Vive Pro device with the Leap Motion controller attached. The main reason for choosing the HTC Vive Pro was that this HMD is equipped with relatively high-resolution display and has a blindspot-free continuous tracking system. The HMD changes the viewing angle according to the user's head movements. A user can freely move around the environment and see all the displayed elements, which makes the experience comfortable and realistic. The system is implemented in Unity 2019.2.10f1 (64-bit) using the C# language and runs on a Windows 10 PC with an i7-8700K processor (3.70 GHz) and a GeForce RTX 2080 Super graphics card.

The system allows users to navigate through two rooms. The first room presents an exhibition of the latest ovens produced by Amica S.A. All virtual home appliances are based on original design models that have been exported to the FBX format and then transferred to Unity, where all related interactions were programmed. All product interactions are based on normal hand gestures. Each oven can be opened, and baking trays can be pulled out (Fig. 1). The ovens also feature fully animated and interactive displays. After a user approaches an oven and points his/her index finger at the oven display for 5 s, it enters a special mode enabling the display control. In this mode, the display is enlarged, and the user can interact with it. For example, by making sweeping movements with his/her hands, a user can move the displayed graphical tiles corresponding to specific oven programs (Fig. 2). The customer has the opportunity to familiarize himself with the capabilities and operation of a given oven. The user can learn, for example, how to set a specific temperature or a given amount of time. After getting acquainted with the product exhibition, the user can go to the second room, which represents a kitchen (Fig. 3). The user can decide which oven from the exhibition should appear in the kitchen. He/she will then be able to see how the chosen oven looks next to various kitchen products.

Fig. 1. Opening the oven using Leap Motion and HTC Vive Pro controllers.

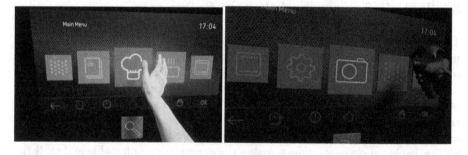

Fig. 2. Interacting with the oven display using Leap Motion and HTC Vive Pro controllers.

The presented system can be operated using all OpenVR devices and the Leap Motion controller. A teleportation mechanism has been implemented to permit users to navigate through the virtual stage (Fig. 4). Using controllers supported by OpenVR software, users can change their position by holding down the button responsible for teleportation and then aiming the controller at the target location. Using the Leap Motion controller, teleportation is done by pointing the index finger for 3 s at the place on the floor where a user wants to go.

4   Experimental Evaluation

An experimental user evaluation of the presented system has been conducted to assess how inexperienced novice users will be able to interact with the exhibition.

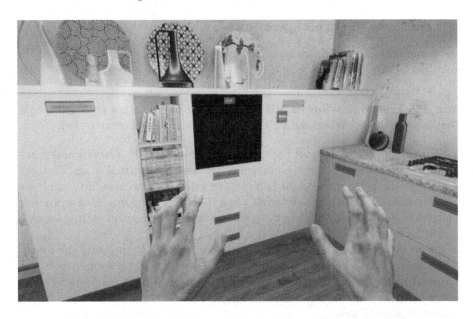

Fig. 3. Virtual kitchen with a selected oven built-in into furniture.

Fig. 4. Teleportation using Leap Motion and HTC Vive Pro controllers.

Tests were performed with the use of HTC Vive Pro and Leap Motion controllers. The following subsections cover the design of the experiment, the characteristics of participants that took part in the study, as well as the collected results, and their analysis.

4.1   Design of the Experiment

The prepared test scenario consists of three separate tasks to be performed, as described below.

Task 1 – User's Motion in VR Space. The user's task was to move to a specific place in the virtual scene. Three methods of motion were tested.

1. Physical movement without the use of controllers (Fig. 5). The physical space prepared for interaction corresponded to the size of the virtual space. The user had to walk 5 m, turning right halfway. For safety reasons, a security grid was set up in the application, informing when the user was approaching a physical obstacle. Additionally, during the tests, we helped users avoid getting tangled in the cables.
2. Teleportation using the Vive Pro controllers (Fig. 4). By pressing the touch-pad under the thumb and pointing to the place of teleportation, a user was moved to the indicated place in the virtual space. Target points to teleport were set every meter. Users had to teleport five times in total to get to the desired place (5 m).
3. Teleportation using the Leap Motion device (Fig. 4). Similar to the motion with the Vive Pro controllers, users had to teleport five times to get to the last point. The users moved to the place by pointing their index fingers at the teleportation point for 2 s.

Task 2 – Interaction with a Virtual Oven. The user's task was to open the oven, slide the rack out of the inside, then grasp the 3D virtual object in the form of a pizza and place it evenly on the rack (Fig. 6). After positioning the pizza, the user had to slide the rack inside and then close the oven. The task was performed twice, using the Vive Pro and the Leap Motion controllers. When using the Vive Pro controllers, the user had to grasp objects by pressing the trigger button located under the index finger. With the use of the Leap Motion device, it was enough to clench a fist naturally close to the object.

Task 3 – Interaction with the Displays. The user's task was to select the appropriate oven program (by moving the interface tiles), set the temperature to 200°, and then accept the settings (Fig. 7). The task was also performed twice, using the Vive Pro and the Leap Motion controllers. Interface tiles can be moved left and right by swinging a hand or a controller in the appropriate direction.

Fig. 5. Physical movement of a user through the virtual scene.

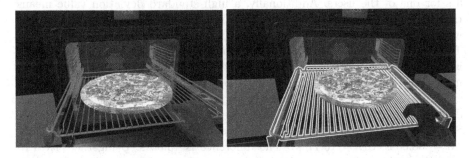

Fig. 6. Putting pizza in the oven using Leap Motion and HTC Vive Pro controllers.

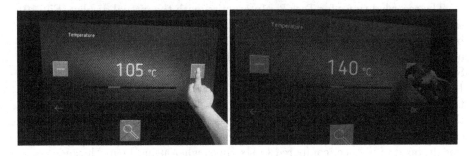

Fig. 7. Setting the temperature on the oven display using Leap Motion and HTC Vive Pro controllers.

4.2   Participants

A total of 20 test subjects (7 females and 13 males) participated in the experiment. The subjects ranged in age from 21 to 26 years (M = 22.50 years, SD =

1.54 years). None of the subjects had earlier experience with Vive Pro or Leap Motion controllers. Before performing a specific task, each user took part in a theoretical discussion of the procedure used within the task.

4.3   Results and Analysis

Within this subsection, the results of the experiment are reported. The results include task completion times, questionnaire data gathered from the participants, as well as an analysis of the collected data.

Task Completion Times. The results collected during Task 1 are shown in Fig. 8. The task was completed fastest using the Vive Pro controllers (M = 12.15 s, SD = 6.42 s). However, the difference between walking the distance on foot (M = 15.85 s, SD = 4.22 s) and teleporting with the use of controllers is not large (3.70 s). Significant differences were noticed in the attempts to teleport using Leap Motion (M = 44.20 s, SD = 28.67 s). This task took as long as 2 min and 5 s for one of the users. Additionally, a high standard deviation value means that the scatter of the results was very large. This task was completed fastest within 13 s, which is still longer than the average for the Vive Pro controllers. The shortest times in the case of Vive Pro controllers and physical movement were 6 s and 8 s, respectively. The longest times (Vive Pro – 34 s and physical movement – 25 s) did not exceed the Leap Motion average.

In the case of Task 2 – Interaction with the virtual oven (Fig. 9), the time differences were also noticeable. Using the Vive Pro controllers (M = 25.60 s, SD = 10.41 s) this task was completed faster than using the Leap Motion device (M = 38.65 s, SD = 10.17 s). The difference is 13.05 s. Using the Vive Pro controllers, the task was completed fastest in 14 s and slowest in 50 s. However, using hand gestures, this task was completed fastest in 21 s and slowest in 62 s.

The recorded times for Task 3 – Interaction with the virtual display (Fig. 10) show only slight differences between the tested devices. It was completed faster by using hand gestures (M = 20.30 s, SD = 4.87 s). It took users an average of 3 s longer to complete this task using the Vive Pro controllers (M = 23.35 s, SD = 5.49 s). Using the Vive Pro controllers, the task was completed fastest in 15 s and slowest in 34 s. Using the Leap Motion device, this task was completed fastest in 14 s and slowest in 33 s. During this task, each time a user dropped the 3D pizza object, a new model appeared in the starting position. However, each time such an error was counted. Using the Vive Pro controllers, the pizza was dropped only once, compared to six times when using Leap Motion.

Questionnaire: Likert Scale Rating. After completing Tasks 2 and 3, the participants were asked to complete a questionnaire with the Likert scale of difficulty of the task – from 1 (very difficult) to 5 (very easy). Figure 11 summarizes the collected results of the assessment questionnaire. Task 2 with the use of Vive Pro controllers was rated as difficult by one person (rating 2). However, interaction with the oven using hand gestures has been rated as difficult by five

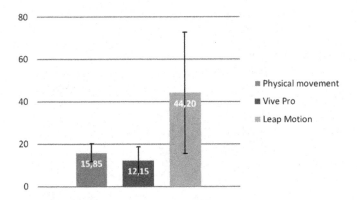

Fig. 8. Average task completion time for Task 1.

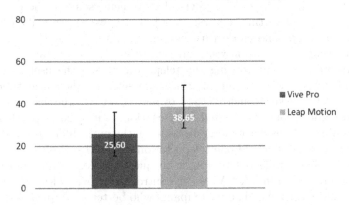

Fig. 9. Average task completion time for Task 2.

people. Several people have reported errors in Leap Motion's finger tracking. As a result, the virtual representation of the user's hand behaved unnaturally, which made the task more difficult to complete. Sometimes Leap Motion lost tracking of several fingers when interacting with an object, which caused the 3D pizza to fall to the ground.

Preferences. Figure 12 summarizes collected responses to a question concerning which method of movement – physical or teleportation using Vive Pro/Leap Motion – was more convenient and user-friendly. No user has stated that using

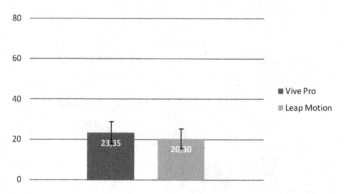

Fig. 10. Average task completion time for Task 3.

hand gestures to navigate through the virtual scene is most convenient. However, when it comes to Vive Pro controllers and physical movement, the votes are evenly distributed. In the case of physical movement, some of the participants indicated the fear of hitting a physical object despite the security grid being displayed. The users who chose this method of movement as the most convenient stated that teleportation was sometimes slightly disorientating. Although the camera did not rotate during the teleportation and the user was moving to the point he/she was looking at, three subjects lost their orientation after teleporting. When asked which method of movement was the least convenient, users almost unanimously indicated Leap Motion. Out of 20 respondents, only three users did not consider hand gestures to be the most difficult. Two subjects chose physical movement and one teleportation using Vive Pro.

Figure 13 shows collected responses to questions concerning which of the methods of interaction in VR – Vive Pro controllers or Leap Motion – was more convenient and immersive. The participants who better performed with the use of the Vive Pro controllers, naturally, have chosen the first option. Only 4 of the subjects stated that when interacting with 3D models, using hand gestures is easier than using controllers. However, when asked which method of interaction seemed more interesting and immersive, 17 subjects chose Leap Motion. Most of the participants indicated the naturalness of hand gestures as the strongest point.

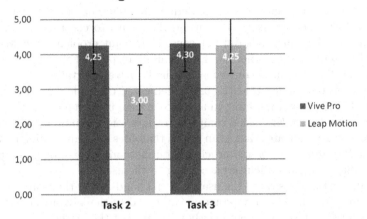

Fig. 11. Ratings given by users to interaction methods in Tasks 2 and 3.

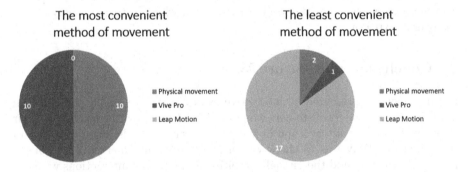

Fig. 12. Votes given by users regarding the method of movement.

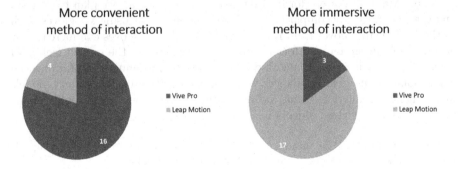

Fig. 13. Votes given by users regarding the method of interaction.

5   Discussion

The first task shows that there is no significant difference in the convenience of transportation in the scene when using the Vive Pro controllers and physical movement. Both methods did not cause significant problems and were well received by users. On the other hand, most users responded that hand gestures are the most difficult and inconvenient method for transportation.

The second task shows that the use of dedicated controllers is an easier and more user-friendly way to interact in a 3D scene than using hand gestures, which is also consistent with the tasks' completion times and the number of failures.

The third task indicates that in an action that does not require high precision, the method of interaction is not crucial. Both methods have similar completion times and have similar difficulties according to the users.

Overall, participants rated the use of virtual hands using the Leap Motion as a more immersive method of interaction compared to the Vive Pro controllers.

The results of the experiment clearly indicate that the method of interaction influences the experience of users in virtual reality. It is important to choose the proper method of interaction for a particular task that needs to be performed in the virtual space. There is also often a need to choose between prioritizing the convenience for users and the level of immersion, which in turn strongly affects the overall experience.

6   Conclusion and Future Work

In this paper, we presented an interactive exhibition of household appliances in VR that can be used by customers who would like to see how the product of their choice will look in a kitchen and how it can be operated. The main objective of the presented study was to check whether potential customers will be able to move efficiently around the virtual exhibition and whether interactions with the products will cause problems. Collected data suggest that users completed tasks without major difficulties. Only a few users reported some technical problems when using the Leap Motion controller.

There are several areas for future research. In particular, we plan to perform an experimental study comparing users' performance while using VR gloves, such as the Forte Data Gloves from BeBop. The use of haptic gloves can increase the accuracy of interactions performed by users and improve the overall feeling of immersion. Another area that could be explored is the connection of a physical exhibition of household appliances with the presentation of 3D product models in augmented reality. It would be interesting to see how users would handle interactions with virtual objects in such an environment.

Acknowledgments. The authors would like to thank Amica S.A. for supporting this research work and providing 3D models of products and graphics.

References

1. Alcañiz, M., Bigné, E., Guixeres, J.: Virtual reality in marketing: a framework, review, and research agenda. Front. Psychol. **10** (2019). https://doi.org/10.3389/fpsyg.2019.01530, https://www.frontiersin.org/article/10.3389/fpsyg.2019.01530
2. Voigt-Antons, J.N., Kojic, T., Ali, D., Möller, S.: Influence of hand tracking as a way of interaction in virtual reality on user experience. In: 2020 Twelfth International Conference on Quality of Multimedia Experience (QoMEX), pp. 1–4. IEEE (2020)
3. Borusiak, B., Pierański, B., Strykowski, S.: Perception of in-store assortment exposure. Stud. Ekon. **334**, 108–119 (2017)
4. Farah, M.F., Ramadan, Z.B., Harb, D.H.: The examination of virtual reality at the intersection of consumer experience, shopping journey and physical retailing. J. Retail. Consum. Serv. **48**, 136–143 (2019). https://doi.org/10.1016/j.jretconser.2019.02.016, https://www.sciencedirect.com/science/article/pii/S0969698918310634
5. Flotyński, J., et al.: An immersive service guide for home appliances. In: 2018 IEEE 8th International Conference on Consumer Electronics - Berlin (ICCE-Berlin), pp. 370–375. IEEE Xplore (2019). https://doi.org/10.1109/ICCE-Berlin47944.2019.8966215, https://ieeexplore.ieee.org/document/8966215
6. Fransen, M., Verlegh, P., Kirmani, A., Smit, E.: A typology of consumer strategies for resisting advertising, and a review of mechanisms for countering them. Int. J. Advert. **34**, 6–16 (2015). https://doi.org/10.1080/02650487.2014.995284
7. Gebhardt, S., flapAssist: how the integration of VR and visualization tools fosters the factory planning process. In: 2015 IEEE Virtual Reality (VR), pp. 181–182, March 2015. https://doi.org/10.1109/VR.2015.7223355
8. Kandaurova, M., Lee, S.H.M.: The effects of virtual reality (VR) on charitable giving: the role of empathy, guilt, responsibility, and social exclusion. J. Bus. Res. **100**, 571–580 (2019). https://doi.org/10.1016/j.jbusres.2018.10.027, https://www.sciencedirect.com/science/article/pii/S0148296318305083
9. Kitson, A., Riecke, B.E., Hashemian, A.M., Neustaedter, C.: Navichair: Evaluating an embodied interface using a pointing task to navigate virtual reality. In: Proceedings of the 3rd ACM Symposium on Spatial User Interaction. pp. 123–126. SUI2015, ACM, New York, NY, USA (2015). https://doi.org/10.1145/2788940.2788956, http://doi.acm.org/10.1145/2788940.2788956
10. Krasonikolakis, I., Vrechopoulos, A., Pouloudi, A.: Store selection criteria and sales prediction in virtual worlds. Inf. Manag.**51**(6), 641–652 (2014). https://doi.org/10.1016/j.im.2014.05.017, https://www.sciencedirect.com/science/article/pii/S0378720614000779
11. Laurell, C., Sandström, C., Berthold, A., Larsson, D.: Exploring barriers to adoption of virtual reality through social media analytics and machine learning – an assessment of technology, network, price and trialability. J. Bus. Res. **100**, 469–474 (2019). https://doi.org/10.1016/j.jbusres.2019.01.017, https://www.sciencedirect.com/science/article/pii/S0148296319300177
12. LaViola, Jr., J.J.: Context aware 3D gesture recognition for games and virtual reality. In: ACM SIGGRAPH 2015 Courses, SIGGRAPH 2015, pp. 10:1–10:61. ACM, New York, NY, USA (2015). https://doi.org/10.1145/2776880.2792711, http://doi.acm.org/10.1145/2776880.2792711

13. Lee, K.C., Chung, N.: Empirical analysis of consumer reaction to the virtual reality shopping mall. Comput. Hum. Behav. **24**(1), 88 – 104 (2008). https://doi.org/10.1016/j.chb.2007.01.018, http://www.sciencedirect.com/science/article/pii/S0747563207000155

14. Loureiro, S.M.C., Guerreiro, J., Eloy, S., Langaro, D., Panchapakesan, P.: Understanding the use of virtual reality in marketing: a text mining-based review. J. Bus. Res. **100**, 514–530 (2019). https://doi.org/10.1016/j.jbusres.2018.10.055, https://www.sciencedirect.com/science/article/pii/S0148296318305368

15. Meißner, M., Pfeiffer, J., Peukert, C., Dietrich, H., Pfeiffer, T.: How virtual reality affects consumer choice. J. Bus. Res. **117**, 219–231 (2020). https://doi.org/10.1016/j.jbusres.2020.06.004, https://www.sciencedirect.com/science/article/pii/S0148296320303684

16. Piumsomboon, T., Lee, G., Lindeman, R.W., Billinghurst, M.: Exploring natural eye-gaze-based interaction for immersive virtual reality. In: 2017 IEEE Symposium on 3D User Interfaces (3DUI), pp. 36–39, March 2017. https://doi.org/10.1109/3DUI.2017.7893315

17. Roupé, M., Bosch-Sijtsema, P., Johansson, M.: Interactive navigation interface for virtual reality using the human body. Comput. Environ.Urban Syst. **43**(Supplement C), 42–50 (2014). https://doi.org/10.1016/j.compenvurbsys.2013.10.003, http://www.sciencedirect.com/science/article/pii/S0198971513000884

18. Sobociński, P., Strugała, D., Walczak, K., Maik, M., Jenek, T.: Large-scale 3d web environment for visualization and marketing of household appliances. In: De Paolis, L.T., Arpaia, P., Bourdot, P. (eds.) Augmented Reality, Virtual Reality, and Computer Graphics, pp. 25–43. Springer, Cham (2021). https://doi.org/10.1007/978-3-030-87595-4_3

19. Statista: Retail e-commerce sales worldwide from 2014 to 2021 (2018), https://www.statista.com/statistics/379046/worldwide-retail-e-commerce-sales/

20. Thomann, G., Nguyen, D.M.P., Tonetti, J.: Expert's evaluation of innovative surgical instrument and operative procedure using haptic interface in virtual reality, pp. 163–173. Springer, Cham (2014). https://doi.org/10.1007/978-3-319-01848-5-13

21. Walczak, K., Flotyński, J., Strugała, D.: Semantic contextual personalization of virtual stores. In: De Paolis, L.T., Bourdot, P. (eds.) Augmented Reality, Virtual Reality, and Computer Graphics, pp. 220–236. Springer, Cham (2019). https://doi.org/10.1007/978-3-030-25965-5_17

22. Walczak, K., et al.: Virtual and augmented reality for configuring, promoting and servicing household appliances. In: Trojanowska, J., Ciszak, O., Machado, J.M., Pavlenko, I. (eds.) Advances in Manufacturing II, pp. 368–380. Springer, Cham (2019). https://doi.org/10.1007/978-3-030-18715-6_31

23. Zielasko, D., Neha, N., Weyers, B., Kuhlen, T.W.: A reliable non-verbal vocal input metaphor for clicking. In: 2017 IEEE Symposium on 3D User Interfaces (3DUI), pp. 40–49, March 2017. https://doi.org/10.1109/3DUI.2017.7893316

TryItOn: A Virtual Dressing Room with Motion Tracking and Physically Based Garment Simulation

Gilda Manfredi[1]([✉]), Nicola Capece[1], Ugo Erra[1], Gabriele Gilio[1],
Vincenzo Baldi[2], and Simone Gerardo Di Domenico[2]

[1] University of Basilicata, 85100 Potenza, PZ, Italy
{gilda.manfredi,nicola.capece,ugo.erra,gabriele.gilio}@unibas.it
[2] SAUTECH S.R.L., 84013 Cava de' Tirreni, SA, Italy
{vincenzo.baldi,simone.didomenico}@sautechgroup.com

Abstract. The interest in the online shopping field has increased considerably nowadays. This has led to emerging technologies being applied in this context. One of the sectors to which particular attention has been paid is the clothing sale. The main reason comes from the problem of physically trying on clothes to choose the correct size. This issue can be addressed using methodologies based on virtual reality and Human-Computer Interaction (HCI). This paper presents a Virtual Dressing Room (VDR) application named TryItOn that allows the user to try on digital clothes. The proposed solution offers an immersive and realistic experience by combining a high degree of photorealism, the presence of an avatar with accurate measurements, the natural interaction with the environment through movements of hands or the entire body, and the use of a real-time physical simulation of the garment.

Keywords: Virtual Dressing Room · Body tracking · Garment physical simulation

1 Introduction

In the last few years, the entire world population has faced a serious epidemic that has led us to gradually change our lifestyles and habits. Fear of contagion has shown people to reduce unnecessary travel and to pay more attention to hygiene. This change is also reflected in the purchase mode of goods such as clothing and footwear. In this regard, many studies conducted in various parts of the world show that there has been an increase in purchases made using e-commerce platforms since the beginning of the pandemic. To confirm this thesis, we conducted a study on consumers' buying habits, which showed that, despite the increase in online purchases, many people still prefer to shop in-store if clothing items have to be purchased. The customer can try on different sizes in the shop and choose the correct one, an action impossible to perform on a standard website for online shopping. As a demonstration of this, it is possible

© Springer Nature Switzerland AG 2022
L. T. De Paolis et al. (Eds.): XR Salento 2022, LNCS 13445, pp. 63–76, 2022.
https://doi.org/10.1007/978-3-031-15546-8_5

to note that, in recent times, fashion brands and retailers have begun to invest in Virtual Shopping (VS). This term bridges the gap between the online and in-store shopping experience. With VS, the customer is not forced to browse a catalogue containing static images of clothes; otherwise, he can have a more interactive and immersive experience thanks to the support of Virtual Reality (VR) and Augmented Reality (AR). Some virtual shopping solutions are already on the market, for example, digital stores and virtual showrooms [1,2], which allow brands to establish an interactive 3D digital store on their website or metaverse platform [3]. Digital stores ensure users a memorable online shopping experience by allowing them to visit the physical store from the comfort of their own homes. The virtual shopping field also includes VDRs, which allow the customer to try on the garment he intends to buy and see how it fits. With VDRs, the user can physically show up in the store and try on virtual clothes using smart mirrors without undressing or touching the clothing. Alternatively, the same VDR solution can be implemented to work on a PC with a webcam or on a smartphone. In this way, the user can try on clothes directly from his own home. As in the previous case, there are VDR solutions on the market. However, these solutions suffer from some limitations, including the absence of dress animations [4], the presence of artifacts due to the incorrect tracking of body measurements [5,6], or clothes that do not adapt to the user's body as their simulation is not based on the physical characteristics of the fabric they are made of [5,6]. Due to these limitations, the users could have an unrealistic experience because they would not be able to see if the chosen cloth size is the correct one. These problems could be addressed by introducing new generation approaches that make real-time execution their strength. Among these, it is necessary to consider the modern depth cameras based algorithms. Through artificial intelligence, they allow not only to acquire an image but also to perform advanced operations on it, such as the identification and segmentation of people and the tracking of their joints' positions, all performed in real-time. The body tracking ensures users an interaction with the virtual environment similar to reality, projecting their movements within the game scene.

The other solutions to consider, concern the algorithms for the physical simulation of garments in real-time. In the literature there are already well-optimized algorithms [7,8] that use force-based methods to simulate the deformation of a fabric and its interaction with the surrounding environment. Physically simulated digital garment can be draped over a 3D character. If this was animated, then the garment would follow its movements.

Our research work is focused precisely on the idea of using these modern solutions to overcome the previously mentioned limitations. We developed a 3D VDR application called TryItOn, having a robust pipeline based on Unreal Engine 4.27 (UE4) [9]. This is a game engine that we have chosen for its ability to generate hyper-realistic environments that guarantee an immersive real-time virtual reality experience. The TryItOn application will allow the user to choose and try on realistic digital garments, faithfully reconstructing the 3D models of both the user and the real garments, the latter available in various sizes.

A single RGB-D camera system supports TryItOn with a dual function: accurately acquire the customer's anthropometric measurements and track their movements in real-time. The anthropometric measurements will be helpful to create a 3D model of the user as faithful to reality as possible. At the same time, the tracking of movements will be used to reconstruct and animate the skeleton of the 3D character. The modeling and simulation of the clothes were entrusted to a third-party UE4 plugin called uDraper. It carries out a real-time simulation of a garment movement similar to reality since it is based on specific physical characteristics of the fabric it is made. The plugin comes with software to model clothes starting from a real-scale tailored pattern.

The remainder of this paper is structured as follow: the Sect. 2 provides a background and methods description; the Sect. 3 shows an overview of the related works; the Sect. 4 contains a description of Tryiton's pipeline; the Sect. 5 opens to final considerations and future works.

2   Background

The solution proposed in this paper was developed using the Microsoft Azure Kinect camera, Blender version 2.92, Unreal Engine 4.27 and the uDraper plugin with its modeling software.

The Microsoft Azure Kinect device [10] is characterized by: a 12-MP BT.601 full-range RGB camera, a 1-Megapixel Time-of-Flight (ToF) depth camera, a CMOS di 12 MP OV12A10 rolling shutter sensor, a motion sensor including an accelerometer and a gyroscope, both sampled at $1.6kHz$, and a 7-microphone array. The device is equipped with a set of SDKs that process the information received from sensors and cameras. Noteworthy is the Sensor SDK [11] that provides access to cameras, sensors, device calibration data, and camera frame meta-data. With this, it is possible to align depth and RGB camera streaming and synchronize multiple devices. Our application also makes use of the Body Tracking SDK [12] which, through segmentation, identifies and estimates 3D joints and control points, resulting in a fully articulated body tracking of multiple skeletons.

Blender [13] is a free, open-source, and cross-platform software (runs on Linux, macOS, and Windows). It offers a wide range of essential tools for modeling, rendering, animation and rigging, video editing, compositing, texturing, and various types of simulation. The peculiarity of this software lies in the possibility of extending its functionality through one or more Python scripts, which can take advantage of tightly integrated APIs.

Lastly, Unreal Engine 4 is a 3D game engine with an editor to develop real-time photorealistic and interactive applications. Photorealism is guaranteed by the possibility of performing dynamic physical simulations and lifelike animations, all rendered using sophisticated lighting techniques. Being written in C++, UE4 is highly portable and supports different platforms such as PCs, consoles, mobile, AR, and VR devices. Like Blender, also UE4 functionalities can be extended via native or third-party libraries.

3   Related Works

The idea of VDR began to develop after a study by Brian Beck [14] which demonstrated that in 1999, online customers were reluctant to buy items that they could not try on. Right after that, F. Cordier et al. [15] presented a web-based virtual-try-on system that produces personally sized bodies and animated garments receiving images or body measurements as input. Their approach is based on using a pre-trained generic database for bodies, garments, and animations to be adapted to personal data. The team made this choice because the operations of body creation and clothes simulation were too heavy to be performed on the web in real-time.

In the following years, various implementations of VDR began to take hold. In 2005, Kjærside et al. [16] provided a marker-based motion tracking technique. Three markers were placed on the user's body and used to identify the torso and arms movements. Subsequently, in 2015, Biswas et al. [17] proposed a 2D webcam real-time tag-less tracking system with face detection technology and hand gesture recognition functions. More and more approaches have been focused on the use of Azure Kinect to implement a VDR [18–20]. The solution of Kotan and Oz [21] uses the joint information given by the Azure Kinect to align the 3D clothes to the model and to trace the user's gestures, which are used to interact with the application.

In 2008, Uğur and Sahiner [22] moved the attention from motion tracking to 3D character creation, presenting an interpolation-based parametric body modeling tool for virtual dressing applications. Estimating the anthropometric measurements of the real user is necessary to model a 3D character as realistic as possible. For this reason, Yoshino et al. [23] defined a methodology to extrapolate the physical measurements of a customer starting from skeleton information provided by the Kinect.

Important was also the study concerning the clothing simulation field. For example, it is worth mentioning the work of Protopsaltou et al. [24] who in 2002 implemented a fast and straightforward cloth simulation system based on implicit integration. Later, in 2008, Zhong [25] proposed a method based on Axis Aligned Bounding Boxes detection to solve the problem of penetration in multilayer garments. In 2015, an analysis of the physical behaviour of different types of fabrics was performed [26]. In 2017 Holte [27] proposed an alternative method of garment modeling which consisted of scanning a real garment using an RGB-D sensor.

4   System Architecture Pipeline

The TryItOn pipeline, shown in Fig. 1, is characterized by two types of operations: one-time and real-time operations. The former are performed only once during the modeling phase. Specifically, the base character is created before the application release, while new garments can be modeled both during the creation and the update phase of the clothes catalogue. On the other hand, real-time operations are performed at the application runtime.

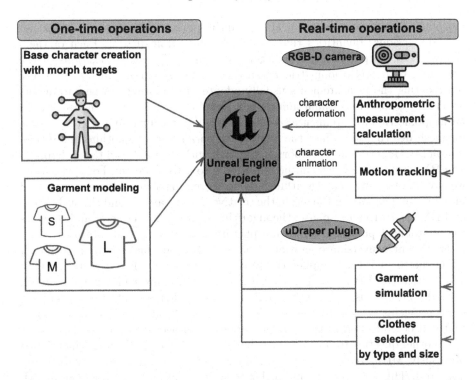

Fig. 1. System architecture pipeline. It shows one-time and real-time operations. The one-time operations concern the modeling of characters and garments that will be loaded into the UE4 project. The real-time operations concern the anthropometric measurements extraction, the user's movement tracking, the physical fabric simulation, and the choice of clothing based on the type and size.

As already mentioned in the introduction, the TryItOn application is based on UE4; therefore the models created during non-runtime operations are loaded into the UE4 project, and the real-time operations are performed in the game engine.

4.1 One-Time Operations

Base Character Creation with Morph Targets. A realistic VDR requires a 3D model of the user as faithful as possible to reality. To achieve this, we have chosen to model the 3D character within Blender, using a third-party add-on called MB-Lab [28]. This tool simplifies the modeling process of a humanoid character - you only have to insert the sex, ethnicity, and, eventually, measurements to generate a mesh with optimized topology and complete with teeth, tongue, and eyes. Finally, the mesh is equipped with a standard skeleton, useful for animations, and with materials that ensure a sense of realism.

For our case study, it is necessary to analyze the values type of the character deformation parameters with particular attention. The add-on has two body morphing parameters: anatomical and anthropometric measures. The former are adimensional quantities that can take values from 0 to 1. Each of them represents a morph target, a structure containing the vertex positions of the deformed mesh. Anthropometric measures are expressed in centimeters or inches, representing the measurements usually adopted in tailoring. These parameters are closely related to the anatomical ones; therefore, the change in the value of an anthropometric measurement also affects the anatomical parameters responsible for mesh deformation. Since the anatomical parameters are nothing more than morph targets, they can be exported, together with the mesh and the skeleton, in an FBX format file, which can be imported into a UE4 project. For this reason, we have implemented an algorithm capable of creating a character with standard measures and exporting the mesh, the relative morph targets, and the skeleton as an FBX file. In the first phase, the algorithm creates the character and converts the anatomical parameters into morph targets that UE4 can interpret. Then it carries out conversion operations from Blender coordinate system to that of UE4 (shown in Fig. 2), applies the same scale factor to the character as UE4 and creates the FBX file. The choice to import a deformable character mesh into UE4 allowed us to untie the application from Blender, but also to overcome some problems related to the real-time garment physical simulation (an issue that will be addressed in the relative paragraph of Sect. 4.2).

Another question to take into account is the skeleton structure. As mentioned previously, MB-Lab also creates a standard skeleton that can be easily imported into UE4. This software is equipped with a 3D creation tool, so it comes with a set of starter contents which includes a rigged mannequin. For this reason, most of the UE4 plugins integrate new features that work on starter contents and consequently on the structure of the UE4 mannequin skeleton. This led to the decision to replace the MB-Lab generated skeleton with the UE4 mannequin one. Therefore, we changed the character creation and export algorithm, adding the skeleton replacement operation. In this phase, the names and orientations of the bones are changed, then some superfluous bones, not present in the UE4

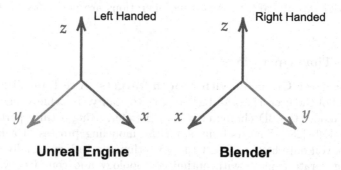

Fig. 2. UE4 and Blender coordinate systems. The first is left-handed and the second is right-handed. Both have the z-vector pointing upward.

skeleton, are eliminated and the same starting pose as the UE4 mannequin is applied to the skeleton.

Finally, it is necessary to make the last but important observation concerning the interaction of the garment with the body mesh. The garment physics engine used performs N collision operations for each frame, with N equal to the number of mesh vertices. Due to this, as the complexity of the mesh increases, N will increase, leading to a noticeable drop in performance in terms of Frame Per Second (FPS). To overcome this problem, we have chosen to create an additional character mesh with a lower definition Level Of Details (LOD) and without head and fingers, to reduce the number of vertices. This is a collision mesh that will be used only by the garment physics engine and, therefore, will be hidden from the user's view. The collision mesh will also have the relative morph targets so that the dress follows the character deformations.

Garment Modeling. The clothes' digital models are created with uDraper modeling software. The modeling process starts with a 2D pattern (Fig. 3(a)). It can be designed in separate software, exported as an SVG or CAD file, and subsequently imported into uDraper. Alternatively, the software offers many features to create a pattern directly through its interface. To ensure that the dress is simulated correctly within UE4, it is necessary to choose and import the character model who will wear the garment. The character model represents the reference point of the 3D scene because, thanks to it, it is possible to understand how to arrange the pieces of the pattern in the 3D scene so that they are correctly sewn together. For the seams to work, they must first be defined on the edges of the pattern (Fig. 3(b)). After this, the garment can be simulated (Fig. 3(c)) and exported as a 3D Garment file.

However, the digital model cannot be said to be complete without the appropriate material. In this regard, for each section of the pattern, it is possible to define a material complete with texture for diffuse color and normal maps. Each material also has a series of physical parameters (weight, damping, friction, thickness, etc.) that define the fabric's behavior. In this regard, we conducted a study on different fabric types (cotton, denim, wool, etc.) to identify the correct set of parameter values associated with each of them. Therefore, we create a collection of cards, each having a scrap of fabric, the main characteristics of the fabric, and the evaluation of the sartorial parameters. The garment can also be enriched with decorative elements such as buttons, zips, and embroidery logos. Finally, the software provides a pattern classification functionality, which creates a range of sizes for the pattern. In this way, it is possible to export clothes of different sizes.

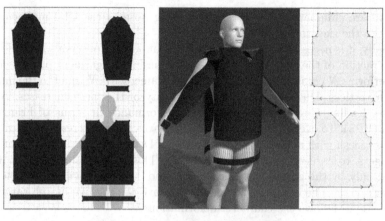

(a) 2D Pattern   (b) 3D cloth parts arrangement + seams

(c) Simulated Garment

Fig. 3. The image shows an example of a 2D pattern (a). Each part of the pattern must be arranged around the character and sewn together. The seams in the 3D view are highlighted in red, while those in the 2D view have different colors for each pair of pattern edges (b). After sewing, the cloth can be draped around the body (c). (Color figure online)

4.2 Real-Time Operations

RGB-D Camera Operations. The RGB-D camera operations play an essential role in our pipeline for the HCI. Indeed, the Azure Kinect provides tools to perform lower-level operations, such as capturing an RGB image, and for higher-level operations, such as identifying skeletons of people in front of the camera. These operations are also performed in real-time: a fundamental requirement to make usable the TryItOn application. The tools mentioned above are provided in the form of SDKs. To use these libraries within UE4, we have implemented a plugin named AzurePlugin, with a dual function: to calculate the anthropometric measurements and track the user's movements. For the calculation of the anthropometric measurement, we designed a REST (REpresentational State Transfer) architecture [29] (Fig. 4) in which UE4 is a client that interacts with a server application via HTTP standard interface. AzurePlugin takes the images provided by the camera and sends them to the webserver within an HTTP message. The web server runs a Python application called Anthropometric Measurement Calculation (AMC), which takes as input a series of user images, calculates the anthropometric measurements, and returns them as a JSON string. The AMC application uses a 3D pose estimation system, named FrankMocap [30], to produce the user's 3D model on which a well-designed algorithm calculates the anthropometric measurements. These are returned as a response to UE4 within another HTTP message.

One of the REST architecture advantages is distributing the calculation among multiple resources, ensuring more remarkable performance in terms of computational cost. Furthermore, as clients and servers communicate via an interface, they work independently. This ensures communication even between applications implemented with different programming languages (i.e., the UE4 C++ application and the AMC Python application). Information exchange between the client and the server takes place only once for each user. However, for the motion tracking operations the AzurePlugin works in a completely different way. First, the plugin opens a new thread to extrapolate, for each frame, the position and orientation of a series of body joints (shown in Fig. 5), using the Azure body tracking SDK. Each joint position and orientation are expressed in the depth camera space; therefore, the Azure plugin makes a conversion from the coordinate system mentioned above to the UE4 one (Fig. 6).

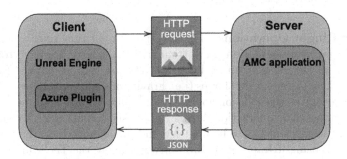

Fig. 4. REST architecture for anthropometric measurements calculation. The Azure Plugin sends an HTTP request containing an image that the AMC application on the server uses to produce the anthropometric measurements, returned as a JSON string.

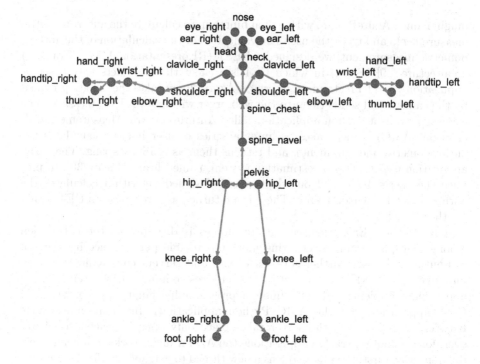

Fig. 5. Azure Kinect joint hierarchy.

The final step is to associate the resulting orientations with the bones of the UE4 skeleton. The Table 1 shows the mapping between the Azure Kinect joints and the bones of the UE4 skeleton.

UDraper Plugin Operations. The uDraper plugin runs operations related to physical garment simulation. In particular, it calculates, for each frame, the deformation of the garment mesh based on internal (i.e., resistance related to bending or shear) and external forces (i.e., gravity or collision volumes). The garment must recognize the collision volume in the character mesh for our case. This is useful to allow their interaction during the physical simulation. To ensure this simulation, the garment has to be modeled and pre-simulated on the character's collision mesh using uDraper modeling software before the TryItOn application deployment. In this way, the clothes can be imported and simulated within the UE4 project at runtime.

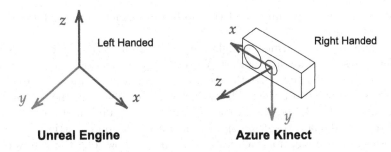

Fig. 6. UE4 and Azure Kinect coordinate systems. The first is left-handed and the second is right-handed with z-vector pointing out of the camera, y-vector pointing downward and x-vector is orthogonal to the other two.

Table 1. Mapping between the Azure Kinect joints and the bones of the UE4 skeleton. For the sake of brevity, only the central and left part of the skeletons have been considered. The association is repeated in a specular way on the right side.

Azure kinect joints	UE4 skeleton bones
pelvis	pelvis
spine_navel	spine_01
spine_chest	spine_03
neck	neck_01
clavicle_left	clavicle_l
shoulder_left	upperarm_l
elbow_left	lowerarm_l
wrist_left	hand_l
hip_left	thigh_l
knee_left	calf_l
ankle_left	foot_l
foot_left	ball_l
head	head

One of the prerequisites of the TryItOn application requires that the character has the exact anthropometric measurements as the user and that they have to be calculated at runtime. It is impossible to know the collision mesh of the user's 3D character before the deployment and execution of the application, and, consequently, it is impossible to model clothes on an unknown mesh. We have chosen to create a base character with deformable mesh to overcome this problem. In this way, the clothes can be modeled a priori on the non-deformed base mesh. At runtime, the clothes are imported into the UE4 project and applied to the non-deformed base character so that the garment physics can begin to work. When a user arrives, the anthropometric measurements are calculated and used to deform the base character. When the character is deformed, the garment simulation is already running, and the clothes can react to the deformation of the character mesh.

In addition to the garment simulation logic, the uDraper plugin offers real-time functions for changing clothes. We used these functions to implement a widget containing buttons that the user, through gestures, can select to choose the clothes and sizes to try on. The widget is a component in the screen space that inputs the hands' positions, calculated by the AzurePlugin, and converts them from world space to screen space. Then a validation is carried out on the new positions, verifying, for each button, if and for how long the values of the (x, y) coordinates of the positions are inside the button box. If the hands are placed inside the button box for 3 s, the button state becomes "clicked", and the relative garment appears on the character.

5   Conclusions

In this paper, we described our VDR solution, named TryItOn. This approach uses the high degree of photorealism of UE4 in combination with the Azure Kinect body tracking algorithms and the real-time garment physical simulation of the uDraper plugin. The user's realistic feeling while using our application is the main advantage compared to the other VDR solutions. Users are immersed in a digital environment with which they can interact using intuitive and natural body movements and hand gestures. The perception of realism is increased by the possibility of trying on digital garments modeled based on 2D patterns related to existing real clothes. Furthermore, the 3D garments interact in real-time with the user's 3D model and the surrounding environment in a way similar to real fabric, thanks to the use of a garment physics model.

Another advantage of our application is that it is not very expensive in computation, despite the high degree of photorealism. This is ensured by the presence of a well-defined algorithm for the physical simulation of the fabric and the possibility of distributing the calculation among multiple resources thanks to REST architecture. This feature would allow the development of both an in-store shopping solution characterized by a smart mirror and an online shopping solution that can run on mobile and desktop devices. Regarding the mobile solution, it is evident that it should use the phone camera, which does not have the SDKs necessary for body tracking. Therefore, for future work, it could be thought of using deep learning [31, 32] to track the user's movements by having a simple RGB camera available.

References

1. Obsess. https://obsessar.com/virtual-store/digital-store/
2. Hero. https://www.usehero.com/
3. Dionisio III, J.D.N., Burns, W.G., Gilbert, R.: 3D virtual worlds and the metaverse: current status and future possibilities. ACM Comput. Surv. **45**(3), 1–38 (2013). https://doi.org/10.1145/2480741.2480751

4. styleme. https://style.me/virtual-fitting/
5. zugara. http://zugara.com/virtual-dressing-room-technology
6. asizer. https://www.asizer.com/
7. Va, H., Choi, M.H., Hong, M.: Parallel cloth simulation using OpenGL shading language. Comput. Syst. Sci. Eng. **41**, 427–443 (2022)
8. Ivanov Vassilev, T.: Real-time velocity based cloth simulation with ray-tracing collision detection on the graphics processor. In: 2021 International Conference on Information Technologies (InfoTech), pp. 1–5 (2021). https://doi.org/10.1109/InfoTech52438.2021.9548602
9. Unreal Engine. https://www.unrealengine.com/en-US/
10. Azure Kinect DK. https://azure.microsoft.com/en-us/services/kinect-dk/#overview
11. Azure Kinect Sensor SDK. https://github.com/Microsoft/Azure-Kinect-Sensor-SDK
12. Azure Kinect Body Tracking SDK. https://docs.microsoft.com/en-us/azure/Kinect-dk/body-sdk-download
13. Blender 2.92. https://docs.blender.org/manual/en/2.92/index.html#
14. Beck, B.: Key Strategic Issues in Online Apparel Retailing, May 1999. https://dan.yourfit.com/
15. Cordier, F., Lee, W.S., Seo, H., Thalmann, N.: From 2D photos of yourself to virtual try-on dress on the web. In: Blandford, A., Vanderdonckt, J., Gray, P. (eds.) People and Computers–Interaction without Frontiers, pp. 31–26. Springer, London (2001). https://doi.org/10.1007/978-1-4471-0353-0_3
16. Kjærside, K., Kortbek, K.J., Hedegaard, H., Grønbæk, K.: ARDressCode: augmented dressing room with tag-based motion tracking and real-time clothes simulation. In: Proceedings of the central European Multimedia and Virtual Reality Conference, pp. 511–515 (2005)
17. Biswas, A., Dutta, S., Dey, N., Azar, A.: A Kinect-less augmented reality approach to real-time tag-less virtual trial room simulation. Int. J. Serv. Sci. Manag. Eng. Technol. **5**, 16 (2015). https://doi.org/10.4018/ijssmet.2014100102
18. Erra, U., Colonnese, V.: Experiences in the development of an augmented reality dressing room. In: International Conference on Augmented and Virtual Reality, pp. 467–474 (2015). https://doi.org/10.1007/978-3-319-22888-4_35
19. Adikari, S.B, Ganegoda, N.C., Meegama, R.G., Wanniarachchi, I.L.: Applicability of a single depth sensor in real-time 3d clothes simulation: augmented reality virtual dressing room using Kinect sensor. Adv. Human Comput. Interact. **2020**, 1–10 (2020). https://doi.org/10.1155/2020/1314598
20. Capece, N., Erra, U., Romaniello, G.: A low-cost full body tracking system in virtual reality based on Microsoft Kinect. In: De Paolis, L.T., Bourdot, P. (eds.) AVR 2018. LNCS, vol. 10851, pp. 623–635. Springer, Cham (2018). https://doi.org/10.1007/978-3-319-95282-6_44
21. Kotan, M., Oz, C.: Virtual dressing room application with virtual human using Kinect sensor. J. Mech. Eng. Autom. **5**, 333326 (2015). https://doi.org/10.17265/2159-5275/2015.05.008
22. Uğur, B., Sahiner, A.V.: A parametric human body modeling tool. In: Proceedings of ISCN 2008 - 8th International Symposium on Computer Networks, January 2008
23. Yoshino, N., Karungaru, S., Terada, K.: Body physical measurement using Kinect for vitual dressing room. In: 2017 6th IIAI International Congress on Advanced Applied Informatics (IIAI-AAI), pp. 847–852, July 2017. https://doi.org/10.1109/IIAI-AAI.2017.207

24. Protopsaltou, D., Luible-Bär, C., Marlene, A., Thalmann, N.: A body and garment creation method for an internet based virtual fitting room. In: Advances in Modelling, Animation and Rendering, pp. 105–122. Springer, London (2002). https://doi.org/10.1007/978-1-4471-0103-1_7

25. Zhong, Y.: Fast penetration resolving for multi-layered virtual garment dressing. Text. Res. J. **79**(9), 815–821 (2009)

26. Poonpong, B., Charlee, K., Salin, B.: realistic simulation in virtual fitting room using physical properties of fabrics. Proc. Comput. Sci. **75**, 12–16 (2015). https://doi.org/10.1016/j.procs.2015.12.189

27. Holte, M.: 3D scanning of clothing using a RGB-D sensor with application in a virtual dressing room. In: Duffy, V. (eds.) Advances in Applied Digital Human Modeling and Simulation. Advances in Intelligent Systems and Computing, vol. 481, pp. 143–153. Springer, Cham (2017). https://doi.org/10.1007/978-3-319-41627-4_14

28. MB-Lab. https://mb-lab-community.github.io/MB-Lab.github.io/

29. Fielding, R., Taylor, R.: Principled design of the modern web architecture. In: Proceedings of the 2000 International Conference on Software Engineering. ICSE 2000 the New Millennium, pp. 407–416 (2000). https://doi.org/10.1145/337180.337228

30. Rong, Y., Shiratori, T., Joo, H.: FrankMocap: a monocular 3D whole-body pose estimation system via regression and integration. In: IEEE International Conference on Computer Vision Workshops (2021)

31. Lugaresi, C., et al.: MediaPipe: a framework for perceiving and processing reality. In: Third Workshop on Computer Vision for AR/VR at IEEE Computer Vision and Pattern Recognition (CVPR) 2019 (2019). https://mixedreality.cs.cornell.edu/s/NewTitle_May1_MediaPipe_CVPR_CV4ARVR_Workshop_2019.pdf

32. Cao, Z., Martinez, G., Simon, T., Wei, S.E., Sheikh, Y.: OpenPose: realtime multi-person 2D pose estimation using part affinity fields. IEEE Trans. Pattern Anal. Mach. Intell. **43**, 172–1861 (2019). https://doi.org/10.1109/TPAMI.2019.2929257

Automatic Generation of 3D Animations from Text and Images

Alberto Cannavò$^{(\boxtimes)}$ ⓘ, Valentina Gatteschi, Luca Macis,
and Fabrizio Lamberti ⓘ

Dipartimento di Automatica e Informatica, Politecnico di Torino,
Corso Duca degli Abruzzi 24, Turin, Italy
{alberto.cannavo,valentina.gatteschi,luca.macis,
fabrizio.lamberti}@polito.it

Abstract. The understanding of information in a text description can be improved by visually accompanying it with images or videos. This opportunity is particularly relevant for books and other traditional instructional material. Videos or, more in general, (interactive) graphics contents, can help to increase the effectiveness of this material, by providing, e.g., an animated representation of the steps to be performed to carry out a given procedure. The generation of 3D animated contents, however, is still very labor-intensive and time-consuming. Systems able to speed up this process offering flexible and easy-to-use interfaces are becoming of paramount importance. Hence, this paper describes a system designed to automatically generate a computer graphics video by processing a text description and a set of associated images. The system combines Natural Language Processing and image analysis for extracting information needed to visually represent the procedure depicted in an instruction manual using 3D animations. It relies on a database of 3D models and preconfigured animations that are activated according to the information extracted from the said input. Moreover, by analyzing the images, the system can also generate new animations from scratch. Promising results have been obtained assessing the system performance in a specific use case focused on printers maintenance.

Keywords: Computer animation · Natural language processing · Image analysis · Virtual prototyping

1 Introduction

Today, the use of computer-generated animations is growing in a number of applications including movie and video-game production, industrial design, product advertising, education, etc. [18,22,29]. However, the process of generating animations or, more in general 3D graphic contents, still represents a time-consuming

This work was developed in the frame of the VR@POLITO initiative. The research was supported by PON "Ricerca e Innovazione" 2014-2020 – DM 1062/2021 funds.

L. T. De Paolis et al. (Eds.): XR Salento 2022, LNCS 13445, pp. 77–91, 2022.
https://doi.org/10.1007/978-3-031-15546-8_6

task requiring numerous skills [5]. Motivations can be found in the need to learn complex software, which require to work with sophisticated interfaces and to tweak many parameters to obtain the intended results [9]. Such constraints can limit the number of potential users involved in the generation and use of these contents, as well as delay their production and exploitation [23].

For these reasons, novel techniques and interfaces able to make the generation process both effortless and immediate are more and more attracting the attention of developers and non-graphics users [9]. Among the various approaches proposed in the literature to tackle this problem, one of the most intriguing is probably represented by the possibility to automatically generate graphics assets starting from text and/or images [4, 23]. Previous works showed the feasibility of generating 3D scenes and computer animations from the said contents in different application domains like, e.g., screenplay writing [11, 15], movie production [19, 28], embodied conversational agents [1, 25], public safety [14], and virtual environment design [4, 7].

The possibility to automatically create these contents would make it possible, e.g., for users with different skills to quickly create proofs of concept and virtual prototypes, speeding up the typical design and development iterations [28]. Besides the above benefits, the automatic generation of animated contents could play a fundamental role in easing the understanding of printed material used today in most of the educational activities. It could be exploited, for instance, to animate contents in school books [21]. It could also be used to create animated versions of traditional instruction manuals [26]. In fact, the possibility to dynamically visualize printed contents would help the cognitive processes of involved subjects, especially when practical abilities are deemed relevant [10]. For instance, videos could be used to represent the steps of a given procedure (e.g., for the maintenance of a complex equipment) showing an operator how to execute it; similarly, 3D animations could be exploited to depict an abstract, theoretical concept (e.g., the spatio-temporal curvature in a physics course) supporting students in the creation of an appropriate mental model for it.

Moving from the above considerations, this paper proposes an automatic text/image-to-3D-animation conversion system. The case of the generation of an animated video starting from an instruction manual is specifically considered. In particular, by providing a manual containing a text description of the steps in a given procedure supported by related illustrations, the system is able to create a computer graphics video showing the above steps animated in 3D. The final goal is not to produce a high-quality rendering, but rather a pre-visualization of the input contents that could help the users to better understand (and perform) the operations described in the manual.

To this aim, two software modules, named Semantic Engine and Rendering Engine have been designed. The first component enables the Natural Language Processing (NLP) and Image Analysis capabilities of the system, which are leveraged to extract text and images from the manual. Data are processed to produce, as the outcome of the overall workflow, a 3D animated video including the animation blocks created, for the various steps of the procedure, in a programmatic way by a scriptable animation software (in the specific case represented by Blender). The generation of the animated contents rendered in the video is carried out by following two different approaches. The first approach consists in activating animations already included in an animation library based on information extracted from the manual by the Semantic Engine. To cope with the possible limitations posed by the use of a library with a limited set of predefined animations, the system also features a mechanism to automatically create animations from scratch based on positional and rotational information extracted from the images in the manual.

The devised system has been developed and tested focusing on a specific use case, in which the input is represented by the instruction manuals of several printers. Besides describing the system architecture, this paper also reports on the results of a preliminary evaluation performed on the considered use case.

2   Related Works

The idea to generate static or animated scenes from texts and/or images is not totally new. Examples are provided by systems like, e.g., NALIG [2] (1993) and PAR [3] (2000), which were designed to convert a text into a static or animated scene. The systems were characterized by some limitations, like the need for the input texts to have a specific format, the limited ability to extrapolate information from the text, and the adoption of small-size databases of 3D models used for populating the scenes.

More recently, some studies partially addressed the limitations of the former works, proposing systems like, e.g., ScriptViz [15], CONFUCIUS [16] and IVELL [13]. The first work describes a system for the visualization of movie scripts in real time through graphics animations. CONFUCIUS consists in a multi-modal text-to-animation conversion system that generates animations from single input sentences. The last work describes an intelligent virtual environment for improving listening and speaking skills of non-native English language learners in which automatically generated animations are used to make a conversational agent get alive.

This domain has been addressed also from other viewpoints. For instance, in [11], a collaborative system was developed for the pre-visualization of screenplays with the final aim of making the movie production process easier. Online datasets were leveraged to improve the analysis of the text, thus enhancing efficiency and accuracy. Moreover, the work presented interesting features like the ability to analyze emotions and a high flexibility in terms of supported text formats. The work developed by Disney Research [28], in turn, focuses on the simplification of the text. The designed architecture based on a state machine is able to analyze texts formatted according to the standard rules for screenplays, texts with formatting errors, or even text not formatted at all, thus making the system flexible in terms of accepted input. The system makes use of linguistic rules for simplifying the text to be analyzed. In order to generate animations, the system combines the advantages offered by NeuralCoref[1] (an extension of the

---

[1] NeuralCoref: https://github.com/huggingface/neuralcoref.

library for advanced NLP named spaCy[2]) which is based on a Support Vector Machine specially trained to segment text with inconsistent indentation, and the animation pipeline adopted in a previous work [19].

The conversion from text to animations was not studied only for animating movies scripts. For example, the system in [8] generates animations of small groups of both people and objects to simulate crowded environments. Animations are created by parsing simple sentences in English through the Stanford Core NLP software [17]. Differently than in the above systems, in this case the information extracted from the text is used to construct structured descriptions about characters' attributes, behaviors, and locations. An interface allows the users to interactively modify, delete or add this information, with the aim of altering the resulting animation. Data that are difficult to extract from the text, such as time, camera positions/framing, animation speed, are defined manually. The work in [27] presents an authoring system for generating animated videos of cooking instructions that was designed to work with simple structured sentences (i.e., containing only subject and verb). The animations are generated through the decomposition rules of a verb in simpler actions referring to predefined animations that were manually generated and added to the system. In this way, the system does not need large libraries containing complex animations, since the output video can be generated by concatenating animation blocks depicting simpler operations.

Especially in the case of animated instruction manuals, text descriptions are usually complemented with images that visually represent actions to be performed. Therefore, it can be helpful to leverage information extracted from the analysis of visual contents, with the goal of obtaining a more reliable representation of the text descriptions. For example, the work in [1] presents a system to enhance the interaction with embodied conversational agents by leveraging human-like co-speech gestures. The mapping between the gesture and the corresponding part of the speech is automatically generated from a publicly available video dataset without the intervention of human experts (that could limit the variety of activated gestures). In [25], an augmented reality system was presented that basically converts the words depicted in a photo taken from a phone's camera into the corresponding sign language gestures. The animations are displayed on the phone's screen to help hearing-impaired people to learn English using the sign language.

If, on the one hand, the use of heterogeneous inputs could improve the fidelity of the generated animation, on the other hand could introduce issues regarding, e.g., the methodology to use for combining the different types of inputs. Indeed, the image analysis could return a large amount of low-level semantic information (e.g., colors, textures, trajectories, etc.) that, nonetheless, needs to be combined with high-level semantic content extracted from the text. These difficulties may be one of the reasons behind the paucity of works in the literature that envisaged the combination of text and images for the generation of animated contents.

---

[2] spaCy: https://spacy.io/.

The proposed work intends to make some steps forward in this direction, by presenting a system designed for converting text and images extracted, in the particular case, from instruction manuals into a video showing the operations to be performed though computer graphics animations. The final purpose is not to replace traditional manuals but rather to offer a complementary visualization tool that can help users in understanding their contents.

3   System Overview

As said, a system has been designed that, once received in input a manual with the text instructions and the images representing the steps to follow in the procedure of interest, is able to automatically generate a video that visually represents the above contents. Figure 1 illustrates the system's workflow.

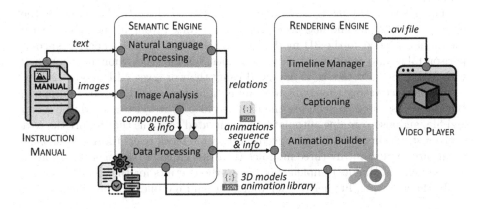

Fig. 1. Workflow of the proposed system.

The resources, i.e., text and images, are automatically extracted from the instruction manual by the Semantic Engine.

More specifically, text is processed by the Natural Language Processing module, which implements a modified version of the framework named Scene Graph Parser[3]. This module is leveraged to extract the *relations* among the terms identified in a sentence. Relations are data structures containing the following information: i) instruction number, ii) subject (i.e., the entity which performs the main action), iii) the predicate expressing the action to be executed, iv) the object/s involved in the action, v) possible modifiers (clauses) used to alter the meaning of the predicate, vi) possible elements indicating where the actions take place.

For what it concerns the images, the Image Analysis module supports the detection of components represented in the figures of the manual through the

---

[3] Scene Graph Parser: http://tiny.cc/dnqpuz.

Mask R-CNN framework[4]. In particular, the following data are made available for each component that is detected in the figure: i) name of the figure, ii) name of the component, iii) the mask to segment the component, iv) position of the component within the figure, and v) the Region of Interest (ROI), i.e., the information about the bounding box of the component.

Once the components are detected, a filtering operation is performed to identify the sub-components to be included in the animation. To this aim, the list of components extracted from the text is compared with those found in the images. This operation removes from the list the components that are not mentioned in the instructions.

Using the recognized relations and components, the Data Processing module tries to automatically find a mapping with the 3D models and animations defined in the Blender file. For each 3D model, a library of animations is available which refer to the most common operations executed in the considered application scenario.

The above mapping is generated by comparing directly the name of the objects/components and actions extracted/recognized from/in the manual with the name assigned to the 3D models and the animations in Blender. The comparison takes into account not only the names, but also the synonyms generated with WordNet[5]. Processing is managed using the word2vec NLP model [20].

Besides activating pre-configured animations based on the above mapping, Blender is also used to generate the output video. The video is produced as an .avi file, and also contains automatically-generated captions that report the text of the instruction to which each specific animation block refers to. All these operations are carried out by three modules (i.e., the Timeline Manager, Captioning and Animation Builder) implemented as Python scripts for Blender.

In the following, further details about the said modules are provided.

3.1   Natural Language Processing

As anticipated, Scene Graph Parser is used to process the text in this part of the workflow. This framework builds onto spaCy for analyzing the natural language.

In order to overcome the limitation regarding the impossibility for this tool to work with texts whose subject is not explicit within the sentence, some modifications have been implemented. Under the hypothesis that actions reported in the instruction manual have to be executed by who is reading it, the pronoun "you" is automatically set as the subject in the sentences in which it is not present. Further modifications have been implemented to process sentences expressed in the negative form (e.g., "check if the product is not already on"), using imperative forms (e.g., "open the front cover"), or containing phrasal verbs (e.g., "push down the component"). Moreover, with the original version of the Scene Graph Parser it was not possible to manage multiple objects associated with the same predicate (e.g., "close the cartridge door and the front cover"). In

---

[4] Mask R-CNN: https://github.com/matterport/Mask_RCNN.
[5] WordNet: https://wordnet.princeton.edu/.

order to deal with this constraint, instructions that are recognized as composed by multiple actions (i.e., containing several predicates) are split into separate instructions. For instance, the instruction "place the new ink cartridge into the cartridge holder with the bottom down, then push down the new ink cartridge until it clicks into place" is split into two parts referring to the predicates "to place" and "to push down", respectively. Finally, the proposed system is able to modify the identified relations when new knowledge is provided. For instance, the sentence "put the cartridge into the slot", is "augmented" by considering the place (i.e., "the slot") in which the action (i.e., "put the cartridge") takes place. The augmentation is not possible with the native version of Scene Graph Parser, since the processing of a relation is stopped after forming the simple sentence "you put the cartridge".

The mentioned tools are used by the proposed system to process the instructions in the manual by following a procedure composed of several steps. First, the entire text is parsed in order to identify the instructions/steps that describe the procedure. Once the individual instructions have been identified, sentences are separated obtaining so-called *noun chunks* (i.e., base noun phrases) that are elaborated individually. The corresponding instruction number is assigned to each sentence. Possible sub-instructions numbering is also managed. Each sentence is provided as input to the Scene Graph Parser to generate a *scene graph*, i.e., a structured representation of the relations. Dependencies among the terms used in a sentence are analyzed through spaCy. Information extracted from spaCy is organized in a data structure named Doc. In this work, the POS (i.e., part-of-speech) and DEP (i.e., the syntactic relation) tags of the Doc object are used, together with manually defined heuristics, for creating the relations. Tokens and their position within the sentence are analyzed in order to identify the (possibly implicit) subject of the actions. Predicates expressed in the negative form are not considered for creating the animation, as they refer to an action not to be executed. Relations that are identified only among objects (without a predicate) are not used in the current version of the system; however, in the future, they could be added to improve the outcome.

As said, the system leverages a set of 3D animated models that have been made available in a Blender file. In order to identify the 3D models and animations a given instruction refers to, the system performs a comparison between the names of the elements (i.e., objects/components and actions) identified in the instruction with the names of the 3D models and animations defined in Blender. In the comparison, synonyms obtained through WordNet are considered to improve the similarity match. In the case of compound nouns (for which Word-Net does not provide adequate results), the synonyms of the individual terms are combined, i.e., concatenated, to form a new compound term exposing the same structure. For instance, the word "paper tray" is split in the words "paper" and "tray", that present as synonyms "newspaper" and "drawer", respectively. The three combinations of the above words (i.e., "newspaper tray", "paper drawer", and "newspaper drawer") are considered in the comparison. The percentages reporting the level of similarity between the terms and their synonyms are computed using word2vec. A threshold equal to 70% was set to consider the mapping between the recognized elements and Blender's 3D models as valid. If the percentage is higher than the threshold, then the predicates are compared to the names of the Blender's animations. In case of a percentage greater than 80%, the match is considered as valid, and the corresponding animation block is added to the video. The values of the two thresholds were obtained empirically.

3.2   Image Analysis

The goal of this part of the workflow is to recognize the components represented in the images appearing in the manual. This operation enables several system's functionalities, namely, reconstructing the point of view from which the final video has to be shot, complementing the text-based recognition of components involved in the actions, and supporting the generation of animations by considering graphics cues (like, e.g., arrows or circles) used in the manual.

Images are analyzed with Mask R-CNN. The pre-trained models available for the above framework were found to be not directly applicable to the images of interest for the considered use case (instruction manuals of printers), as they are generally trained on images representing objects of common use and they are not meant to recognize specialized components (like printer's parts). Moreover, the existing models faced difficulties at recognizing images with a low resolution and in grayscale, which are very common in the instruction manuals. For these reasons, a TensorFlow model was trained by using a small-size dataset containing 500 images of printers, which were manually annotated. The model was trained to recognize 34 classes of objects.

In order to annotate the images, the VGG Image Annotator[6] tool was leveraged. With the trained model, the system is able to detect printer components through a component detection process based on image and instance segmentation. Figure 2 shows an example of the results that can be obtained with the component detection. In particular with the R-CNN framework, the following data are retrieved: the ROIs containing the identified components (i.e., the dashed boxes in the figure around the components), the labels representing the recognized class (e.g., paper output tray, flipped arrow, front cover, etc.), the similarity of the identified object with respect to the trained model (e.g., the paper output tray had a similarity equal to 0.951 in the considered example), and the masks to segment the objects (e.g., the red area highlighting the paper output tray component, in this case).

Generally, movements described in the instruction manual are also depicted in the images, e.g., using arrow signs. The image analysis also enables, in principle, the reconstruction of these movements. At the present time, the system assumes that the images show the final poses that the components have to reach in the animation. Thus, by analyzing the positions of the components with respect to the printer's body, it is possible to generate animations that represent rotation and translation transformations. For this reason, the positions of the components are also leveraged.

---

[6] VGG Image Annotator: http://tiny.cc/fnqpuz.

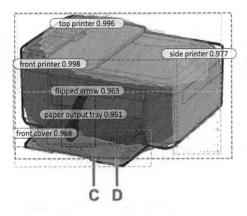

Fig. 2. Examples of the component detection output.

As mentioned, images provided as input to the system are also used to detect the points of view that will be used to frame the components in the generation of the video. This operation is done in order to provide the users with a visualization of the components which is, as much as possible, similar to that shown in the manual. To this aim, the user is requested to select a subset of images from the manual that frame the printer from a desired point of view. These images are then elaborated through a computer vision algorithm implemented using OpenCV that is based on the Harris Corner Detection [12], the Canny Edge Detection [6] and the corner detection method described in [24]. The output of this algorithm allows the system to choose which camera has to be used for shooting the video among those defined in the Blender's scene. In particular, once extracted the corners of the printer's body in the input images, the system tries to identify the camera in the scene from which it is possible to observe the most similar layout of the corners (relative positions and distances of the points) by testing all the cameras defined in Blender.

3.3 Video Generation

After the camera calibration, the three modules of the Rendering Engine, i.e., Blender, are exploited to assemble the complete animation, produce the video, and add the captions with the text of the instructions which the various animation blocks refer to.

The communication between the Rendering Engine and the Data Processing module of the Semantic Engine is based on network communications over HTTP. In the devised network architecture, the role of the server is played by the Rendering Engine. The module of the Semantic Engine, which acts as the client, is designed to request data through HTTP GET messages, and to use HTTP POST messages to communicate how to update the Blender's scene and produce the animations according to the results of the data processing. In particular, once the system receives the instruction manual as input, a HTTP GET

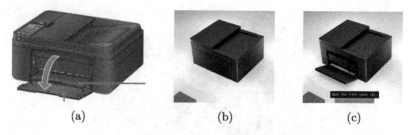

(a)   (b)   (c)

Fig. 3. Example of animation generated based solely on information extracted from an image of the manual: a) source image, b–c) two keyframes of the animated video.

request is sent to Blender by the Semantic Engine asking the names of all the 3D models representing the considered printer and its components, as well as the list of available animations. Data are formatted in JSON. After elaborating the received information, a HTTP POST request is sent to Blender along with a JSON file containing the following data: i) a list of relations identified by the Natural Language Processing module, ii) a list containing the name, position, and ROI of all the components detected by the Image Analysis module, iii) a list of animations reconstructed from the analysis of the images. Once the above lists have been extracted from the JSON file, Blender proceeds with the selection or the generation of the corresponding animations based on received data.

In the first case (selection), the mapping between a relation and the corresponding 3D models/animations to be used/activated has already been identified by the Data Processing module. Hence, the Timeline Manager module is programmed to add the corresponding animation block in the correct position of the Blender's timeline.

In the second case (generation), the animation blocks are automatically produced by the Animation Builder module of the Rendering Engine using data obtained from the Image Analysis module. An approach based on keyframes is pursued, which creates the animations by programmatically setting the amount of rotation and/or translation to be applied to the selected 3D models, as well as the axes to consider for the transformations. In the current implementation, the transformations managed by the system are constrained to a single axis. The newly generated animations are finally added to the timeline. Figure 3 shows an example of animation automatically generated by the system.

The animation blocks (both the newly generated ones and those selected from the library) are concatenated using the Blender's NonLinear Animation (NLA) Editor. This tool is also used to add the captions to the video, thus implementing the Timeline Manager and Captioning modules. For what it concerns the captioning, the first row of each caption (with the text in white over a black background, as depicted in Fig. 3c) indicates the corresponding instruction identified in the manual, whereas the second row (in red over a gray background, in the figure shown just for debugging purposes) provides the name of the animation activated in Blender.

At the end of the process, a video is rendered and saved as an .avi file.

4 Use Case

In this section, the results obtained in preliminary system evaluation will be presented in order to show the performance of the proposed approach for the automatic generation of an animated video showing common operations performed during the maintenance of some printers. The printers used for the considered use case include models of common brands for which instruction manuals or user guides are freely available online. The selected printers are the Canon PIXMA-MX495[7], Epson WF-7010[8], HP Deskjet 3000[9]. The 3D models as well as a number of predefined animations were manually created for each printer using the images in the manual as a reference. The models include, on average, 23 components and 30 predefined animations. The animation library encompassed common operations regarding printers maintenance like, e.g., opening/closing the cover or paper tray, inserting/removing the ink cartridge, etc.

The procedure to be animated was the same for the three printers: the replacement of the ink cartridge. With the aim to study the generalization capabilities of the devised approach, the text instructions extracted from the manual of a given printer (e.g., the Epson) were used to generate a video for each of the other two printers (e.g., Canon and HP). In this way, the names associated with the components and animations in the input instructions differed from those used in the Blender's files. Some adaptations to the original instructions were required in order to deal with the different numbering schemes and component types of the printers. The aim of this experiment was to evaluate the capability of the devised system to recognize and associate elements that, despite the possibly different name, still represent the same component or animation.

The six videos generated for the three printers using the other two manuals are available for download[10]. Figure 4 shows some sample frames extracted from the videos. In particular, the frames on top (Figs. 4a–4c) refer to different time instants of the same video, generated for the Canon printer using one of the two manual of the other printers. Frames at the bottom (Figs. 4d–4e), instead, depict the same operation (precisely, the insertion of the new cartridge) for the three printers, again animated using the manual of a different printer.

Performance of the devised system was analyzed by means of the data reported in Table 1, which describe in objective terms the results obtained with the three printers. The differences between the number of instructions in the manual and the extrapolated relations can be explained by the presence of complex text that the system was able to recognize and simplify by generating sub-instructions. The similarity values represent the average scores obtained by computing the similarity between the words used for referring to objects/components and actions in the manual, and the most similar 3D models and animations defined in Blender. These scores provide an indication of the differences in the

---

[7] Canon PIXMA-MX495 manual: https://bit.ly/3hxeohx.
[8] Epson WF-7010 manual: https://bit.ly/3pxLNNu.
[9] HP Deskjet 3000 manual: https://bit.ly/3hw1nVv.
[10] Video generated in the experiments: http://tiny.cc/iiopuz.

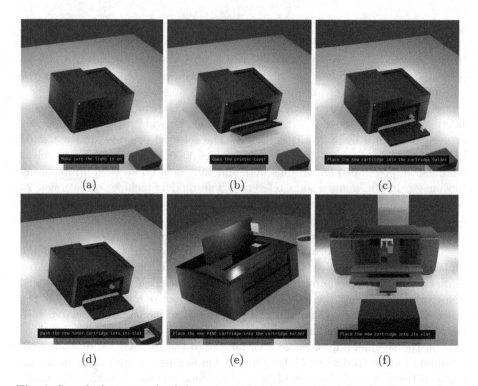

Fig. 4. Sample frames a–c) of the animated video generated for the Canon printer with the manual of another printer, and frames showing the animation of the same instruction for the d) Canon, e) Epson e), and f) HP printers animated with a manual which is different from the given printer.

Table 1. Results obtained by generating the videos using for each printer the manuals of the other two.

	Canon		Epson		HP	
No. instructions	7	5	8	10	10	10
No. extrapolated relations	8	10	11	14	11	11
No. images	9	2	4	6	7	3
Avg. similarity [%]	90.77	80.73	88.18	85.15	89.75	84.47
Selected animations [%]	75.00	50.00	81.82	71.43	90.91	54.55
Generated animation [%]	12.50	10.00	9.09	0.00	9.09	0.0
Not animated instr. [%]	12.50	40.00	9.09	28.57	0.00	45.45

wording used in the two contexts. Results also show that the system was able to activate or generate an animation for most of the instructions, as the number of instructions that were not animated is generally low. However, the small number of images used to train the models led to a reduced ability of the system to detect the components pictured in the images. This difficulty translated into a limited capability of identifying the position and/or rotation of the components in the image, thus making it hard for the system to reconstruct the offsets that should be applied to the 3D models for automatically generating the corresponding animation block. This limitation reduced the number of animations belonging to the generated category. In fact, the percentages for these animations are below 13.00% for all the printers. Despite the low values, this result can nonetheless be regarded as promising, considering that, at least in the selected use case, the majority of the instructions lack a corresponding visual representation in the manual, i.e., the corresponding animations could not be generated that way.

5   Conclusion and Future Work

In this work, a system was proposed to automatically generate an animated video based on descriptions of actions expressed in natural language and supported by images. In particular, the operations regarding the maintenance of printers were considered as a use case, and their instruction manuals used as input data.

The system combines the activation, based on the provided text and images, of animations included in a library containing a limited number of prepared 3D models, together with an algorithm designed to automatically generate new animations based solely on image data.

The obtained results show the ability of the devised system to create a mapping between the information available in the instruction manuals of the considered printers and the elements in the library, even when the terms used to refer to them are different. Moreover, the automatic generation of animations from images lets the system introduce in the output video animations which were not available in the library.

Future work could consider the possibility to enhance the size of the dataset used to train the Image Analysis module in order to improve the percentage of components detected within the images, thus possibly increasing the number of automatically generated animations. The Natural Language Processing module could benefit from the use of mechanisms for simplifying the sentences (as done in [28]) to improve the ability of the system to process the natural language. It would also be interesting to devise a user study aimed to evaluate the system's usability and check if the generated videos can actually improve the users' understanding of the information contained in manuals. Finally, efforts could be focused on the generalization of the proposed approach, in order to possibly use it also for the generation of animations outside the considered context (e.g., instruction manuals of other products, school books, etc.).

References

1. Ali, G., Lee, M., Hwang, J.I.: Automatic text-to-gesture rule generation for embodied conversational agents. Comput. Anim. Virtual Worlds **31**(4–5), e1944 (2020)
2. Armando, A., Pecchiari, P.: NALIG: a CAD system for interior design with high level interaction capabilities. In: Proceedings of the IEEE Conference on Tools with AI, pp. 446–447 (1993)
3. Badler, N.I., Bindiganavale, R., Allbeck, J.: Parameterized Action Representation for Virtual Embodied Conversational Agents. MIT Press, Cambridge (2000)
4. Cannavò, A., et al.: An automatic 3D scene generation pipeline based on a single 2D image. In: De Paolis, L.T., Arpaia, P., Bourdot, P. (eds.) AVR 2021. LNCS, vol. 12980, pp. 109–117. Springer, Cham (2021). https://doi.org/10.1007/978-3-030-87595-4_9
5. Cannavò, A., Lamberti, F.: A virtual character posing system based on reconfigurable tangible user interfaces and immersive virtual reality. In: Proceedings of the Conference on Smart Tools and Applications in Graphics, pp. 1–11 (2018)
6. Canny, J.: A computational approach to edge detection. IEEE Trans. Pattern Anal. Mach. Intell. **6**, 679–698 (1986)
7. Chang, A.X., Eric, M., Savva, M., Manning, C.D.: SceneSeer: 3D scene design with natural language. arXiv preprint arXiv:1703.00050 (2017)
8. Chen, C.Y., Wong, S.K., Liu, W.Y.: Generation of small groups with rich behaviors from natural language interface. Comput. Anim. Virtual Worlds **31**(4–5), e1960 (2020)
9. Coyne, B., Sproat, R.: WordsEye: an automatic text-to-scene conversion system. In: Proceedings of the 28th Annual Conference on Computer Graphics and Interactive Techniques, pp. 487–496 (2001)
10. Denis, M., Logie, R., Cornoldo, C., de Vega, M., EngelKamp, J.: Imagery, Language and Visuo-spatial Thinking, vol. 1. Psychology Press, Hove (2012)
11. Hanser, E., Mc Kevitt, P., Lunney, T., Condell, J.: SceneMaker: automatic visualisation of screenplays. In: Mertsching, B., Hund, M., Aziz, Z. (eds.) KI 2009. LNCS (LNAI), vol. 5803, pp. 265–272. Springer, Heidelberg (2009). https://doi.org/10.1007/978-3-642-04617-9_34
12. Harris, C., Stephens, M.: A combined corner and edge detector. In: Proceedings of the 4th Alvey Vision Conference, pp. 147–151 (1988)
13. Hassani, K., Nahvi, A., Ahmadi, A.: Design and implementation of an intelligent virtual environment for improving speaking and listening skills. Interact. Learn. Environ. **24**(1), 252–271 (2016)
14. Johansson, R., Williams, D., Berglund, A., Nugues, P.: Carsim: A system to visualize written road accident reports as animated 3D scenes. In: Proceedings of the 2nd Workshop on Text Meaning and Interpretation, pp. 57–64 (2004)
15. Liu, Z.Q., Leung, K.M.: Script visualization (ScriptViz): a smart system that makes writing fun. Soft Comput. **10**(1), 34–40 (2006)
16. Ma, M.: Automatic conversion of natural language to 3D animation. Ph.D. thesis, University of Ulster (2006)
17. Manning, C.D., Surdeanu, M., Bauer, J., Finkel, J.R., Bethard, S., McClosky, D.: The Stanford CoreNLP natural language processing toolkit. In: Proceedings of the 52nd Annual Meeting of the Association for Computational Linguistics: System Demonstrations, pp. 55–60 (2014)
18. Mansor, N.R., et al.: A review survey on the use computer animation in education. IOP Conf. Ser. Mater. Sci. Eng. **917**, 012021 (2020)

19. Marti, M., et al.: Cardinal: computer assisted authoring of movie scripts. In: Proceedings of the 23rd International Conference on Intelligent User Interfaces, pp. 509–519 (2018)
20. Mikolov, T., Chen, K., Corrado, G., Dean, J.: Efficient estimation of word representations in vector space. arXiv preprint arXiv:1301.3781 (2013)
21. Özdemir, S.: Supporting printed books with multimedia: a new way to use mobile technology for learning. Br. J. Educ. Technol. **41**(6), E135–E138 (2010)
22. Preim, B., Meuschke, M.: A survey of medical animations. Comput. Graph. **90**, 145–168 (2020)
23. Seversky, L.M., Yin, L.: Real-time automatic 3D scene generation from natural language voice and text descriptions. In: Proceedings of the 14th ACM international Conference on Multimedia, pp. 61–64 (2006)
24. Shi, J., et al.: Good features to track. In: Proceedings of the IEEE Conference on Computer Vision and Pattern Recognition, pp. 593–600 (1994)
25. Soogund, N.U.N., Joseph, M.H.: Signar: A sign language translator application with augmented reality using text and image recognition. In: Proceedings of the IEEE International Conference on Intelligent Techniques in Control, Optimization and Signal Processing, pp. 1–5 (2019)
26. Wolfartsberger, J., Niedermayr, D.: Authoring-by-doing: animating work instructions for industrial virtual reality learning environments. In: Proceedings of the IEEE Conference on Virtual Reality and 3D User Interfaces - Abstracts and Workshops, pp. 173–176 (2020)
27. Yadav, P., Sathe, K., Chandak, M.: Generating animations from instructional text. Int. J. Adv. Trends Comput. Sci. Eng. **9**(3), 3023–3027 (2020)
28. Zhang, Y., Tsipidi, E., Schriber, S., Kapadia, M., Gross, M., Modi, A.: Generating animations from screenplays. arXiv preprint arXiv:1904.05440 (2019)
29. Zyda, M.: From visual simulation to virtual reality to games. Computer **38**(9), 25–32 (2005)

Design Process of a Ceramic Modeling Application for Virtual Reality Art Therapy

Carola Gatto[1(✉)], Kim Martinez[2], and Lucio Tommaso De Paolis[3]

[1] Department of Cultural Heritage, University of Salento, Lecce, Italy
`carola.gatto@unisalento.it`
[2] Department of History, Geography and Communication, University of Burgos, Burgos, Spain
`kmartinez@ubu.es`
[3] Department of Engineering for Innovation, University of Salento, Lecce, Italy
`lucio.depaolis@unisalento.it`

Abstract. In the last years, teletherapy has provided the possibility of improving the accessibility to the therapy itself, by means of digital platforms. Of all the technologies that make up e-health, Virtual Reality is the one that creates the sense of presence, using immersive, interactive and collaborative virtual environments. From this perspective, this paper presents the preliminary study for a Virtual Reality (VR) Art Therapy application. It concerns one module of a project called Ermes, aimed at providing psychological support for remote practice for hospitalized patients, by means of Mindfulness and Art therapy practice. This perspective research starts with the aim of experimenting with a new system of interaction in Virtual Reality for the practice of Art Therapy. In particular, the medium that we want to adopt for the practice is the modeling of ceramics with traditional techniques. In this paper, we introduce the methodology and the design of this VR Art Therapy application, by explaining the gamification choices we made, in terms of mechanics, dynamics (visual responses), and aesthetics. The output is the definition of an optimal experience for the implementation of the Art Therapy scenario.

Keywords: Virtual Reality · Art Therapy · User experience · Gamification

1 Introduction

In this paper we present the preliminary study for a Virtual Reality (VR) Art Therapy application. The VR Art Therapy is one module of a project called Ermes, aimed at providing psychological support for remote practice to hospitalized patients, by means of Mindfulness and Art therapy practice. According to the 2019 World Health Organization (WHO) report, the role of arts and culture in empowering well-being and quality of life has been demonstrated, since more than 3000 studies have highlighted their effect on public health [1]. Previous research [2] has therefore shown that the topic of e-health to support psychological therapy is of great interest to the scientific community. Therefore, the aim of the project is to measure the impact of VR Art Therapy on patients' wellbeing, in terms of stress reduction. This perspective research starts with the aim of

L. T. De Paolis et al. (Eds.): XR Salento 2022, LNCS 13445, pp. 92–103, 2022.
https://doi.org/10.1007/978-3-031-15546-8_7

experimenting a new system of interaction in Virtual Reality for the practice of Art Therapy. In particular, the medium that we want to adopt for the practice is the modeling of ceramics with traditional techniques. In this paper we introduce the methodology and the design of this VR Art Therapy application, by explaining the gamification choices we made, in terms of mechanics, dynamics (visual responses), and aesthetics. Even if this paper takes in exam just the Art Therapy section, we underline that the User eXperience (UX) aspects need to be considered later in the design of the complete application. After defining the state of art of VR Art Therapy, we studied the most common elements of UX and gamification in Virtual Reality. The output is the definition of an optimal experience for the implementation of the Art Therapy scenario.

2   What is Art Therapy and Why in Virtual: A Brief State of Art

Acting on people's well-being means acting on a complex system made of layers, in which besides a physical component, there are emotional, intellectual-cognitive, spiritual, social and professional ones. All these categories coincide with the holistic idea of well-being promoted by the World Health Organization. This report supports the correlation between culture and well-being as a priority in the idea of the creation of cultural policies that include public administrations, institutions, museums and organizations. For instance, social isolation is an increasing social issue that does not regard only the emergency due to the pandemic: loneliness among young, middle-aged, and older adults is a serious public health concern of our time because, and it is demonstrated to have a strong correlation with cardiovascular, autoimmune, neurocognitive, and mental health issues. Social isolation is a condition that often for physical or psychological obstacles and prevents people from moving around, performing creative activities, traveling and visiting cultural places. From this point of view, the technology of Virtual Reality (VR) has been identified as an expansion of physical space and it can represent a decisive paradigm of innovation both in an emergency period and in normal life [3]. Of all the technologies that make up e-health, Virtual Reality is the one that creates the sense of presence, using immersive, interactive and collaborative virtual environments. This media is a useful tool to restore the sense of presence where physical presence is not possible, due to contingencies related to the individual. VR has proven useful for applications of learning [4, 5], training [6, 7] and psychology [8]. Therefore, the effectiveness of this technology can be explored to provide a psychological support tool for therapeutic practice, as in the case of Art Therapy. Art Therapy is based on the idea that art is the most accessible form of communication for human experience, since it makes use of visual symbols and images [9]. It is a form of psychotherapy that employs artistic creation for integrative personality processes [10]. Art therapy consists of an interaction of an individual or group with a therapist who supports self-expression through various artistic mediums [11]. The psychological impact can be measured both in the artistic practice [12] and in oral reflection on art [13].

Art Therapy practice in museums has become increasingly popular for the well-being of vulnerable individuals, seen as active members of a social context. This practice was born in Canada in 1996 as part of a project aimed to provide assistance to cancer patients by helping them, through the museum path, to visually express their experiences on different levels. The program was developed at the McMichael Canadian Art Collection in partnership with the Toronto-Sunnybrook Regional Cancer Centre-Bayview Support Network [14]. From that moment, numerous experiments followed, arriving in 2018, also in Canada, to talk about the possibility of allowing doctors to "prescribe" guided visits to museums for patients with chronic disorders and depression as an effective therapy. In the last years, teletherapy has provided the possibility of improving the accessibility to the therapy itself, by means of digital platforms. The debate quickly accelerated when closure orders surrounding COVID-19 forced many therapists to adopt the practice of online art therapy [15].

Virtual Reality is a specific kind of teletherapy and it can include different artistic media, such as three-dimensional painting, immersive creative experience, dynamic scaling, and embodied expression and it can actually figure as an innovative medium for therapy practice. In particular the application can be combined with a measurement system that actually can provide on time neuro or biofeedback. The implementation of VR application for psychotherapy purpose is also customized to the specific disorder and patient being treated. Multiple techniques employing simulative controlled exposure (e.g., anxiety, phobias, fear of flying), embodied technologies (e.g., eating disorder), cue exposure (e.g., addictions), or distraction (e.g., pain management) have been explored.

An interesting study is provided in [16], where a pilot qualitative research has been conducted on 17 participants with VR art-making tools, to determine its relevance to art therapy practice and research. Results indicate that VR-based self-expression is embodied visual expression, generates novel artistic and imaginative responses, and requires a developmental trajectory in terms of self-expression and skills.

In [17] it has been explored the potential of artistic creation in VR for art therapy (VRAT) from the perspective of expert art therapists. In particular, this methodology has been followed: seven art therapy experts experimented with creating visual art in VR and as observers. After the VR experience, a semi-structured test has been conducted to collect fundamental data about their experience both as creators and as observers. The results pointed out that therapists expect substantial value in the new VR medium for art therapy.

In some cases, specific targets have been focused on, in order to find out the most effective practice related to the disorder, for instance, in [18] Virtual reality (VR) technology has been combined with traditional art therapy to treat adolescents suffering from anxiety and social difficulties. This study showed that this type of technology can lead to a better understanding of adolescents' needs by employing their perspective and therefore better results.

As we described so far, the scientific literature has shown that the topic is of great interest to the scientific community. This perspective research starts with the aim of experimenting a new system of interaction in Virtual Reality for the practice of art therapy. In particular, the medium that we want to adopt for the practice is the modeling of ceramics with traditional techniques.

3 Definition of UX and Gamification Elements

UX can be defined as the effect created by hardware and software on users' perceptions and interactions [19]. It is a very important aspect of the design because it determines if the experience is pleasant and if the desired effect of the therapy is achieved. UX design has to focus on the interaction with the application, between the user's actions and the graphic interface. There are some general characteristics that these UX elements must meet [20]:

- Attract and motivate to perform the actions of the application.
- Give freedom in their interactions and awareness of their effects.
- Offer a sense of increasing control from the start of the application.
- Propose a graphic interface that offers a pleasant sensory experience.

An important UX design choice is the used VR headset and controllers [21]. Each one has different characteristics of sensor data process, computational power and quality of visual representation. Another important aspect is the possibility of positional tracking and degrees-of-freedom (DoF) interaction. For art therapy applications the best choices are Oculus Rift or Quest, and HTC Vive headsets that have good visual and computational performance, as well as hand sensors. These devices have 6 DoF (rotational and translational motion tracking) which increases spatial consistency for the user in the virtual and physical environment. Additionally, users need to become familiar with controllers or hand gestures to feel in control and focus on the app without distraction [16]. Several works [18] have proven that the best way to guide the user through this learning is verbal communication. Therefore, the instructions should be audible, and also written for accessibility.

Other controls of the space, such as visualization or perspectives, must be taken into account. The most useful point of view for VR therapy is the first person since it affects emotions directly, and the interaction with virtual elements is more realistic [18]. The main configurations with respect to the user's body that can be applied are sitting or standing positions. Adapting the height and motion with which the user feels most comfortable allows for choosing both options [22]. The results regarding application performance, intrinsic motivation, and motion sickness were studied by [23]. Being seated can make it more difficult to use body gestures, and even making movements in the environment can be more dizzying. Therefore, controls should be adapted to both positions to avoid motion sickness.

On the other hand, gamification is defined as the use of game elements in non-game contexts to improve engagement in users and create richer and more fun experiences [24]. For this design, the Mechanics, Dynamics and Aesthetics (MDA) framework [25] is followed, which identifies the 3 main layers of playability elements. Mechanics are the virtual items, and the actions that the user can perform; dynamics are the responses and behaviors towards those actions; aesthetics are the audiovisual representations that evoke emotions in the user [26]. From these layers, game elements for VR art therapy applications can be defined [27]:

- Virtual elements that are interactive and help to recreate the feeling of presence in a virtual environment.
- Objectives and points that motivate the user to carry out the actions with a good performance.
- Responses to positive user actions to encourage their achievement.

- Audio and visual effects in the virtual environment that evoke feelings of beauty and delight.

There are also other aspects of VR art therapy that affect MDA layers, such as the ways to control mechanics [28]. The first and most basic use is through controllers with buttons and joysticks that the user presses and moves to perform actions. It offers a more reliable and familiar interface for people not used to a VR environment. The second way uses gestures and movements of the user to perform the actions. Selected VR headsets (Oculus Rift or Quest, and HTC Vive headsets) can track hands using optical tracking with a camera system.

Art therapy applications in VR have some advantages over face-to-face activities that can be applied to their dynamics. The modification of the artwork is possible in all its interactions, skipping the traditional permanence. Users are not afraid of error and can focus on freedom of creative expression and exploration [16]. However, these applications need feedback when interacting with the virtual world. Especially, virtual tools' feedback is important to point out each interaction that the user must perform. Moreover, sensory stimulation in the virtual environment should also help to focus on the task [29]. These sensations give the user a feeling of challenge, but never have to make controls difficult or uncomfortable [30].

Regarding aesthetics, users enjoy the feeling of being transported to an imaginary space, away from the pressure and stress of the real world [16]. They even prefer experiences that cannot be carried out in the normal world, such as jumping from heights or floating through the air [22]. As applications dedicated to art, visual elements like lines, shapes, marks and colors become very important. These virtual representations do not have physical feedback or occupy real space. However, its 3D representation offers other advantages such as being able to observe the work from multiple angles. The app can also simulate materials without having to conform to the laws of physics or limited spaces [18].

4   Design Process of UX and MDA for VR Art Therapy

4.1   User Experience

The first UX aspect to design is the graphic interface with which the user interacts to access the application. The most basic interface is a menu through which the user accesses different modules or activities of the application. It has to be visually pleasing, and indicate by visual and sound effects when an option is selected. Interface has to be simplified as much as possible, as Fig. 1 shows, to avoid distractions and make interactions easier. If it is necessary to display a menu while using the activities, the interface has to be schematic, with little text and the use of symbols and sounds.

The VR headset for the development of this module is Oculus Quest, so this application allows good visual quality and 6 DoF. The point of view is the first person so that the user perceives their actions in a realistic way, with a greater effect on their emotions. Since the target is hospitalized patients, it can be controlled in a standing or sitting position, adapting its height. The user is able to choose in the interface the position in which he or she prefers to carry out the experience, an option that is explained in the tutorial.

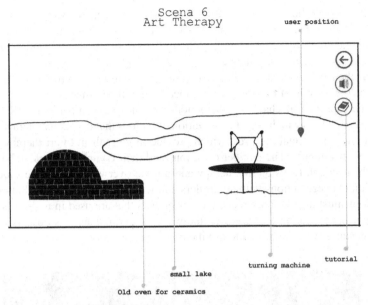

Fig. 1. Interface design for Art Therapy module

Movement in the virtual space is done by teleportation, being able to move freely around the virtual items. In this way, any physical movement that is uncomfortable is avoided, in addition to motion sickness.

The Art Therapy module has been designed in order to start with a first tutorial module to explain movement and controls. The user adapts to the virtual environment and obtains a growing sense of control over the experience. The tutorial explains in a textual and auditory way the objective of the application and how to interact with its graphic interface. The possibility of movement in the virtual environment and interaction with objects is especially important. The use of controllers or hand gestures are introduced here, making the user repeat them one by one to learn them. The user can press X or A buttons of Oculus controllers and a line appears to mark the point they move to, and when they release the button, they appear there. To grab objects, they use the controllers' triggers, while for pottery modeling the interaction is done through the virtual collision of the controllers or the hands with the mesh inside the application. If different controls are used throughout the application, these have to be explained beforehand to avoid confusion in the experience.

4.2 Mechanics

VR art therapy combines the use of techniques that correspond to painting, drawing, collage and sculpture. Virtual elements that are introduced in these applications must emulate the real objects that are used for art. The realism with which they are represented increases immersion and engagement with the application. Furthermore, the sense of presence also increases when these items are interactive. The user must be able to move around them, pick them up and observe them from different perspectives. This allows them to visualize their details and size, as well as obtain information about each one. In this application, direct interaction with controllers or the user's hands is required to model a vessel. The controllers use the tracking included in their sensors, while for the hands the trackers of Oculus headset are used. The use of controllers or hands will depend on the version of the application, since both will be tested.

A vital aspect of mechanics is the actions that the user can perform. VR headsets often use controllers which need the definition of buttons that trigger an interaction. The second option is manual gestures, which provide more realism to art therapy since it is based on handcrafts. The number of actions and their complexity have to be limited so that the user can focus on the therapy and not get overwhelmed. There should be a correlation between actions with controllers and with hand gestures. In addition, these interactions must take as a reference the movements that are used in reality, as seen in Fig. 2. For the modeling of the vessel, the work of a craftsman was observed and the manual gestures were simplified to use them in the application.

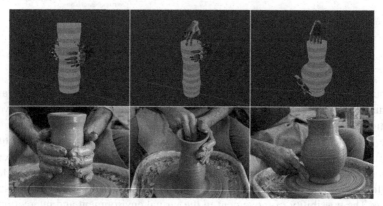

Fig. 2. Comparison of artisan movements with gestures in application

Mechanics also refer to the objectives that are set within the application and that must be met as part of the therapy. To make them interesting, the application must create a narrative that raises a need for which the user must perform the actions. In this case, the context and the place where ceramics were produced in the past and the replication of ancient techniques. Some very engaging mechanics are badges and points that are awarded when the user successfully completes their mission. This application also rewards the accuracy with which the vessel is modeled in reference to the original object that it has to replicate. The more exact it is, the user receives more points as a prize.

4.3 Dynamics

Dynamics are related to the UX characteristic of giving freedom of action and awareness of its effects. Once users learn the controls, they should be free to move around the virtual space because the immersion and presence are increased. However, the application has to guide the direction and indicate the next action to perform with visual or sound elements. This module uses visual highlighted indications of the process to produce the vessel.

The VR application allows the user to modify the vessel as much as wanted, which in reality would be much more laborious. To guide the modeling, the pottery is divided into small strips as shown in Fig. 2, that show where the hands should be placed. When both hands are on the same strip, the user can modify their size, widening or narrowing the pot with total freedom of interaction. To give feedback on the relationship of the model with the vessel to be imitated, auditory stimulation is given, in addition to the points. When each stripe approaches the ideal size, the user hears the sound of a meditation bell. The volume is higher the more precise the pot is and the lower the further it gets from the exact size.

4.4 Aesthetics

Aesthetics encompass all the audiovisual representations of the virtual environment. To help users create a positive and relaxed emotional state, any space can be recreated. In order to increase the feeling of presence, we adopt an aesthetic that reproduces a natural environment in which we collocate the outdoor workshop of the ceramist, as shown in Fig. 3. This is not an imaginary place, since the virtual environment is based on the historical reconstruction of the archaeological site of Cavallino, in the Apulia region (Italy). This choice starts from the consideration that the archaeological site of Cavallino shows the remains of an old oven (V century B.C.) for pottery production. This is a visually pleasing place that encourages the user's curiosity, immersion and abstraction in therapy. In addition, they are accompanied by harmonious and relaxing melodies and sound effects that intensify positive emotions. In this way, the user is induced to relax through a manual activity, which reproduces traditional ceramic working techniques, which have their roots in the history of the territory. Moreover, the user, thanks to

Fig. 3. Reconstruction of an outdoor workshop of the ceramist in Cavallino scenario

learning by doing activities, can get important archaeological content, concerning the history of the territory. Today, another very important center of ceramic production, which has certain longevity, is that of Cutrofiano (Lecce), also in Salento, not far from Lecce. In a center of artisanal ceramic production in Cutrofiano, gestures for the working of ceramics in a virtual environment have been studied.

The vase that we take as an example for the modeling takes the name of "Trozzella", typical of the Messapians' production (Fig. 4), attested in different archaeological sites of Salento, including Cavallino, around VI-III century B.C. The characteristic shape of the Trozzella is that of a pot-bellied krater, with a small foot, a truncated cone neck, more or less high, and two vertical ribbon handles, surmounting the mouth. The peculiarity of the form is given by the small round disks placed at the top and bottom along with the handles.

Fig. 4. Trozzella's shape, Blender 3D model

There are other aesthetic elements that are related to art such as shapes and colors. They participate with the UX function of attracting and motivating the user to perform the actions. These elements don't have to fit the appearance or physics of the real materials, taking advantage of the virtual world. Design can change the perspective or size of objects, or highlight the colors or sounds that are emitted. These are useful tools to fix the user's attention and motivate them to complete the activity.

5   Conclusions and Future Work

This paper identifies the main elements of UX and gamification for the design of a VR Art Therapy application. A review of the state of the art is performed to study the current uses of this medium for the practice of art therapy. Next, the main User Experience needs are identified: attractive and motivational actions, a sense of freedom and control, and a graphic interface with a pleasant sensory experience. Gamification design is based on the MDA model, which has to enhance presence, user's performance, achievements, and feelings of beauty and delight.

This work is applied to the design of a VR art therapy application to model pottery as in ancient centuries. It has been designed for Oculus Quest headset that allow the use of controllers or hand gestures for interactions, which are learned in a tutorial. The mechanics that the hands must replicate to model the vessel reproduce the work of a craftsman to increase realism. In the same way, ceramic objects and tools are interactive to simulate presence. To engage the user, the application introduces a narrative and a rewarding points system for the similarity to the original vessel. The dynamics of the module constantly guide the process, indicating with colored strips and sounds the dimensions that must be modeled. To create a positive and relaxed emotional state, harmonious and relaxing melodies are introduced while the user performs the actions. In addition, the aesthetic environment recreates the historical reconstruction of the archaeological site of Cavallino, in Apulia region (Italy), promoting curiosity and immersion. A trozzella is replicated, being able to observe it from different perspectives and highlighting its interactions to fix the user's attention.

Future work of this project will finish the development of this application following the design explained. Afterward, tests with different users will be performed to measure the quality of user experience and its adaptation to the gamification elements. These trials will allow assessing the adequacy of this design and the possible changes that the application could need. In addition, tests will be carried out with biofeedback sensors to measure the emotional reactions of the users to prove the objective of this art therapy application. Another point of the study will be the comparison of the UX and biofeedback measures between the version that uses controllers and the one with hand gestures. In this way, the type of interaction that gives the greatest sense of control, realism and presence will be chosen for future developments. Depending on the result, the integration of haptic sensors for gesture interactions to feel virtual objects and enhance realism will be considered. At the end, the implementation of the Virtual Reality Art Therapy application will be completed by the integration of the virtual brush, for the pictorial decoration of pottery itself, so that the user can enjoy a high realistic process of ceramic production.

References

1. United Nation Report, Policy Brief: The Impact of COVID-19 on older persons (2020)
2. Gatto, C., D'Errico, G., Nuccetelli, F., De Luca, V., Paladini, G.I., De Paolis, L.T.: XR-based mindfulness and Art Therapy: facing the psychological impact of COVID-19 emergency. In: De Paolis, L.T., Bourdot, P. (eds.) Augmented Reality, Virtual Reality, and Computer Graphics. Lecture Notes in Computer Science, vol. 12243, pp. 147–155. Springer, Cham (2020). https://doi.org/10.1007/978-3-030-58468-9_11
3. Gatto, C., D'Errico, G., Paladini, G., De Paolis, L.T.: Virtual reality in Italian museums: a brief discussion. In: De Paolis, L.T., Arpaia, P., Bourdot, P. (eds.) Augmented Reality, Virtual Reality, and Computer Graphics. Lecture Notes in Computer Science, vol. 12980, pp. 306–314. Springer, Cham (2021). https://doi.org/10.1007/978-3-030-87595-4_22
4. Checa, D., Bustillo, A.: Advantages and limits of virtual reality in learning processes: Briviesca in the fifteenth century. Virtual Real. 24(1), 151–161 (2019). https://doi.org/10.1007/s10055-019-00389-7
5. Checa, D., Miguel-Alonso, I., Bustillo, A.: Immersive virtual-reality computer-assembly serious game to enhance autonomous learning. Virtual Real. 1–18 (2021).https://doi.org/10.1007/s10055-021-00607-1
6. Checa, D., Martinez, K., Osornio Ríos, R.A. Bustillo, A.: Virtual reality opportunities in the reduction of ocuppational hazards in industry 4.0. DYNA. 96(6), 620–626 (2021). https://doi.org/10.6036/10241

7. Checa, D., Saucedo-Dorantes, J.J., OsornioRios, R.A., AntoninoDaviu, J.A., Bustillo, A.: Virtual reality training application for the condition-based maintenance of induction motors. Appl. Sci. **12**(1), 414 (2022). https://doi.org/10.3390/app12010414

8. Martinez, K., Menéndez-Menéndez, M.I., Bustillo, A.: Awareness, prevention, detection, and therapy applications for depression and anxiety in serious games for children and adolescents: systematic review. JMIR Ser. Games **9**(4), e30482 (2021). https://doi.org/10.2196/30482

9. Ford-Martin, P.: Art therapy. Gale Encyclopedia of Psychology, 2nd Edn., pp. 48–49. Gale Group, New York (2011)

10. Guttmann, J., Regev, D.: The phenomenological approach to art therapy. J. Contemp. Psychother. **34**, 153–162 (2004). https://doi.org/10.1023/B:JOCP.0000022314.69354.4

11. Hacmun, I., Regev, D., Salomon, R.: The principles of art therapy in virtual reality. Front Psychol. **31**(9), 2082 (2018). https://doi.org/10.3389/fpsyg.2018.02082. PMID:30429813; PMCID: PMC6220080

12. Rubin, J.A.: Art is the therapy. In: Rubin, J.A. (ed.) Approaches to Art Therapy, pp. 33–48. Routledge, New York, London (2016). https://doi.org/10.4324/9781315716015

13. Case, C., Dalley, T.: The Handbook of Art Therapy. Routledge, New York (2014)

14. Deane, K., Carman, M., Fitch, M.: The cancer journey: bridging art therapy and museum education. Can Oncol. Nurs. J. **10**(4), 140–146 (2000)

15. Snyder, K.: The digital art therapy frame: creating a 'magic circle' in teletherapy. Int. J. Art Ther. **26**(3), 104–110 (2021). https://doi.org/10.1080/17454832.2020.1871389

16. Kaimal, G., Carroll-Haskins, K., Berberian, M., Dougherty, A., Carlton, N., Ramakrishnan, A.: Virtual reality in art therapy: a pilot qualitative study of the novel medium and implications for practice. Art Ther. **37**(1), 16–24 (2020). https://doi.org/10.1080/07421656.2019.1659662

17. Hacmun, I., Regev, D., Salomon, R.: Artistic creation in virtual reality for art therapy: a qualitative study with expert art therapists. Arts Psychother. **72**, 101745 (2021). https://doi.org/10.1016/j.aip.2020.101745

18. Shamri, Z.L.: Making art therapy virtual: integrating virtual reality into art therapy with adolescents. Front Psychol. **4**(12), 584943 (2021)

19. Schell, J.: The Art of Game Design: A Book of Lenses. Elsevier, Burlinton (2008)

20. Ferrara, J.: Playful Design: Creating Game Experiences in Everyday Interfaces. Rosenfeld Media, New York (2012)

21. Checa, D., Bustillo, A.: A review of immersive virtual reality serious games to enhance learning and training. Multimed. Tools App. **79**(9–10), 5501–5527 (2019). https://doi.org/10.1007/s11042-019-08348-9

22. Haeyen, S., Jans, N., Glas, M., Kolijn, J.: VR health experience: a virtual space for arts and psychomotor therapy. Front. Psychol. **12**, 704613 (2021). https://doi.org/10.3389/fpsyg.2021.704613

23. Xu, W., Liang, H.N., He, Q., Li, X., Yu, K., Chen, Y.: Results and guidelines from a repeated-measures design experiment comparing standing and seated full-body gesture-based immersive virtual reality exergames: within-subjects evaluation. JMIR Ser. Games **8**(3), e17972 (2020). https://doi.org/10.2196/17972

24. Deterding, S., Dixon, D., Khaled, R., Nacke, L.: From game design elements to gamefulness. In: Proceedings of the 15th International Academic MindTrek Conference on Envisioning Future Media Environments - MindTrek 2011 (2011). https://doi.org/10.1145/2181037.2181040

25. Hunicke, R., Leblanc, M., Zubek, R.: MDA: a formal approach to game design and game research. In: Proceedings of the AAAI Workshop on Challenges in Game AI (2004)

26. Kim, J.T., Lee, W.-H.: Dynamical model for gamification of learning (DMGL). Multimed. Tools App. **74**(19), 8483–8493 (2013). https://doi.org/10.1007/s11042-013-1612-8

27. Martinez, K., Menéndez-Menéndez, M.I., Bustillo, A.: Considering user experience parameters in the evaluation of VR serious games. In: De Paolis, L.T., Bourdot, P. (eds.) Augmented Reality, Virtual Reality, and Computer Graphics. Lecture Notes in Computer Science, vol. 12242, pp. 186–193. Springer, Cham (2020). https://doi.org/10.1007/978-3-030-58465-8_14
28. Yin, J., Hinchet, R., Shea, H., Majidi, C.: Wearable soft technologies for haptic sensing and Feedback. Adv. Func. Mater. **31**(39), 2007428 (2020). https://doi.org/10.1002/adfm.202007428
29. Aldridge, A., Bethel, C.L.: A systematic review of the use of art in virtual reality. Electronics **10**(18), 2314 (2021). https://doi.org/10.3390/electronics10182314
30. Baron, L., Wang, Q., Segear, S., Cohn, B.A., Kim, K., Barmaki, R.: Enjoyable physical therapy experience with interactive drawing games in immersive virtual reality. In: Symposium on Spatial User Interaction (2021). https://doi.org/10.1145/3485279.3485285

Computer Simulation of a Spectrum Analyzer Based on the Unity Game Engine

Ye. A. Daineko, A. Z. Aitmagambetov, D. D. Tsoy$^{(\boxtimes)}$, A. E. Kulakayeva, and M. T. Ipalakova

International Information Technology University, Almaty, Kazakhstan
{y.daineko,a.aitmagambetov,d.tsoy,a.kulakayeva,
m.ipalakova}@iitu.edu.kz

Abstract. At present, computer information systems are of great interest in such fields of activity as education and science. Moreover, the impact of the pandemic that had swept the whole world has led to the emergence of new information systems, as well as to the development and improvement of existing ones. Concerning education, the introduction of new technologies, as well as comprehensive modernization, are the main issues that receive special attention throughout the world.

The article discusses the use of information computer systems in the educational process in the form of virtual laboratory work. The advantages and disadvantages of virtual laboratory work for studying radio engineering disciplines are considered. An example of a computer simulation of a spectrum analyzer based on the Unity game engine is given for inclusion in the general composition of the virtual laboratory. Physical and mathematical support, tools, as well as the process of implementing the program, its main elements, and the logic of work are described. It is shown that modern information technologies make it possible to carry out any form of experiment and open broad prospects in modelling and developing relevant and fundamentally important radio engineering devices.

Keywords: Unity 3D · Virtual laboratory · Spectrum analyzer · 3D modelling · C# (CSharp) · Fourier transforms

1 Introduction

The pandemic caused by the coronavirus has led Kazakhstan to a forced transition to distance education [1]. In some cases, its main consequence was limited access to information resources due to several reasons, such as the lack of devices (computers, tablets, smartphones), weak Internet connection, and poor learning conditions. Children with special needs were deprived of special care, provided by specialists who cannot be replaced by parents.

However, this problem is relevant not only to the Kazakh education system but can be applied to almost any region of developing countries, and remote or sparsely populated regions of developed countries. The problem begins at the level of secondary education, where the weakest point is remote and small schools.

© Springer Nature Switzerland AG 2022
L. T. De Paolis et al. (Eds.): XR Salento 2022, LNCS 13445, pp. 104–112, 2022.
https://doi.org/10.1007/978-3-031-15546-8_8

Narbekova G.A. in her work identifies three levels of factors affecting the accessibility of education in Kazakhstan [2]. The first one is socio-economic inequality, the second is the state of the educational system in general and the third factor is the operation of the internal university system of each institution.

In mid-2017, the state program "Digital Kazakhstan" was launched, within which the informatization of the educational system has become one of the most important priorities. The goal of this strategy was to provide equal access to the distance education system throughout the curriculum. Certain success has been achieved, for example, the number of students per PC unit has been reduced from 41 to 11 [3]. However, other problems have been discovered, such as obsolete equipment and poor Internet connection or sometimes its absence. The same problems are observed in the system of higher education.

The unexpected transition to distance learning has led to the introduction of many online courses in various subject areas. Thus, according to Sun et al. [4], 24,000 online courses have been launched only in China during that period. However, there is an issue that it is impossible to obtain practical experience remotely. The technical courses suffered the most due to the need for specialized equipment to conduct practical and laboratory classes [5].

If a student is introduced to theoretical material at lectures, this theory must be necessarily applied in laboratory classes. Practical skills and abilities are formed only by carrying out physical measurements and experiments, processing and presenting results. And during the pandemic and distance learning, students of engineering educational programs in Kazakhstan did not have access to that kind of laboratory work.

One of the ways out of this situation is the use of virtual laboratory work, which is a computer application or a related set of applications that perform computer simulations of some processes [6]. Additionally, the use of technologies such as virtual and augmented reality makes it possible to demonstrate the visualization of the processes more clearly by immersing the student in a virtual environment [7, 8]. Using the same example with China, 401 courses of virtual experimental simulations operating on 22 platforms were created and introduced in this country.

2   Related Work

Examples of the development and introduction of virtual laboratories can be found in many areas of education such as medicine, technical, natural science and even humanitarian [6]. The author's project is focused on the development of a virtual laboratory for studying Radio Engineering courses. Several papers discuss the same issue.

The lack of equipment [9], and as a result the inability to produce experimental simulations has led to the creation of the LabVIEW project. It is a system of virtual experiments in the field of electronics. Among the created equipment there is a simulation with an asynchronous binary counter and a spectrum analyzer. This system is designed in a way that it can be modified, expanded, and easily scaled. It is available due to its digital nature, which also reduces the cost of real equipment and resources for its maintenance. Such an innovative approach, according to the authors, makes learning more interesting and changes the very technology of teaching. The authors suggest that the introduction of such tools into the educational process can reform it and is dominant in higher education institutions.

An integrated approach to the organization of virtual laboratory work is described by Aydin and Cagiltay [10]. The proposed approach was introduced within the Radio Frequency and Microwave Engineering course. It allows conducting remote virtual experiments along with real ones. Within this approach, a computer-aided design system was employed that allows to design and manufacture of high-frequency filters.

Volovyk *et al.* in their paper [11] describe the experience with the lack of equipment necessary for conducting composite complex experiments. The authors chose virtual instruments as a solution to this problem. Their advantage is that with this approach it is possible to endow them with any necessary properties, and certain functionality. And therefore, to work on the experiment, it will be enough to have a personal computer and appropriate software. The authors described their experience in developing a system for studying the signal spectrum. Their work is based on a variety of libraries that allow them to perform various tasks, process, collect, analyze, and present information of various kinds.

However, one should not forget about the shortcomings of virtual analogues and virtual laboratory work. Budai and Kuczmann in their work [12] describe the two most significant drawbacks of such projects. The first one is the lack of physical interaction with the equipment. When working through a computer monitor and input means, students do not acquire the necessary motor skills. This may affect their performance while using the real equipment. The second disadvantage of this approach is the lack of a serious attitude when working with virtual devices, and as a result, inattention, and inaccuracy in completing tasks.

Okoyeigbo *et al.* present the experience of increasing students' attention to educational material [13]. New generations of students perceive information differently, and therefore the old ways of its delivery seem boring and outdated to them. Consequently, the level of course understanding suffers, and the degree of involvement in the study of the topic and the performance of tasks decreases. In this regard, the authors came up with a system that, by working with simulations, allows to demonstrate the material being studied in an interesting and accessible way, to make students more interested and independent. It is also noted that to work with such material, students may not have special skills in programming or equipment operation.

The results of a study on the influence of the interface of a virtual lab on students' perception are presented by Marquez-Barja *et al.* [14]. The control group was offered four types of interfaces: Web-based point and click, Web-based rich interactive, Command line, and Traditional in-lab. The results of the survey of the participants in the experiment revealed that the most convenient type of interface for students was a Web-based rich interface, which allowed them to control and set the parameters of the experiment, to observe the output data obtained in real-time.

The International Information Technology University (IITU, Almaty, Kazakhstan) also faced a sudden transition to a distance-learning format. For the lecturers in the Radio Engineering Department, it was almost impossible to conduct laboratory and practical classes because there was no access to the measuring and other equipment. At the same time despite the presence of virtual laboratories on the market, they could not be applied within classes at IITU due to several reasons. One of them is that the content of the existing virtual solutions does not correspond to the syllabuses of the Radio Engineering courses at IITU. Another reason is that neither of those virtual labs supports the Kazakh language. If it is still possible to find suitable information in English and Russian languages, the acceptable learning materials in Kazakh are completely absent. In addition, the existing software implementations of virtual labs do not make it easy to integrate and study new radio systems and devices and explore the results of the latest scientific achievements, because they are based on "hard-coded" algorithms of work. To solve this problem, it was decided to create our own digital multilingual (Kazakh, Russian, English) educational platform for remote laboratory work within studying the modern telecommunication systems. The developed digital educational platform allows studying and researching the complex processes of transmitting centimetre and millimetre-wave radio signals, studying the designs and characteristics of radio channel elements, and studying methods for measuring the main characteristics of microwave and EHF band systems.

This article is devoted to the development of a spectrum analyzer based on numerical and mathematical modelling that is included in the virtual laboratory of the created digital educational platform. The main requirements set to the simulated virtual devices are the ability to integrate them into the virtual lab, and the realism of the interface, i.e., a complete analogy of an actual device. Also, the functionality of the virtual simulator must correspond to the real device and allow a user to make all the necessary measurements, in our case, to study the spectrum of the input signal. The developed computer model of the spectrum analyzer makes it possible to obtain primary skills in performing measurements with this device. At the same time, the student becomes a direct participant in the process being studied.

3   Spectrum Analyzer Simulation

To develop a spectrum analyzer model that will work in the virtual environment, the process was divided into the following stages:

- system development and planning;
- 3D modelling;
- numerical and mathematical modelling;
- scene development.

In the first stage, a set of tools was selected to implement the necessary functionality. The modular system was chosen as the approach to the project logic. Its essence lies in the fact that each developed device is considered as a separate module, consisting of input and output functions. They determine the behaviour of our models. For example, to create a virtual spectrum analyzer, the functions that are often used by students during laboratory work were selected. This approach makes it similar to real-life practical tasks, where each device performs its own set of functions but is part of the big picture.

Autodesk Maya was used to create 3D models. The creation of the model was based on the photo and video materials of a real analyzer, which is available in the laboratory of the University. As a result, the following model was developed, shown in Fig. 1.

a) A spectrum analyzer   b) 3D model of the analyzer

Fig. 1. 3D model of the analyzer

Numerical and mathematical modelling of the spectrum analyzer was carried out based on the Fourier transform. This device allows to visualize the frequency spectrum of signals, and measure the frequency and signal level, occupied bandwidth, noise level, and signal-to-noise ratio. The basis of numerical and mathematical modelling was the basic function of signal transformation. The developed spectrum analyzer leads to the appearance of a spectral signal necessary to determine the programmable function. One of them was the following transformation:

$$U_{FM}(t) = U_m * \cos(\omega t + M\sin\vartheta t) \tag{1}$$

where U_m is the amplitude of the carrier wave, M is the index of frequency modulation, ω is the frequency of the carrier wave. As a result, an expression was obtained for the frequency spectrum of modulated signals.

To obtain the spectrum of the signal, the input signal was converted. In this case, the fast Fourier transform was used, which makes it possible to simplify the work with data, namely, to expand the signal into a trigonometric series. To do this work, in the application the Cooley-Tukey algorithm (2) was used. The essence of its work is to apply the fast Fourier transform with sequences of dimension 2.

$$X_k = \sum_{m=0}^{\frac{N}{2}-1} x_{2m} e^{-\frac{2\pi}{N}(2m)k} + \sum_{m=0}^{\frac{N}{2}-1} x_{2m} + 1 e^{-\frac{2\pi}{N}(2m+1)k} \tag{2}$$

The development of the scene implied creating an environment similar to the laboratory environment at the University. Since the project is aimed primarily at the students of our University, the similar environment in the virtual space will provide them with a more comfortable experience when working in the real laboratory.

Unity version 2020.3.4f1 was used as the development environment since this version is LTS (Long Time Supported) and fits the requirements and development time of this project, which will simplify its support in the future. This engine was chosen because the authors have sufficient experience in it. Also, the wide functionality of the platform includes cross-platform, and the ability to import the tools necessary for XR development.

4   Results

As a result of the current part of the project, the computer simulation of the spectrum analyzer was created (Fig. 2). The user can enter and change signal parameters (frequency) and modify the signal display mode (Fig. 3). The analyzer provides students with the ability to measure the amplitudes and frequencies of oscillations, change the parameters of the modulating signal, and perform other procedures necessary for frequency analysis.

Fig. 2. Device launch screen in a scene

As was mentioned before, the spectrum analyzer is built into the system of the educational platform for training specialists of the Radio Engineering Department at IITU.

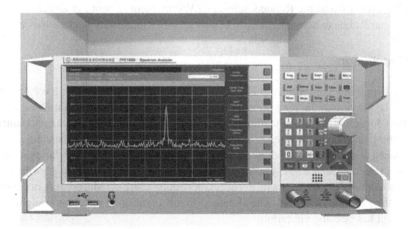

Fig. 3. Frequency spectrum display screen

Figure 4 shows the dependency between the components of the project being developed. As mentioned earlier, when creating this system, a modular approach was chosen, which implies the development of each device used in the laboratory as a separate module. As a result, each lab has its equipment, behaviour scenarios, materials, and additional resources to ensure the operation of the system.

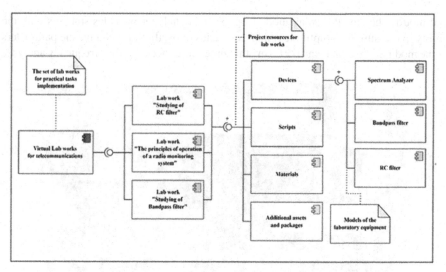

Fig. 4. The component diagram of a set of labs to study telecommunication systems

Now, the following virtual experiments have been implemented in the project: "Studying the RC filter", "Studying the filter on a rectangular waveguide" and "Studying the principles of a radio monitoring system using the example of a small spacecraft". The set of special equipment that the student must work with depends on the topic of an assignment. However, due to the independence of each of the developed devices within these systems, such as the Rohde&Schwarz ZVA40 vector network analyzer or the RC filter, or our Rohde & Schwarz FPC1500, new labs configurations can be easily created.

5   Conclusion

The pandemic has brought many issues to the world, but some of them have pushed a part of the previously lagging areas to develop. Now, the market for online education and tools for remote communication is one of the growing priorities in many countries. Some companies completely change their strategies to match the new tendency.

Against the backdrop of these events, the development of a modular system for studying telecommunication systems turned out to be one of the highest priorities. The inability to physically interact with the necessary equipment has reduced students' awareness of their professional field. The already difficult situation of different availability of equipment has become ubiquitous.

This paper highlights the issue of developing new tools that allow getting real experience even under such restrictions. In addition, such virtual devices can be either separate models suitable for study, or components of complex systems.

The studied world experience suggests that this approach is not only more interesting for the new generation of students, but also allows them to acquire the skills of independent work.

This article provides an example of developing a spectrum analyzer that is included in the structure of the previously developed virtual laboratory. The computer model of the measuring device is identical to the actual equipment in terms of the user interface. The developed model of the spectrum analyzer will be used to perform virtual laboratory work within the courses "Electromagnetic Compatibility and Management of the Use of the Radio Frequency Spectrum", "Systems and Devices for Satellite and Radio Relay Communications", "Networks and Systems for Mobile Communications", "Television and Radio Broadcasting Systems", and "Satellite Communication Systems" for educational programs 6B06201 – "Telecommunication Systems and Networks" and 6B06202 – "Radio-Technical Systems for Transmitting Information" in the training field 6B062 – "Telecommunications" at the International Information Technology University.

The testing process will be organized at the beginning of the autumn semester of the 2022–2023 academic year. It is planned to conduct a survey about the effectiveness of the spectrum analyzer among students who already have worked with the actual equipment within their courses and the students who have not study those subjects yet. Such approach allows comparing various types of students' opinions having different experience.

Given that the interface and content of the developed virtual laboratory are implemented in Kazakh, Russian, and English, the target consumer market is not limited to Kazakhstan but expands to the international level.

Acknowledgment. This research has been funded by the Science Committee of the Ministry of Education and Science of the Republic of Kazakhstan (Grant No. AP08857146).

References

1. Order of the Minister of Education and Science of the Republic of Kazakhstan dated April 1, 2020 No. 123 Strengthening measures to prevent the spread of coronavirus infection COVID-19 in educational institutions, for the period of the pandemic. https://online.zakon.kz/Document/?doc_id=39049590. Accessed 10 Nov 2021
2. NAS R.K. National Academy of Sciences of the Republic of Kazakhstan. http://iph.kz/ru/izd aniia/stati/narbekova_ga-problema_dostupnosti_obrazovaniia_v_kazahstane/. Accessed 13 Nov 2021
3. State program for the development of education and science of the Republic of Kazakhstan for 2011–2020. https://adilet.zan.kz/rus/docs/U1000001118. Accessed 15 Nov 2021
4. Sun, L., Tang, Y., Zuo, W.: Coronavirus pushes education online. Nat. Mater. **19**, 687 (2020)
5. Daineko, Y., et al.: Development of virtual laboratory work on the base of unity game engine for the study of radio engineering disciplines. In: De Paolis, L.T., Arpaia, P., Bourdot, P. (eds.) AVR 2021. LNCS, vol. 12980, pp. 419–427. Springer, Cham (2021). https://doi.org/10.1007/978-3-030-87595-4_31
6. Daineko, Y., Dmitriyev, V., Ipalakova, M.: Using virtual laboratories in teaching natural sciences: an example of physics courses in university. Comput. App. Eng. Educ. **25**(1), 39–47 (2017)
7. Daineko, Ye., Ipalakova, M., Tsoy, D., Bolatov, Zh., Baurzhan, Zh., Yelgondy, Ye.: Augmented and virtual reality for physics: experience of Kazakhstan secondary educational institutions. Comput. App. Eng. Educ. **28**, 1–12 (2020)
8. Daineko, Ye., Ipalakova, M., Tsoy, D., Seitnur, A., Zhenisov, D., Bolatov, Zh.: Virtual reality technologies as a tool for development of physics learning educational complex. In: DePaolis, L.T., Bourdot, P. (eds.) AVR 2020. LNCS, vol. 12242, pp. 194–202. Springer, Cham (2020). https://doi.org/10.1007/978-3-030-58465-8_15

9. Wang, W., Quan, X.: Design of electronic virtual experiment system based on LabVIEW. IOP Conf. Ser. Mater. Sci. Eng. **490**(4), 042024 (2019)
10. Aydin, E., Cagiltay, N.: A new RF and microwave engineering course enriched with advanced technologies. Comput. Appl. Eng. Educ. **20**(4), 634–645 (2012)
11. Volovyk, A., Havrilov, D., Koval, L., Vasylkivskyi, M., Yarovyi, D., Semenov, A.: Design of spectrum analyzer for radio signals. In: 2021 IEEE 16th International Conference on the Experience of Designing and Application of CAD Systems (CADSM). IEEE (2021)
12. Budai, T., Kuczmann, M.: Towards a modern, integrated virtual laboratory system. Acta Polytechn. Hung. **15**(3), 191–204 (2018)
13. Okoyeigbo, O., Agboje, E., Omuabor, E., Samson, U.A., Orimogunje, A.: Design and implementation of a java based virtual laboratory for data communication simulation. Int. J. Elect. Comput. Eng. (IJECE) **10**, 5883–5890 (2020)
14. Marquez-Barja, J.M., Kaminski, N., Dasilva, L.A.: Assessing the impact of user interface abstraction on online telecommunications course laboratories. IEEE Access **6**, 50394–50403 (2018)

The Influence of Method of Control and Visual Aspects on Exploratory Decisions in 3D Video Games Environments

Aneta Wiśniewska[(✉)] [ID], Jedrzej Kołecki, Adam Wojciechowski[ID], and Rafał Szrajber[ID]

Institute of Information Technology, Lodz University of Technology,
215 Wólczańska Street, Lodz 90-924, Poland
aneta.wisniewska@dokt.p.lodz.pl,
{adam.wojciechowski,rafal.szrajber}@p.lodz.pl
http://it.p.lodz.pl

Abstract. Computer games are currently the most complex interactive medium. Understanding how to manipulate the player's attention avoids getting lost in the environment while the player is receiving a significant amount of audiovisual stimuli. By appropriately selecting the visual aspects of the environment, player navigation can be aided. This article focuses on the examination of selected visual aspects such as lighting and colour, movement on the scene (animations and special effects), space composition and attempts to analyse their effectiveness in influencing the players' decision-making process during exploration. The research compared two methods of control - keyboard and controller - to see what additional effect on the player's route choice this will have. The results of the study show how the different methods supporting navigation and methods of control influence the gameplay.

Keywords: Video games · Navigation · Visual aspects · Input device · Games design · Interaction · User behavior

1 Introduction

This paper focuses on analysing the visual aspects of three-dimensional environments, comparing their effectiveness in directing the player's attention, and the influence of control methods on path selection. Level design in the context of the work is understood as the creation of an environment in which there is a way for the player to get from A to B through intermediate points [15]. The designer's task is to provide level flow [3], i.e. to predict the path or paths leading to the goal and suggest them to the players. During exploration, these choices are often made based on experience with various other computer games [5,13]. However, research suggests that these may be primarily due to ongoing processes

© Springer Nature Switzerland AG 2022
L. T. De Paolis et al. (Eds.): XR Salento 2022, LNCS 13445, pp. 113–120, 2022.
https://doi.org/10.1007/978-3-031-15546-8_9

related to visual perception and subconscious selection of elements that stand out from the background [12], which directly affect the player's decision-making. Additionally, the mode of control may also affect immersion and movement.

The experiment was conducted to compare the effectiveness of different visual aspects in controlling the player's attention in a first person perspective game, and to compare whether the type of control has an effect on the decision-making regarding route choice. The visual aspects were selected on the basis of various articles on human psychology in the context of visual perception and emotion and game level design. Two modes of control were selected for comparison: the first using the keyboard, the second using a gamepad. In the case of the experiment prepared in this paper, a corridor single-player linear game is analysed. To test the effectiveness of the visual aspects, a simple simulation was developed in the Unity game engine, in which the player, placed in a dangerous situation, has to escape through branching corridors and constantly have to choose between two paths.

2   Related Works

The author in his work [3] refers to visual aspects as mechanisms for controlling the flow of a game level. The term level flow, or "flow through a level", generally refers to the pace and progression during a game, or the balance between action sequences and rests during gameplay [1]. The primary function of the visual aspects of the environment is to attract or draw players away from given locations, possibly subconsciously guiding them according to the designer's intent. They are to assist in navigation and to help achieve the goal. Common procedures used by designers are exploiting the human eye's sensitivity to movement, natural attraction towards light and the composition of objects in space. They are supported by the theory of action of perception and visual intelligence. The visual aspects of a virtual space should be selected in such a way as to focus the eye, so they must have features unique to the overall image and be easily associated by the player with other media and experiences of real navigation [11,17].

The perception of movement has been essential throughout history to be able to read an approaching threat from the environment. For example, in the popular FPS (First Person Shooter) game genre, we are able to locate an opposing player running between the curtains in a visually complex environment. It is the movement that contrasts with the environment, which remains static or inanimate. The movement does not have to be sudden or fast - the contrast is enough for the player to notice it and focus their attention on it.

Lighting is a key visual aspect that has a direct impact on gamers' experience of emotions and the mood of games. Light determines our perception of a scene. The same scene with different light settings can be perceived differently, and its implementation without considering the importance of highlighting different key points can cause the player to have difficulty navigating the scene. An illuminated section may indicate a safe area. It may also indicate the opposite, i.e.

an area where the player is visible to opponents and should be avoided. Genre conventions may therefore change the task focus and the player will look for other areas.

How information is communicated and conveyed through space is an issue studied in both architecture and visual design. The article [14] refers to the use of architectural knowledge in the design process of game level space navigation. In visual design or communication design, techniques for the effective arrangement and distribution of elements in space are defined by the seven Principles of Design. The purpose of the creation of this discipline is to explore the relationship between the art of graphic design and the communication of information. These principles apply to traditional paper-based communication or architecture as well as to new media arts, and thus to exploration in video games.

The most common control methods in computer games are keyboard and mouse or a gamepad. The device with which we move can change our perception of the environment or the way we move within it. The authors in the papers [2,4,6,8] compared the two control methods in games also selected for our study. Keyboard and mouse performed better in games where fast and dynamic decisions had to be made and precise movements had to be made, while pad was better suited for exploration games.

3 Methodology

The prepared research method is an extension of the method developed in articles and papers [3,7,9,10,15,16]. The method is based on the development of an environment with a linear layout, where bifurcations are the place where decisions are made, leading to the next stages of the game. In this way, corridor-like levels with bifurcations were proposed, whose design was referred to as "Y-bifurcation". Each branch presents a different explored visual aspect to influence the players' decisions in choosing a path. Their final choices are monitored to determine the visual aspects selected.

It is important to create a sterile environment in the sense that the visual aspects are not mixed with each other. Amount of stimuli from the environment that can influence the decision-making and the choice of the spur is limited. A separate level was created for each type of visual aspect. Thus, levels were created to examine the influence of light, motion perception and geometry. Each study level is repeated by duplicating and mirroring the corridors. The individual Y forks are separated from each other by doors. The bifurcations where the player makes decisions about the direction of exploration consist of a section of a straight corridor and two branches containing a selected type of visual aspects that shape the environment. After passing through each module, the doors close. Y-bifurcation provide an area with a field of view that allows the two visual aspect options to be perceived evenly. By separating the corridors from the intersections with doors, these options will only be shown to the player when the next door opens. Each level was repeated in mirror image to see if the subject retained their bias of choices.

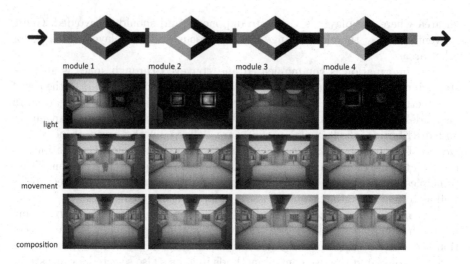

Fig. 1. At the top, the structure of the level is demonstrated, split into modules. Each level consists of four modules presented below divided into light, movement and composition.

The examined visual aspects are divided into three types - lights, movement and composition. The modules are described as follows and showed in Fig. 1:

- light—module 1 - no light vs static light; module 2 - static light vs dynamic light; module 3 - yellow light vs red light; module 4 - light at the beginning of the corridor vs light at the end of the corridor
- movement—module 1 - inanimate movement (on the floor) vs inanimate movement (on the floor) activated by the player; module 2 - inanimate movement (on the ceiling) vs no movement; module 3 - no movement vs animated movement (human); module 4 - animated movement (human) vs inanimate movement (on the floor)
- composition—module 1 - artimicity vs rhythmicity; module 2 - expression, smoke and blockades vs no effect; module 3 - framing vs no effect; module 4 - glass doors vs metal doors

Conclusions are drawn on the basis of the data collected from the levels completed by the participants. In addition, before the test, the participant is given a questionnaire to fill in, which determines factors such as age, gaming experience and whether they are right or left-handed.

4   Procedure

The experiment was conducted in a remote form. The participant himself downloaded the file with the launched version of the study and filled in the questionnaire. At the beginning of the test, participants are given a brief introductory story and explained the gameplay and controls. However, they do not know the purpose of the experiment or what aspects are being investigated.

The study took place in two rounds. In the first round, participants navigated using a keyboard and mouse, and in the second round with a game pad. The same set of modules were used in both rounds to make the levels. Participants did not repeat in the rounds. In the first round 50 participants with an average age of 21 years took part, 90% of the participants were right-handed . In the second round there were 84 participants with an average age of 24 years of which 92% were right-handed.

5   Results

The results presented here relate to repeat elections. This is understood as the repeated selection of a corridor containing the selected visual aspect. The assumption for duplicating levels with effects appearing in different order and located in the opposite corridor to the previous one was to see if, under different conditions, the player would repeat his choice of a visual aspect.This is understood by whether their preference was due to choosing the right or left side, whether their exploration method is pre-trained or whether they choose a different path due to curiosity about what is in the second corridor (the previous one they had already explored in the previous level). The repetition tendency was divided into four categories, where tendency means at least 75% of the choices of a method were repeated after changing sides. These are: General repetition of choices; Repeating a decision under the influence of light; Repeating a decision under the influence of movement; Repeating a decision under the influence of the composition of the environment. As the aim of the study is also to compare whether the control type influences the choice of route, separate summaries were produced for each variant. Figure 2 shows the results in the case of keyboard navigation. It can be seen that in this case the respondents mostly repeated the path containing the light guided method. In Fig. 3 , on the other hand, we see the results in the case of moving with the gamepad. Here we can see an overall greater tendency to repeat choices of paths containing methods. In this case, paths containing movement guidance were the most likely to be repeated.

Keyboard control			
Repetition of choices for all visual aspects	Repetition of light	Repetition of movement	Repetition of composition
10%	35%	20%	20%

Fig. 2. Table showing the trend results for the variant where control was done by keyboard. The top row represents the number of subjects with a trend, while the bottom row represents the percentage of subjects.

The tendency of the choices of the left and right paths was also checked on an overall basis with no breakdown by aspect. As can be seen in Fig. 4, there was

Pad control			
Repetition of choices for all visual aspects	Repetition of light	Repetition of movement	Repetition of composition
13%	33%	36%	24%

Fig. 3. Table showing the trend results for the variant where control was done with a pad. The top row represents the number of subjects having a trend, while the bottom row represents the percentage of subjects.

an advantage in choosing the right side. A greater disproportion was obtained with the keyboard variant than with the gamepad.

Keyboard control		Pad control	
Left side choice	41,7%	Left side choice	45,6%
Right side choice	58,3%	Right side choice	54,4%

Fig. 4. Table showing the percentage distribution for left and right path choices by type of control.

6   Discussion

Looking at the trend results for the selected visual aspects, respondents mostly repeated their choices in the case of light for the keyboard, and movement for the gamepad. In both cases, the composition caught the least attention of the respondents. This may have to do with the fact that in the case of composition, the differences in the corridors were more subtle than in the previous two cases. The differences in choices in the variant containing movement for both control modes were the largest. The visual aspect associated with movement was more often chosen when moving with using a gamepad. The apparent differences in the orientation of players by means of movement open the field for more detailed research and an attempt to understand the resulting difference.

As many as 90% of the respondents were right-handed. Decisions made in a modular, repetitive environment may have caused players to feel less inclined to decide and they started to complete levels automatically (mainly by walking on the right side all the time). This conclusion comes from the analysis of the transition maps, which show a higher degree of involvement in the first and second level a tendency to change corridor can be observed, and in later stages right corridors dominate.

Looking at and comparing the results obtained for the test where the control method was the keyboard, and for the test where one moves using a gamepad, it can be concluded that the control method does not significantly influence the decision making regarding path selection for most of the visual aspects used. The players' choices for both control methods are also similar in terms of the overall distribution of left and right path choices.

7   Conclusions

The aim of the study was to test the effectiveness of using three visual aspects of three-dimensional environments to aid navigation: light, motion and space composition, and to compare whether the type of control influences route choice. The results demonstrated how the repetition of the environment influences players' fatigue and decisions in the later phases of the game. This aspect seems to be an interesting field for further research to test the emergence of this phenomenon over time or number of repetitions.

Similar results for route choice according to control type suggest that it does not influence route choice decisions. Both for the use of aided navigation methods and for the overall summary of left and right hand split path selection.

Additionally, the problem encountered as expected was a preference for the right-hand side, which may (or may not) be due to the fact that 90% of the study participants were right-handed. From the moment the phenomenon of automatic play began to emerge, right-handed corridors were almost always selected. This happened often enough to be noticeable in the overall results.

It took about seven minutes to get through the entire game if the player did not look around and immediately made a decision when entering a crossroads. The monotony of the environment, which stemmed from the assumption of a sterile environment where a single type of visual aspect of the environment is tested and there are repetitive stages, contributed to the auto-play that began to occur after passing the first two levels exploring the effects of light. Going through the same stage twice showed that players went through the second stage much faster and paid less attention to it than the first time. Further studies of this phenomenon should take into account the acceleration of the pace and the variation of the spatial structure of the developed environment. Verification of the effect of repetition and the lack of influence of the experience of previous stages on subsequent choices should be based on an experiment divided into shorter stages with different effects that would be tested on different days.

The experiment ended with very interesting conclusions - despite the fact that it was not possible to confirm the effectiveness of methods of controlling the player's choices based on visual aspects of the environment, resulting from the analysis of the state of knowledge, it indicated the lack of influence of the method of steering on the player's decisions and clearly showed the phenomenon of automatic play and preference for the right side. The above conclusions provide guidelines for further research and the influence of further visual aspects on exploration decisions in the environment.

Acknowledgment. This article has been completed while the first author was the Doctoral Candidate in the Interdisciplinary Doctoral School at the Lodz University of Technology, Poland.

References

1. Eliasson, D.: What level design elements determine flow? How light and objects guide the player in overwatch and doom (2017)
2. Gerling, K.M., Klauser, M., Niesenhaus, J.: Measuring the impact of game controllers on player experience in fps games. In: Proceedings of the 15th International Academic MindTrek Conference: Envisioning Future Media Environments, pp. 83–86 (2011)
3. Hoeg, T.: The invisible hand: Using level design elements to manipulate player choice. Masters of Interactive Technology in Digital Game Development with a Specialization in Level Design, Guildhall at Southern Methodist University (2008)
4. Isokoski, P., Martin, B.: Performance of input devices in FPS target acquisition. In: Proceedings of the International Conference on Advances in Computer Entertainment Technology, pp. 240–241 (2007)
5. Joosten, E., Lankveld, G.V., Spronck, P.: Colors and emotions in video games. In: 11th International Conference on Intelligent Games and Simulation GAME-ON, pp. 61–65. sn (2010)
6. Kavakli, M., Thorne, J.R., et al.: A usability study of input devices on measuring user performance in computer games. In: Proceedings of First International Conference on Information Technology and Applications, pp. 291–295 (2002)
7. Knez, I., Niedenthal, S.: Lighting in digital game worlds: effects on affect and play performance. CyberPsychology Behav. 11(2), 129–137 (2008)
8. Lapointe, J.F., Savard, P., Vinson, N.G.: A comparative study of four input devices for desktop virtual walkthroughs. Comput. Hum. Behav. 27(6), 2186–2191 (2011)
9. Liszio, S., Masuch, M.: Lost in open worlds: design patterns for player navigation in virtual reality games. In: Proceedings of the 13th International Conference on Advances in Computer Entertainment Technology, pp. 1–7 (2016)
10. Nowak, P.: Virtual reality in investigation of human navigational skills. J. Appl. Comput. Sci. 26(2), 131–146 (2018)
11. Podhorecka, M., Andrzejczak, J., Szrajber, R., Lacko, J., Lipiński, P.: Virtual reality-based cognitive stimulation using GRYDSEN software as a means to prevent age-related cognitive-mobility disorders-a pilot observational study. Hum. Technol. 17(3), 321–335 (2021)
12. Rensink, R.A.: The Management of Visual Attention in Graphic Displays. Cambridge University Press, Cambridge (2011)
13. Rogers, S.: Level Up! The Guide to Great Video Game Design. Wiley, Chichester (2014)
14. Szrajber, R., Wojciechowska, J.: Odczytac wirtualna przestrzeń - komunikacja przez przestrzen w grach wideo (2019)
15. Wadstein, E.: Artistic techniques to influence navigational behavior in 3D-games (2013)
16. Winters, G.J., Zhu, J.: Guiding players through structural composition patterns in 3D adventure games. In: FDG (2014)
17. Wojciechowski, A., Wiśniewska, A., Pyszora, A., Liberacka-Dwojak, M., Juszczyk, K.: Virtual reality immersive environments for motor and cognitive training of elderly people-a scoping review. Hum. Technol. 17(2), 145 (2021)

Collaborative Virtual Reality Environment for Training Load Movement with Overhead Bridge Cranes

David Checa[✉], Ines Miguel-Alonso, Henar Guillen-Sanz[✉], and Andres Bustillo

Departamento de Ingeniería Informática, Universidad de Burgos, Burgos, Spain
{dcheca,imalonso,hguillen,abustillo}@ubu.es

Abstract. In the last decade, the rapid development and the price reduction of immersive Virtual Reality (iVR) devices allow its application to a wide range of applications. The sense of immersion and presence that these iVR devices produce surpasses any other display. These unique characteristic opens up new ways of training in Occupational Risk Prevention (ORP). iVR can create applications in collaborative training environments that mimic real situations and reinforce collaborative work and avoids unnecessary risks to the user in their training, as well as to other people or equipment that would exist if working with real equipment. Overhead cranes are one of the most interesting elements for the application of iVR training simulators. Firstly, because they are present throughout the production space and their movement involves the displacement of heavy loads that are not always well balanced. In addition, these movements occur in areas where other operators might be present and, in some cases, their collaboration is necessary during the movement stage. This research presents the design of a collaborative iVR application for training the movement of loads with overhead cranes. This developed application focuses on providing the user with the ability to proficiently operate an overhead crane. The usefulness of the iVR application was tested with 3 experienced overhead crane operators and 29 undergraduate students. These users reported that the experience was enjoyable and felt that the iVR environment was realistic and that the application would be useful to train how to handle an overhead bridge crane.

Keywords: Virtual Reality · Overhead crane · Training · Collaborative environments

1 Introduction

Virtual reality was described as early as 1965, as "a room in which a computer controls the existence of matter" [1]. This definition already foreshadowed the great potential of this technology, although the technological challenges it faced hindered it from becoming a reality for the general public for more than half a century. This slow maturation accelerated definitively in the second decade of this century, and Virtual Reality Head Mounted Displays (HMDs) have become available on the market in the last five years at an affordable price. These devices have been complemented by other technologies such as hyper-realistic video game engines that have been developed at the same time

© Springer Nature Switzerland AG 2022
L. T. De Paolis et al. (Eds.): XR Salento 2022, LNCS 13445, pp. 121–129, 2022.
https://doi.org/10.1007/978-3-031-15546-8_10

[2]. This fusion of technologies is what we currently define as Immersive Virtual Reality (iVR).

IVR outperforms other computer-generated image display systems in terms of the sense of immersion and presence it produces in the user. After a few minutes of immersion in the virtual environment, it becomes practically indistinguishable from the real one. These characteristics make it a particularly suitable technology for training. Firstly, it allows a first-person experience with a very high degree of interaction in real time and a sense of presence in the environment impossible to achieve with other technologies; these characteristics increase motivation and therefore the effectiveness of training in end users [3]. In addition, it allows the user to work autonomously and receive immediate feedback on their performance [4].

These unique features of immersive Virtual Reality open a new way of understanding Occupational Risk Prevention (ORP) training. iVR avoids unnecessary risks to the user in their training, as well as to other people or equipment, that would exist if working with real devices. Even high-risk situations can be simulated with great realism that are too difficult to achieve with desktop applications and impossible to do with real equipment. In addition, this type of training requires regular updating, making the use of iVR simulators an easy, flexible and dynamic solution compared to traditional training [7]. Within the multifaceted scope of the ORP, the machinery responsible for moving loads, such as bridge cranes, is one of the most interesting elements for the application of Immersive Virtual Reality. Firstly, because they are always present throughout the production space and their movement involves the displacement of heavy loads that are not always well balanced. Moreover, this movement takes place in areas where other operators are present.

Early applications of Virtual Reality in training were not focused on ORP. These first academic works, more than a decade old, were oriented towards describing the potential advantages of these VR technologies [5]. In 2015, iVR experiences began experimenting and demonstrating the improvement of learning and training [6, 7]. Although the technological problem remains unresolved because the devices were still relatively expensive and produced with some regularity dizziness in long experiences. With the emergence of low-cost HMDs, iVR applications are beginning to be applied in industries. The general purpose of these applications is to provide practical utility regarding a suitable work-force training for certifying new operators to work under dangerous and complex environments [8, 9].

The logical evolution is to turn these applications into collaborative training and learning environments that mimic real-life situations. These environments are intended to reinforce collaborative work. iVR environments reinforce collaborative work, and the sense of immersion can be enhanced when users are also present in a shared physical space [11]. Therefore, this research is based on the development of a collaborative immersive virtual reality application for training the movement of loads with overhead cranes. The structure of this paper will be organized as follows: in Sect. 2, the development of the collaborative VR environment will be described. In Sect. 3, the usability evaluation will be analyzed with its procedure and results. Finally, the main conclusions and future lines will be exposed in Sect. 4.

2 Development

This iVR application is intended to instruct in the prevention of occupational hazards in the interaction with overhead bridge cranes. Overhead cranes are the most widespread method of transporting loads in industrial environments. This heavy machinery is operated with remote controls, so the training can be simulated in iVR with a high degree of fidelity to the real training. Furthermore, in this case, the iVR allows us to face dangerous situations such as unbalanced loads, operators passing under the load or transit through poorly lit areas. This type of training is rarely carried out in real environments because of its high level of risk. Therefore, this training solution prepares the user to deal with such dangerous situations.

For the development of this application a framework of key aspects of iVR experience design and optimization for the prevention of occupational hazards has been followed [10]. This strategy is divided into 4 levels: 1) instruction, 2) interface, 3) simulation and 4) evaluation. Figure 1 shows the proposed strategy for the design of a collaborative iVR application for training the movement of loads with overhead cranes.

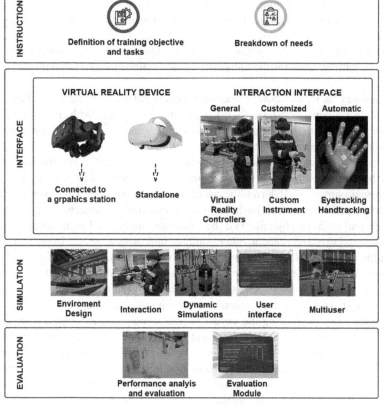

Fig. 1. Proposed strategy for the design of a collaborative immersive virtual reality application for training the movement of loads with overhead cranes.

In the first level of instruction, the definition of the tasks to be performed by the users in the iVR environment is carried out. In order to achieve this objective, operations and risks present in the handling of overhead cranes were defined. It has been taken into account that they can be trained autonomously or with the help of another user in a collaborative environment. Among the most common risks detected are the following:

- Risk of overturning and falling objects or equipment.
- Poor handling of equipment due to lack of operator training.
- Risk of entrapment caused by equipment transported on the traffic lanes.
- Risk of entrapment or dragging due to incorrect handling and/or load conduction.
- Collisions with other work equipment due to: Simultaneous and uncoordinated work of several pieces of work equipment in close proximity to each other or because a lack of signaling.

The following operations were also identified as particularly useful for simulation and training in individual or collaborative iVR environments:

- Transporting loads without visibility aided by another user or with lighting conditions affecting visibility (low luminosity, zenithal lights…)
- Hearing impairment (high ambient noise, communication problems between different users, etc.)
- Technical complications (carrying loads with a mass greater than that allowed by the crane or tooling, transporting unbalanced loads, balancing loads in motion)

In this way, as well as how to operate the overhead crane proficiently, the user will learn to detect occupational hazards, especially those associated with crushing accidents, as part of a work team, coordinating with co-workers and dealing with problems arising from working in a team and with complex machinery.

To maximize the naturalness of the interaction with the iVR environment, several approaches have been developed to allow the user a natural and trustworthy interaction with the environment. First, an ad-hoc custom controller interface was developed for this simulator: a real bridge crane pushbutton controller that is connected to the simulator. Likewise, and with the objective that the simulator can be used in any context and not only with specialized equipment, other available interfaces were also integrated, such as the Oculus Touch and HTC Vive controllers. As well as the integration of the user's hand tracking through the front cameras of the HTC Vive and Oculus Quest. This is necessary for some collaborative tasks such as communicating by signals with your co-worker.

In the next stage, the requirements to create the simulation are detailed. This phase included the tasks of creating the virtual environments, programming the interactions with this environment, with the objects and with the interfaces to be used by the user. Regarding the creation of the environment, generic factories were created. These factories had to meet the requirement of being modular in order to be able to adapt to the widest range of possible situations that can arise in the handling of overhead cranes in different industries. Figure 2 shows the modularity of these environments. In addition, it was also necessary to model the overhead cranes, controls, slinging and lifting accessories, as well as connection elements between accessories or load grips with high detail and fidelity.

Fig. 2. Example of the modular factory, recreating a single building on the left and a double building on the right.

For the development, Unreal Engine was used in conjunction with a previously created framework [12] that, by means of predesigned tools, simplifies the development of the iVR application. In particular, this framework includes tools for creating interactions with the scenario and objects. It also facilitates the creation of tasks and their objectives. Finally, it also facilitates the extraction of data and user performance indicators.

The multi-user support has been realized with the help of Epic Online Services which provides the online infrastructure for the multiplayer integration. A basic lobby was created to set up multiplayer and the replication, since all actors whose position or other properties are relevant in multiplayer must replicate to ensure synchronization between all the clients. At the same time the system supports the presence of viewers, used by managers or technicians to evaluate in real time the user's performance. These can be visible or invisible to the user depending on the desired effect.

3   Usability

The usability of the iVR application was tested on 3 experienced overhead bridge crane operators. The equipment used in these tests is made up of a workstation equipped with Intel Core i7-10710U, 32 GB RAM, with NVIDIA GTX 2080 graphics card connected to the HTC Vive Pro Eye HMD. This is an HMD that includes a high-quality display, 6DOF controllers, eye tracking and sensors to calculate the user's position in the virtual environment. Thanks to its integrated eye-tracking system, it allows real-time analysis of the user's performance, as well as detecting improper behavior, for example, if the user is not monitoring the load being carried continuously. The experience was executed in one session. First a brief explanation of the iVR system and HMD was given as introduction. Then, participants began the iVR experience with a tutorial on how to use the virtual environment and interaction devices before moving on to a test in which they had to complete a circuit by handling a load. Subsequently, users were faced with different tasks that varied according to the slinging accessory chosen, the type of load and the movement conditions, among others, sequentially increasing the difficulty throughout the different levels. These experienced crane operators used both types of interaction devices as shown in Fig. 3.

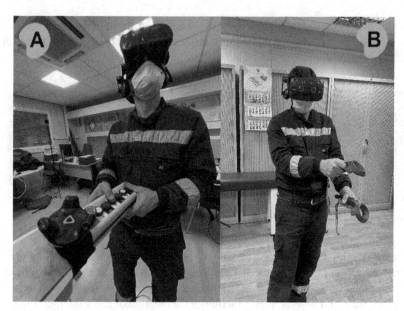

Fig. 3. Crane operator testing the different methods of interaction. A: real bridge crane controller. B: general virtual reality controllers.

In relation to the validation experience, the survey is comprised of 11 questions to measure cybersickness, satisfaction and usability. Eight multiple choice questions (MCQs) were used, rating each aspect with 1 to 5 points on a Likert scale, where 1 means not at all and 5 means very much. In the survey, there are included additionally three open questions for giving the positive and negative aspects and suggestions of the iVR experience. The 8 MCQ were divided into categories to evaluate 5 different aspects of the iVR experience. These aspects are satisfaction, usefulness perception, usability, presence, and immersion, using a validating and unified questionnaire on user experience in immersive virtual environment (IVEQ) [13]. None of these users had used an iVR device before, and they did not report any dizziness. Satisfaction with the application was very high, as well as the usefulness perceived by the user, because of their good opinions that the simulator would help in learning how to operate a bridge crane. Regarding realism, users gave an average of 7.5 out of 10 to the recreation of the factory and 8.5 to the level of presence experienced. Reported usability was much higher with the customized device (9.1) than with the general controllers (7.9), although in both cases reasonably high. In addition, after completing the survey, these crane operators were given a personal interview while using the simulator again to receive more direct feedback. Possible improvements to the simulator were also addressed at this time. Small bugs were corrected, such as the correct crane speed when using two-speed push buttons or the increased braking distance when moving large loads.

The usability was also tested on 29 undergraduate students. This sample group is balanced in terms of gender. Its average age is 22.86 years. The experience was run in 3 sessions. In the first one, a brief explanation of the iVR system and HMD was given. Then, participants began the iVR experience with a tutorial on how to use the virtual environment and the interaction devices, before moving on to a test in which they had to complete a circuit by handling a load, as shown in Fig. 4.

Fig. 4. Example of skill test that students used in the usability test.

After this first session, the users used the simulator two more times in the following weeks. In these sessions the participants performed the same circuit, but with different complications while the difficulty was being increased. At the end of it, participants were asked to complete the usability and satisfaction survey. Cybersickness was only reported by 4 of the 29 participants. One of the participants considered his cybersickness event as "moderate". The other 3 participants rated their cybersickness as "low level". As it can be seen in the Table 1, the participants' satisfaction was high (4.55) as well as the presence (4.43). In the contrary, their usefulness perception, usability and immersion have the lowest rates (3.84 in usefulness perception, 3.90 in usability and 3.83 in immersion). This difference between the classification of the questions means that the experience was enjoyable, and they felt that the iVR environment was real, but the handling of the bridge crane was difficult and make them get distracted from their tasks during the iVR experience.

Table 1. Mean (M) and Standard Deviation (SD) of satisfaction and usability surveys.

	M	SD
Satisfaction	4.55	0.63
Usefulness perception	3.84	0.94
Usability	3.90	1.26
Presence	4.43	0.84
Immersion	3.83	1.14

Moreover, the open questions demonstrate the results of the 8 MCQ. Participants commented as positive aspects that the application was useful to train how to handle a bridge crane and the iVR environment was realistic. However, as negative aspects, they considered that the use of the virtual control of the bridge crane was not intuitive, and they had little precision when pressing the virtual buttons. In addition, some participants asked for more obstacles and variety of circuits. These negative aspects and your suggestions will be taken into account for future improvements of this application as well as in research.

4 Conclusions and Future Research Lines

This paper proposed an immersive and collaborative virtual reality application for training the movement of loads with overhead cranes. This application focuses on providing the user with the ability to proficiently operate an overhead crane. In addition, the user will learn to detect occupational hazards, to be part of a work team, to coordinate with colleagues and to deal with problems arising from working in a team and with complex machinery. The usefulness of the iVR application was tested with 3 experienced overhead crane operators and 29 undergraduate students. The experience was enjoyable, and they felt that the iVR environment was real.

Future works will be focused in expanding the scope of applicability of this application, as well as integrating intelligent systems in its evaluation. Occupational Risk Prevention training can be much more effective if immersive Virtual Reality devices become serious games with artificial intelligence. In this case, training can be adapted to the skills, habits and knowledge of each user, and training gaps or improvements can be identified semi-automatically. Virtual Reality 3D visualization equipment is particularly suitable for incorporating artificial intelligence, given that it always reflects the way the user interacts with the virtual environment, by means of haptic or manual interfaces, and what is being visualized at any given moment, given the tendency of human beings to focus on the fovea on what they are focusing their attention.

Acknowledgments. This work was partially supported by the ACIS project (Reference Number INVESTUN/21/BU/0002) of the Consejeria de Empleo e Industria of the Junta de Castilla y León (Spain) and the Erasmus + RISKREAL Project (Reference Number 2020-1-ES01-KA204-081847) of the European Commission. This work has been made possible thanks to the support received from Nicolas Correa S.A. where the validation tests with final users were performed.

References

1. Sutherland, I.E.: The ultimate display. In: Proceedings of the Congress of the International Federation of Information Processing (IFIP) (1965). https://doi.org/10.1109/MC.2005.274
2. Das, S., Maiti, J., Krishna, O.B.: Assessing mental workload in virtual reality based EOT crane operations: a multi-measure approach. Int. J. Indust. Ergon. **80**, 103017 (2020). https://doi.org/10.1016/j.ergon.2020.103017
3. Bustillo, A., Alaguero, M., Miguel, I., Saiz, J.M., Iglesias, L.S.: A flexible platform for the creation of 3D semi-immersive environments to teach cultural heritage. Digital App. Archaeol. Cult. Herit. **2**, 248–259 (2015). https://doi.org/10.1016/j.daach.2015.11.002

4. Checa, D., Bustillo, A.: A review of immersive virtual reality serious games to enhance learning and training. Multimed. Tools App. **79**(9–10), 5501–5527 (2019). https://doi.org/10.1007/s11042-019-08348-9

5. Dong, H., Xu, G.: An expert system for bridge crane training system based on virtual reality. In: Proceedings - International Conference on Artificial Intelligence and Computational Intelligence, AICI 2010 (2010). https://doi.org/10.1109/AICI.2010.247

6. George, A.K., McLain, M.L., Bijlani, K., Jayakrishnan, R., Bhavani, R.R.: A novel approach for training crane operators: serious game on crane simulator. In: Proceedings - IEEE 8th International Conference on Technology for Education, T4E 2016 (2017). https://doi.org/10.1109/T4E.2016.030

7. Moreland, J., Zaraliakos, J., Wang, J., Zhou, M., Zhou, C.: Interactive Training for Fall Protection and Crane Safety (2016)

8. Müller, D., Ferreira, J.M.M.: MARVEL: a mixed reality learning environment for vocational training in mechatronics. In: T.E.L. 2003 Proceedings: International Conference on Technology-enhanced Learning (2004)

9. Travassos Valdez, M., Machado Ferreira, C., Martins, M.J.M., Maciel Barbosa, F.P.: Virtual labs in electrical engineering education-The VEMA environment. In: ITHET 2014 - 13th International Conference on Information Technology Based Higher Education and Training (2014). https://doi.org/10.1109/ITHET.2014.7155714

10. Checa, D., Martínez, K., Osornio-Ríos, R., Bustillo, A.: Virtual Reality opportunities in the reduction of occupational hazards in industry 4.0. DYNA. **96**, 620–626 (2021). https://doi.org/10.6036/10241

11. Beck, S., Kunert, A., Kulik, A., Froehlich, B.: Immersive group-to-group telepresence. IEEE Trans. Visual Comput. Graph. **19**, 616–625 (2013). https://doi.org/10.1109/TVCG.2013.33

12. Checa, D., Gatto, C., Cisternino, D., De Paolis, L.T., Bustillo, A.: A framework for educational and training immersive virtual reality experiences. In: De Paolis, L.T., Bourdot, P. (eds.) Augmented Reality, Virtual Reality, and Computer Graphics. LNCS, vol. 12243, pp. 220–228. Springer, Cham (2020). https://doi.org/10.1007/978-3-030-58468-9_17

13. Tcha-Tokey, K., Christmann, O., Loup-Escande, E., Richir, S.: Proposition and validation of a questionnaire to measure the user experience in immersive virtual environments. Int. J. Virtual Real. **16** (2016). https://doi.org/10.20870/ijvr.2016.16.1.2880

A VR Multiplayer Application for Fire Fighting Training Simulations

Irene Capasso[1,2], Chiara Bassano[1(✉)], Fabrizio Bracco[2], Fabio Solari[1], Eros Viola[1], and Manuela Chessa[1]

[1] Department of Informatics, Bioengineering, Robotics and Systems Engineering, University of Genoa, Genoa, Italy
irene.capasso@scenariosrl.com, chiara.bassano@dibris.unige.it, {fabio.solari,manuela.chessa}@unige.it, eros.viola@edu.unige.it
[2] Department of Education Sciences, University of Genoa, Genoa, Italy
fabrizio.bracco@unige.it

Abstract. The need to guarantee employees good training in the field of safety in workplaces, risk assessment, fire prevention and fire fighting, or management of dangerous situations is a priority in different sectors, from maritime, airport and military to schools, offices. The application of Virtual Reality (VR) technologies, as a substitute or complement to traditional teaching methods, is a relevant topic both for researchers and companies specialized in the organization of training courses. Here, we present a multiplayer immersive VR application for safety and fire prevention training, developed in collaboration with experts adopting a user-centered design approach. A preliminary usability test on 20 subjects showed promising results regarding the usability and the efficacy of the VR intervention but a low level of sense of presence, maybe due to the non-photo realistic graphic rendering or to the fact that participants were unfamiliar with the interaction methods and frequently asked questions disrupting the immersion. Feedback received will be used to modify and improve the application.

Keywords: Virtual Reality · Human-computer interaction · Hand interaction · Navigation · Simulation · Training · Fire fighting

1 Introduction

Health and safety in workplaces is a fundamental topic in Italian law: a legislative decree states that the employer is obliged to adopt all fire prevention measures and to guarantee its employees adequate training through highly specialized courses. In general, companies specialized in training use ad-hoc designed buildings and structures capable of hosting simulations of different scenarios. The aim is to recreate situations as much similar as possible to those that could arise in the real workplace of interest and, ideally, simulations should be organized on site: the fire would be simulated in places where the risk is actually higher, workers would be familiar with the setting, aware of the actual arrangement of the necessary tools (fire extinguishers, hoses, clothing) and of the escape routes and transfer of the learned concepts would be immediate. However, on site training is unpractical, because of the need for highly specialized structures and fire resistant artifacts (furniture, machinery, mannequins, etc.) and because of the logistics costs, which include travel and accommodation, since courses are often held over several days.

The application of technologies for immersive Virtual Reality (VR) to these contexts could have a very strong impact, for several reasons [6,8,11,13,14]. Firstly, immersion within the Virtual Environment (VE) allows removing external distractions and the physical exploration of simulated spaces facilitates active learning, i.e. the consolidation of theoretical knowledge through practical experience. Secondly, the use of VR is more engaging and enjoyable, thanks to gamification, and less frustrating, since simulations take place in controlled and safe settings and users can stop whenever they feel uncomfortable. Thirdly, VR scenarios could replicate the real workplace and specific situations or events by simulating an on site training in a more affordable way. Lastly, during simulation it is possible to record videos, body and head position, speed, gaze, interaction actions, task completion time and other information from external wearable sensors (e.g., heart rate, skin conductance). These data allow the analysis of participants behavior, decisions, errors and progresses.

In the current work, we propose a multiplayer immersive VR application for teaching safety at work and fire prevention to inexperienced low risk personnel, novice with fire and with the use of fire extinguishers. The application has been designed in collaboration with Masterfire Antincendio[1], a Genoa's company specialized in the supplement of systems and devices for fire safety and in the organization of training courses in different fields, among which fire prevention. The VR simulation is conceived as a complementary tool to be used in combination with traditional learning methodologies, i.e. theoretical lessons and practice in the Training House, a complex structure used by Masterfire Antincendio company for training courses. Indeed, experts has observed an inconsistency between the proactive attitude of participants during lessons and their behaviour during practice, which is often negative and unproductive and may be due to the fear and anxiety caused by the fact of facing an unknown dangerous situation. Thus, the developed VR application represents an intermediary step, which allows participants to familiarize with fire in a safe environment and consolidate their basic knowledge. The idea of a multiplayer platform arises from the fact that offices usually hold more than one person and collaboration is an essential factor to achieve safety and security. During the design phase, we adopted a user-centered design approach. Hence, we did not solely focus on information technologies aspects, but also took into account key factors such as usability, sense of presence, participants learning rate, individual behaviour and social dynamics within the group.

---

[1] https://masterfireantincendiogenova.com.

In the following, we propose an overview of related literature (Sect. 2) and describe the proposed system (Sect. 3.2). We then illustrate the usability test procedure (Sect. 3.3 and 3.4), recorded data (Sect. 3.5) and preliminary results obtained (Sect. 4). Finally, we discuss limitations and future developments of the designed system (Sect. 5).

2   State of the Art

The application of VR technologies to the field of training for safety, fire and risk reduction in workplaces has been a relevant topic in the literature in the last decades.

In the 90's US Navy, introduced VR simulations as a substitute of traditional practices for fire testing and training, which used to take place on the decommissioned ship Shadwell [14]. A VR scenario with the 3D model of the ship has been implemented and tested. Results highlight a marked improvement in participants performance with respect to traditional training. Sidh, a training system for the CAVE has been developed by [1] and successfully tested on firefighter students. Recently, authors in [10] have proposed Immersive Safe Oceans, an immersive VR training technology, for ship personnel aimed at enhancing risk assessment and decision making skills and improving the management of accidents such as fires in the engine room. Similarly, authors in [7], combine VR and AI technology in the design of a training application for airport staff addressing fire safety knowledge, safety awareness of staff and passengers and emergency response ability. Finally, a research conducted by RelyOn Nutec, a company that offers safety training courses to personnel in the Norwegian oil and gas sector, has assessed the effectiveness, usability and acceptability of a mixed reality fire extinguisher training [11].

VR fire training simulations are also diffused in other contexts. Authors in [13] propose VR as a mean to improve children's awareness of fire hazards and rehearse evacuation techniques. The study highlights a high level of engagement and motivation. Another work on road tunnel evacuation compares the effects of training based on subjective questionnaires, information sheets and VR simulation [6], by dividing participants in three groups. A week after training, they took a trip through a real tunnel, where a car accident was simulated. The third group have evacuated the area more reliably and safely than those in the other groups. Finally, authors in [8] conduct an experiment to compare the effectiveness of a traditional non-interactive training based on watching videos and an innovative VR application in teaching non-experts to use and manipulate fire extinguishers. The amount of information preserved during the follow-up test, three/four weeks after the intervention, is significantly higher in the second case.

Also many companies have specialized in the creation of VR solutions for safety and firefighting training for personnel working in various sectors: for example, the start-up launched by Deakin University which produced the FLAIM

Systems[2], OneBonsai[3], Luminous[4], Virtual Safety Lab[5], IGAEM[6], STI - Servizi Tecnologico Industriali[7], SCENARIO[8] and VStep[9].

3   Materials and Methods

3.1   Virtual Reality Application

The proposed VR simulation system has been developed using Unity 2020.3.17f1 and runs on Oculus Quest 2. The 3D model of the Training House, shown in Fig. 1c, has been created in Blender[10], while other accessories and tools models have been imported from Unity Asset Store and Turbosquid[11] and avatars and their animations from Mixamo[12]. Focusing on fire extinguishers (Fig. 1b), we considered three different categories, namely powder, CO_2 and foam. 3D models have been further modified in Blender, since they did not fully comply with the Italian regulations for the labels and originally consisted of a single object, which had to be divided in different parts (body, rope, handle and safety pin) for manipulation. In fact, users have to grab the fire extinguisher from the handle with one hand, remove the safety pin with the other hand, then grab the rope, press the handle to let the flow out and direct it towards the flames. Particles effects for fire, smoke and fire extinguishers flows were created in Unity.

The application is composed of a single player training scene and a multiplayer simulation scene. In the first case, there is no avatar and interaction can be achieved both by using the Oculus controllers or the Oculus Custom Hands Integration for hand tracking. The playing area is limited and all interactable objects can be easily reached by stretching the arms. In the second case, an avatar is associated to each player and since users are asked to explore a building, controllers thumbsticks, buttons and triggers are used for objects manipulation and environment exploration. In fact, hand tracking would be impractical since user would often have to handle the controllers to move in the VE and release it to interact with virtual objects.

In the literature works comparing controllers based and hand tracking based interaction still show controversial results. For example, hand tracking has been found to be more usable and effective with respect to controllers in tasks such as grabbing objects and typing keys [16] and has been already successfully applied to firefighting contexts [9]. Instead, with small objects, controllers result to be

---

[2] https://flaimsystems.com.

[3] https://onebonsai.com/.

[4] https://www.luminousgroup.co.uk/project/premier-partnership-vr-fire-training/.

[5] https://virtualsafetylab.com/.

[6] https://igeam.it/.

[7] https://www.sti-consulting.it/.

[8] https://scenariosrl.com/.

[9] https://www.vstepsimulation.com/.

[10] https://www.blender.org/.

[11] https://www.turbosquid.com/.

[12] https://www.mixamo.com/.

more appreciated by the users [15]. Nonetheless, a research comparing HTC Vive controllers and Leap Motion shows better performance and usability with controllers even if learning curve is slower [3]. Thus, we decided to use controllers for fire extinguisher interaction. Furthermore, considering the exploration of the virtual scenario, the two main solutions currently available are continuous motion and teleportation. They both cause cybersickness, mainly characterized by disorientation, even if with teleportation is associated to milder effects [4]. However, we chose continuous motion because teleportation causes discomfort and determines a lower sense of presence and experienced realism [5].

The multiplayer platform has been implemented using the TCP network protocol. In the multiplayer scene there are three fundamental components: the Network manager, responsible for managing the network aspects; the Host, i.e. the user wearing the HMD connected to Unity through USB cable which acts as a server; the Client, the second player wearing a standalone HMD, managed by the ClientManager, which searchs the server and connects to it.

Finally, the system proposes two different interfaces, one for the players, who perform the task in an immersive VE by wearing a head-mounted display (HMD), and the other for the instructor, who supervises task execution from a computer running the Unity application. The supervisor can, in real-time, add or delete fire at specific positions through raycasting and resize flames, increasing or decreasing the particle effect size from the Inspector Window in the Unity Editor.

3.2 Gameplay

After wearing the HMD, the experience begins with a short training inside a virtual warehouse. Participants are asked to choose the correct fire extinguisher among three different options, according to the flames type, namely a small fire originating from an electrical panel. In this case, the correct choice is the CO_2 one. A feedback is given to users when they try extinguishing the fire, a green light if they are using the correct extinguisher and a red light on the contrary. In the first case, they can continue the exercise and extinguish the fire, whereas in the second case, they can try again until they choose the correct fire extinguisher. When the fire has been completely extinguished, the training phase finishes and the actual simulation starts. Even if no limit to players number exists, we tested the application with couples. In the beginning, the two firefighters are warned of the fire in the Training House, but, before leaving the warehouse, they must choose the correct equipment. Then, they are asked to follow the smoke, find the fire origin and extinguish it. Stressors, such as the sound of a siren, are added to increase the realism of the experience. The simulation ends when the goal is achieved and the two firefighters have evacuated the building. The instructor supervises the process and can in real-time manipulate smoke and fire intensity to increase the difficulty level, if the exercise is having a positive outcome and a high level of collaboration is observed, or decrease it, if one or both of the participants show difficulties. Exposure to VR, is followed by a debriefing phase with the students, where the instructor shows and comments simulation recordings.

A workflow diagram of the proposed gameplay is shown in Fig. 1a and a sample video is available[13].

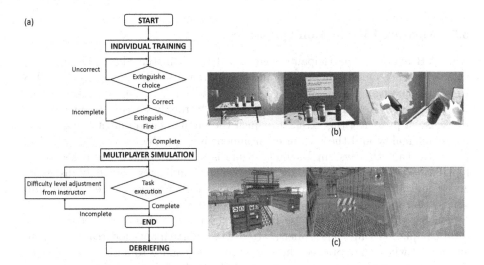

Fig. 1. (a) Workflow diagram of the gameplay with screenshots of the application referred to (b) the individual training inside the warehouse and (c) the multiplayer simulation inside the Training House.

3.3 Participants

20 volunteer healthy subjects, 10 males and 10 females, aged between 18 and 65, took part in the experimental session. They all had no or a very basic level of expertise in the firefighting field. Only 2 of the participants had already used VR. Before starting the experiment, all participants were explained the goal of the research and given instructions about the tasks and the hardware involved. Since a person abandoned the VR simulation because of simulator sickness, data presented below are referred to 19 participants.

3.4 Procedure

Participants took part to a training course lasting four hours. First of all, they followed lessons providing theoretical notions on fire, fire prevention and protection and procedures to be adopted in case of fire. Next, they performed the VR simulation task, where they were asked to put into practice the knowledge previously acquired. Subsequently, they filled in the questionnaires described in Sect. 3.5. The day after, they performed a simple exercise in the real Training House, aimed at assessing the effects of VR training. Participants had to take a fire extinguisher, find the fire origin and simulate its extinguishing. Due to technical and logistical

---

[13] https://youtu.be/V5rPBSRTW2I.

reasons, it was not possible to use real fire, hence a panel representing the fire was placed on a wall. In addition, so-called stressors, i.e. alarms, sirens, obstacles, were introduced to increase stress and make the simulation more realistic.

3.5 Measured Evaluation Quantities

After VR exposure, participants were asked to fill in the Slater, Usoh, Steed (SUS) Presence Questionnaire [12] and the System Usability Scale [2]. The SUS Presence Questionnaire is based on 6 items, rated in a 7-point Likert scale, where 1 indicates "Strongly disagree" and 7 "Strongly agree". It investigates the sense of presence, the extent to which the virtual environment becomes the dominant reality and the virtual environment is remembered as a real physical place. Instead, the System Usability Scale is a questionnaire composed of 10 items, rated using a 5-point Likert scale, where 1 indicates "Strongly disagree" and 5 indicates "Strongly agree". It evaluates the effectiveness, efficiency and satisfaction with which users achieve task completion.

During the practical exercise in the real Training House, we recorded the total completion time. The timer started when participants felt ready to begin and ended when they pressed the fire extinguisher lance to activate the jet. In addition, an expert instructor supervised the task execution and provided an objective and professional judgment. He assigned a score from 1 to 5 to each participant, where 1 indicated "Incorrect procedure together with inappropriate behavior" and 5 indicated "Correct procedure together with adequate behavior". In particular, he focused on the extent to which subjects recognized what they had to do and seemed concentrated, determined and self-confident.

4 Results

Results obtained from the analysis of acquired parameters are shown in Table 1. For the SUS Presence Questionnaire, we first considered the number of times each item was rated with scores 6 and 7 and averaged across all participants (SUS Count); then, sums of scores 6 and 7, for each participant, were transformed into means, dividing them by the total number of items (SUS Mean). Observing results, we can notice that the resulting scores are moderate to high, which means that the three dimensions of the sense of presence are experienced in a normal measure. This could be due to the non-photo realistic graphic rendering or to the fact that some participants had difficulties in using the controller and asked questions to the instructor, disrupting the immersion in the VE. Better results have been obtained from the System Usability Scale. In fact, since the average score as reported by the authors corresponds to 68, we can state that our application complies with usability standards.

Total completion time and the instructor evaluation, referred to the practical exercise in the real Training House, can be used as a measure of participants learning level. Taking into account that the average time to perform the procedure in a complete and correct way is usually 17 s, we can state that participants have achieved the objectives of the course in a quite satisfactory way. Similarly, scores assigned by the instructor demonstrate that the proposed procedure can be usefully and effectively adopted for teaching safety and fire prevention.

Table 1. Mean and standard deviation of parameters acquired.

Parameter	Reference value	Mean	Std
SUS count	6	3	1.45
SUS mean	1	0.6	0.29
System usability scale	100	73.42	16.84
Expert evaluation	5	4.05	1.23
Total completion time (sec)	17 s	18.02 s	2.78 s

5   Conclusions

The current work presents the design and implementation of a simulation system for teaching safety at work and fire prevention to inexperienced low risk personnel, based on the most recent technologies for immersive VR. The system has been conceived in collaboration with experts, specialized in the fields of safety and security training courses, and adopting a user-center design, since we took into account usability, sense of presence, participants learning rate, behaviour and social dynamics. A preliminary usability test on 20 subjects has been conducted. Results show a moderate degree of sense of presence but promising outcomes on usability and efficiency of the learning method. This test gave us the opportunity to re-evaluate some aspects of the application, which will be reviewed and tested again in the near future. In particular, we plan to integrate hand tracking, in order to allow free hands interaction and manipulation of the fire extinguisher. Furthermore, a between group experimental design comparing the effect of traditional and VR based training is needed for better assessing the benefits of immersive VR.

Acknowledgements. The authors would like to thank Alessandro Ferrando, owner and instructor at Masterfire Antincendio, who supervised the experiments, and all volunteers who participated in the experimental sessions.

References

1. Backlund, P., Engstrom, H., Hammar, C., Johannesson, M., Lebram, M.: SIDH-a game based firefighter training simulation. In: 2007 11th International Conference Information Visualization (IV2007), pp. 899–907. IEEE (2007)
2. Brooke, J.: SUS: a "quick and dirty" usability scale. Usab. Eval. Ind. **189**(3), 4–7 (1996)

3. Caggianese, G., Gallo, L., Neroni, P.: The Vive controllers vs. leap motion for interactions in virtual environments: a comparative evaluation. In: De Pietro, G., Gallo, L., Howlett, R.J., Jain, L.C., Vlacic, L. (eds.) KES-IIMSS-18 2018. SIST, vol. 98, pp. 24–33. Springer, Cham (2019). https://doi.org/10.1007/978-3-319-92231-7_3

4. Clifton, J., Palmisano, S.: Comfortable locomotion in VR: teleportation is not a complete solution. In: 25th ACM Symposium on Virtual Reality Software and Technology, pp. 1–2 (2019)

5. Clifton, J., Palmisano, S.: Effects of steering locomotion and teleporting on cybersickness and presence in HMD-based virtual reality. Virtual Real. **24**(3), 453–468 (2019). https://doi.org/10.1007/s10055-019-00407-8

6. Kinateder, W., et al.: Human behaviour in severe tunnel accidents: effects of information and behavioural training. Transp. Res. Part F Traffic Psychol. Behav. **17**, 20–32 (2013)

7. Li, J., Mei, X., Wang, J., Xie, B., Xu, Y.: Simulation Experiment Teaching For Airport Fire Escape Based On Virtual Reality and Artificial Intelligence Technology. In: 2020 IEEE 2nd International Conference on Civil Aviation Safety and Information Technology (ICCASIT), pp. 1014–1017. IEEE (2020)

8. Lovreglio, R., Duan, X., Rahouti, A., Phipps, R., Nilsson, D.: Comparing the effectiveness of fire extinguisher virtual reality and video training. Virtual Real. **25**(1), 133–145 (2020). https://doi.org/10.1007/s10055-020-00447-5

9. Luimula, M., Ranta, J., Al-Adawi, M.: Hand tracking in fire safety-electric cabin fire simulation. In: 2020 11th IEEE International Conference on Cognitive Infocommunications (CogInfoCom), pp. 000221–000222. IEEE (2020)

10. Markopoulos, E., Luimula, M.: Immersive safe oceans technology: developing virtual onboard training episodes for maritime safety. Fut. Internet **12**(5), 80 (2020)

11. Saghafian, M., Laumann, K., Akhtar, R.S., Skogstad, M.R.: The evaluation of virtual reality fire extinguisher training. Front. Psychol. **11**, 3137 (2020)

12. Slater, M., Usoh, M., Steed, A.: A depth of presence in virtual environments. Presence Teleoperat. Virtual Environ. **3**(2), 130–144 (1994)

13. Smith, S., Ericson, E.: Using immersive game-based virtual reality to teach fire-safety skills to children. Virtual Real. **13**(2), 87–99 (2009)

14. Tate, D.L., Sibert, L., King, T.: Virtual environments for shipboard firefighting training. In: Proceedings of IEEE 1997 Annual International Symposium on Virtual Reality, pp. 61–68. IEEE (1997)

15. Viola, E., Solari, F., Chessa, M.: Small objects manipulation in immersive virtual reality. In: VISIGRAPP (2022)

16. Voigt-Antons, J.N., Kojic, T., Ali, D., Möller, S.: Influence of hand tracking as a way of interaction in virtual reality on user experience. In: 2020 Twelfth International Conference on Quality of Multimedia Experience (QoMEX), pp. 1–4. IEEE (2020)

Effects of Head Rotation and Depth Enhancement in Virtual Reality User-Scene Interaction

S. Livatino[1]([✉]), A. Zocco[2], Y. Iqbal[1], P. Gainley[1], G. Morana[1], and G. M. Farinella[3]

[1] SPECS, University of Hertfordshire, Hatfield, UK
s.livatino@herts.ac.uk
[2] ELT, Elettronica Group, Rome, Italy
[3] DMI, University of Catania, Catania, Italy

Abstract. Immersive experiences with virtual reality systems are normally connected to user-scene interaction. The immersive system interprets movement commands and updates its output accordingly. When operating on PC and console games, interaction is typically triggered by hand-controllers' buttons, including joysticks. When wearing a head-mounted display (HMD), user's head-position can also prompt interaction, e.g. viewpoint changes. This is a major difference between operating on a HMD and on a desktop monitor. Changing observation viewpoint through head-rotation contributes to the user's immersion in the observed world, as it comes naturally. However, this may lead to visual disturbances and loss of concentration in some applications, hindering tasks like scene overviewing, especially in complex dynamic environments. The latter would call for joystick use instead. This paper assesses the use of head-rotation and controller joystick to generate differences in observation viewpoint. Our application context is a three-dimensional dynamic scene where users must identify and discover threats represented by unmanned aerial vehicles (UAVs) entering a protected area. Two distinct levels of depth enhancements are provided using stereoscopic-3D visualization (S3D). Our focus is to see the effects of the two interaction modalities (head-rotation and joystick) and two S3D levels. We evaluate user performance in terms of mission success and action timing, and assess how they relate to learning and memorization. Eye movements are also analyzed to help understand user interaction patterns and focus of attention.

Keywords: Virtual Reality · Head mounted display · Head rotation · 3D visualization · Command and control · Eye-tracking

1 Introduction

User interaction in Virtual Reality (VR) environments is crucial as it affects the sense of presence and user performance. Therefore, user interaction needs to be well thought out in applications where careful comprehension of the scene and timely responses are critical. For example, effective decision-making is crucial in military defense command and control applications.

© Springer Nature Switzerland AG 2022
L. T. De Paolis et al. (Eds.): XR Salento 2022, LNCS 13445, pp. 139–146, 2022.
https://doi.org/10.1007/978-3-031-15546-8_12

Interaction in VR involves both sensing user's action and providing commands. The technology for sensing users' actions typically includes tracking movements, e.g., head, hand, eye positions, and, more recently, voice commands. The technology for providing commands typically includes pushing buttons on keyboards or controllers and moving joysticks, while hand gestures have become more popular, so is eye movements.

Situation awareness has been investigated in various studies addressing interaction [1]. Prior work in interaction attempts to understand different aspects, including: understanding controllers that are either different or the same changing visual aspects [2–4]; analyzing movements such as head, body or eye movement [5–7]; comprehending ergonomics and VR sickness [8]; understanding interaction role by performing a task [9, 10]; and, understanding the connection performance-interaction [11].

When assessing interaction technology in VR, the specific application requires consideration as this may affect user performance. For example, in using VR headsets for command-and-control operations [12], there is a need to overview scenes and events, perform focused observations, and act and provide commands. Very few works in the literature focus on interaction related to military defense, and nearly no literature to our knowledge focuses on large-scale remote battlefield and the use of VR headsets (besides, e.g. Zocco et al. using Augmented reality [2]).

The use of VR headsets has grown in the last years, and this technology has become dominant in VR. This can certainly help achieve higher user presence and involvement because of the greater sense of isolation due to the provided immersion. Furthermore, it allows users to discover and explore the surrounding environment through the simple and natural gesture of head rotation. Depth discrimination can be very helpful in tasks of identification and discovery [12], and HMDs naturally support S3D viewing as users look at scenes through separate displays. Nonetheless, different S3D settings can be applied, which affects user performance.

This paper aims to understand the effects of using head-rotation to change observation viewpoint compared to using a controller joystick and the effect of varying scene depth discrimination. In addition, our analysis looks at aspects of learning and memorization and how these related to user performance in terms of mission success and action timing. This research also explores eye-tracking data to understand user interaction patterns and focus of attention.

2   Literature Review

2.1   Head Rotation in VR

One of the affordances of virtual reality is movement can play a part in learning. The psychological aspects of learning and memorization are relevant for completing various tasks using movement within VR. For example, researchers are increasingly exploring sensorimotor experiences to understand their contribution to learning. Ratcliffe and Tokarchuk [13] review 14 experimental sensorimotor studies. The review supplied positive learning outcomes using different approaches while discussing problems and the lack of methods for sensorimotor engagement within Virtual Reality.

Paired with the psychological aspects are the physical aspects of movement. Penumudi et al. [14] explore the effect of location on performance and physical load and discomfort, revealing that neck movement is more optimized for looking left and right and not up and down, as validated by subject discomfort measurement. In another study, Sargarnum et al. [6] investigate the concept of guided head rotation and amplified head rotation with VR viewing. The concept is to reduce physical strain by avoiding large head movements. The authors compare natural head rotation in VR to amplified head rotation with gamers and non-gamers. They discover that gamers perform better for their preference and lower sickness when amplifying movement.

One aspect in addition to gross motor skills of neck movement is eye tracking. This tracking records how the eyes move and where a person fixates their eyes. This eye-tracking measurement is achieved by bouncing light off the back of the eye and recording its refraction. Researchers believe eye-tracking records attention. Carter and Luke [15] describe eye-tracking and different methods to understand fixations – where the eyes focus for a short time, saccades – the movement of the eyes and smooth pursuits – slowly tracking an object. Although, the accuracy and precision of these devices can vary based on technology and how its configured and then used.

In another study by Christou et al. [7], gaze-directed and pointing motions are compared in the control of navigation tasks. In their evaluation, both head-rotation and eye-tracking are tested during the evaluation to assess the effectiveness of gazing alone while static or separating gazing from movement. Results showed control separated from gazing provided the least errors.

Understanding where eye-tracking and situational awareness correlates influences the study design approach. Zhang et al. [16] provided a review and proof by linking situational awareness and eye-tracking when focusing on an area of interest using metrics such as fixation rate, fixation count and dwell time. However, most studies focus on a static scene to allow a more straightforward implementation.

As objects get further away, the angle and range between eye-position reduce. Lamb et al. [17] discuss the challenges and approaches, implementation and verification of eye-tracking. They discovered that accuracy and precision varied based on object distance for up to ten meters. Although the study does not mention any information above ten meters, the effects on performance are not known. This suggests that if objects are far away, then accuracy and precision will be worse with distance. Therefore, the mapping between performance and eye-tracking data may need to be custom based on scale changes. There is no evidence to understand the effect of scale changes.

2.2 Depth Discrimination

The concept of depth discrimination has been around for many years. However, much research is concerned with estimating distances and less about using this depth discrimination or any underlying mechanics that go into decision making. Similarly, head rotation and locomotion affordance are studied to provide natural interaction with the virtual environment. Part of task completion requires understanding the role of depth discrimination, learning and memorization and how to explain user behavior through eye-tracking.

Depth discrimination is attained via human-vision binocular and monocular cues. These cues can be recreated in graphical rendering through S3D and can be adjusted to provide different levels of depth impression. For example, Lamb et al. [18] use depth ranking, relative depth judgement and path tracing tasks in two stereoscopic rendering techniques: (a) closest object, and (b) furthest object. The paper studies response time and error magnitude as objective measurements. As the static object focus is close, researchers discovered that performance response times are similar in complex path tracing tasks from one node to another, but the time taken is slower. However, the investigated tasks could be too simple to highlight their differences.

In another study, S3D parameters were adjusted to understand the effects of retinal displarity, the tiny amounts of depth-dependent image shifts on the eye when observing scenes. Konrat et al. [19] seek to understand depth detection and discrimination. The results show that ocular parallax can prove an effective depth cue and realism of a scene. Although, one considerable limitation of their work is using a static environment with only one object.

Levac et al. [20] explore how humans learn and how training skills learnt in virtual environments are applied to the real world. The literature suggests that virtual environments should enable the transfer of skills into the real world. However, some tasks require another way to represent them more abstractly than the real world. In this abstraction, a person is not directly involved but applies telemonitoring and teleoperation. Teleoperation is providing remote commands, and telemonitoring is the ability to assess a remote area. One example of this is the work of Zocco et al. [21]. The task is a command-and-control operation where a physical battlefield is represented as a virtual battlefield with symbols representing objects to identify risks in the virtual battlefield scenario. The author discovered that performance is faster using S3D viewing.

As part of the S3D viewing, the eyes focus on a particular object using the accommodation and convergence processes. One use of this process is depth discrimination, which attempts to answer the question of knowing the distance of things. Naceri et al. [22] discussed the role of accommodation and convergence cues between distances between 1.4–2.5 m, with the performance significantly different between natural and virtual environments. However, what is less known is virtual environments with varying levels of discrimination.

Focusing on a particular object could be more difficult in an immersive-based environment if the scene changes. Tahimi et al. [23] provided an experiment on automatic scene transitions and teleportation in Virtual Reality and explored the implications for spatial awareness and sickness. The study discusses switching between different types of automatic transitions from one type of viewport to another to understand its effectiveness while using a HMD. What is not known is the effectiveness of switching between different viewpoints in a manual effort using varying depth discrimination. It would be interesting to understand the use of switching between views vs performance to understand if there is an effect.

3 Proposed Investigation

The paper aims to build knowledge on the role played by head-rotation and depth discrimination when a scene is observed through a HMD. We focus on their effect towards user performance. Our application context is command and control in military defense operations. This type of application calls for careful monitoring of actions and effective decision-making.

We evaluate user performance in cases when a controller joystick is used in place of head-rotation, to change the observation viewpoint. We also assess performance when head-rotation is used with two levels of S3D depth enhancement.

The user performance is estimated in terms of mission success and action timing. We also observe how this performance relates to situation awareness and short-term memorization. Eye-position data is also gathered to explore pattern differences among the different conditions.

Our experimental scenario shows two clusters of drones represented through graphical icons, which move towards the observer. Each cluster includes hostile and friendly drones (those hostile are colored red). The two clusters occupy two regions in space far apart, e.g. to the right and left of the user's view, therefore calling for changes in observation viewpoint to be seen and monitored. Figure 1 shows instances of our operating scenario. The drones are represented by graphical icons and spread over a geographical area. The user needs to monitor them and understand when a drone is entering the area to be protected (red circle).

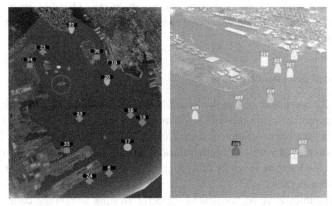

Fig. 1 Top and perspective views of different instances of an operating scenario. Drones are represented by graphical icons of different colors. The drones move while being observed. (Color figure online)

During experiment trials, users are asked to monitor hostile drone movements and record when they enter a protected area. The success of this identification and the time employed by the user to identify the drone are noted. Questions are also asked during observation, in an adapted-SAGAT[1] approach (including scenes freeze and blind views) to test user's event and objects memorization using a short mission time.

Difference instances of the above-described scenarios are executed on different trials (in a counter-balanced fashion), while observing the scene through the HMD. The hardware to run the experiments includes high-specs PC with *nVidia* GPU GeForce RTX

---

[1] Situation Awareness Global Assessment Technique (SAGAT) – a freeze probe technique to test memory of the current task.

3080Ti graphic card. The software uses the *Unity ArcGis* SDK beta 0.3 and the proprietary *ELT simulator* [24] to design and playback mission scenarios. The virtual reality headset *HTC Vive Pro Eye* features a *Tobii* eye-tracking system.

3.1 Interaction in VR Environment

In our first experiment, users use two different interaction modalities (head-rotation or joystick) to change the observation viewpoint when searching and monitoring the two drone clusters while also looking at their configuration and positioning. Interacting through a joystick is performed through a typical console-game controller (*Sony PS5* dual-controller).

Although viewpoint change by head-rotation is more natural than operating a joystick, it may affect comfort, e.g. in terms of cyber-sickness or neck pain, when such operation is continuously and rapidly performed. Furthermore, our monitoring actions include overviewing, which is normally considered more suitable when on stable views. The above makes us wonder whether a joystick-based control would be more convenient. If this is not the case, we wish to assess the advantage of head-rotation to have certainty that head-rotation-based viewpoint change is always preferred performance-wise, despite possible discomfort.

3.2 Enhanced 3D Visualization

In our second experiment, we use only head-rotation to change observation viewpoint while users perceive scenes through standard or enhanced S3D settings. The standard S3D setting is the one our graphical software (*Unity3D*) sets automatically. This results in sceneries displayed with low (and comfortable) screen-parallax. On the other hand, the enhanced S3D setting is set by our program, resulting in a much higher (five times increase) screen-parallax.

Previous studies have demonstrated the S3D viewing advantage compared to 2D viewing during teleoperation in terms of accuracy (at times at the expense of some comfort and operation delays [25]). However, those studies were sometimes conducted on what can now be considered old HMD models. We deem the S3D advantage is consolidated, while 3D viewing has become a standard feature in modern HMD systems. The S3D viewing effect can be adjusted and enhanced with further potential benefits in accuracy and scenery comprehension. Again, this may have the side effect of reducing viewing comfort.

In this paper we are interested in conducting experiments with an enhanced S3D viewing and assess user performance in terms of mission success, time of operation and comfort. The experimentation involves the latest HMD systems. We specifically wish to investigate with an application calling for continuous and rapid viewpoint changes. We aim for this experiment to provide insight on the role of S3D effect on applications where a strong 3D effect is expected to be beneficial, but also on an S3D effect combined with the head-rotation movement.

While conducting both the above experiments we track user's eye position and process it towards the focus of attention, identification of eye-movement patterns and correlation to interaction type. We are interested in relating eye position to control navigation tasks [7] and situational awareness [22].

References

1. Endsley, M.R.: A systematic review and meta-analysis of direct objective measures of situation awareness: a comparison of SAGAT and SPAM. Hum. Factors. **63**, 124–150 (2021). https://doi.org/10.1177/0018720819875376
2. Ali, M., Cardona-Rivera, R.E.: Comparing gamepad and naturally-mapped controller effects on perceived virtual reality experiences. In: ACM Symposium on Applied Perception 2020, pp. 1–10. Association for Computing Machinery, New York, NY, USA (2020). https://doi.org/10.1145/3385955.3407923.
3. Seibert, J., Shafer, D.: Control mapping in virtual reality: effects on spatial presence and controller naturalness. Virtual Real. **22**, 1–10 (2018). https://doi.org/10.1007/s10055-017-0316-1
4. Ebnali, M., Lamb, R., Fathi, R., Hulme, K.: Virtual reality tour for first-time users of highly automated cars: comparing the effects of virtual environments with different levels of interaction fidelity. Appl. Ergon. **90**, 103226 (2021). https://doi.org/10.1016/j.apergo.2020.103226
5. Ragan, E.D., Scerbo, S., Bacim, F., Bowman, D.A.: Amplified head rotation in virtual reality and the effects on 3D search, training transfer, and spatial orientation. IEEE Trans. Vis. Comput. Graph. **23**, 1880–1895 (2017). https://doi.org/10.1109/TVCG.2016.2601607
6. Sargunam, S.P., Moghadam, K.R., Suhail, M., Ragan, E.D.: Guided head rotation and amplified head rotation: evaluating semi-natural travel and viewing techniques in virtual reality. In: 2017 IEEE Virtual Reality (VR), pp. 19–28 (2017). https://doi.org/10.1109/VR.2017.7892227
7. Navigation in virtual reality: Comparison of gaze-directed and pointing motion control. https://ieeexplore.ieee.org/abstract/document/7495413/. Accessed 15 Mar 2022
8. Sharples, S., Cobb, S., Moody, A., Wilson, J.R.: Virtual reality induced symptoms and effects (VRISE): Comparison of head mounted display (HMD), desktop and projection display systems. Displays. **29**, 58–69 (2008). https://doi.org/10.1016/j.displa.2007.09.005
9. Bayramova, R., Valori, I., McKenna-Plumley, P.E., Callegher, C.Z., Farroni, T.: The role of vision and proprioception in self-motion encoding: an immersive virtual reality study. Atten. Percept. Psychophys. **83**, 2865–2878 (2021). https://doi.org/10.3758/s13414-021-02344-8
10. Ragan, E.D., Kopper, R., Schuchardt, P., Bowman, D.A.: Studying the effects of stereo, head tracking, and field of regard on a small-scale spatial judgment task. IEEE Trans. Vis. Comput. Graph. **19**, 886–896 (2013). https://doi.org/10.1109/TVCG.2012.163
11. Ragan, E., Bowman, D., Kopper, R., Stinson, C., Scerbo, S., McMahan, R.: Effects of field of view and visual complexity on virtual reality training effectiveness for a visual scanning task. IEEE Trans. Vis. Comput. Graph. **21**, 1–1 (2015). https://doi.org/10.1109/TVCG.2015.2403312
12. Zocco, A., Zocco, M.D., Greco, A., Livatino, S., De Paolis, L.T.: Touchless interaction for command and control in military operations. In: De Paolis, L., Mongelli, A. (eds.) AVR 2015. LNCS, vol. 9254, pp. 432–445. Springer, Cham (2015). https://doi.org/10.1007/978-3-319-22888-4_32
13. Ratcliffe, J., Tokarchuk, L.: Sensorimotor learning in immersive virtual reality: a scoping literature review. In: 2021 IEEE International Conference on Artificial Intelligence and Virtual Reality (AIVR), pp. 276–286 (2021). https://doi.org/10.1109/AIVR52153.2021.00061

146   S. Livatino et al.

S. Livatino et al.

14. Penumudi, S.A., Kuppam, V.A., Kim, J.H., Hwang, J.: The effects of target location on muscu-loskeletal load, task performance, and subjective discomfort during virtual reality interactions. Appl. Ergon. **84**, 103010 (2020). https://doi.org/10.1016/j.apergo.2019.103010
15. Carter, B.T., Luke, S.G.: Best practices in eye tracking research. Int. J. Psychophysiol. **155**, 49–62 (2020). https://doi.org/10.1016/j.ijpsycho.2020.05.010
16. Zhang, T., et al.: Physiological measurements of situation awareness: a systematic review. Hum. Factors. 0018720820969071 (2020). https://doi.org/10.1177/0018720820969071
17. Lamb, M., Brundin, M., Perez Luque, E., Billing, E.: Eye-tracking beyond peripersonal space in virtual reality: validation and best practices. Front. Virtual Real. **3**, 1–19 (2022)
18. Kulshreshth, A., LaViola, J.J.: Dynamic stereoscopic 3D parameter adjustment for enhanced depth discrimination. In: Proceedings of the 2016 CHI Conference on Human Factors in Computing Systems, pp. 177–187. Association for Computing Machinery, New York, NY, USA (2016).
19. Computational Imaging Gaze-Contingent Ocular Parallax Rendering for VR | TOG 2020. https://www.computationalimaging.org/publications/gaze-contingent-ocular-parallax-rendering-for-virtual-reality/. Accessed 24 Apr 2022
20. Levac, D.E., Huber, M.E., Sternad, D.: Learning and transfer of complex motor skills in virtual reality: a perspective review. J. NeuroEng. Rehabil. **16**, 121 (2019). https://doi.org/10.1186/s12984-019-0587-8
21. Zocco, A., Livatino, S., De Paolis, L.T.: Stereoscopic-3D vision to improve situational aware-ness in military operations. In: De Paolis, L., Mongelli, A. (eds.) AVR 2014. LNCS, vol. 8853, pp. 351–362. Springer, Cham (2014). https://doi.org/10.1007/978-3-319-13969-2_26
22. Naceri, A., Moscatelli, A., Chellali, R.: Depth discrimination of constant angular size stimuli in action space: accommodation and convergence cues. Front. Hum. Neurosci. **9**, 511 (2015)
23. Rahimi, K., Banigan, C., Ragan, E.D.: Scene transitions and teleportation in virtual reality and the implications for spatial awareness and sickness. IEEE Trans. Vis. Comput. Graph. **26**, 2273–2287 (2020). https://doi.org/10.1109/TVCG.2018.2884468
24. LOKI | Elettronica Roma. https://www.elt-roma.com/product/loki. Accessed 11 May 2021
25. Livatino, S., Muscato, G., Sessa, S., Neri, V.: Depth-enhanced mobile robot teleguide based on laser images. Mechatronics. **20**, 739–750 (2010). https://doi.org/10.1016/j.mechatronics.2010.01.011

Are We Ready for Take-Off ? Learning Cockpit Actions with VR Headsets

S. Livatino[1(✉)], M. Mohamed[1], G. Morana[1], P. Gainley[1], Y. Iqbal[1], T. H. Nguyen[2], K. Williams[1], and A. Zocco[3]

[1] SPECS, University of Hertfordshire, Hatfield, UK
s.livatino@herts.ac.uk
[2] Department of Engineering, HCMC University of Technology and Education, Ho Chi Minh City, Vietnam
[3] ELT, Elettronica Group, Rome, Italy

Abstract. Pilot training is crucial for learning and practicing operations and safety procedures. The sooner pilots become acquainted with flight deck instrumentation and actions, the faster, safer, and cost-effective the training. Active learning with pilot training includes searching tasks and memorization ability. These aspects then need to be incorporated into the flight simulator training. The use of virtual reality (VR) technologies can in principle take pilot training to the next level. VR technologies such as head-mounted displays can provide a higher sense of presence in the observed sceneries and a more natural interaction than traditional (non-immersive) display systems (e.g. 2D monitors). There is, however, some reluctance towards using immersive VR systems in aviation training and a lack of knowledge on its effectiveness, which results in slow take-up of VR solutions and the dominant use of 2D monitors. This paper aims to assess the performance advantage an immersive system such as a head-mounted display (HMD) brings to pilot training. The focus is on presence, search tasks and memorization. We experiment with actions of learning instrumentation and procedures in the cockpit. We run the same activities on both a HMD and 2D monitor. We gather data on users' performance in terms of accuracy, the success of actions, completion time and memorization through objective measurements. We also acquire data on presence and comfort through subjective rating.

Keywords: Virtual reality · Immersion · Head mounted display · Pilot training · Visual search · Memorization

1 Introduction

The aviation industry expects to hire a hundred thousand new pilots in the coming years [1–3]. The potential pilots will need training, which is a costly but needed activity. Operating an aircraft represents significant challenges for pilots, with a crucial aspect being the familiarization of dashboard instruments and their correct operation. One critical use case is take-off and landing in normal and emergency situations where pilots must act promptly and precisely. These activities call for fast decision-making based (among

© Springer Nature Switzerland AG 2022
L. T. De Paolis et al. (Eds.): XR Salento 2022, LNCS 13445, pp. 147–153, 2022.
https://doi.org/10.1007/978-3-031-15546-8_13

other things) on relevant warnings identification and instrument reading interpretation [4]. Therefore, the skills acquired during pilot training play a very relevant role. In addition, the complexity of cockpit panel instrumentation and related actions depend on search tasks and memorization, which are therefore critical aspects to train on.

There has been significant development of VR systems in the last decades. In particular, VR headsets (also referred to as head-mounted displays, HMDs) have recently evolved, becoming capable of providing wide field-of-view (FOV), high pixel-resolution, lightweight, wireless connection, accurate position tracking and low visual latency. Such VR systems are immersive, enhancing the user's sense of presence, typically defined as the feeling of "being there" [5], which is expected to affect the user's performance positively. As a result, Immersive VR systems could significantly facilitate learning flight procedures, including search tasks and place memorization. There has been a greater effort both in research and commercial projects to understand the effects of training for pilots [6–9]. These projects represent a formidable opportunity to take pilot training to a new level both in research and commercial investment [10, 11].

The use of VR technologies has been proposed in literature works, but its impact on user performance call for further investigation, including its role in pilot training. The impact of presence to search task performance and memorization in pilot training appears underrepresented in the literature. This has prompted the authors of this paper to assess the contribution of HMDs in pilot training and the role of presence in search and memorization. Search task performance may represent an important success metric for training programs, which needs to be understood.

2 Literature Review

The concept of immersion or presence has been around for many years. However, there is some confusion due to varying definitions from a) hardware fidelity, b) psychological aspects that could be: i) what the person sees, ii) what the person experiences from the virtual environment [12]. Furthermore, this immersion can help or hinder performance [13, 14].

2.1 Search and Distractors

Accurate and time-critical decision-making is a topic of paramount importance when piloting an aircraft. Coupled with this is finding the right instrument on a control panel and being able to operate it promptly. Visual search is a fundamental aspect in which efficiency depends on the amount of information presented to a user. What may hinder visual search efficiency is the presence of "distractors". They represent objects and features present in the user's visual field that is not of interest to the user. In other words, they represent obstacles in finding the target object.

Emani et al. [15] discussed the effect of "visual distractors" and how these affect cognitive load. They conclude that any visual stimuli that were not relevant to the task significantly increase the objective measure of cognitive load on the parietal channels (alpha and theta brain waves) using EEG-BCI technology. Furthermore, the linear relationship was strongest for the lowest performing group where subjective cognitive load was greatest then there is a decrease in BCI performance.

Olk et al. [16] investigates measuring visual search in immersive VR and on a 2D monitor. In this work, users search for an item while several distractors represent objects familiar to the user. At times an object is placed in the scene that is either similar or dissimilar, to understand how it effects user performance. Reaction time is slower when placing an object that is dissimilar. This slower reaction time could be because the objects are familiar to the user, despite the objects being a distraction. The same result exists both in the VR and 2D monitor conditions.

The effect of using different display settings in an AR system is investigated by Marquard et al. [17]. This paper compares limited FOV to audio-tactile approaches on situational awareness. It discovers that the visual approach is the fastest, but the audio approach provides the best improvement on situational awareness.

Xu et al. [18] study reaction time when examining similar and different symbols to understand the cognitive processes involved that may explain performance. It is found that symbols near each other interact in some way which affects performance. Secondly the processes that affect searching in homogeneous search also affect heterogeneous searches. It is believed that while searching interactions occurs when objects are similar to each other slow down distraction supported by previous research [18].

Focused on pilot training is the work of Walters and Walton [3]. It underlines the lack of literature works addressing links between search task performance, collaboration and sense of presence when using VR systems.

2.2 Memorization

Makranski and Peterson [19] address learning in an immersive environment. It presents a conceptual model by synthesizing existing literature and demonstrating the model factors that lead to learning in an immersive environment. There is a link between learning in a traditional manner and an immersive environment. The taxonomy suggests that the technological factors match affordances, cognitive factors and learning outcomes.

Connected to learning are memorization approaches. Memory palaces are among the most popular types of traditional memorization that also applies to VR. Krokos et al. [20] uses virtual reality to look around a spatial environment to test recall compared to a desktop environment. It discovers that immersion aids help recall within a specific layout within a familiar indoor environment. Staton et al. [21] argue people don't use their memory.

Memorization effectiveness depends on the technique and the approach used. Changing one aspect of the experience can affect performance that relies on memory and learning. Johnson-Glenberg et al. [22] compare 2D desktop and 3D virtual reality STEM environment with different levels of embodiment and test time. Embodiment is defined as watching or interacting. There is significant proof for a high-level embodiment, with the VR group performing the best.

3 Proposed Investigation

We aim to investigate connection between presence, search task performance, and memorization. We deem this aspect is crucial to better understand and demonstrate the immersion advantage in pilot training. This paper investigates the advantage immersive technology brings to pilot training, with a specific focus on searching and memorization. Our approach consists of gathering empirical data in pilot training when performing typical cockpit actions naturally involving searching and memorization. We replicate the same training procedures while operating through an immersive and non-immersive display.

The immersive display is an HMD (*HTC Vive Pro Eye*), whereas the non-immersive display is a 55″ 2D monitor. The aircraft represented dashboard is a *Cessna 152* (Fig. 1).

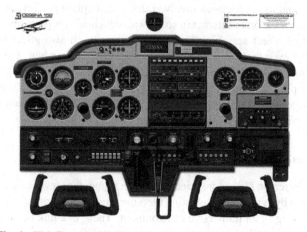

Fig. 1. The *Cessna 152* aircraft dashboard used in our experiments.

Figure 2 illustrates the proposed operating procedure. The same procedure runs on HMD and monitor following a counterbalanced schedule to avoid learning effects. The proposed user' actions include typical movements pilots are asked to perform in real flight deck training. Testing starts with an introduction and practice steps, they then perform a "search & find" step where are asked to search for specific objects in the cockpit dashboard and indicate where they are located. The check-list procedure is then performed where user needs to operate yoke and throttles and push few buttons. Those proposed users' actions include typical movements pilots are asked to perform in real flight deck training. Memorization questionnaires are administrated soon after operation (short-memory) and later on after presence and comfort questionnaire are administrated.

The gathered data are objective measurements, consisting of accuracy and success of actions, completion-time, and search and memorization-related aspects, and subjective rating, consisting of presence and comfort. Data are then processed to detect significant differences and trends and investigate the correlation between the perceived sense of presence and search tasks, and memorization performance.

Our research investigates the following three hypotheses:

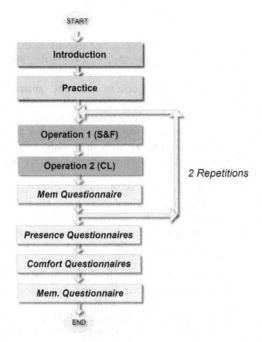

Fig. 2. The proposed operating procedure for our experiments (see text).

1. Higher Presence, Accuracy and Timing. Presence will be higher when using a HMD, leading to higher accuracy and a longer observation time. This hypothesis is supported by VR-related literature which has shown users perceive higher sense of presence when using immersive technologies [3]. Task accuracy, which in our case indicates the number of actions successfully completed is also expected to be higher [23]. However, we expect task time completion will be higher too. Livatino et al. [24] works shows slower actions with immersive and S3D observations compared to 2D.

2. Effective Search Task. The first hypothesis indicates higher operation accuracy, which we expect leads to a more effective search task. Effectiveness is indicated by a high success-rate when finding the search object. This seems supported by the work of Pomplun et al. [25], which investigates search strategies on 3D monitors. We will observe with interest about the search time. This is an element we find no indications in the literature.

3. Greater Memorization. We hypothesize memorization will score higher with HMD. However, we find no evidence in the literature about different scenarios or environments in a dynamic environment. The work of Wallet et al. (2011) [26] can be of reference. It provides an urban representation of a street. Memorization is then assessed by varying immersion and interaction quality and by then providing tasks outside of the VR experience. We feel this is weakest of our hypothesis.

References

1. Lutte, B.: Pilot supply at the regional airlines: airline response to the changing environment and the impact on pilot hiring. J. Aviat. Educ. Res. **27**, 1–22 (2018). https://doi.org/10.15394/jaaer.2018.1749
2. Losey, S.: The Air Force is revolutionizing the way airmen learn to be aviators. https://www.airforcetimes.com/news/your-air-force/2018/09/30/the-air-force-is-revolutionizing-the-way-airmen-learn-to-be-aviators/. Accessed 25 Apr 2022
3. Walters, W.T., Walton, J.: Efficacy of virtual reality training for pilots: a review of links between user presence, search task performance, and collaboration within virtual reality. Proc. Hum. Factors Ergon. Soc. Annu. Meet. **65**, 919–922 (2021). https://doi.org/10.1177/1071181321651347
4. Pritchett, A.R., Nix, D.C., Ockerman, J.J.: Empirical evaluations of pilot planning behavior in emergency situations. Proc. Hum. Factors Ergon. Soc. Annu. Meet. **45**, 6–10 (2001). https://doi.org/10.1177/154193120104500201
5. Slater, M., Wilbur, S.: A framework for immersive virtual environments (FIVE): speculations on the role of presence in virtual environments. Presence Teleoper. Virtual Environ. **6**, 603–616 (1997). https://doi.org/10.1162/pres.1997.6.6.603
6. Dymora, P., Kowal, B., Mazurek, M., Romana, S.: The effects of virtual reality technology application in the aircraft pilot training process. IOP Conf. Ser. Mater. Sci. Eng. **1024**, 012099 (2021). https://doi.org/10.1088/1757-899X/1024/1/012099
7. Hight, M., Fussell, S., Kurkchubasche, M., Hummell, I.: Effectiveness of virtual reality simulations for civilian, Ab Initio pilot training. J. Aviat. Educ. Res. **31**, 1 (2022). https://doi.org/10.15394/jaaer.2022.1903
8. The Air Force's Virtual Reality Fighter Training Is Working Best for 5th-Gen Pilots | Military.com. https://www.military.com/daily-news/2021/03/26/air-forces-virtual-reality-fighter-training-working-best-5th-gen-pilots.html. Accessed 25 Apr 2022
9. US Air Force trials virtual reality for crew chief course - Airforce Technology. https://www.airforce-technology.com/analysis/us-air-force-trials-virtual-reality-for-crew-chief-course/. Accessed 25 Apr 2022
10. Are VR flight simulators the future of pilot training? https://www.aircharterservice.com/about-us/news-features/blog/are-vr-flight-simulators-the-future-of-pilot-training. Accessed 25 Apr 2022
11. Jaakola, M.: Current Virtual Reality Solutions and Possibilities for Training Within Aviation 58
12. Nilsson, N., Nordahl, R., Serafin, S.: Immersion revisited: a review of existing definitions of immersion and their relation to different theories of presence. Hum. Technol. **12**, 108–134 (2016). https://doi.org/10.17011/ht/urn.201611174652
13. Baceviciute, S., Cordoba, A.L., Wismer, P., Jensen, T.V., Klausen, M., Makransky, G.: Investigating the value of immersive virtual reality tools for organizational training: an applied international study in the biotech industry. J. Comput. Assist. Learn. **38**, 470–487 (2022). https://doi.org/10.1111/jcal.12630
14. Nash, E., Edwards, G., Thompson, J., Barfield, W.: A review of presence and performance in virtual environments. Int. J. Hum. Comput. Interact. **12**, 1–41 (2000). https://doi.org/10.1207/S15327590IJHC1201_1
15. Emami, Z., Chau, T.: The effects of visual distractors on cognitive load in a motor imagery brain-computer interface. Behav. Brain Res. **378**, 112240 (2020). https://doi.org/10.1016/j.bbr.2019.112240
16. Olk, B., Dinu, A., Zielinski, D.J., Kopper, R.: Measuring visual search and distraction in immersive virtual reality. R. Soc. Open Sci. **5**, 172331 (2018). https://doi.org/10.1098/rsos.172331

17. Marquardt, A., Trepkowski, C., Eibich, T.D., Maiero, J., Kruijff, E., Schöning, J.: Comparing non-visual and visual guidance methods for narrow field of view augmented reality displays. IEEE Trans. Vis. Comput. Graph. **26**, 3389–3401 (2020). https://doi.org/10.1109/TVCG. 2020.3023605
18. Lleras, A., Wang, Z., Madison, A., Buetti, S.: Predicting search performance in heterogeneous scenes: quantifying the impact of homogeneity effects in efficient search. Collabra Psychol. **5**, 2 (2019). https://doi.org/10.1525/collabra.151
19. Makransky, G., Petersen, G.B.: The cognitive affective model of immersive learning (CAMIL): a theoretical research-based model of learning in immersive virtual reality. Educ. Psychol. Rev. **33**(3), 937–958 (2021). https://doi.org/10.1007/s10648-020-09586-2
20. Krokos, E., Plaisant, C., Varshney, A.: Virtual memory palaces: immersion aids recall. Virtual Real. **23**(1), 1–15 (2018). https://doi.org/10.1007/s10055-018-0346-3
21. Stanton, N.A., Salmon, P.M., Walker, G.H.: Let the reader decide: a paradigm shift for situation awareness in sociotechnical systems. J. Cogn. Eng. Decis. Mak. **9**, 44–50 (2015). https://doi. org/10.1177/1555343414552297
22. JohnsonGlenberg, M.C., Bartolomea, H., Kalina, E.: Platform is not destiny: embodied learning effects comparing 2D desktop to 3D virtual reality STEM experiences. J. Comput. Assist. Learn. **37**, 1263–1284 (2021). https://doi.org/10.1111/jcal.12567
23. Cooper, N., Milella, F., Pinto, C., Cant, I., White, M., Meyer, G.: The effects of substitute multisensory feedback on task performance and the sense of presence in a virtual reality environment. PLoS ONE **13**, e0191846 (2018). https://doi.org/10.1371/journal.pone.0191846
24. Livatino, S., et al.: Stereoscopic visualization and 3-D technologies in medical endoscopic teleoperation. IEEE Trans. Ind. Electron. **62**, 525–535 (2015). https://doi.org/10.1109/TIE. 2014.2334675
25. Pomplun, M., Garaas, T.W., Carrasco, M.: The effects of task difficulty on visual search strategy in virtual 3D displays. J. Vis. **13**, 24 (2013). https://doi.org/10.1167/13.3.24
26. Wallet, G., Sauzéon, H., Pala, P., Florian, L., Zheng, X., Bernard, N.: Virtual/real transfer of spatial knowledge: benefit from visual fidelity provided in a virtual environment and impact of active navigation. Cyberpsychol. Behav. Soc. Netw. **14**, 417–423 (2011). https://doi.org/ 10.1089/cyber.2009.0187

Virtual Reality as a Collaborative Tool for Digitalised Crime Scene Examination

Vincenzo Rinaldi$^{(\boxtimes)}$, Lucina Hackman , and Niamh NicDaeid

Leverhulme Research Centre for Forensic Science, University of Dundee, Dundee, UK
{VRinaldi001,LHackman,NNicdaeid}@dundee.ac.uk

Abstract. Crime scene investigation is a multidisciplinary response that involves the identification and securing of physical and trace material that may have evidential value. In this context, accurate documentation of the scene(s) is fundamental, when subsequent analysis is required for comparison and evaluative purposes.

This technical note reports a virtual reality framework developed in Unity 3D targeting a low-cost Virtual Reality (VR) head-mounted display (HMD), which enables the exploration of virtualized crime scenes and supports collaborative investigation through an online shared repository of 3D reconstructions. The system is agnostic at the source, implying that several types of 3D imaging sensors can provide recording of the scenes. Data are presented via an immersive virtual-roaming VR application to enhance spatial perception and telepresence. The virtualized environment is accompanied by original photographs and reference information, enabling validation and contextualization of the three-dimensional spatial data. The developed framework was employed in the context of a training operation spread between Scotland, UK and Denmark, demonstrating the feasibility of the deployment of the platform independent of location at the early stages of a forensic investigation.

Keywords: Virtual Reality · Forensic science · Crime scene investigation · 3D reconstruction · Collaborative systems · Multimodal interfaces

1 Introduction

The analysis of a crime scene is cross-functional work that requires multi-skilled teams to cooperate often with limitations due to environmental restrictions and temporal constraints. In complex cases, first responders and investigators may seek help from other forensic science experts [1]. This carries the inevitable need to enlarge the pool of specialized personnel operating at the crime scene whilst, at the same time there is a need to cause minimal contamination of the scene through the presence of these individuals. Streefkerk et al. [2] also report on limitations hindering staff's ability to attend crime scenes in a timely manner, such as *"officers availability, proximity to the incident and incident priority"*. In addition, other exceptional circumstances, for example, the Covid-19 pandemic, can also hamper the expert's mobility and impact their availability to attend at the scene. This highlights both the need, and the opportunity, to develop a system that

L. T. De Paolis et al. (Eds.): XR Salento 2022, LNCS 13445, pp. 154–161, 2022.
https://doi.org/10.1007/978-3-031-15546-8_14

enables experts to remotely perform a rapid inspection of the scene, providing immediate support to first responders before the experts may be able to reach the site themselves.

In the context of incident response, early documentation and evaluation of the scene are vital. Techniques such as sketching, photography, and videography are traditional and trusted methods of site processing [3]. In the last decade, new technologies and sensors began to emerge which supplemented the traditional approach to crime scene documentation, including but not limited to, photogrammetry and scanners incorporating different light sources [4, 5]. The data collected with modern imaging devices hold multifold information, which is still mostly accessed through traditional screens displaying 3D content through 2D devices, thereby missing depth, understanding and spatial perception.

Previous works reported in the scientific literature on the use of immersive headsets as a means of navigation of virtualized crime scenes, mainly target witness interrogation [6] and post-analysis incident reconstruction [7, 8], however to the knowledge of the authors, no previous work has explored the integration of a VR tool to facilitate decision making at the early stages of a forensic investigation.

In this work, we wanted to assess the feasibility of virtualizing a crime scene enabling visualization of the 3D data in a collaborative Virtual Environment (VE) during the initial phase of an investigation. We introduce a framework to create a reproduction of the incident locus and have developed a Crime Scene VieweR (CSVR) application to enable navigation of the virtual spaces, whilst also addressing several issues which render current commercial 3D viewers unsuitable for forensic employment. A calibration tool component was devised to complement the viewer in facilitating scale accurate calibration of the 3D models. A separate component enhances reconstructions produced using photogrammetry-based methods allowing automated incorporation of the photographs that were the source for this modelling method. A dedicated repository was deployed to ensure secure data access, using security certificates that guarantee the authenticity and reliability of the communicating parties. These components grant secure access of scale correct models to the developed application. Therefore, once the initial images of the crime scene have been captured, the user can perform remote analysis of an accurate digital representation of the scene without accessing areas at risk of contamination. A key advantage of creating a virtual space is that it allows the experience to be shared amongst multiple devices, providing live collaboration amongst professionals and scientific experts located at different locations.

We present a full proof of concept demonstration carried out between Scotland in the UK and Denmark that adopted the proposed framework and demonstrated the feasibility of the process. An analysis of the benefits and drawbacks is presented, with an outlook on the integration of new measurement and presentation tools into the suggested process.

2 Materials and Methods

The whole pipeline of integration of the CSVR system consists of two clear phases, as seen in Fig. 1, the data preparation phase, and the data utilization phase.

The data preparation phase concerns the documentation of the site using one (or a combination of) digitalization technique(s). The availability of equipment, the skills

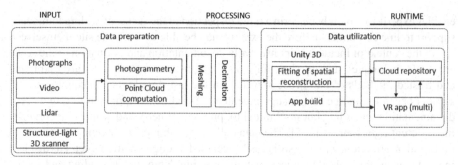

Fig. 1. Workflow of the process that enables full visualization of the scene.

of those involved, and environmental factors (i.e. space and light conditions) typically determine the choice of the imaging method utilised. The tools listed at the first stage of the data preparation phase, composing the 'Input' step in Fig. 1, typically produce data in a raw format requiring further processing before utilisation in any application. Most commercial 3D processing software allow refinement and conversion of unprocessed data into formats suitable for visualization or integration in any of the 3D engines commercially available. This step is shown in Fig. 1 as the initial stage of the processing, in which cleaning of the data takes place, commonly removing outliers and low-confidence points. Then, the creation of meshes and decimation of triangles produce a simplified model, to offer the highest quality whilst considering the performance limits of the target platform.

In our tests, imaging of scenes using several 3D imaging tools including photogrammetry, videogrammetry and Matterport 3D were undertaken, and the data produced was successfully used to render the environments as textured meshes. When using a Terrestrial Laser Scanner and a Handheld Mobile Scanner, spatial data was registered as point clouds. To achieve smooth visualization, point clouds were converted into 3D models using the surface remeshing tool of the software CloudCompare [9].

It should be noted that even when imaging the same environments, computation for the point clouds required longer times compared to the tools natively outputting meshed surfaces. Furthermore, methods applying format conversion [10] introduce approximations whose uncertainty should be estimated, although this topic is beyond the scope of this paper.

The last part of the processing of the data phase takes place in the 3D engine. The CSVR was developed in the game engine Unity 3D, targeting the OpenXR open standard and deployed on the HMD Meta Quest 2. Given the resources at hand, the extent of the virtualized space and the resolution of data, the 3D models were cleaned up by removing redundant information, and a dedicated shader was created to meet the hardware requirements of the platform of choice [11]. To enable multi-platform support, a modified version of the software targets computers with traditional 2D displays.

The fitting of the spatial reconstruction models (i.e. calibration and the integration of source information) constitutes the first part of the data utilization phase. This operation ensures the correct alignment of the 3D models, as they often lack information regarding scale and orientation, due to a change in the reference system at import time.

We tackled this critical issue by creating a tool for systematic rigid transformation and scale calibration. Firstly, three points in space are declared for the alignment (Fig. 2). Optionally, the alignment points determine the vertical offset to match the height of the virtual floor. Secondly, two supplementary positions are assigned to define a scalebar of reference.

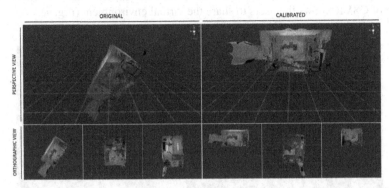

Fig. 2. Model calibration tool: exocentric view (above), lateral, top, and frontal views (below). The red dots highlight the selected alignment points. (Color figure online)

Outliers in the source data, occlusion at scan time, and imprecise sensor calibration can often produce artefacts in the geometry. As a result of this, the user may require the provision of supplemental data to validate or disprove the reconstruction. In the case of photogrammetry, for example, software such as Agisoft Metashape can be utilised to embed the position of input photographs that generated the 3D geometry into the exported model as individual entities. We exploit this information by rendering the photographs as floating pictures. A placemark for each photograph reveals the location of the camera that was used to take the images (Fig. 3). The user can grasp and handle photographs as physical stills and validate the 3D reconstruction by examining the source images, also identifying artefacts and areas lacking detail.

Fig. 3. View of a reconstructed site with source photographs. The displayed photo was selected by the user for inspection.

After the model(s) positioning, a catalogue bundles the fitted data with descriptive properties, such as registration method, generation setting, etc. Ultimately, the arranged data is published on a dedicated server accessible only to the signed application.

CSVR Multi-users Instance

The Unity 3D offers several tools to enable multi-user experiences. The client-server feature of CSVR allows the users to share the virtual environment (Fig. 4).

Fig. 4. First-person snapshot of a reconstruction shared amongst three users.

Each user session starts with the selection of the role. The designated host user begins the session by creating a host session. Then, the host shares the connection information with other users, who can join the shared virtual space. Both parts, server, and host, can run on any supported platforms. The external cloud repository ensures the participants of the joint space can share the same version of the catalogue bundling the reconstructions (Fig. 5).

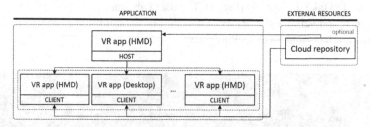

Fig. 5. Distributed Client-Server application structure with optional cloud catalogue.

In the case of the unavailability of a cloud repository, an alternative version of the catalogue can be embedded into the application, storing the data locally on the device, ensuring privacy in scenarios where a secure connection is not guaranteed.

A unique identifier is associated with each 3D reconstruction and assigned prior to the bundle creation phase. This enables each instance to exchange packets containing only an operation and object identifier, limiting the amount of data to transfer during virtual roaming. The reason for this design choice is twofold. Firstly, the data exchanged between the application instances is text-only, avoiding sensitive data transfer when using unsecured connections. Secondly, the framework addresses use at unknown locations without assumptions about the available bandwidth, therefore, small message exchange has been preferred to the peer-to-peer distribution of files, i.e. 3D models and source photographs.

3   Test of the Concept

A pilot test was performed using photogrammetry, during a collaboration between the University of Dundee and The Danish National Police Forensic Centre [12]. The main goal of the work was to evaluate the feasibility of the developed solution, focusing on the total deployment time from the beginning of the data collection to the availability of the final 3D render, quality of output and practicality of the distributed approach.

The approach is illustrated in Fig. 6, and the time taken for each task is shown in Table 1.

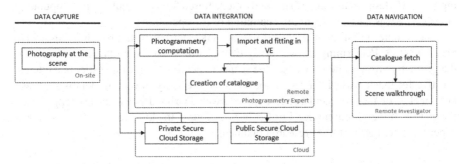

Fig. 6. Dataflow diagram with corresponding domains.

Table 1. Results of processes and times.

Process	Data capture (a)	Transfer (b)	Photogrammetry (c)	Fitting (d)	Upload (e)	Download (f)
Time	1 h 18 m	23 m	29 m	10 m	<1 m	<1 m
Size	160 images	1.87 GB	55 MB	–	290 MB	290 MB
Hardware capacity	Intel®Core™i7–7800X CPU @3.50 GHz, 6 cores, 12 threads, 64.0 GB RAM Internet bandwidth (b), (e), (f): 11 Mbps					

A member of staff without specialized training in photography or crime scene investigation performed the documentation of a mockup fire crime scene in Denmark (a) using a standard operating procedure devised by the research team. Photography was undertaken using a Canon EOS 5D Mark III, a traditional 22.3 megapixels full-frame camera The timestamps of the first and last photos were used to obtain the time taken for this task. Once imaging was completed, the photographs were extracted from the memory card to a laptop, and a copy of the data was uploaded to a remote server using a secure cloud repository (b). Once uploading to the cloud repository was complete, a remote technician in Scotland, UK retrieved the data from the server and computed the photogrammetric model and texture of the room using the Agisoft Metashape software [13] version 1.6.3.10732 (c). The settings selected for the mesh generation were the 'Depth map generation' method with a 'High' level of detail for both alignment and mesh generation, subsequently decimating the model down to 750 thousand faces. Then, preparation and data utilization were conducted as described in the previous section (d). At this stage, a digital catalogue containing the 3D reconstruction was bundled and uploaded to a server (e), exposing a public endpoint of the repository only accessible to the signed CSVR application.

Lastly, a remote fire investigator located in Scotland, UK tested the CSVR application. The bootstrap phase of the client checked against the repository, downloading the latest version of the catalogue (f), enabling the expert to perform a walkthrough of the digitalized indoor environment. The total time required for data acquisition, computation, and sharing was 142 min from the beginning of the operations.

The remote investigator accessed the site via a virtual walkthrough using a Meta Quest headset. Performing a solo survey of the virtualized room, the level of detail of the geometry allowed them to assess the scene, indicating areas of investigative interest. Positive feedback was given regarding the texture quality, revealing details such as a broken glass of a window and a visible spider's web. During this test, the user appreciated the quality of the virtual model. Further tests regarding the knowledge transfer and user experience are part of future research planned.

4   Conclusions

We have shown the basic procedure required to perform rapid crime scene virtualization using commercially available equipment. A framework to enable the digitalization of the sites has been presented, and a dedicated multi-platform application to perform intuitive navigation of the reconstructed environment is described.

We evaluated the feasibility of the developed approach during a simulated crime scene investigation, to demonstrate the capability of current state-of-the-art methods and tools that can enable remote experts to experience the scene whist also enhancing telepresence. The devised framework has demonstrated that an accurate model of an indoor scene can be obtained at the early stages of a crime scene investigation, allowing a remote expert to perform preliminary analysis and decision making using this software as a tool. Expansion of the tools available in the application is planned, to enable users to perform accurate measurements, add annotations and record actions. We expect to enlarge the pool of 3D imaging techniques, such as commercially available Time-of-Flight sensors and neural rendering models. We also wish to perform more in-depth tests regarding the uncertainty estimation of the reconstructions.

References

1. Merck, M.D.: Crime Scene Investigation. Vet. Forensics Anim. Cruel. Invest. 17–35 (2013). https://doi.org/10.1002/9781118704738.ch2

2. Streefkerk, J.W., van Esch-Bussemakers, M., Neerincx, M.: Context-aware team task allocation to support mobile police surveillance. In: Schmorrow, D.D., Estabrooke, I.V., Grootjen, M. (eds.) FAC 2009. LNCS (LNAI), vol. 5638, pp. 88–97. Springer, Heidelberg (2009). https://doi.org/10.1007/978-3-642-02812-0_11

3. Fish, J.T., Miller, L.S., Braswell, M.C., Wallace, E.W.: Crime scene investigation. Crime Scene Invest. 1–433 (2013).https://doi.org/10.4324/9781315721910

4. Sansoni, G., et al.: Scene-of-crime analysis by a 3-dimensional optical digitizer a useful perspective for forensic science. Am. J. Forensic Med. Pathol. 32(3), 280–286 (2011). https://doi.org/10.1097/PAF.0b013e318221b880

5. Galanakis, G., et al.: A study of 3D digitisation modalities for crime scene investigation. Forensic Sci. 1(2), 56–85 (2021). https://doi.org/10.3390/forensicsci1020008

6. Sieberth, T., Dobay, A., Affolter, R., Ebert, L.C.: Applying virtual reality in forensics – a virtual scene walkthrough. Forensic Sci. Med. Pathol. 15(1), 41–47 (2018). https://doi.org/10.1007/s12024-018-0058-8

7. Wang, J., et al.: Virtual reality and integrated crime scene scanning for immersive and heterogeneous crime scene reconstruction. Forensic Sci. Int. 303 (2019). https://doi.org/10.1016/j.forsciint.2019.109943

8. Ebert, L.C., Nguyen, T.T., Breitbeck, R., Braun, M., Thali, M.J., Ross, S.: The forensic holodeck: an immersive display for forensic crime scene reconstructions. Forensic Sci. Med. Pathol. 10(4), 623–626 (2014). https://doi.org/10.1007/s12024-014-9605-0

9. CloudCompare (version 2.12.0) [GPL software] (2021). www.cloudcompare.org

10. Estellers, V., Scott, M., Tew, K., Soatto, S.: Robust Poisson surface reconstruction. In: Aujol, J.-F., Nikolova, M., Papadakis, N. (eds.) SSVM 2015. LNCS, vol. 9087, pp. 525–537. Springer, Cham (2015). https://doi.org/10.1007/978-3-319-18461-6_42

11. Performance and Optimization, Oculus Developers (2022). https://developer.oculus.com/documentation/unity/unity-perf/

12. Rinaldi, V., Nic Daeid, N., Yu, S., Thomsen, B., Ljungkvist, E.: Udgård 2021 Raw Dataset (2021). https://doi.org/10.15132/10000174

13. Agisoft Metashape. https://www.agisoft.com/

A Virtual Reality Application for Stress Reduction: Design and First Implementation of ERMES Project

Carola Gatto[1]($\boxtimes$), Giovanni D'Errico[2], Fabiana Nuccetelli[3], Benito Luigi Nuzzo[4], Maria Cristina Barba[4], Giovanna Ilenia Paladini[4], and Lucio Tommaso De Paolis[4]

[1] Department of Cultural Heritage, University of Salento, Lecce, Italy
carola.gatto@unisalento.it
[2] Department of Applied Science and Technology, Politecnico di Torino, Turin, Italy
giovanni.derrico@polito.it
[3] Casa di Cura Prof. Petrucciani, Lecce, Italy
[4] Department of Engineering for Innovation, University of Salento, Lecce, Italy
{benitoluigi.nuzzo,cristina.barba,ilenia.paladini,
lucio.depaolis}@unisalento.it

Abstract. Recent studies have shown how Virtual Reality is one of the most effective innovative means for acting on the psychological well-being of patients with different health problems, in situations of isolation, burnout, and under high-stress levels. This paper presents the current state of work on the development of the ERMES project, which involves the creation of immersive, interactive virtual scenarios with the possibility of performing several individuals and participatory therapeutic activities through the use of Virtual Reality, promoting the psychological and physical well-being of patients in hospital wards. In particular, it aimed at providing patients with a tool that allows them to reduce stress levels, by practicing Mindfulness sessions, virtual museum exploration, and Art Therapy activities, with the possibility of safely sharing the experience with other patients.

Keywords: Virtual Reality · Mindfulness · Art Therapy · Well-being · Virtual Museum

1 Introduction

The latest events related to the spread of the Covid-19 virus in Italy have seen an important part of our population particularly affected: people in hospitals for receiving care, such as rehabilitation. This project aims to create a methodology that safeguards the target population by intervening in their psychological well-being. This scenario leads us to reflect and asks the question: "How can improve well-being and reduce stress related to the emotional state of the people in hospitals?".

Among all the technologies that make up e-Health, Virtual Reality (VR), a technology that enables the creation of immersive, interactive, and collaborative virtual environments, can be a decisive paradigm of innovation. The goal is to break down the social

© Springer Nature Switzerland AG 2022
L. T. De Paolis et al. (Eds.): XR Salento 2022, LNCS 13445, pp. 162–173, 2022.
https://doi.org/10.1007/978-3-031-15546-8_15

and physical barriers that some patients may encounter during their hospitalization, and thus promote the preservation of mental health. Therefore, an interdisciplinary working group was set up for the purpose of conducting a pilot project inside the cardiology rehabilitation department of the Hospital "Casa di Cura Prof. Petrucciani". The experimentation will involve the use of an innovative virtual and participatory care protocol, proposed through special Virtual Reality viewers. The project, specifically, exploits these technologies to create an innovative methodology for the guided practice of Mindfulness and participation in Art Therapy experiences, with the possibility of sharing playful and recreational paths with other patients in total safety.

2 Virtual Reality and Mental Health: Related Works

Recent studies [1, 2] have shown how Virtual Reality is one of the most effective innovative means to act on the psychological level of patients with various mental health problems, or in situations of isolation and burnout. Immersing oneself in telepresence, interacting in a 3D format as opposed to a 2D layout, having a sense of fun and involvement, and activating an affective-motivational state are the main features that make VR an efficient and valuable psychological intervention tool.

As recognized by the World Health Organization (WHO), the epidemic posed a significant threat to global mental health, perpetuating effects over time [3]. A large-scale study showed a significant increase in mental distress among the UK population compared with the previous year, especially among young adults, women, and people living with young children [4].

From this perspective, Virtual Reality (VR) technology has been identified as the medium through which this experimentation can be carried out since it can provide another, continuous and coherent dimension to physical space. It can be a decisive paradigm of innovation both in an emergency period and in normal life [5]. VR technology can be seen as a means of restoring a sense of presence where physical presence is not possible due to contingencies related to the individual or society. For example, through this technology, the museum collection can be "broken down" and reassembled for the purpose of acting on the well-being of individuals. VR can also be seen as a tool for practicing playful and therapeutic activities such as Art Therapy.

Among the strategies that can adopt VR as a means of fruition for therapies devoted to well-being are Mindfulness and Art Therapy, the subject of this project.

The therapeutic effects of Mindfulness meditation practices in clinical interventions, particularly in the treatment of stress, anxiety, depression, and chronic and acute pain are scientifically well-founded. In [6] it was found that, according to most experiments, VR ensures the increase of relaxation self-efficacy, the reduction of mind wandering and the preservation of attention resources. The study concludes that VR has potential favorable features to support mindfulness practice, especially immersive and multisensory VR. The use of bio/neurofeedback sensors enables real-time adaptive experience. A design proposal for upcoming trends in VR-supported mindfulness was presented and the need for more rigorous randomized controlled trials in the future was highlighted.

Recent studies have shown how museum enjoyment can provide significant health benefits for people, as the experience is able to act on a sense of identity, resulting in an impact on positive emotions and self-esteem.

The United Kingdom is one of the spokespersons for the culture-wellbeing pairing and has promoted the establishment of the National Alliance for Museums Health and Wellbeing [7], which has 5,800 members, including freelance creatives and museum managers, for the purpose of encouraging active citizenship and promoting practices for subjective well-being. Interestingly, art therapy emerges as an important strand within this scenario [8]. Studies demonstrating the benefit to the art therapy field of embracing VR as a tool for therapeutic creative expression are presented in [9]. With the development of new media, and the experimentation of the same as expressive media, new digital arts have emerged, which have reflexively given rise to new forms of practice for art therapy [10, 11].

3 Conceptualization of ERMES Project: Virtual Immersive Reality for Mindfulness and Art Therapy

3.1 Project Methodology

Based on what has been presented so far, the project aims to offer an alternative, engaging, and stimulating therapy tool, aimed at improving the well-being state for people in hospitals. To achieve this goal, the project intends to decline into the following specific objectives:

- To emotionally engage and cognitively stimulate the user (reduce stress, induce pleasant-relaxing emotional states, stimulate cognitive abilities, such as memory, attention, and learning);
- Increase intergenerational exchange, through the use of virtual play activities to be shared with other patients or family members, in order to break down physical and social barriers in the hospital and increase socialization opportunities;
- Detect the level of the user's quality of life before and after the execution of the protocol by monitoring, through specific sensors, the progress of physiological responses to the proposed activities.

In particular, the project will use VR to implement Mindfulness sessions, museum tours and Art Therapy activities, all under the guidance and continuous mediation of trained operators who are physically present alongside each user. Through VR headset equipped with controllers for interaction, such as the Oculus Quest 2, a participatory and collaborative approach will be provided, giving the possibility to safely share some virtual experiences with other patients or family members who are outside the hospital.

In addition, psychophysiological sensors are intended to be used as a noninvasive tool for monitoring, collecting, and analyzing the psychophysical state of patients involved in the experience. This module is intended to be preparatory to the future development of a Biofeedback tool, aimed at helping the users become more aware of his or her reactions, participate actively in the project, and learn to use his or her mental abilities to balance his or her psychophysical state.

Through VR, the user is confronted with immersive virtual stimuli that can induce the feeling of actually being inside the virtual world. The use of specific virtual environments (especially those that immerse the user in nature scenarios, in accordance with the so-called Attention Restorative Theory) can, therefore, reduce mind wandering in the form of distracting thoughts (mind wandering), because the subject's attention is drawn to specific virtual elements, promoting an experiential focus on the present moment. Ultimately, by limiting the distractions of the real world, increasing the sense of presence, and offering people a stimulating and suitable place to practice, VR can certainly facilitate the practice of mindfulness. Many studies have shown the beneficial contribution of a museum visit, and likewise art therapy, especially related to the observation of a museum collection. From this point of view, Art therapy and museum virtual tours complete the methodology, by providing other kinds of stimuli to the patient. Art therapy is becoming increasingly popular acting on people's well-being. It originated in Canada in 1996 as part of a project that aimed to provide assistance to cancer patients by helping them, through the museum journey, to visually express their experience on different levels. Since that time numerous experiments followed, arriving in 2018, again in Canada, to talk about allowing doctors to "prescribe" museum tours for patients with chronic conditions and depression. In the study conducted by the Research Centre for Museum Studies, at Leicester University in 2014, titled "How Museum impact health and wellbeing" [12] it becomes clear how museums are able to respond to public health needs, using their collections to improve people's health and wellbeing, to counter health inequalities within communities and to contribute positively to the goals of public health agencies. The aim was precisely to keep these people physically and mentally active by intervening in the emotional well-being of the target population.

3.2   The Role of Measurements: Psychometric Scales and Biosignals Analysis

In the literature, both states and traits related to Mindfulness are measured through self-assessment instruments, so the standard approach to assessing the effects of Mindfulness makes use of mainly psychometric scales [13]. This shows clear advantages in terms of simplicity, convenience and speed of administration, but they are mainly empirical instruments [14] and, by their very nature, are based on introspective self-perception [15]. The development of such assessment instruments has also been supported by the evolution of various therapeutic approaches that start from Mindfulness-based protocols (such as Mindfulness-Based Stress Reduction (MBSR) [16] and Mindfulness-Based Cognitive Therapy (MBCT) [17].

In terms of psychometric evaluations, the assessment of the effects that Mindfulness practices and protocols have on both physical and mental health that is perpetrated in this study makes use of instruments such as the SF-12 questionnaire [18]. This tool was originally developed in the United States to provide a short form alternative to the sf-36 questionnaire and consists of 12 items (taken from the 36 items of the original SF-36 questionnaire) that produce two measures of two different aspects of health. The SF-12 consists of 4 scales (physical functioning, role and physical health, role and emotional state, and mental health) each measured by 2 items and 4 scales each measured by 1 item (physical pain, vitality, social activities, and general health). This questionnaire investigates the perception of individuals' psychophysical conditions. The synthesis of the scores makes it possible to construct two indices of health status, one concerning the synthesis of the physical component (Pcs), the other the synthesis of the psychological component (Mcs). A low psychological health index indicates "frequent psychological distress; significant social and personal disability due to emotional problems; health is judged to be poor".

Another instrument used in the assessment phase in the present work is the Perceived Stress Scale (PSS) [19], one of the most widely used psychological instruments to measure the perception of stress. It is a measure of the degree to which certain situations are assessed as stressful by the subject. The scale also includes a series of direct questions about current levels of stress experienced. The questions are general in nature and therefore relatively free of content specific to any subpopulation group.

The UCL Museum Wellbeing Measures Toolkit can measure the impact on the well-being of activities carried out within museums or cultural venues. This is a set of measurement scales used to assess levels of well-being resulting from participation in museum and gallery activities that have been piloted in the United Kingdom. The Toolkit is designed to help people involved in managing internal or external museum projects assess the impact of this work on the psychological well-being of their audiences. The Toolkit synthesizes known and validated psychometric scales such as the PANAS and VAS, and was produced by researchers at University College London (UCL) Museums & Public Engagement and funded by the Arts & Humanities Research Council (AHRC) [20]. The Toolkit measures psychological well-being as an indicator of an individual's mental state.

The Toolkit consists of two generic well-being Questionnaires (short and full versions), four Umbrellas of well-being measures (positive, negative, older adult, and young adult) with instructions on the same page, and a separate sheet for comments. Although these are activities experienced in VR and not in the presence of the museum, this tool is an excellent psychometric scale that is well suited to the needs of the project.

Both for Mindfulness and Museum/Art-related wellbeing assessment, objective psychophysiological measurement is more and more requested by researchers and clinicians in order to consolidate psychometric data. Therefore, the ERMES project will consider a series of biosensors for the primary purpose of collecting data from the subject and, on a purely research level, corroborating and supporting psychometric inferences. The EEG-based passive brain-computer interface is a growing technology in this field for the measurement of mental states [21]. Emotiv Epoc is the headset envisaged within the project, a portable, flexible, lightweight and low-priced BCI-EEG device that has been exploited in the literature for these purposes [22]. From the EEG signal it is possible to extract features in the power domain (in the alpha, beta, gamma, delta and theta bands) and infer important information about the levels of valence and arousal experienced by the subject [23]. An Empatica E4 WRISTBAND device, allows the acquisition of additional physiological data in real time, such as heart rate variability (HRV) and Skin Conductance Level (SKL), values generally associated with a direct measurement of the subject's levels of activation and stress [24].

4 User Experience Design

We considered all aspects of user experience (UX), calibrating choices based on the characteristics of our target audience. In fact, by UX we mean all those choices that can influence the user's perception and interaction, and that concern both software and hardware. The main goal of the whole application is to induce a state of relaxation, by means of breath-conscious meditation and Art Therapy tools.

The UX and gamification aspects such as mechanics, dynamics, and aesthetics were all designed to be able to meet these needs and will be detailed in the next sections.

4.1 Hardware Evaluation

First and foremost, the important choice was the Virtual Reality device: each visor on the market has different processing characteristics, computing power, and quality of visual representation. Another important aspect to consider is the interaction of degrees of freedom (DoF). After a series of evaluations Oculus Quest was chosen because of its visual quality, the presence of the two integrated controllers, and because of its 6 DoFs. For a specific module, we worked on the use of Hand tracking, specifically to carry out Art Therapy activities in the virtual environment. Hand Tracking enables the use of hands as an input method for the Oculus Quest headsets. When using hands as input modality, it delivers a new sense of presence, enhances social engagement, and delivers more natural interactions with fully tracked hands and articulated fingers. Hand tracking analyzes discrete hand poses and tracks the position of certain key points on your hands, such as knuckles or fingertips, in real-time as your hands are moving. When you use hands as input, the hand's pose drives a laser cursor-pointer that behaves like the standard controller cursor. You can use the cursor-pointer to highlight, select, click, or write your own app-level event logic. Integrated hands can perform object interactions by using simple hand gestures such as point, pinch, unpinch, scroll, and palm pinch. The idea being developed aims to expand the system gesture library so as to provide customized gestures to be employed in the Art Therapy activity.

4.2 Software Choice: From the Modelling to the Development

Currently, the entire design of the application has been completed and we passed to the modeling phase, both landscape and 3D objects, and also to the implementation of some scenes. Development involves the use of Unity, a cross-platform graphics engine by Unity Technologies that is used mostly for video games and Virtual Reality development. The version used is 2020.3.14. The 3D models have been done on Blender 3.0, in part by integrating Unity tools, provided by its asset store.

The 3D contents of the Museum scene (pottery collection), on the other hand, have been created by photogrammetry, through Metashape 1.5.2. Details on the photogram-metric processing of these contents will be the subject of a subsequent paper since due to the characteristics of the artifacts, they required specific image processing.

4.3 Design and Storyboard

The VR application was developed with a first-person point of view, as it makes the personal and emotional experience, and interaction with virtual elements, more realistic. The main configurations with respect to the user's body position that can be applied are sitting or standing. The application is designed for a seated user, keeping the gaze in the virtual environment at half height, in order to enjoy the scenarios to the fullest.

The solution to be tested makes use of gamification paradigms in which the patient is asked to perform certain tasks during single, collaborative sessions that may also involve simultaneous involvement of multiple users.

With reference to mindfulness, efforts were made to commensurate the level of engagement, affect and motivation, with discrete and contextual design to keep the experience effective and not to add additional distracting elements that may be detrimental to the practice.

For Art Therapy, on the other hand, the focus was on a more dynamic and interactive experience that makes use of gamification techniques (e.g., rewarding with results, holding certain choices accountable, etc...). The storyboard for the application consists of seven scenes, and was created through co-design involving experts in psychology and mindfulness, experts in museums and archaeology, and experts in immersive technologies.

- **Start Scene**: this scene has the function of leading the user to the Home where he/she will have the menu of all the scenes, or to the Tutorial scene, to learn the modes of interaction on the practice in VR.
- **Home scene**: in this scene the user has the option to start the therapeutic path, starting from the first scenario and following the suggested order, or, in agreement with their therapist, they can access a specific scenario of their choice, based on the practice they intend to implement. The aesthetics are simple and functional, the colors soft and soothing. Interaction with the buttons is through the pointer provided by the controllers.
- **Tutorial**: essential scene that aims to instruct the user to use the application, through mini videos and voice instructions
- **Neutral scene** - introduction to meditation: The function of this scene is to introduce the subject to mindful meditation. Mindful breath meditation represents the easiest way to begin a formal meditation practice. It consists of focusing attention on the breath and observing what happens as we try to maintain it. The aesthetics of the scene are therefore neutral, with dim light and soothing color. There is no distracting element present, and the subject is immersed in a monotonous virtual environment in which the only element he or she perceives is the voice providing initial instructions on how to conduct the meditation.
- **Mountain Meditation**: Mountain meditation is a visualization practice that is intended to evoke in us the same almost archetypal qualities, of a solid and majestic mountain, stable in the midst of the seasons, the weather, as we can be in the midst of life's many changes. Within this scene, the user is immersed in a virtual environment that represents precisely a natural environment: he or she is surrounded by mountains, forests, and a stream. The vantage point is from observing the largest mountain, from base to summit, which is revealed as majestic and imposing (Fig. 1). The tools of UX in this environment are, in addition to the virtual environment, the guiding voice and the metamorphoses of the landscape that follow the course of the seasons and the cycle of the sun, with alternating day and night. These landscape changes are provided by animations that are synchronized with the audio of the voice. For example, the Skybox

of the scene changes to match the passage of time and alternates between moments when the sky is clear and other specific weather phenomena, always in harmony with what the guiding voice says.

- **Lake Meditation**: This is a visualization practice used to offer participants the opportunity to compare themselves to the surface of a lake (Fig. 2). The latter can be clear and calm or murky, slightly rippled and dark, like the human mind. As in the previous scene, in this scene the user is immersed in a virtual environment that represents a natural setting: he or she is surrounded by mountains and forests. The vantage point is from observing the lake, and the stream that flows into it. The user is sitting on a pier in observation of the water surface.

Fig. 1. Mountain meditation environment

Fig. 2. Lake meditation environment

The UX tools in this environment are, in addition to the virtual environment, the guide voice and the metamorphoses of the landscape that follow the course of the seasons and the cycle of the sun, with alternating day and night. These landscape changes are provided by animations that are synchronized with the audio of the guide voice. Specifically, in addition to the metamorphosis of the sky, in this scene emphasis has been given to the animations that create the metamorphoses of the lake surface: this, in reflection to the alternation of weather phenomena, changes and adapts, in relation to what the guide voice says. For example, the voice says, "When it rains, the water of the lake is rippled by the falling rain. When autumn comes, the lake takes in the leaves that fall from the trees. When winter comes, the lake welcomes the low temperatures and freezes." With each transformation narrated by the voice, the surface of the lake changes in its essential components of material and texture, and an animation is built up that runs throughout and in sync with the meditation.

- **Pure Awareness Group Meditation**: this type of meditation, also called unfocused awareness, means practicing mindfulness by pausing in awareness itself, without any specific object to focus on. In this case the scenario is similar to that of the Neutral Scene, with an environment that is precisely neutral and without distractions, with a guiding voice saying the instructions for relaxation. In this scene, however, the user can see the avatar of other users who are performing the same exercise. This is in fact a collaborative environment.
- **Museum Scene**: In this scene, the user moves through an indoor scenario. It is a reconstruction of a virtual museum within which users can browse and enjoy selected artifacts from the collection of the Sigismondo Castromediano Museum. The museum location has soft tones and a spotlight on points of interest (Fig. 3).

Fig. 3. A museum room

- The aesthetic is based on two different styles: the first hall is the simplification of the actual museum, eliminating distracting elements but maintaining the philological coherence of the location, the second is a reconstruction of the first location of the museum, and it looks like an Antiquarium. In the first hall, the collection is arranged around in cyrcle, each object is placed on a cube with a light pointed on. There are six objects: as noted above, these objects were chosen from within the collection of the Sigismondo Castromediano Museum, and come from different archaeological sites in Salento. The storytelling is based on the figurative themes of ancient ceramics, particularly the myths or convivial scenes depicted on them. In this case, the user can interact by means of controllers with buttons that turn audio on and off. Such audios are sounds that evoke the scenes depicted on ancient artifacts. The user can also listen to tracks that narrate the artifact, like an emotional audio guide. The voice tells about the myths depicted, each of which has a particular connection to an aspect of human psychology. In this scene, the user has a task to actively perform; in fact, by activating the "Game" mode, the artifacts disappear from the vitrines, and the purpose of the task is to search for the artifacts by following the sound they emit, collect them, and arrange them at their own glass vitrine, which has a specific caption for that artifact. The gamefication strategy put in place for this scene is based on this paradigm "The collection cares for you, take care of the collection!"

- **Art Therapy Scene**: the scene is set in the ancient Messapian settlement of Cavallino, in Apulia (Italy). It is a reconstruction of an outdoor scenario that contextualizes some artifacts within the site of discovery, thus telling the social story from the objects. In fact, following the narration of the previous scene, the user is now taken to an ancient pottery production center, where he or she gets to see how the artifacts on display in the museum were worked. In order to increase the feeling of presence, we adopt an aesthetic that reproduces a natural environment in which we place the outdoor workshop of the ceramist (Fig. 4).

Fig. 4. Ceramist ancient laboratory

This choice starts from the consideration that the archaeological site of Cavallino shows the remains of an ancient oven (V century B.C.) for pottery production. This visually pleasing place encourages the user's curiosity, immersion, and abstraction in therapy. Within this scenario, the user is asked to perform a task: to induce relaxation, a Virtual Reality Art Therapy technique will be used, namely the modeling of ceramics using ancient techniques. Moreover, the user, thanks to learning by doing activities, can get important archaeological content, concerning the history of the territory. The purpose of the task is to virtually "decorate" or "model" an artifact found within the archaeological context, with instructions that come from experimental archaeology. The performance of the task is set within an outdoor virtual scenario, namely the archaeological site itself. Interaction is designed for it to occur without the use of controllers but only through the use of specific gestures. This part of the study is still in progress and will cover a subsequent in-depth study.

5 Conclusions and Future Work

This paper presents the current status of work on the development of the ERMES project. The project involves the creation of immersive, interactive virtual scenarios with the possibility of performing various individual and participatory therapeutic activities through the use of Virtual Reality. Specifically, it is intended to provide patients with a tool that allows them to implement activities of meditation (Mindfulness), museum exploration and observation, and art practice (art therapy). Specifically, the project leverages VR to create an innovative methodology for guided Mindfulness practice and participation in Art Therapy experiences, with the possibility of safely sharing playful and recreational paths with other patients.

The project aims to raise the level of quality of life, in terms of well-being, of people in hospitals, who experience situations of stress. To objectively detect the beneficial effects of virtual reality on users and monitor the status of the Project noninvasive neurophysiological signal recording sensors (biofeedback and Neurofeedback) will be applied during the activities.

Future work of this project concerns the development of this application following the explained design and integrating the 3d content so far made into the VR environments. Then, tests will be performed with different users to measure the quality of the user experience and the impact on stress levels. These tests will allow assessing the adequacy of what has been designed and the possible modifications that the application might require. An informed consent form for data processing and therapy administration will be completed for each patient. Each patient will be registered in a special database in which his or her clinical data will be stored at the same time as the test data derived from VR therapy.

Depending on the result, remodeling aspects related to the development of the application itself will be considered. Another test will be aimed at the therapists themselves, who will go on to validate the usability of the system and suggest potential improvements.

Acknowledgements. The 3D models of the archaeological findings have been produced thanks to the authorization of the Soprintendenza Archeologia Belle Arti e Paesaggio of Lecce, for Carola Gatto's PhD research project, and thanks to the collaboration with Sigismondo Castromediano Museum in Lecce.

References

1. Hatta, M.H., et al.: Virtual Reality (VR) technology for treatment of mental health problems during COVID-19: a systematic review. Int. J. Environ. Res. Public Health **19**, 5389 (2022). https://doi.org/10.3390/ijerph19095389
2. Siani, A., Marley, S.A.: Impact of the recreational use of virtual reality on physical and mental wellbeing during the Covid-19 lockdown. Heal. Technol. **11**(2), 425–435 (2021). https://doi.org/10.1007/s12553-021-00528-8

3. World Health Organization: Mental health and psychosocial considerations during the COVID-19 outbreak. https://www.who.int/publications/i/item/WHO-2019-nCoV-Mental Health-2020.1 (2020). Accessed 25 July 2021
4. Pierce, M., et al.: Mental health before and during the COVID-19 pandemic: a longitudinal probability sample survey of the UK population. The Lancet Psychiatry (2020)
5. Gatto, C., D'Errico, G., Nuccetelli, F., De Luca, V., Paladini, G.I., De Paolis, L.T.: XR-based mindfulness and art therapy: facing the psychological impact of Covid-19 emergency. In: DePaolis, L.T., Bourdot, P. (eds.) AVR 2020. LNCS, vol. 12243, pp. 147–155. Springer, Cham (2020). https://doi.org/10.1007/978-3-030-58468-9_11
6. Arpaia, P., D'Errico, G., De Paolis, L.T., Moccaldi, N., Nuccetelli, F.: A narrative review of mindfulness-based interventions using virtual reality. Mindfulness 13, 1–16 (2021). https://doi.org/10.1007/s12671-021-01783-6
7. The Culture, Health & Wellbeing Alliance. https://www.culturehealthandwellbeing.org.uk/who-we-are/about-alliance (2022). Accessed 12 Apr 2022
8. Silverman, L.H.: The Social Work of Museums, 208 p. Routledge, New York (2010). 978-0-415-77521-2
9. Winkel, M.: Virtual Art Therapy: Research and Practice. 1st edn. Routledge, New York (2022). https://doi.org/10.4324/9781003149538
10. Garner, R.: Digital Art Therapy: Material, Methods, and Applications. Jessica Kingsley Publishers, London (2016)
11. Lohrius, J., Malchiodi, C.: Virtual reality art therapy. In: Malchiodi, C., (ed.) Handbook of Art Therapy and Digital Technology, pp. 215–229. Jessica Kingsley Publishers, London; Philadelphia (2018)
12. Dodd, J., Jones, C.: Mind, Body, Spirit: How museums impact health and wellbeing. University of Leicester. Report (2014). https://hdl.handle.net/2381/31690
13. Sauer, S., et al.: Assessment of mindfulness: review on state of the art. Mindfulness 4(1), 3–17 (2013)
14. Chiesa, A., Calati, R., Serretti, A.: Does mindfulness training improve cognitive abilities? A systematic review of neuropsychological findings. Clin. Psychol. Rev. 31(3), 449–464 (2011)
15. Grossman, P.: On measuring mindfulness in psychosomatic and psychological research. J. Psychosom. Res. 64(4), 405–408 (2008)
16. Kabat-Zinn, J.: Full Catastrophe Living: Using the Wisdom of Your Body And Mind to Face Stress, Pain, and Illness: How to Cope With Stress, Pain and Illness Using Mindfulness Meditation. Delta, New York (1990)
17. Williams, J.M.G., Russell, I., Russell, D.: Mindfulness-based cognitive therapy: further issues in current evidence and future research. J. Consult. Clin. Pschol. 76, 524–529 (2008)
18. Ware, J.E., Jr., Kosinski, M., Keller, S.D.: A 12-Item Short-Form Health Survey: construction of scales and preliminary tests of reliability and validity. Med. Care. 34, 220–233 (1996)
19. Cohen, S., Kamarck, T., Mermelstein, R.: Perceived stress scale. Measur. Stress: Guide Health Soc. Sci. 10(2), 1–2 (1994)
20. University College of London (2022). https://www.ucl.ac.uk/museums/research/touch
21. Aricò, P., Borghini, G., Di Flumeri, G., Sciaraffa, N., Babiloni, F.: Passive BCI beyond the lab: current trends and future directions. Physiol. Measur. 39(8), 08TR02 (2018)
22. Sánchez-Reolid, R., et al.: Artificial neural networks to assess emotional states from brain-computer interface. Electronics 7(12), 384 (2018)
23. Roy, R.N., Frey, J.: Neurophysiological markers for passive brain–computer interfaces. Brain–Comput. Interfaces 1: Found. Methods. 85–100 (2016)
24. Ollander, S., Godin, C., Campagne, A., Charbonnier, S.: A comparison of wearable and stationary sensors for stress detection. In: 2016 IEEE International Conference on systems, man, and Cybernetics (SMC), pp. 004362–004366. IEEE (2016)

Efficient and Secure Transmission of Digital Data in the 5G Era

Bruno Carpentieri[✉] and Francesco Palmieri

Università di Salerno, 84084 Fisciano, SA, Italy
{bcarpentieri,fpalmieri}@unisa.it

Abstract. With the arrival of new smartphones and new social networks and with the speed of the new 5G communication the network traffic of multimedia documents has significantly increased, and it becomes necessary to preserve privacy when using digital images or videos, for example in the current social networks or, even more, in those based on Virtual and Augmented reality that soon will take the place of the current ones. In this paper we explore a unified approach to compression and privacy by considering both one-dimensional and two-dimensional data by implementing a secure protocol for interactive data compression and by presenting a new algorithm for scrambling the Region of Interest (ROI) of an image.

Keywords: Compression · Privacy · Social networks

1 Introduction

We live in a digital era in which a huge amount of digital data travels, in compressed form, and it is often strictly connected to people, describing what we do, what we see and photograph, were we go, who we meet and, specifically, every instant of our life.

With the arrival of new smartphones and new social networks and with the speed of 5G, the network traffic of multimedia documents has significantly increased. The identification of users through the data circulating on social networks is a current problem and malicious people or even government agencies could often use these channels to spy on subjects. It therefore becomes necessary to protect privacy when using digital images or videos, for example in current social networks and, even more, in those based on virtual and augmented reality that soon will take the place of the current ones.

In fact, one of the greatest perceived dangers of these new platforms based on Virtual Reality (VR) or Augmented Reality (AR) relates to privacy. The user's privacy is at risk because virtual and augmented reality technologies can see what he is doing. The software that design these new realities can easily collect a lot of information about the user's identity and his behavior, to a much greater extent than, for example, social networks or other forms of technology. This raises concerns and questions about the need to protect the privacy of the users and the multimedia digital contents that are transmitted to provide the new experiences.

Data Compression is essential for storing and transmitting this gigantic amount of information and therefore there is a strong need to pair compression and security together when dealing with this peculiar data.

L. T. De Paolis et al. (Eds.): XR Salento 2022, LNCS 13445, pp. 174–182, 2022.
https://doi.org/10.1007/978-3-031-15546-8_16

In this paper we explore a unified approach to data compression and privacy by considering both one-dimensional and two-dimensional data.

The next Section deals with protection and compression of text, and present, as a case study, the maintaining of privacy in interactive data compression. Section 3 is devoted to two-dimensional data and presents a scrambling technique to maintain privacy in the Region of Interest in digital images. Section 4 outlines our conclusions and describe possible new research directions.

2 Privacy and Compression of One-Dimensional Data

Generally lossless algorithms are used for the compression of one-dimensional data, such as text, programs, object codes, and all data for which the correlation is intended as one-dimensional: i.e. sample x is strictly correlated with the previous and the following samples. One dimensional data often needs to be safely and securely transmitted, for example when using mobile devices, we want to ensure the confidentiality of the messages and data we transmit (see [1] and [2]).

Privacy and security of lossless data compression algorithms that are dictionary based can be achieved by reordering in a secret way the indices that point to dictionary elements. Kelley and Tamassia in [3] present a formal framework for proving security when data compression is combined with encryption and discuss the security of the LZW compression algorithm when the dictionary management is randomized.

In [4] it is presented a way to provide security combined to data compression in the BZIP family of compression algorithms.

Bzip2 is an open source lossless data compression algorithm. Developed by Julian Seward, it was first published in July 1996 (version 0.15). Its popularity increased in a short time as the compression was high and stable: version 1.0 was published in 2000. The latest version, 1.0.6, was published on September 20, 2010.

Bzip2 generally produces very small compressed files having a better compression with respect to other lossless compression algorithms like gzip or ZIP, however it "pays" in performance being slightly slower. Bzip2 uses the Burrows-Wheeler transform to convert sequences of recurring characters into strings of identical letters. In bzip2 the blocks are in plain text and all of the same size. The approach presented in [4] alters the Burrows-Wheeler transform (BWT) by using a permutation of the input symbols that is selected randomly. In order to develop a coding solution for holographic data, it is necessary to know how the current coding behaves and how much the characteristics of the hologram affect the coding performance. The statistical characteristics of the samples obtained from a hologram are different from that of the samples obtained from conventional two-dimensional images, therefore, it is not possible to directly apply the same compression algorithms for the reduction of associated information.

2.1 Security of Interactive Compression

If we compress and send messages from a data source that is well known to both Sender and Receiver, then lossless, dictionary based, data compression algorithms can use the same (static) dictionary for both Sender and Receiver: at the beginning of the communication the Sender will send its dictionary to the Receiver. For example, in Vector Quantization compression algorithms the compressor constructs its dictionary on a training set of images. This dictionary will successively be used to compress new data. Of course, the compressor must send this dictionary to the decompressor so to make the communication possible. This is true also when similar techniques are applied to digital images (see [5]).

A large part the compression methods used in practice that are based on dictionaries are not static dictionary methods but dynamic dictionary methods: they grow up the Sender and the Receiver dictionary at run time. They start with dictionaries that are empty and then they grow the dictionaries by considering data in the already compressed part of the data stream.

The compression performance could be improved if, in a dynamic, dictionary based, compression method, Sender and Receiver could start with a common, full, dictionary.

El Gamal and Orlistky in [6] study this problem: "Given two random variables X and Y with entropies H(X) and H(Y) and joint entropy H(X,Y), and two persons PX and PY, such that PX knows X and PY knows Y, suppose that the two persons wish to communicate over a noiseless two-way channel so that at the end of the communication process they both know X and Y. How many bits on the average must they exchange and what are the optimal codes?".

They discover that not less than $H(X|Y) + H(Y|X)$ bits must be transmitted on the average and that $H(X,Y) + 2$ bits are sufficient and that if the joint probability p(x,y) is uniform then the average number of bits needed is close to $H(X|Y) + H(Y|X)$.

Moreover, they present randomized protocols that limit the amount of data exchanged in the communication if we can accept a limited possibility of communication errors.

Carpentieri in [7] and [8] presents an effective method to solve this problem in the framework of compressed communication. When a compressor and a decompressor have already a good experience of a given source, because in the past the compressor has compressed many messages from that source and the decompressor has itself decompressed other many messages (not necessarily all the same messages that the compressor has compressed) and if there is an interaction between the communication factions, then it is possible to improve the data compression operations when compression is used for data transmission. The cost paid is an extremely low chance of decoding errors. If we can accept this, then we can design interactive protocols that permit to a Sender and to a Receiver to benefit of the information they already have of the data source that produces the messages to exploit their interaction so to minimize the cost of communication.

As an example of everyday usage of this method consider a user that downloads regularly a file (an upgrade, a report, a newsletter, etc.) from a given data source, or a system manager who often downloads an update or a patch for an application or an antivirus, or a mirroring internet site that has to be systematically updated, etc.

In [7] was described a communication protocol to allow a "learned" Sender and a "learned" Receiver to be in communication, by using a dynamic dictionary method where dictionaries are, at the beginning, single-handedly built, starting by prior (and may be conflicting) instances of source messages that Sender or Receiver have at hand. This protocol improves compression and pays a small, almost zero, chance of communication errors.

When this protocol is used in practice, Sender and Receiver possess many messages from a given information source (not necessarily the same messages and, independently, build up their dictionaries, *SenderDictionary* and *ReceiverDictionary*, including in the dictionaries what each of them supposes are the m most common words of the information source.

Sender will transmit a compressed message to the Receiver by means of the *SenderDictionary* and Receiver shall decode the message by means of the *ReceiverDictionary*. The Receiver can interact with the Sender by sending acknowledgment messages.

The first time a new word is transmitted Sender and Receiver use a protocol based on Karp and Rabin's fingerprinting for the transmission, the subsequent times the word is indexed univocally in both dictionary and that index is sent from the Sender to the Receiver, and it is univocally decoded.

To maintain the communication privacy when using interactive data compression, we can add to the dictionary management of the encoder and decoder a RandomSwap operation similar to the one introduced in [3] in the context of LZW compression.

In particular when Sender finds a word for which there is already a common index in the dictionaries it sends the index to the Receiver and after that, independently but consistently, they both do a RandomSwap on the dictionaries (using both Sender and Receiver the same random number generator and the same seed) by randomly swapping the transmitted word with another in the common dictionary, so that next time the word will be used a different index will be sent. In this way it is possible to prove the security of Interactive Compression by using the same theoretical framework used in [3].

We have also implemented and tested this new secure interactive compression algorithm by compressing some of the books in test data set used in [8].

Table 1 shows the results obtained. We have compared the original Interactive Compression Algorithm (12 bits hash) and this new Secure Interactive Compression Algorithm (12 bits hash): the compression performances are almost identical to the original approach.

Table 1. Secure interactive compression.

Book title	Original dimensions	Interactive protocol	Secure interactive protocol
		Compressed size	Compressed size
20000 Leagues Under The Sea	875,5 KB	306,2 KB	306,3 KB
The Wealth of Nations	2273,1 KB	602,9 KB	602,9 KB
Catcher in the Rye	384,3 KB	122,4 KB	122,4 KB
For Whom The Bell Tolls	937,4 KB	288,2 KB	288,2 KB
The Grapes of Wrath	935,3 KB	310,8 KB	310,8 KB

The very small differences in compressing the book "20000 Leagues Under The Sea" depend on the fact that the cost of sending a single pointer it is now randomly changed (but in average it is almost the same as before).

3 Privacy and Compression of Bi-dimensional Data

The number of digital images shared by the most disparate devices has reached proportions that were unimaginable just 10 years ago: every day, in fact, more than 2 billion pictures are downloaded on social networks or traded through messaging or cloud-based sharing services.

Advances in image sharing have raised serious privacy concerns as photos can potentially reveal a large amount of delicate info on the persons depicted.

Several approaches to ensuring privacy have been proposed in the past, many of them are based on the encryption or permutation of the entire image content but these approaches can negatively impact the usefulness and diffusion of the images and the possibility of sharing them.

In many cases users want to share their photos online and they would prefer to protect specific regions of the images by applying, for example, masking, blurring, or scrambling of sensitive areas.

3.1 Scrambling the Region of Interest (ROI) of an Image

In this paper we are interested in obtaining privacy through data manipulation: this technique does not delete the pixels to be hidden but modify them in a reversible way that will allow a complete decoding only by whoever owns the associated secret key. The method is simple and does not significantly affect the file size: it is not necessary to maintain great deals of information to allow full decoding (i.e., original pixels must not be kept).

We are particularly interested in *scrambling*. Scrambling involves the use of two main players: the scrambler and the descrambler who share a key. Before sending the data, the scrambler manipulates the data flow by using the secret key (shared with the descrambler) and then forwards it to the receiver. Once the data has arrived at its destination, the descrambler uses the key to perform the reverse operation and thus obtains the original image to show to the receiver.

We will apply the scrambling to images encoded with the JPEG (Joint Photographic Experts Group) coding algorithm by using an approach called *JPEG transcoding*: that is, the scrambling will be carried out starting from the compressed JPEG image and in particular it will be applied after the calculation of the DCT (Discrete Cosine Transform) coefficients.

Descrambling, on the other hand, will be performed after decoding the JPEG image but before calculating the DCT coefficients.

The basic idea of our approach is to select a region of interest (ROI) within the JPEG image and to apply the scrambling operation to that region. The descrambling process will perform the same operations as scrambling, but in reverse order.

Specifically, the main steps of our algorithm are the following:

1. In the first phase, the ROI is identified and selected, for example through the Viola-Jones algorithm;
2. Scrambling is applied, block by block, by modifying the values of the DCT coefficients already quantized during the JPEG compression process;
3. The modification of the DCT coefficients depends on the selected scrambling level (the value of the scrambling level can vary from 0: no coefficient is modified, to 64: all the coefficients are involved in the modification);
4. A seed is generated to obtain a pseudorandom binary sequence and the signs of the DCT coefficients are inverted for each value corresponding to 1 in the pseudorandom string;
5. The seed for the generation of the pseudorandom sequence is encrypted before being inserted together with the information on the ROI within the JPEG metadata. Due to this procedure, the image size will increase by a few bytes (about 0.37 Kb in the case of a single ROI);
6. At this point, the JPEG encoding process continues normally.

3.2 Experimental Results

Figure 1 shows the algorithm applied to the image Lena (225×400 pixels, 24 bits for pixel), by using in step 3 a value of the scrambling level of 8.

Fig. 1. Scrambling *Lena*.

Our approach can also be applied to images that have multiple ROIs. Figure 2 shows an example of an image with 21 ROIs and the result of applying our algorithm with a scrambling level of 50. The goal here was to identify, as ROIs, the human faces.

Fig. 2. Scrambling multiple ROIs.

We have performed experiments to validate the effectiveness of our approach by using the Group4a [9] and BaoDataset [10] datasets as test datasets. The goal here was again to identify, as ROIs, the human faces.

We have tested our method (with scrambling level values of 8, 16, 32 and 64) and, at the end of the execution, we have launched the initial script for the detection of faces again (this time on the scrambled dataset as input), noting the number of faces identified both before and after scrambling. Table 2 and Table 3 show the results obtained on the two datasets.

Table 2. Experiments on *Group4A*.

Scrambling level	n. of human faces	n. of human faces after scrambling
8	4334	3502
16	4334	3001
32	4334	1780
64	4334	170

Table 3. Experiments on *BaoDataset*.

Scrambling level	n. of human faces	n. of human faces after scrambling
8	1357	1024
16	1357	870
32	1357	581
64	1357	71

The two results in Table 2 and Table 3 shows the effectiveness of our approach in masking the faces: the higher is the scrambling level value the more difficult is to identify the ROI as a face (and of course it shall be harder or practically impossible, to recognize the face).

4 Conclusions and Future Work

In this paper we have explored a unified approach to compression and security.

We have discussed, implemented, and experimentally tested new ideas connected to one-dimensional data (security of interactive data compression) and to two-dimensional data (JPEG image scrambling).

Future research includes an extensive experimentation of the ideas presented here both for the secure lossless compression of images (see, for example, [11] and [12]) and new approaches to the combination of lossy compression and security for holograms, three-dimensional data, i.e.: digital video or hyperspectral or three-dimensional medical images (see [13] and [14]) and for multidimensional data.

References

1. Pizzolante, R., Carpentieri, B., Castiglione, A., Castiglione, A., Palmieri, F.: Text compression and encryption through smart devices for mobile communication. In: Proceedings of the 7th International Conference on Innovative Mobile and Internet Services in Ubiquitous Computing (IMIS), pp. 672–677 (2013)
2. Pizzolante, R., Carpentieri, B.: Copyright protection for images on mobile devices. In: Proceedings of the 6th International Conference on Innovative Mobile and Internet Services in Ubiquitous Computing (IMIS). IEEE Press, pp. 585–590 (2012)
3. Kelley, J., Tamassia, R.: Secure Compression: Theory & Practice. IACR Cryptology EPrint Archive (2014)
4. Oğuzhan, K.M.: On scrambling the Burrows-Wheeler transform to provide privacy in lossless compression. Comput. Secur. **31**(1), 26–32 (2012)
5. Rizzo, F., Storer, J.A., Carpentieri, B.: Overlap and channel errors in adaptive vector quantization for image coding. Inf. Sci. **171**(1–3), 125–143 (2005)
6. El Gamal, A., Orlitsky, A.: Interactive data compression. In: Proceedings of the 25th Anniversary Symposium Foundations Computer Science (FOCS), pp. 100–108 (1984)

7. Carpentieri, B.: Sending compressed messages to a learned receiver on a bidirectional line. Inf. Process. Lett. **83**(2), 63–70 (2002)
8. Carpentieri, B.: Interactive compression of digital data. Algorithms **3**, 63–75 (2010)
9. http://chenlab.ece.cornell.edu/people/Andy/ImagesOfGroups.html
10. https://facedetection.com/datasets/
11. Rizzo, F., Storer, J.A., Carpentieri, B.: LZ-based image compression. Inf. Sci. **135**(1–2), 107–122 (2001)
12. Motta, G., Storer, J.A., Carpentieri, B.: Adaptive linear prediction lossless image coding. In: Proceedings of the 1999 Data Compression Conference (DCC), pp. 491–500 (1999)
13. Pizzolante, R., Carpentieri, B.: Lossless, low-complexity, compression of three-dimensional volumetric medical images via linear prediction. In: Proceedings of 18th International Conference on Digital Signal Processing (DSP), pp. 1–6 (2013)
14. Pizzolante, R., Carpentieri, B.: Visualization, band ordering and compression of hyperspectral images. Algorithms. **5**(1), 76–97 (2012)

Augmented Reality

Hand Interaction Toolset for Augmented Reality Environments

Ilias Logothetis$^{(\boxtimes)}$, Konstantinos Karampidis, Nikolas Vidakis,
and Giorgos Papadourakis

Department of Electrical and Computer Engineering, Hellenic Mediterranean University,
71004 Heraklion, Crete, Greece
{iliaslog,karampidis,nv,papadour}@hmu.gr

Abstract. As Augmented and Virtual Reality (AR/VR) technologies become nowadays very popular, there is the need for better interaction in these environments. In this paper, a toolset that facilitates the process of creating interaction in AR and VR environments is presented. The toolset is mainly targeted on mobile devices as the majority of AR and VR applications are exported. The toolset is divided into two main parts; the first part presents the components that are utilized inside the Unity 3D game engine, and the second part involves a webservice to handle the hand tracking task. The separation of hand tracking into a different part allows changes of the algorithms without the need to update the entire package. To evaluate the proposed toolset, a scenario of usage was fabricated in which users -with a computer science background- were shared a package and were asked to complete three tasks and evaluate their experience of using the toolset to create applications. Furthermore, the resulting applications were tested in real case scenarios to examine the overall performance and experience.

Keywords: Augmented reality · Toolset · Human-computer interaction

1 Introduction

Augmented reality (AR) and virtual reality (VR) are two technologies with great potential that have started to be incorporated in almost every task of our daily lives. These technologies allow a user to display virtual content into the real world (AR) [1], blend the real world with a virtual (Mixed Reality - MR) [2] or completely immerse into the virtual world (VR) [3]. As these technologies grow, a new term has been introduced to serve as an umbrella for technologies that blend real and virtual worlds, i.e., the Extended Reality (XR) [4]. This advancement has led to the need for better interaction in their corresponding applications has arisen. The conventional ways of using a mouse and a keyboard, a touchscreen or a controller, limits the immersive experience they offer as well as the realism that users expect [5]. Furthermore, using external devices of interaction needs training and time to acclimatize with, and using them can swift focus from the content to the operation of such devices [6].

To that end, more natural and realistic means of interaction in these environments are currently under research [7–10]. Hardware devices able to track the hands' movement

© Springer Nature Switzerland AG 2022
L. T. De Paolis et al. (Eds.): XR Salento 2022, LNCS 13445, pp. 185–199, 2022.
https://doi.org/10.1007/978-3-031-15546-8_17

have been developed, such as Microsoft's Kinect [11], Leap Motion [12], and various wearables like gloves [13]. These devices can achieve high accuracy, but they are either limited to a specific location, or they need special equipment to set them up. For these reasons, a modern approach is to utilize a camera - typically found in almost every smart device - to detect and track the hands. While this approach does not require external hardware to operate, it does require the hands to be on the capturing frame otherwise the tracking will not work. Each technique has its merits and disadvantages and depending on the use-case scenario one can be favored over the others.

Regardless of the approach utilized to detect and track the hands, there are techniques able to recover the exact hand pose, providing the ability to perform actions that demand high precision. These methods are demanding in computational power as they include many algorithms to predict and reconstruct the exact hand. Another - not so computationally demanding - technique is to recognize specific hand gestures. The latter method is mostly preferred in tasks where high precision is not needed, and the hardware resources are limited. As both methods are used to provide a natural way of interaction, the required functionalities are common. Such functionalities have to do with the behavior of the hand in the virtual world like grabbing an item, moving an object, detecting a collision with an item, etc. The aforementioned actions are simple tasks that every application in a three-dimension environment incorporates with the traditional techniques of interaction. Therefore, the need of developing tools to facilitate the creation and integration of such actions in the XR environments and the setting of the natural interaction through hand tracking, is getting compulsory.

In this paper, a novel toolset for the Unity3D game engine [14] that aims to provide the core features necessary for the creation of interactive content in XR environments is presented. Interactions between virtual objects and hands, visualization of the hand in the virtual space, and actions such as grabbing, and pushing, are some of the functionalities exposed through the toolset. Moreover, the toolset is created in a way to allow the future extension of each feature and to allow developers to include or create their preferred behaviors. The main objective of the toolset is to be used for applications running on mobile devices; for that reason, the hand tracking algorithms are separated from the toolset and into a web service to lessen the processing duty that these algorithms may add on mobile devices. Another advantage of this separation is that it is easier to change the hand tracking algorithms. Moreover, the broad usage of XR in the future is almost guaranteed as it is a fascinating technology with a lot to offer.

Currently, the lack of frameworks and libraries to facilitate that process can discourage developers to engage with this technology at this stage. Existing technologies, both software and hardware tend to change rapidly, obliging developers to continuously learn new tools and not being able to reuse existing components [15], or companies forcing the utilization of specific tools as they have paid for them. Thus, this study provides an agile toolset that exposes functionalities invariant to the adopted hand tracking technique. The toolset exposes a module for hand tracking that can be customized by the user or completely ignored in the case of the incorporation of external hardware as the hand tracking technique.

The contribution of this study is an agile toolset that can be used by developers to include interactions with physical hands mainly in AR but also extending to XR environments as well. A similar toolset as reported in [15] is currently missing from the market. Furthermore, due to the agile nature of the toolset it can adapt to changes on the hand tracking technologies that constantly changing.

The rest of the paper is organized as follows: in Sect. 2 state of the art approaches are reviewed, while in Sect. 3 the methodology of the proposed method is described. In Sect. 4 the experimental results on the algorithms chosen for the evaluation of the toolset are presented, and finally a discussion on the results and directions for future work are given in Sect. 5.

2 State of the Art

With the wide adoption of XR in various fields and the introduction of new applications each day, there is a need for frameworks and tools to facilitate the development of those applications. These frameworks and tools will enable developers to get involved with the technology in a guided way, making it easier to adapt. To that end, ZeusAR [16] proposes an architecture for the development of Augmented Reality Serious Games. The authors developed tools that through a wizard guide a user to convert or create a serious game in AR. JavaScript libraries were chosen for this process to allow the material to be hosted on the web. The result from this study was that within 10 min a non-professional user can create such content. Another study in [17] proposed an architecture based on the incorporation of smart glasses and external hardware for hand tracking as the Leap Motion [10]. An approach [10] for real-time drawing in AR using ARCore and Leap Motion was developed for mobile devices. In this work the Leap Motion manages the hand gesture recognition, and the authors focused on exposing the right tools for a drawing application.

More studies on interaction with physical hands in AR include the accurate grasp gesture and visualization [18, 19], gaze-based hand interactions [20], and gesture-based system to interact with virtual objects in museums [21]. While all these studies rely on Leap Motion for the tracking of the hands, this indicates a preference for the employment of external hardware for such a task rather than using a camera sensor approach. This preference can be due to the automated procedures that Leap Motion offers for hand tracking and gesture recognition, which allows researchers to focus on their tasks without having complicated configurations and setups. Another reason could be that external hardware handles the required computations without the need for a high-end device for that purpose.

To address this issue, researchers in the field of hand tracking and pose estimation have swift their attention on developing models that are able to run on a mobile device in a real-time setting. The study in [22] presents an architecture based on the collaboration of two models to track the hands. The first model is responsible for tracking the palm, while the other detects 2.5D landmarks based on the palm model. This research was based on the MediaPipe framework [23]. Authors in [24] had a very similar approach to the problem by using the same framework. A study using 802.11ad 60 GHz (mmWave) technology to recognize 5 gestures [25] is reported. This approach can provide results within 100 ms and additionally it provides a frame drop stabilizer. The aforementioned studies show promising results that a modern mobile device can support, but libraries that include such methods are not available to make use of them.

3 Methodology

The architecture of the proposed toolset is presented in Fig. 1. The toolset is divided into two modules, each one implemented into a different application. The hand tracking module consists of a web service that receives a stream of photos and tries to recognize where the hand is located. Afterwards, it sends back a response with a list containing recognized hand points. The module responsible for interaction functionalities is the Unity Toolset. This module captures and sends a stream of images to the hand tracking module, where the retrieved hand points are assigned to a virtual hand, allowing interaction between the virtual hand and virtual objects.

The modules are divided into two separate applications because this clarifies the responsibilities of each module and ensures that changes to one module do not affect the other and eventually the entire toolset. Separating the hand tracking module provides flexibility on changing the algorithms utilized for the hand tracking process, while keeping the Unity toolset unaware of the changes and without requiring an update if the exchanged data formats remain the same. Another reason for separating the hand tracking module is due to the currently limited processing power of mobile devices that cannot support both environment tracking (required by AR) and hand tracking in real-time. If the hand tracking module was included on the Unity toolset, the mobile device would not be able to handle the processing burden included in the hand tracking algorithms, the Augmented Reality functionality, and the content of the created application in real-time.

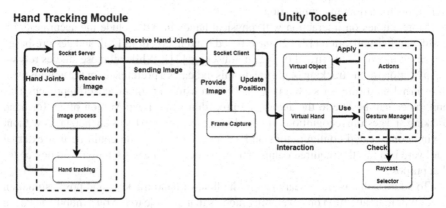

Fig. 1. Proposed toolset architecture

3.1 Unity Toolset - Interaction Module

The implementation of the interaction module (Fig. 2) for the Unity 3D game engine is in C# and consists of the components described below in this section. During development, Object-Oriented Programming principles and Design Patterns were applied appropriately to ensure the extensibility of the toolset without breaking or altering parts that are not necessary.

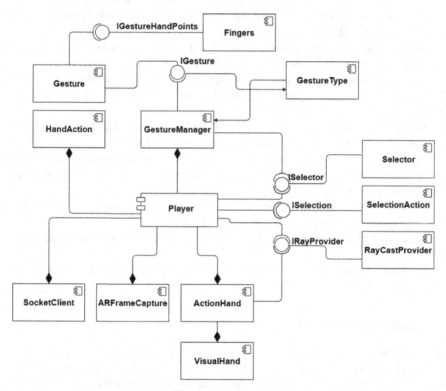

Fig. 2. Unity toolset

Gesture is a component that describes a hand gesture and provides functionality to check if a certain gesture is performed at the current time. Each gesture implementation must implement the IGesture Interface to ensure that every gesture has the same behaviour.

Fingers is a component that describes which of the retrieved hand points correspond to each finger. By using this component, the points of a specific finger can be retrieved all together as a list which in the first place of the list is the base finger point and on the last is the fingertip point.

GestureType is an enumerated value that defines a type of gesture. The gesture types defined in this enumerated value are the types that are assigned to each gesture component.

GestureManager is a component that manages all the gestures. Using this class facilitates access to the gesture classes. Additionally, it can check when a specific gesture is completed and return the object currently interacting.

HandAction is an abstract class created to act as a guideline for the future implementation of action classes. These action classes are the result of successful interaction with an object. Sample actions include movement and rotation. Developers can implement more action classes depending on their needs.

SocketClient is a simple client responsible for sending the images from the device camera to the hand tracking module and receiving the recognized hand points.

ARFrameCapture is responsible for capturing the image from the camera of the device. The next step is to transform the image into a form that can be sent to and processed by the hand tracking module.

ActionHand contains the functionality of the virtual hand. The logic of retrieving the how and when the hand can interact with an object is defined here.

VisualHand is the visualization of the retrieved hand points from the hand tracking module. This component is responsible for placing the virtual hand on top of the user's hand in the device viewport.

Selector is a component responsible for containing the mechanism that will check if an interaction between the hand and an object is triggered.

SelectionAction is a component that visually notifies the user about interactions with objects.

RayCastProvider is a component providing the required ray caster for the corresponding task.

3.2   Hand Tracking Module

The hand tracking module (Fig. 3) is implemented in python due to the plethora of frequently updated, and supported libraries. The design approach of this module does not follow the Object-Oriented Programming paradigm and thus the code is structured in functions and not on classes and interfaces. It consists of the following components:

Socker Server is the module's server. It waits for devices using the Unity toolset to connect and receive messages.

Image Process handles the processing of the image received from the devices. It shapes the decoded image in the correct form for the hand tracking algorithms.

Message Receiver is a function responsible to receive and decode the messages sent from the devices.

Hand Tracking Algorithm is the algorithm used to recognize and track the hand on the images. This algorithm is in an isolated component that makes the replacement of it an easy task.

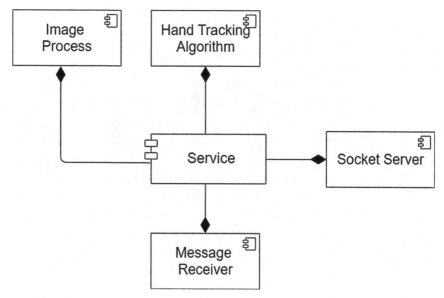

Fig. 3. Hand tracking module

4 Experimental Setup

To evaluate the usability of the toolset, a package containing the toolset with short documentation, and three tasks, was publicly available for people to download and use. After the completion of the tasks the users could fill a form to express their impressions about the toolset and possible improvements that can be made. 14 users-with a background in software engineering-downloaded the toolset and completed the tasks to develop an application by using the toolset.

The first step in creating the application was to create a scene and define the objects that were involved in it. To facilitate this step some sample scenes and objects were provided (Fig. 4), so the users could choose to open an already created scene. After the setup of the scene, users had to use the toolset's components on their scene. In this step, the interaction conditions of the application were defined. Next, the users were asked to create new components using the interfaces provided by the toolset as guidelines. This step allowed to evaluate the validity of the design choices for the toolset as well as the interface definitions and naming. The resulting scene of the users should be similar as the scene shown in Fig. 5.

Before the start of the application, users should tweak the python module to possibly change hand tracking algorithms, add extra interchangeable messages between client and server, or add extra filtering and validation on the hand tracking algorithms' results. Moreover, users were asked to start the server and launch the application after completing these steps in order to test the results. Following the users' testing of the resulting application, brief feedback was asked from the users to discuss their overall impression and give them the opportunity to communicate their suggestions for improving the toolset.

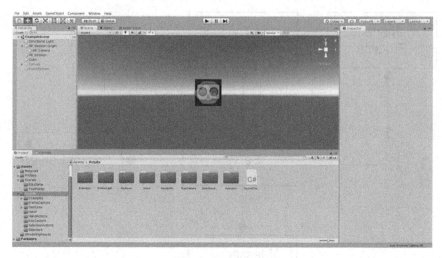

Fig. 4. Initial scene

Fig. 5. Resulting scene

Each user could complete the tasks in their own space for their convenience. Following the tasks and survey completion, users were asked to test the resulting application on their mobile devices and provide feedback about their experience. Since users completed the evaluation from their location, they were asked to describe the environment and light conditions as part of their feedback. Such conditions could comprise the lighting volume, the weather conditions, the color of the walls, or similar information users believe influences the execution of the application. This would help to understand when and how the hand tracking, and AR environment tracking, performed well or poorly. Moreover, information about the devices used for the execution of the application was requested in order to detect possible incompatibilities or limitations. Most of the devices were mid-range smart phones.

4.1 Evaluation

To measure the usability of software the System Usability Scale (SUS) [26] was utilized. SUS is a Likert scale that includes ten questions with five response options ranging from "strongly disagree" to "strongly agree" with three choices in between. The selection of SUS was because it can provide reliable results even with a small sample size (even with two users) that other questionnaires lack. It has been tested in almost 500 studies with over 5000 students [27] to measure the usability of software. ZeusAR [16] used SUS to evaluate the process of creating an AR serious game through the proposed wizard. Another study based on SUS for the evaluation of its usability is the MAT for ARLearn [28], which is an authoring tool for mobile environments for educational resources. LAGARTO [29] relied upon SUS also to evaluate the system and compare the users' performance.

Table 1. SUS questionnaire

Question number	Question
1	I think that I would like to use this system frequently
2	I found the system unnecessarily complex
3	I thought the system was easy to use
4	I think that I would need the support of a technical person to be able to use this system
5	I found the various functions in this system were well integrated
6	I thought there was too much inconsistency in this system
7	I would imagine that most people would learn to use this system very quickly
8	I found the system very cumbersome to use
9	I felt very confident using the system
10	I needed to learn a lot of things before I could get going with this system

To calculate the score from the SUS questionnaire (Table 1) users' answers were converted on a scale of 0 to 4 where 0 represents the "strongly disagree" and 4 the "strongly agree" options. Using this scale, as instructed by SUS, followed a subtraction of one point from the user responses for the odd-numbered questions, and a subtraction of the user responses from 5 for the even-numbered questions. Finally, to calculate the overall score, the sum of all the converted responses from users is multiplied by 2.5. This converts the range of the result from 0 to 40 to a scale of 0 to 100. Although the scale ranges from 0 to 100 it is important to note that it is not a percentage value.

5 Results

Figure 6 presents the technical background of the 14 users who participated in the experiments. One (1) denotes zero knowledge or familiarity with the technology, while five (5) denotes expertise. The answers indicate that while users have a strong background in software engineering, they lack experience with Unity 3D game engine and python programming language. Table 2 shows the average score of each question derived from the users' answers and calculated with the formula described previously. The even-numbered questions are changed to represent the result of the converted score based on the instructions interpreting the SUS scores. The overall usability score of the toolset is 74.65, which on the SUS scale is above average (the average score in SUS is 68). Based on this score, it can be assumed that the toolset is easy to learn and use.

Table 2. SUS questionnaire with average scores

Question	Average score
I think that I would like to use this system frequently	2.78
I did not find the system unnecessarily complex	3
I thought the system was easy to use	2.92
I think that I would not need the support of a technical person to be able to use this system	2.42
I found the various functions in this system were well integrated	3.2
I did not think there was too much inconsistency in this system	3.7
I would imagine that most people would learn to use this system very quickly	3
I did not find the system very cumbersome to use	3.2
I felt very confident using the system	3.07
I did not need to learn a lot of things before I could get going with this system	2.57

Figure 7 shows the responses from users on the SUS questionnaire. It can be observed from the answers to questions 4 and 10, that most of the users would most likely require technical support for the toolset. Questions 1 and 3, followed by question 9 have the lowest scores. The answers to these questions, combined with the users' familiarity and experience with the toolset's technologies, lead to the requirement for a simpler interface for the addition of the toolset's components. This improvement will assist users that are not familiar with such technologies to include them in the development process. Answers to question 8 indicate that the toolset was designed correctly. That conclusion is supported by questions 5 and 6, with question 6 scoring 3.7 indicating that the system's architecture is well structured. Finally, users' score for questions 2 and 7 is 3, which means that users believe that someone can learn and use the tool with ease.

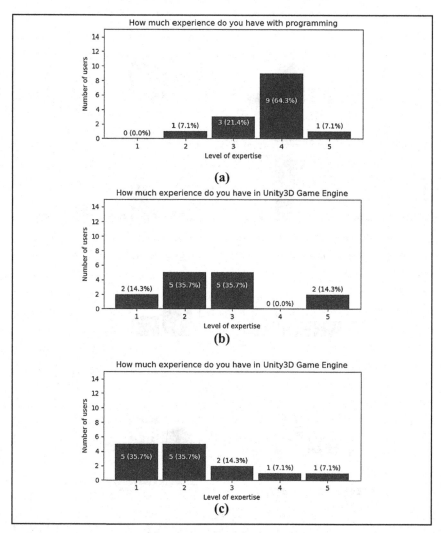

Fig. 6. Users' background: a) Software background, b) familiarity with Unity 3D game engine, c) familiarity with python programming language

After calculating the standard deviation of each question, it is observed that the answers in questions 4 and 10 have substantial variations with values of 1.178 and 0.903 respectively. These variations are from the least experienced users with Unity 3D and Python. It is expected for these users to report that they need more time and effort to familiarize themselves. Furthermore, from analyzing the coefficient of variation of the questions, it is observed that question 4 has the most spread values. The rest of the questions indicate a tendency towards a specific answered value, with questions 1, 3, and 6 having the majority of the users' answers concentrated in one value.

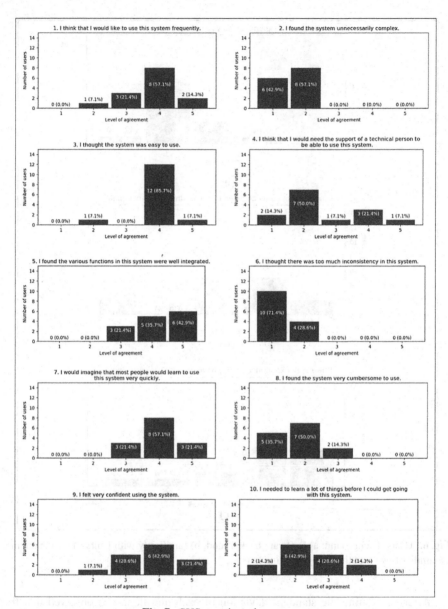

Fig. 7. SUS questionnaire answers

6 Discussion

Having 14 users that evaluated the usability of the toolset, the acquired results are promising. The rating depends on the software engineering background of the users, and their familiarity with the Unity3D game engine and python programming language. Users familiar with both technologies found the toolset very easy to use, while users with no experience found it harder to adapt. Most users who answered the survey were more familiar with the Unity3D game engine, which explains why most of them commented that they need a very straightforward way to set up the python server. Some users commented that they would have preferred to find the server already up and running and only connect to the service. Many users got confused while placing the components on the *Gameobject* by their interface classes. This confusion is interesting as it was not anticipated. The users tried to add the interface instead of the implemented classes. In future versions of the toolset, it will be handled accordingly. Placing the interface classes in another directory from the components available for usage, therefore changing the structure of the folders can solve this issue. Misconceptions with the naming conventions of some methods that the components expose were also detected. The reason is that different users can comprehend the meaning of a word differently. Consequently, their expectations about the purpose of this method would be other than the current. Users with a weak background in software engineering and not familiar with Unity3D or python would prefer already configured components ready to be used inside the scene. These users also recommended the option to include a visual options panel with simple drop-down menus for possible configurations. This visual representation of the toolset's options is requested both in Unity and in python modules. The overall score of the toolset can be considered satisfying as the documentation provided for the evaluation was very limited in order to assess how well defined the classes and naming conventions were. The fact that all of the users managed to complete and successfully run the application (even if limitations due to the desktop or mobile device specifications did not let the users experience the final application) shows that the toolset is capable to provide an easy-to-use interface for the purpose of applying physical hand interaction into AR Unity Scenes. Finally, users reported errors that occurred when the hand-tracking algorithm did not correctly recognize the hand, or the AR camera failed to detect the environment. These kinds of errors require better handling from the toolset to provide a more stable outcome.

7   Conclusion and Future Work

In this paper, a toolset-mainly targeted on mobile devices-that facilitates the process of creating interaction in such environments was presented. The toolset is divided into two main parts; the first part presents the components that are utilized inside the Unity 3D game engine, and the second part involves a webservice to handle the hand tracking task. An evaluation of the toolset's usability was conducted to assess how easy one can use the toolset to add physical hand interaction in their applications using the Unity3D game engine. Although the obtained results were promising, many open issues must be considered in the future. More studies regarding the usability and the performance of the toolset must be made. Furthermore, the development of the hand tracking module should be addressed in terms of improving and optimizing a server-client communication. Another part for improvement is the way that the algorithms are changed. A visual approach allowing a more plug-and-play experience needs to be investigated. For this task, the development of wrapper functions is necessary to include as many as possible formats of the algorithms. Finally, the visualization of the hand needs to be improved and potentially include a 3D model of the hand with depth perception. After these changes another evaluation of the toolset will start and for a better assessment of the two modules, they will be evaluated separately as from this study the results shows that users have strong knowledge in one of the two technologies required for the full system.

References

1. Azuma, R., Baillot, Y., Behringer, R., Feiner, S., Julier, S., MacIntyre, B.: Recent advances in augmented reality. IEEE Comput. Graph. Appl. **21**(6), 34–47 (2001). https://doi.org/10.1109/38.963459
2. Milgram, P., Kishino, F.: A taxonomy of mixed reality visual displays. IEICE Trans. Inf. Syst. **E77-D**, 1321–1329 (1994)
3. Coomans, M.K.D., Timmermans, H.J.P.: Towards a taxonomy of virtual reality user interfaces. In: Proceedings 1997 IEEE Conference on Information Visualization (Cat. No. 97TB100165), pp. 279–284 (1997). https://doi.org/10.1109/IV.1997.626531
4. Doolani, S., et al.: A review of extended reality (XR) technologies for manufacturing training. Technologies **8**(4), 77 (2020). https://doi.org/10.3390/technologies8040077
5. Alalwan, N., Cheng, L., Al-Samarraie, H., Yousef, R., Alzahrani, A.I., Sarsam, S.M.: Challenges and prospects of virtual reality and augmented reality utilization among primary school teachers: a developing country perspective. Stud. Educ. Eval. **66**, 100876 (2020). https://doi.org/10.1016/j.stueduc.2020.100876
6. Christinaki, E., Vidakis, N., Triantafyllidis, G.: A novel educational game for teaching emotion identification skills to preschoolers with autism diagnosis. Comput. Sci. Inf. Syst. **11**(2), 723–743 (2014)
7. Ghazwani, Y., Smith, S.: Interaction in augmented reality: challenges to enhance user experience. In: Proceedings of the 2020 4th International Conference on Virtual and Augmented Reality Simulations, pp. 39–44 (2020). https://doi.org/10.1145/3385378.3385384
8. Che, Y., Qi, Y.: Detection-guided 3D hand tracking for mobile AR applications. In: 2021 IEEE International Symposium on Mixed and Augmented Reality (ISMAR), pp. 386–392 (2021). https://doi.org/10.1109/ISMAR52148.2021.00055
9. Wang, L., et al.: WiTrace: centimeter-level passive gesture tracking using OFDM signals. IEEE Trans. Mob. Comput. **20**(4), 1730–1745 (2021). https://doi.org/10.1109/TMC.2019.2961885
10. Ismail, A.W., Fadzli, F.E., Faizal, M.S.M.: Augmented reality real-time drawing application with a hand gesture on a handheld interface. In: 2021 IEEE 6th International Conference on Computing, Communication and Automation (ICCCA), pp. 418–423 (2021). https://doi.org/10.1109/ICCCA52192.2021.9666439
11. Microsoft: Azure Kinect DK. https://azure.microsoft.com/en-us/services/kinect-dk/. Accessed 17 Mar 2022
12. LeapMotion: Ultraleap for Developers. https://developer.leapmotion.com/. Accessed 17 Mar 2022
13. Sensoryx: VRfree - VRfree® glove - intuitive VR interaction. https://www.sensoryx.com/products/vrfree/. Accessed 17 Mar 2022
14. Unity: Unity. https://unity.com/. Accessed 11 Mar 2022
15. Krauß, V., Boden, A., Oppermann, L., Reiners, R.: Current practices, challenges, and design implications for collaborative AR/VR application development (2021). https://doi.org/10.1145/3411764.3445335

16. Marín-Vega, H., Alor-Hernández, G., Colombo-Mendoza, L.O., Bustos-López, M., Zatarain-Cabada, R.: ZeusAR: a process and an architecture to automate the development of augmented reality serious games. Multimed. Tools Appl. **81**(2), 2901–2935 (2021). https://doi.org/10.1007/s11042-021-11695-1

17. Mccallum, S., Boletsis, C.: Augmented reality & gesture-based architecture in games for the elderly. Stud. Health Technol. Inform. **189**, 139–144 (2013). https://doi.org/10.3233/978-1-61499-268-4-139

18. Tian, H., Wang, C., Manocha, D., Zhang, X.: Realtime hand-object interaction using learned grasp space for virtual environments. IEEE Trans. Vis. Comput. Graph. **25**(8), 2623–2635 (2019). https://doi.org/10.1109/TVCG.2018.2849381

19. Liu, H., et al.: High-fidelity grasping in virtual reality using a glove-based system. In: Proceedings - IEEE International Conference on Robotics and Automation, pp. 5180–5186, May 2019. https://doi.org/10.1109/ICRA.2019.8794230

20. Han, S., Kim, J.: A study on immersion of hand interaction for mobile platform virtual reality contents. Symmetry **9**(2) (2017). https://doi.org/10.3390/sym9020022

21. Kyriakou, P., Hermon, S.: Can I touch this? Using natural interaction in a museum augmented reality system. Digit. Appl. Archaeol. Cult. Herit. **12**, 1–9 (2019). https://doi.org/10.1016/j.daach.2018.e00088

22. Zhang, F., et al.: Mediapipe hands: on-device real-time hand tracking. arXiv Preprint arXiv:2006.10214 (2020)

23. Lugaresi, C., et al.: MediaPipe: a framework for building perception pipelines. arXiv Preprint arXiv:1906.08172 (2019)

24. Chunduru, V., Roy, M., Dasari Romit, N.S, Chittawadigi, R.G.: Hand tracking in 3D space using mediapipe and PnP method for intuitive control of virtual globe. In: 2021 IEEE 9th Region 10 Humanitarian Technology Conference (R10-HTC), pp. 1–6 (2021). https://doi.org/10.1109/R10-HTC53172.2021.9641587

25. Ren, Y., et al.: Hand gesture recognition using 802.11ad mmWave sensor in the mobile device. In: 2021 IEEE Wireless Communications and Networking Conference Workshops (WCNCW), pp. 1–6 (2021). https://doi.org/10.1109/WCNCW49093.2021.9419978

26. Brooke, J.: SUS: a quick and dirty usability. Usability Eval. Ind. **189**(3) (1996)

27. Sauro, J.: Measuring usability with the system usability scale. https://measuringu.com/sus/. Accessed 04 Apr 2022

28. Tabuenca, B., Kalz, M., Ternier, S., Specht, M.: Mobile authoring of open educational resources for authentic learning scenarios. Univ. Access Inf. Soc. **15**(3), 329–343 (2014). https://doi.org/10.1007/s10209-014-0391-y

29. Maia, L.F., et al.: LAGARTO: a LocAtion based games AuthoRing TOol enhanced with augmented reality features. Entertain. Comput. **22**, 3–13 (2017). https://doi.org/10.1016/j.entcom.2017.05.001

Assessing Visual Cues for Improving Awareness in Collaborative Augmented Reality

Francesco Strada(✉)🆔, Edoardo Battegazzorre🆔, Enrico Ameglio,
Simone Turello, and Andrea Bottino🆔

Dipartimento di Automatica e Informatica, Politecnico di Torino, Turin, Italy
{francesco.strada,edoardo.battegazzorre,enrico.ameglio,simone.turello,
andrea.bottino}@polito.it

Abstract. Augmented Reality (AR) is an emerging technology that offers new and compelling design opportunities for Computer Supported Cooperative Work (CSCW). To foster collaboration and communication in AR-based CSCW, users should be able to understand how others interact with the shared environment. One of the most effective ways to support this awareness is to link user interactions to visual cues (VCs) that provide immediate cognitive feedback about the actions of other users (e.g., pointing, annotating, or manipulating objects). However, AR-based CSCW is in many ways still in its infancy in terms of visual language, and further research is needed, especially to evaluate the effectiveness of different VCs in improving user awareness in collaborative, co-located AR scenarios. To this end, this paper presents an evaluation of different VCs based on previous literature. Experiments were conducted with different scenarios covering the main purposes for which VCs are used and in which users had to perform tasks with increasing complexity. Results show that volunteers positively evaluated the VCs offered, as they effectively supported user awareness and provided contextual and spatial information to all participants.

1 Introduction

In CSCW, recent advances in AR technologies have enabled the introduction of disruptive innovations thanks to their ability to overlap the task space with the communication space [20], leading to more effective collaboration [4,37]. The key element currently being explored in AR-based CSCW (hereafter AR-CSCW) is the promotion of user awareness and, in particular, the effective use of visual and auditory information to support collaboration [9]. These two aspects are closely related. To communicate (and collaborate) efficiently, users must be able to understand how others interact with the shared environment. An effective way to support this awareness is to associate user interactions with visual cues (VCs) that provide immediate cognitive feedback on actions taken, e.g., pointing, annotating, or manipulating objects [17]. Examples of such VCs

L. T. De Paolis et al. (Eds.): XR Salento 2022, LNCS 13445, pp. 200–218, 2022.
https://doi.org/10.1007/978-3-031-15546-8_18

include displaying digital replicas of each user, visualizing their attentional focus, and highlighting the objects with which the user interacts.

Given the importance of VCs in increasing awareness in AR-CSCWs, the choice of VCs to make available and how to implement them are design decisions that are also related to the configuration in which these collaborative systems will be used. To capture and describe such configurations, researchers have developed several taxonomies such as the *time-space* matrix [14], which categorizes collaborative approaches based on two dimensions: *time* (i.e. *synchronous* when user interaction occurs at the same time, and *asynchronous* otherwise), and *space* (i.e. *co-located* when users share the same space, and *remote* otherwise). Another dimension for categorization is *symmetry*, first proposed by [3], which is further distinguished into two subclasses [32]. The first is *technological symmetry*, which can be either *symmetric* if all users use the same hardware devices, or *asymmetric* if they use different devices. For example, head-mounted displays (HMD) and handheld devices (HHD) imply different interaction and visualization tools available to each participant. The second subclass is *role symmetry* and indicates when users experience a shared workspace with different roles, each with different tasks, responsibilities, and available actions that can be performed.

Based on these dimensions (i.e., *time, space,* and *symmetry*), recent reviews [9,25,32] analyzed the state of the art in AR-CSCW and identified areas where further research is needed. In particular, two main issues were raised. First, the scenarios involving *symmetric technologies* and *asymmetric roles* are largely unexplored compared to other settings [32]. Second, while there is evidence that a team working in a shared location and synchronously across time is more productive [21], recent research has focused primarily on remote experiences (mainly with symmetric configurations), and studies addressing the *co-located context* are significantly older, being published primarily between 1995 and 2004 [9]. However, in the last fifteen years, AR technologies have made tremendous progress, moving from an emerging to a mature status [2,16], necessitating new analyses of the AR-CSCW domain.

In light of these considerations, this research proposes to address the two aforementioned issues through an analysis aimed at evaluating the effectiveness of different VCs in improving users' awareness and supporting their communication in collaborative AR scenarios with the following characteristics: *co-located, synchronous,* use of *symmetric technologies* (e.g., using HHDs for all users), and involvement of users in both *symmetric and asymmetric-role tasks*. To the best of our knowledge, such an analysis has not been presented in the literature before, and therefore our work aims at filling this gap.

In our work, we analyzed VCs inspired by solutions proposed in the literature through quantitative measurements obtained from 40 volunteers performing various collaborative tasks with different combinations of VCs. These data were then complemented with visual observations collected by the researchers. The experimental results show that the proposed VCs supported user awareness in a co-located environment by providing contextual and spatial information to all participants and that users rated most of the proposed VCs positively.

2   Related Works

In addition to the results of the studies presented in the Introduction [9,25,32], the survey of [20] highlights that (i) co-located AR-CSCWs allow users to interact with AR content as naturally as with real-world objects and (ii) AR improves communication by reducing the separation between task and communication spaces. Nevertheless, [20] reports that further research is needed to analyze how VCs can improve *awareness* in CSCWs, defined as the awareness of people and their interaction with the workspace, rather than just the awareness of the workspace itself, i.e., the perception and understanding of relevant elements in the environment [12]. This element is particularly important in shared AR environments, where it is not always easy to understand where users are looking or what virtual objects they are interacting with.

Given the relevance of VCs in AR-CSCW, several authors have attempted to propose and evaluate various forms of VCs for improving users' awareness. For example, [13] analyze the effectiveness of different VCs in promoting spatial awareness. In the study, a local user (through a projector-based spatial AR setup) interacts with different remote VR and AR users. The experiments show that with only two users a combination of many VCs improves awareness, but as the number of collaborators increases, excessive visual clutter can become confusing and detrimental to awareness. Another study analyzing different combinations of VCs to promote awareness in remote collaboration between AR and VR users has been carried out by [27]. According to the results, displaying the Field of View and pointing with a Gaze Ray are the most effective.

Pointing is one of the most important elements for awareness since it can draw attention to objects and locations where an action or task is being performed or planned to be performed [25]. In AR, pointing is managed through egocentric and exocentric metaphors [5]. Egocentric pointing VCs are synchronized with the user's point of view [23,27,33] and usually represented as 2D overlays [18]. On the contrary, exocentric metaphors detach VCs from the user's point of view. One solution is to anchor the VCs in the environment, ensuring spatial coherence from every point of view. [10] developed a system where a *remote-expert* can create spatial pointing annotations for a local user in AR. A comparison with a 2D egocentric VCs solution resulted in a higher preference (80%) for the spatial VCs. However, the authors emphasized some limitations. The most notable is that annotations could only be instantiated by the remote expert, highlighting the need to extend this exocentric pointing approach to a multi-user setup. [34] discuss different approaches to positioning label placeholders, resulting in a general appreciation of the proposed VCs, although the small number of participants (six volunteers) prevented generalization of these results. In line with these findings, the review of [32] points out the lack of evaluations of exocentric spatial pointing solutions validated in co-located multi-user settings.

However, despite ongoing research in AR-CSCW, the authors of [9] conclude that great efforts have been made to explore the use of VCs in VR, while the visual language of VCs for spatial awareness in AR is in many ways still in its infancy. This conclusion is also supported by the recent survey presented by

[29], which describes a list of design features for AR-HMD collaborative experiences gathered from 92 papers, and concludes that further evidence is needed to evaluate the effectiveness of the various features in promoting awareness.

Moreover, we would like to emphasize that these conclusions, as well as those of [32], are the result of an analysis of the literature from the point of view of the *time*, *space* and *symmetry* dimensions. Therefore, the authors were able to highlight in which of these areas (or a combination thereof) evidence was lacking. As a result, the research community has proposed a variety of VCs that can serve many purposes and use different interaction metaphors. However, to the best of our knowledge, there is only one work [8] that has proposed a comprehensive taxonomy to categorize this wide variety of VC. By analyzing various VCs in 49 commercial video games, the Authors explored their potential use in AR systems categorizing VCs along three dimensions: *purpose* (what the cue is for), *trigger* (how and when it is activated), and *markedness* (its visual representation). While *markedness* can be characterized by different nuances, the main classes for their *purpose* are three: *Look* (tell the user where to focus their attention), *Discover* (highlight points of interest), and *Go* (to aid navigation). VCs can also have different *triggers*: *user-triggered* (the user actively decides when and where to display the hint), *context-triggered* (the VC is generated by the system in response to a specific event), *agent-triggered* (the VC is triggered by another agent or user), or *persistent* (the VC is always visible and usually not spatially registered, e.g., a navigation map or compass superimposed on the displayed image in 2D).

Given these observations, the main goal of this paper is to determine whether and to what extent three VCs inspired from the literature and a novel exocentric spatial pointing technique called Shared Point of Interest (SPOI) can improve user collaboration and mutual awareness. These VCs and the evaluation scenarios used to assess them were designed according to the *purpose* and *trigger* dimensions proposed by [8]. This analysis was performed in the specific context of users collaborating in a co-located space via AR-HHD, a scenario for which there is currently no evidence, as recently pointed out by [38].

3 Methods

To summarize the rationale of our work, the main research question that guided our research was to investigate whether (and which) VCs are effective in increasing user awareness and facilitating communication in collaborative AR scenarios. Specifically, we focused our research on *co-located* AR environments in which all users interact via AR-HHDs (i.e., using *symmetric technologies*) and perform their assigned tasks with either *symmetric* or *asymmetric roles*.

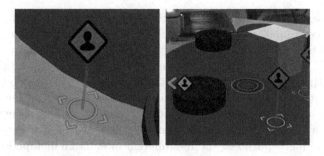

Fig. 1. Shared Point of Interest (*active* visual cue). *Left:* visual representation of the SPOI when it falls within the FOV. *Right:* Color-coded multi-user visualization showing different SPOIs placed by different users; note the blue cursor on the left side of the image, signaling an SPOI outside the FOV. (Color figure online)

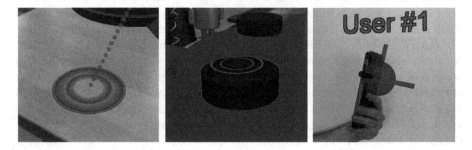

Fig. 2. *Passive* visual cues. *Left:* LoS. *Center:* Highlight. *Right:* Avatar

3.1   Implemented VCs

For our study, we defined three basic scenarios (described in detail in Sect. 3.2), which cover the purposes defined in the taxonomy of [8] (i.e., *Go*, *Look*, and *Discover*) and involve users in simpler symmetric tasks and more complex asymmetric tasks where a combination of VCs supports the users' activities. To improve understanding and information transfer, each user's VCs are uniquely colored.

In the following, we categorize the VCs offered to users in these scenarios into the two classes of *active* and *passive* VCs, based on the *trigger* taxonomy defined by [8], where *active* VCs (i.e., the VCs that require the active intervention of an agent to be deployed) include the *user* and *agent-triggered*, and the *passive* include the *context-triggered* and *persistent*.

The first VC offered to users is an *active* VC called **Shared Point of Interest** (SPOI). The adjective "shared" indicates that the POI is visible to all collaborators in the shared augmented environment, not just in the private space of the user who owns it. The SPOI is an exocentric pointing VC, registered in the 3D virtual space. Double-tapping the screen instantiates the SPOI and determines its 3D position in the augmented environment using a raycasting technique (Fig. 1, left). Tapping on a placed SPOI (owned by the user) deletes it. The SPOI allows users to determine the location where they want to attract the attention of their peers. To avoid visual clutter, each user has only one SPOI available. Since the presence of a placed SPOI should be obvious to all users, a cursor on the HHD screen side (Fig. 1, right) draws the attention of other users to any SPOI outside their (often limited) field of view (FOV).

SPOI is then combined with other passive VCs. Inspired by previous literature [8,9,13,27,36] and taking into account the specificity of the scenarios, we selected the following passive VCs as the most suitable ones:

- **Line of Sight (LoS):** (*persistent*) a segmented ray that highlights the user's line of sight, emanating from and perpendicular to the HHD screen and terminating at the intersection with a virtual object or plane in the environment. The ray has a limited extent if it does not intersect with anything. Otherwise, a cursor consisting of two concentric circles is displayed at the intersection point (Fig. 2, left). A similar visual cue was previously implemented in [27] for gaze tasks similar to our own, and was praised by users (and preferred over the alternative Field-of-View cone). Moreover, in the study conducted by [38] on co-located collaborative hand-held AR applications, they strongly recommend providing the users with clear visual feedback on where the other users are looking.
- **Highlight:** (*context-triggered*) this VC highlights any interactive object in the user's line of sight by adding a colored outline to the object (with the same color as the user). The same VC is used to signal peers (with the appropriate color) when a user picks up and manipulates a virtual object (Fig. 2, center). Highlighting an object of interest (either with an outline, glow or color change), is very common in both games [8] and AR applications [13,30,36].
- **Avatar:** (*persistent*) a colored sphere (with the same color assigned to the user) rendered at the HHD position and topped by the user's name (Fig. 2, right). While the *avatar* is a necessary VC in remote settings [27], it can also be useful in co-located environments to verify that the correct user is moving to the expected location or when spatial occlusions are present. In addition, avatars can be used in asymmetric tasks to explicitly and unambiguously convey the role of each user.

3.2   Evaluation Scenarios

In this section, we detail the scenarios used in our analysis (Fig. 3), focusing on the *Go, Look,* and *Discover* purposes of the taxonomy proposed by [8]. We emphasize that these are not simple toy scenarios, but reflect a variety of real-world use cases of collaborative AR applications. We exemplified some of these use cases in Table 1, taken both from literature and industrial applications where collaborative AR is used for tour guides [30], maintenance training [6,28], collaborative design [1] and classroom support [35]. In the following, we named each scenario according to the main activities assigned to the users and also indicated the purpose category to which the scenario refers.

Fig. 3. Virtual Environments for each scenario. *Left:* Navigation Scenario (*Go*). *Center:* Gaze Scenario (*Look*). *Right:* Manipulation Scenario (*Discover*).

Each scenario is divided into different tasks. The first ones are less complex and assign the same role to all users (symmetric role tasks). The last task involves role asymmetry and presents users with the greatest challenges in communication and collaboration.

Since we are also interested in exploring the relationships between passive (LoS, Highlight, Avatar) and active VCs (SPOI), we defined two different visual configurations: V0, which provides users with only the passive VCs, and V1, which combines active and passive VCs. As described later, we asked users to repeat each scenario for each visual configuration (i.e., twice).

Navigation Scenario (NS), Focus on *Go*. In this scenario, VCs are used to get users to physically reach a specific location in the real-world environment. Real-world use cases include any application where navigational assistance is required. Similar collaborative navigation tasks can be found in [19,30] and in the literature on Collaborative Virtual Environments.

The Navigation Scenario consists of eight platforms arranged in a circle on the floor (Fig. 3, left), which users must physically reach to complete the assigned task.

The Navigation Scenario is divided into three tasks:

– *NS-Task 1*: a platform is randomly selected and marked with a red beacon. All users must simultaneously position themselves around it for a few seconds. The task is repeated three times, each time selecting a different platform.
– *NS-Task 2*: the application highlights n platforms (where n is the number of users collaborating), each with the color assigned to a user. Users must position themselves on the platform of their color. The task is repeated three times.
– *NS-Task 3*: Activation and coloring of the platforms are the same as in NS-Task 2. However, only one user (*guide*) can see the colored information, while others (*followers*) can only see the inactive platforms. The *guide*'s goal is to direct each *follower* to the correct platform (i.e., the platform with the same color as the followers). This task is repeated n times (where n = number of users collaborating), with the *guide* role assigned to a different user at each iteration.

Table 1. Examples of practical use cases for each evaluation scenario and specific task (asymmetric-role tasks are indicated with "*").

Scenario	Task	Use cases examples
Navigation (*Go* purpose)	*NS-Task 1*	AR-based Tour Guide: all members must reach the next landmark while visiting a city [30]
	NS-Task 2	Collaborative Design: collaborators must look at an item from different viewpoints [1]
	NS-Task 3*	AR-based Tour Guide: a tour guide informs tourists where they should go next [30]
Gaze (*Look* purpose)	*GS-Task 1*	Maintenance: workers must understand how a specific part of a machine works [6]
	GS-Task 2	Collaborative Design: each user focuses on a different part of an item [1]
	GS-Task 3*	Classroom AR Support: teacher highlights a problem and suggests solutions to the students' assignment [35]
Manipulation (*Discover* purpose)	*MS-Task 1*	Maintenance: a worker must use the correct tool on a specific part of machinery [6,28]
	MS-Task 2*	Assembly: a remote expert guides a worker through an assembly process [28]

Gaze Scenario (GS), Focus on *Look*. In this scenario, we evaluate the effectiveness of VCs in directing the user's visual attention to a specific object or part of the environment that requires timely action. For more examples of similar tasks in the literature, see [10,13,19,22,33,38].

In the Gaze Scenario, users must synchronously or asynchronously direct their gaze to one or more cubes arranged on a 4×4 grid (Fig. 3, center). This scenario is divided into the following tasks:

- *GS-Task 1*: all users must collectively (and for a few seconds) focus their gaze on the cube highlighted by the application. This task is repeated three times selecting a different random cube at each iteration.
- *GS-Task 2*: the application selects n random cubes (where n is the number of users), each marked with a different color. To complete the task, all users must simultaneously fix their gaze on the cube of their corresponding color for a few seconds. The task is repeated three times with a different cube selection.
- *GS-Task 3*: the activation and coloring of the cubes is done as in GS-Task 2, but only one user (the *guide*) can see the coloring information on his/her screen and must guide the other users to gaze the correct cube. The task is repeated n times, where n is the number of users, and at each repetition a different user takes the role of the *guide*.

Manipulation Scenario (MS), Focus on *Discover*. In various scenarios, user attention needs to be directed to objects that are interactive and can be manipulated. The most important use cases are collaborative maintenance and assembly tasks where specific objects or parts of an object need to be interacted with or correctly aligned and placed in a specific location to complete the operation. More generally, the ability to clearly show users which objects they can interact with to complete their tasks (or which others can interact with for the same purpose) is of utmost importance in any (collaborative) AR environment. For more examples of similar tasks, see [10,11,13,19,22,33].

The Manipulation Scenario provides several virtual objects and holes (Fig. 3, right) with three different shapes (i.e., square, rectangle, or triangle). Holes and objects are also associated with a number, a constant for a hole and a variable for an object, which can be changed by interacting with a dial on the side of the object. Users have to correctly orient the object and insert it into the hole after matching the hole and object values. For our experiments, we defined the two following tasks:

- *MS-Task 1*: the user must place the object with her color in the correct hole and with the correct number. The task is repeated three times with different combinations of objects and numbers per user.
- *MS-Task 2*: the *guide* sees a 4×4 grid with holes, while the *followers* only see the grid outline and the objects, but not the object colors and the holes. The *guide* must instruct the *followers* to place their object in the correct location, with the appropriate orientation and number. The task is repeated n times with a new user taking the *guide* role at each iteration.

4   Experimental Protocol

To evaluate the effectiveness of the VCs under analysis (and their combinations), we conducted a user study with 40 volunteers (11 females and 29 males, aged 18 to 34 years), all of which are students and researchers of the Polytechnic of Turin. The technological competence of the volunteers was assessed though a pre-questionnaire, the results of which are discussed in the following. Volunteers were divided into 20 groups, each consisting of two users and one researcher. The researcher acted as a facilitator, introducing the scenarios, explaining the procedures required for each task, and addressing any technical issues that arose during the session. The facilitator (which did not play the role of *guide* in the asymmetric tasks) was instructed not to interfere with the users' choices and to follow their input promptly. In order to minimize potential differences in interaction with subjects, communication of information, and presentation of sessions and tasks, the same researcher assumed the role of facilitator in all experimental sessions.

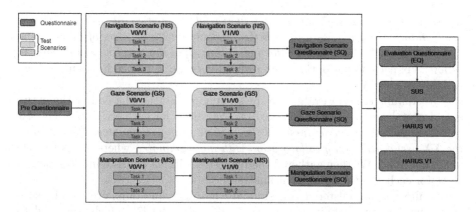

Fig. 4. Summary of the evaluation protocol. After filling a pre-questionnaire, the groups complete two iterations of a scenario (using a different visual configuration at each round) and then fill the SQ. At the end of the experimental tests, users complete the EQ and three usability questionnaires (SUS, and HARUS for both V0 and V1).

4.1   Methodology

After giving volunteers an overview of the goals of the experiment and explaining the use of key terms in the experiment (e.g., visual information and visual cues), the scenarios were administered in increasing order of complexity (i.e., first Navigation, then Gaze and finally Manipulation). Each experiment began with a simple training task to help volunteers become acquainted with the VCs and scenario interactions. As previously stated, each scenario was repeated twice, using either the V0 or V1 configuration. To reduce the possibility of learning effects biasing the results (especially the performance metrics), we pseudo-randomly shuffled the order of the executed configurations (i.e., V0–V1 vs V1–V0), ensuring a final balance (50%–50%) of volunteers' groups between the two options.

4.2   Evaluation Metrics

Figure 4 summarizes the steps of the evaluation protocol. The evaluation included observational data, objective measurements (completion times for each task), and subjective measurements. Concerning the latter, we asked volunteers to complete a *pre-questionnaire* that included exploratory questions about their personal data (username, gender, and age) and prior experiences with AR technologies. We delivered a questionnaire (*scenario questionnaire*, SQ) immediately after completing the two iterations of each scenario to collect volunteers' opinions about using the proposed VCs in that specific context (i.e., we collected one such questionnaire per scenario). This questionnaire begins by asking users to express explicitly whether they prefer the V0 (without SPOI) or V1 (with SPOI) configuration. Then, we included three questions about the usefulness of the available visual information in raising awareness and promoting collaboration (*Q1 - For collaboration purposes, I have found the presence of visual information to be significant for the successful completion of tasks; Q2 - The visual information allowed me to better understand the actions of other users; Q3 - The availability of visual information improved the effectiveness of collaboration*). For each scenario, these three questions were combined into a multi-item *collaboration score.*

We administered an evaluation questionnaire (EQ) at the end of the entire experimental session, which included two questions for each VC (*Q1 - The use of XX helped me better understand the actions of my teammates; Q2 - I found the XX useful during my collaboration with my teammates*, where XX is the VC under analysis). We then gathered these questions into a multi-item *effectiveness score* for each VC for subsequent analysis.

Finally, we administered two standard usability questionnaires to the subjects, the System Usability Scale (SUS), described by [7], which was used to obtain an overall usability assessment of the application, and the Handheld Augmented Reality Usability Scale (HARUS) questionnaire proposed by [31], which assesses the comprehensibility and manipulability of AR-HHD applications. The HARUS aimed to assist us in gaining a thorough understanding of the comprehensibility of the two proposed visual configurations (V0 and V1), and it was thus administered to users once for each configuration. We emphasize the relevance of usability since, as highlighted by [25], we can only assume a certain amount of technical literacy on the average user, leading to lower adoption due to frustration if usability is not maximized.

Except for HARUS, scored on a scale of 1 to 7, and the question about the preferred visual configuration (which can assume only the value V0, V1 or none of the two), all questionnaire items were scored on a Likert Scale from 1 (strong disagreement) to 5 (strong agreement). SUS and HARUS final scores are computed on a 0–100 scale.

5   Results and Discussion

The shared AR experience has been implemented with the Unity game engine. This section will first discuss the results concerning the overall application usability and the comprehensibility of V0 and V1 visual configurations (Sect. 5.1). Then, we will assess the users' evaluation of the proposed VCs (Sect. 5.2). Finally, we will discuss the completion times recorded for each collaborative task using V0 and V1 configurations (Sect. 5.3).

5.1   Usability and Comprehensibility

A summary of the usability scores (SUS and HARUS), is shown in Fig. 5, left. The SUS scores differed significantly (two-sample t-test, $p = 0.007$) between the V1–V0 (i.e., those who perform the two iterations beginning with V1 and concluding with V0) and V0-V1 (i.e., those who use the reverse order) groups, but both were high, 83.38 ($SD = 8.52$) and 90.13 ($SD = 6.41$), respectively, highlighting the excellent usability [7] of the application and consequently of the

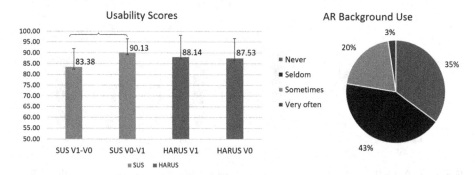

Fig. 5. *Left:* SUS and HARUS average scores on a scale of 1–100. SUS is reported for the two configuration orders (V1-V0 and V0-V1), whereas HARUS for the two configurations (V0 and V1). Standard deviations are expressed through error bars and significantly different scores through curly brackets. *Right:* frequency of responses to the question: "how often do you use an AR application?".

proposed VCs. One possible explanation for the SUS differences between the two groups is that the V1-V0 users had to simultaneously learn to perform the tasks and use the SPOI in the specific scenario context during the first iterations. In contrast, the V0-V1 users were first introduced to the scenario context, so they had enough time to become familiar with the environment, the application interface, and the other VCs before they started using the SPOI.

In terms of comprehensibility, we found no significant differences between the V0-V1 and V1-V0 groups, so we reported the average V0 and V1 ratings per user. The results show that the V1 configuration received a slightly higher HARUS score (88.14, $SD = 9.97$) than the V0 configuration (87.53, $SD = 9.14$), and both can be classified as very positive (i.e., very understandable). The literature emphasizes that combining an appropriate number of different VCs only helps to increase awareness if designers can maintain a clear and simple visualization [13]. Our results suggest that our design successfully achieved this goal. Furthermore, we believe that the higher V1 score is indicative of the effectiveness of SPOI in improving the overall comprehensibility of the VC set.

Finally, we emphasize that the positive usability and comprehensibility scores are even more impressive considering that our testers had no experience with AR, as 43% and 35% of them had rarely and never used an AR application, respectively (Fig. 5, right). Thus, we were able to design a collaborative AR system and provide a set of VCs that were easy to learn and simple to use, which made the users feel in control and ultimately sparked their interest to use a similar system again in the future.

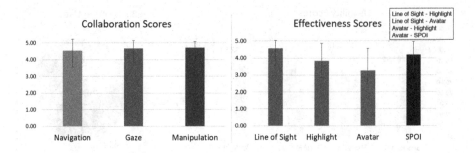

Fig. 6. *Left:* Collaboration scores organized per evaluation scenario. *Right:* VC Effectiveness as rated by users. On the top right box of the graph we report couples of VCs which show significant differences. Significance ($p < 0.05$) was evaluated through a Tukey's post-hoc test performed after a One-Way ANOVA test. Standard deviations are expressed through error bars.

5.2   VCs Assessment

The *collaboration score* (i.e., the multi-item score obtained from the *scenario questionnaire*, summarizes the overall users' evaluation of the extent to which, for each experimental scenario, the offered VCs contributed to foster collaboration. The final average collaboration scores, Fig. 6 left, are high (Navigation: 4.56, $SD = 0.67$, Gaze: 4.68, $SD = 0.45$, Manipulation: 4.72, $SD = 0.35$), have relatively high internal consistency (Cronbach's Alpha is 0.91 for Navigation, 0.65 for Gaze and 0.60 for Manipulation), and are not significantly different between themselves (One-Way ANOVA, significance at $p = 0.05$). The slightly higher values recorded in the Gaze and Manipulation scenarios can be attributed to the higher complexity of their collaborative tasks, which the users found to be positively supported by the available VCs. Our observations of user behavior provide another indication of how VCs facilitated collaboration. As a matter of fact, during the experimental sessions, participants engaged in active discussion, often relying on the VCs for help (e.g., pointing out objects or locations involved in the discussion). Although communication does not always lead to collaboration, the team cannot work together to achieve a goal without sharing knowledge and ideas, and this sharing was facilitated in our case by the available VCs. However, since the sessions were not videotaped, we were not able to collect detailed metrics on the time involved in (and the quality of) different types of communication.

User evaluations of the VCs' effectiveness (i.e., the *effectiveness score*, which summarizes the two *evaluation questionnaire* questions for each VC) are summarized in Fig. 6, right. It can be seen that the LoS and SPOI are highly rated (4.58, $SD = 0.45$, and 4.20, $SD = 0.77$, respectively). Since both VCs are used for the same function (namely, pointing), we believe that their different scores are due to the ease and speed with which large objects (such as the cubes in the "Gaze" scenario) or locations (such as in the "Navigation" scenario) can be highlighted with the LoS by simply pointing the device. In contrast, performing

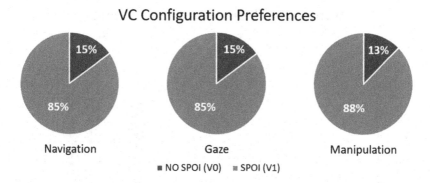

Fig. 7. VC configuration preferences organized per evaluation scenario.

the same operation with SPOI requires an additional operation (i.e., explicitly instantiating the SPOI). Nonetheless, one finding that suggests greater "real" effectiveness of SPOI is the higher percentage of users who prefer the V1 configuration (85% for gaze and navigation tasks and 88% for manipulation tasks, Fig. 7), i.e. the configuration where SPOI is the key feature.

Highlight was less appreciated than other VCs (3.83, $SD = 1.04$), which was an unexpected result given its potential utility in some scenarios (especially for Manipulation). Observational analysis allowed us to identify an issue with the information conveyed by this VC. *Highlight* is used both in our implementation and in similar approaches [8,15,24,26] to indicate to a user the objects that can be interacted with, and at the same time to signal peers when the user manipulates a virtual object. Despite the color coding used to distinguish the two cases, this mix of messages (the personal ones and the ones for peers) made the communication less immediate and clear. This observation points to a design element that can be improved in future implementations, which we think is a helpful hint that other researchers can benefit from.

Finally, *Avatar* received the lowest appreciation (3.26, $SD = 1.29$). This result confirms the lower relevance of this VC in a co-located environment, which is definitely better suited for scenarios where remote peers need to be digitally present in the shared environment.

5.3 Completion Times

Although not indicative of the quality of the collaboration and the extent of the increase in awareness mediated by the VCs, completion times are an objective measure of user performance that can shed light on experimental results and facilitate their interpretation.

In all test scenarios, the results show different trends between symmetric and asymmetric-role tasks. For the tasks with *symmetric roles*, there was no statistical difference in the completion times for the first and second iterations between the V0–V1 and V1–V0 groups. On the contrary, for tasks with *asymmetric roles*,

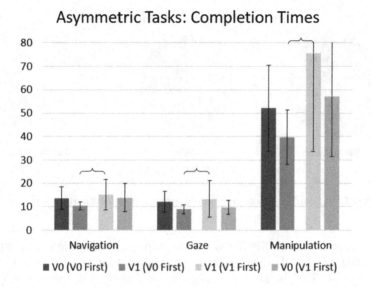

Fig. 8. Completion times (in seconds) for asymmetric tasks organized by visualization configuration and configuration order. Significantly different configurations are reported through curly brackets. Standard deviations are expressed through error bars.

significant differences between the completion times of the first and second iteration between the V0–V1 or V1–V0 groups are evident (Fig. 8). We believe that one possible explanation for these observations is that in symmetric tasks, users need tools that support awareness but do not rely on VCs to convey directional information. Conversely, in asymmetric tasks, it is critical to support guides with tools that allow them to provide timely cues (and commands) to help followers accomplish the task. In this context, the different characteristics and number of VCs available in the two configurations justify the observed differences in completion times. These differences deserve a detailed analysis.

In all scenarios, we observed lower completion times in the second iteration of the asymmetric tasks, which can be attributed to the users' knowledge acquired in the first iteration. In the Gaze and Navigation scenarios, the difference between the completion times of the first iterations using V1 and V0 is not significant. On the contrary, the completion times of the second iterations are significantly different. In particular, the second iterations with V1 consistently take less time than those with V0. Since the pointing VCs are probably the most important VCs for controlling activities in asymmetric tasks, these results seem to indicate the contribution of SPOI (which is only available in V1 and not in V0) in supporting effective communication, spatial information sharing, and awareness, ultimately leading to shorter completion times.

The results of the Manipulation scenario are quite different and more difficult to interpret. For the V0–V1 group, the second iteration (with V1 and the SPOI) had the lowest average completion time among all iterations (Fig. 8). In contrast, starting with V1 seems to have a negative effect on completion time. A possible explanation arises from visual observations. In Manipulation scenario, users were asked to explain (*guides*) and adjust (*followers*) the correct orientation of the object. In the first iteration (V0 having only LoS as pointing VC), most *guides* in the V0-V1 group performed this process by pointing (with the LoS VC) a specific corner of the hole and telling the follower which corner of the object it corresponded to. In the second iteration, the higher visual stability of SPOI compared to LoS led *guides* to prefer this VC for highlighting a suitable hole landmark. In turn, the stable visual reference provided by SPOI resulted in a shorter processing time.

Instead, for the V1–V0 group, in the first iteration (V1, with SPOI and LoS as pointing VCs), *guides* generally began by placing the SPOI in the center of the hole and using it as a reference to tell followers how to find the correct orientation (e.g. "turn slightly to the left" or "move the object slightly to the right"). However, these voice commands often increased the cognitive load on participants, who had to correctly interpret the relative position cues (with the possibility of misunderstanding them). We also noted a kind of "mental laziness" on the part of the guides, who relied too long on the placed SPOI without immediately understanding that canceling and moving the SPOI to select a better reference for object placement (e.g., a hole corner), or combining the cues offered by the SPOI and LoS, could simplify verbal communication and speed up activities. Then, in the second iteration (with V0), the guides could only use the LoS as a visual reference. However, the reduced visual stability resulted in a slight loss of clarity in the information conveyed (and higher completion times than in the second iteration with V1 of the V0-V1 group). In summary, we believe that these empirical observations both illustrate the initial mental load required to master the SPOI and support its effectiveness in this scenario.

6   Conclusions

We investigated the effectiveness of different VCs in increasing user awareness and facilitating communication in collaborative HHD-based AR scenarios where co-located users are involved in both symmetric and asymmetric-role tasks. This work contributes to the state-of-the-art by filling a gap in the AR-CSCW literature, where studies addressing *co-located context* are significantly older and do not reflect current advances in AR technologies.

For our study, we designed and developed three assessment scenarios in which users could use two different VC configurations. The first includes various passive VCs selected from previous solutions in the literature. The second combines passive VCs with an active and exocentric pointing VC (called SPOI). We collected quantitative and observational data to evaluate the proposed VCs and their configurations. The experimental results highlight the contribution of all VCs (and the SPOI in particular) in improving user awareness and supporting collaborative activities. The positive results are consistent with previous research examining the use of VCs in remote scenarios [27], and provide additional evidence for their effectiveness in co-located settings, evidence that was lacking in the current literature. Our observations have also uncovered some issues with the standard design of Highlight that may reduce the effectiveness of the information conveyed by this VC and require improvements in its design.

In conclusion, we note that some of our findings can be applied with similar benefits in other settings, e.g., remote environments, where we expect (based on previous research) a more significant contribution from the Avatar, which is an almost mandatory VC in such scenarios. Similar comments can be made in settings involving other devices such as AR-HMD, with the only exception of LoS in co-located environments, whose usability and effectiveness are affected by the fact that HMDs force users to direct their gaze to the point where they want to draw the attention of other users, unlike HDD, where the user's gaze is separated from the device's line of sight, allowing users to highlight a point while actually looking in another direction (e.g., to look other users in the eye during communication).

Future work will address more challenging evaluation scenarios inspired by real-world use cases (e.g., maintenance or collaborative design). We believe that by requiring more "collaborative intense" activities from users, richer and more detailed data can be obtained, allowing novel insights into the problem.

References

1. Arvizio, I.: Arvizio (2022). https://www.arvizio.io/. Accessed 21 Apr 2022
2. Batuwanthudawa, B., Jayasena, K.: Real-time location based augmented reality advertising platform. In: 2020 2nd International Conference on Advancements in Computing (ICAC). IEEE, December 2020. https://doi.org/10.1109/icac51239.2020.9357261
3. Billinghurst, M., Bee, S., Bowskill, J., Kato, H.: Asymmetries in collaborative wearable interfaces. In: Digest of Papers. Third International Symposium on Wearable Computers, pp. 133–140. IEEE (1999)
4. Billinghurst, M., Kato, H., Kiyokawa, K., Belcher, D., Poupyrev, I.: Experiments with face-to-face collaborative AR interfaces. Virtual Reality 6(3), 107–121 (2002). https://doi.org/10.1007/s100550200012
5. Bleeker, T., Lee, G., Billinghurst, M.: Ego-and Exocentric interaction for mobile AR conferencing. In: 2013 IEEE International Symposium on Mixed and Augmented Reality (ISMAR), pp. 1–6. IEEE (2013)
6. BOSCH: Bosch common augmented reality platform (2022). https://www.re-flekt.com/portfolio-item/bosch-common-ar-platform. Accessed 21 Apr 2022
7. Brooke, J.: SUS: a retrospective. J. Usability Stud. 8(2), 29–40 (2013)
8. Dillman, K.R., Mok, T.T.H., Tang, A., Oehlberg, L., Mitchell, A.: A visual interaction cue framework from video game environments for augmented reality. In: Proceedings of the 2018 CHI Conference on Human Factors in Computing Systems, pp. 1–12 (2018)
9. Ens, B., et al.: Revisiting collaboration through mixed reality: the evolution of groupware. Int. J. Hum Comput Stud. 131, 81–98 (2019)

10. Gauglitz, S., Nuernberger, B., Turk, M., Höllerer, T.: World-stabilized annotations and virtual scene navigation for remote collaboration. In: Proceedings of the 27th Annual ACM Symposium on User Interface Software and Technology, pp. 449–459 (2014)
11. Guo, A., Canberk, I., Murphy, H., Monroy-Hernández, A., Vaish, R.: Blocks: collaborative and persistent augmented reality experiences. Proc. ACM Interact. Mob. Wearable Ubiquit. Technol. **3**(3), 1–24 (2019). https://doi.org/10.1145/3351241
12. Gutwin, C., Greenberg, S.: A descriptive framework of workspace awareness for real-time groupware. Comput. Support. Coop. Work (CSCW) **11**(3–4), 411–446 (2002). https://doi.org/10.1023/a:1021271517844
13. Irlitti, A., Piumsomboon, T., Jackson, D., Thomas, B.H.: Conveying spatial awareness cues in XR collaborations. IEEE Trans. Vis. Comput. Graph. **25**(11), 3178–3189 (2019)
14. Johansen, R.: Groupware: Computer Support for Business Teams. The Free Press (1988)
15. Kantonen, T., Woodward, C., Katz, N.: Mixed reality in virtual world teleconferencing. In: 2010 IEEE Virtual Reality Conference (VR), pp. 179–182. IEEE (2010)
16. Kim, K., Billinghurst, M., Bruder, G., Duh, H.B.L., Welch, G.F.: Revisiting trends in augmented reality research: a review of the 2nd decade of ISMAR (2008–2017). IEEE Trans. Vis. Comput. Graph. **24**(11), 2947–2962 (2018). https://doi.org/10.1109/tvcg.2018.2868591
17. Kim, S., Lee, G., Huang, W., Kim, H., Woo, W., Billinghurst, M.: Evaluating the combination of visual communication cues for HMD-based mixed reality remote collaboration. In: Proceedings of the 2019 CHI Conference on Human Factors in Computing Systems, pp. 1–13 (2019)
18. Kim, S., Lee, G., Sakata, N., Billinghurst, M.: Improving co-presence with augmented visual communication cues for sharing experience through video conference. In: 2014 IEEE International Symposium on Mixed and Augmented Reality (ISMAR), pp. 83–92. IEEE (2014)
19. Kolkmeier, J., Harmsen, E., Giesselink, S., Reidsma, D., Theune, M., Heylen, D.: With a little help from a holographic friend: the openimpress mixed reality telepresence toolkit for remote collaboration systems. In: Proceedings of the 24th ACM Symposium on Virtual Reality Software and Technology, pp. 1–11 (2018)
20. Lukosch, S., Billinghurst, M., Alem, L., Kiyokawa, K.: Collaboration in augmented reality. Comput. Support. Coop. Work (CSCW) **24**(6), 515–525 (2015). https://doi.org/10.1007/s10606-015-9239-0
21. Marai, G.E., Forbes, A.G., Johnson, A.: Interdisciplinary immersive analytics at the electronic visualization laboratory: lessons learned and upcoming challenges. In: 2016 Workshop on Immersive Analytics (IA), pp. 54–59. IEEE (2016)
22. Müller, J., Rädle, R., Reiterer, H.: Remote collaboration with mixed reality displays. In: Proceedings of the 2017 CHI Conference on Human Factors in Computing Systems. ACM, May 2017. https://doi.org/10.1145/3025453.3025717
23. Nancel, M., Chapuis, O., Pietriga, E., Yang, X.D., Irani, P.P., Beaudouin-Lafon, M.: High-precision pointing on large wall displays using small handheld devices. In: Proceedings of the SIGCHI Conference on Human Factors in Computing Systems, pp. 831–840 (2013)
24. Pereira, V., Maftos, T., Rodrigues, R., Nóbrega, R., Jacob, J.: Extended reality framework for remote collaborative interactions in virtual environments. In: 2019 International Conference on Graphics and Interaction (ICGI), pp. 17–24. IEEE (2019)

25. Pidel, C., Ackermann, P.: Collaboration in virtual and augmented reality: a systematic overview. In: De Paolis, L.T., Bourdot, P. (eds.) AVR 2020. LNCS, vol. 12242, pp. 141–156. Springer, Cham (2020). https://doi.org/10.1007/978-3-030-58465-8_10

26. Pinho, M.S., Bowman, D.A., Freitas, C.M.D.S.: Cooperative object manipulation in collaborative virtual environments. J. Braz. Comput. Soc. **14**(2), 53–67 (2009). https://doi.org/10.1007/BF03192559

27. Piumsomboon, T., Dey, A., Ens, B., Lee, G., Billinghurst, M.: The effects of sharing awareness cues in collaborative mixed reality. Front. Robot. AI **6** (2019). https://doi.org/10.3389/frobt.2019.00005

28. PTC: Vuforia chalk (2022). https://www.ptc.com/en/products/vuforia/vuforia-chalk. Accessed 21 Apr 2022

29. Radu, I., Joy, T., Bowman, Y., Bott, I., Schneider, B.: A survey of needs and features for augmented reality collaborations in collocated spaces. Proc. ACM Hum. Comput. Interact. **5**(CSCW1), 1–21 (2021). https://doi.org/10.1145/3449243

30. Reitmayr, G., Schmalstieg, D.: Scalable techniques for collaborative outdoor augmented reality. In: 3rd IEEE and ACM International Symposium on Mixed and Augmented Reality (ISMAR 2004), Arlington (2004)

31. Santos, M.E.C., Taketomi, T., Sandor, C., Polvi, J., Yamamoto, G., Kato, H.: A usability scale for handheld augmented reality. In: Proceedings of the 20th ACM Symposium on Virtual Reality Software and Technology, pp. 167–176 (2014)

32. Sereno, M., Wang, X., Besançon, L., McGuffin, M.J., Isenberg, T.: Collaborative work in augmented reality: a survey. IEEE Trans. Vis. Comput. Graph. **28**(6), 2530–2549 (2020)

33. Teo, T., Lee, G.A., Billinghurst, M., Adcock, M.: Investigating the use of different visual cues to improve social presence within a 360 mixed reality remote collaboration. In: The 17th International Conference on Virtual-Reality Continuum and Its Applications in Industry. ACM, November 2019. https://doi.org/10.1145/3359997.3365687

34. Väyrynen, J., Suoheimo, M., Colley, A., Häkkilä, J.: Exploring head mounted display based augmented reality for factory workers. In: Proceedings of the 17th International Conference on Mobile and Ubiquitous Multimedia. ACM, November 2018. https://doi.org/10.1145/3282894.3289745

35. Villanueva, A., Zhu, Z., Liu, Z., Peppler, K., Redick, T., Ramani, K.: Meta-AR-app: an authoring platform for collaborative augmented reality in STEM classrooms. In: Proceedings of the 2020 CHI Conference on Human Factors in Computing Systems, pp. 1–14 (2020)

36. Volmer, B., et al.: A comparison of predictive spatial augmented reality cues for procedural tasks. IEEE Trans. Vis. Comput. Graph. **24**(11), 2846–2856 (2018)

37. Wang, X., Dunston, P.S.: Comparative effectiveness of mixed reality-based virtual environments in collaborative design. IEEE Trans. Syst. Man Cybern. Part C (Appl. Rev.) **41**(3), 284–296 (2011)

38. Wells, T., Houben, S.: CollabAR-investigating the mediating role of mobile AR interfaces on co-located group collaboration. In: Proceedings of the 2020 CHI Conference on Human Factors in Computing Systems, pp. 1–13 (2020)

Human Augmentation: An Enactive Perspective

Agnese Augello[1], Giuseppe Caggianese[2(✉)], and Luigi Gallo[2]

[1] Institute for High Performance Computing and Networking, CNR, Palermo, Italy
[2] Institute for High Performance Computing and Networking, CNR, Naples, Italy
{agnese.augello,giuseppe.caggianese,luigi.gallo}@icar.cnr.it

Abstract. In this work, we frame the area of research known as Human Augmentation (HA) from an enactive perspective. According to Enactivism, cognition arises through dynamic interaction between organism's sensorimotor capacities and its environment. In this perspective, it is important to evaluate how an augmentation of users abilities introduced by HA systems can affect their cognitive processes. We propose an architecture as a blueprint for designing and implementing HA systems. In our vision, the user and the system are intertwined: the system envelops and enhances the user's abilities with a combined augmentation on sensorial, motor and mental dimensions in a HA space. We discuss how many existing systems are more situated on augmentation planes and why a holistic vision covering the whole HA space is important. The architecture can drive HA systems' design, by introducing XR and AI solutions that can effectively expand the possibilities of human beings while ensuring low friction and high transparency in information access.

Keywords: Human augmentation · Augmented cognition · Enactivism · Mixed reality

1 Introduction

Technology has redefined the way we retrieve and access information; it has increasingly become embedded in our lives and support us in performing different tasks, extending our perception, memory, and processing capabilities. AR further enables such a process by superimposing digital objects and information on physical reality. The growing trend to intertwine the human being with smart devices and systems has led to the emergence of an interdisciplinary research field called both Human Augmentation (HA) and Augmented Humanity (AH) [18,24,26]. Among the several definitions [18], Raisamo et al. describe Human augmentation as *"An interdisciplinary field that addresses methods, technologies and their applications for enhancing sensing, action and/or cognitive abilities of a human. This is achieved through sensing and actuation technologies, fusion and fission of information, and artificial intelligence (AI) methods"* [24]. In addition to providing this insightful definition and an in-depth analysis of Human Augmentation and the related ethical risks, they observe that despite the existence

© Springer Nature Switzerland AG 2022
L. T. De Paolis et al. (Eds.): XR Salento 2022, LNCS 13445, pp. 219–228, 2022.
https://doi.org/10.1007/978-3-031-15546-8_19

of several systems augmenting human senses, actions and cognition, the vision of human augmentation is not yet established. According to the authors, there is a lack of architectures and models that integrate individual contributions in a holistic approach that could be considered the basis for practical applications. In addition to the above considerations, in our opinion, it is necessary to refer to a cognitive theory that could drive the design, implementation and evaluation of human augmentation systems. This is especially important in consideration that one of the intended outcomes of HA systems is to support and enhance the user's cognitive processes effectively. To the best of our knowledge, from what we observed in mixed reality literature, most of the current systems act mainly on a level of senses and partially on a level of action augmentation, while the potential that a cognitive augmentation can offer is not enough exploited. The primary purpose of MR systems is generally to support the user in performing a task by superimposing the necessary information on the physical world in real-time, information that can be therefore accessed and deepened through immediate and straightforward interactions, such as the use of gestures or verbal interaction with virtual assistants. In a prospective of HA, it is important to exploit the potential offered by new MR technologies and AI methodologies to not only extend/increase the user's perceptive and interactive experience, but also to naturally support and augment the user's cognitive processes while performing a task.

In the specific, starting from a brief analysis of the main theories of cognition, we propose a holistic, enactive view of HA, where user capabilities and cognition can be augmented as the effect of an increase of sense-motor possibilities in a mixed reality environment, and as a consequence of the introduction of AI modules. We'll discuss in detail our enactive perspective in Sect. 2, also proposing a blueprint architecture for the design of HA systems. In particular, considering three different dimensions of augmentation, we'll examine existing systems insisting more on "planes of augmentation", or on the whole augmentation space. Finally, in Sect. 3, we address the importance of such a holistic approach identifying some requirements that are necessary to obtain an effective HA.

2   An Enactive Human Augmentation Architecture

Our position is that HA Systems should be designed and implemented considering human cognition at its heart, to define the most appropriate technologies and methodologies to support and, in a sense, augment it. Modern cognitive theories, considers cognition situated in the physical and social context. According to approaches known as 4Es, cognition is embodied in our bodies (Embodied Cognition), embedded in the physical and socio-cultural context (Embedded Cognition), enacted through the active perception of the environment (Enactive Cognition) or extended by using extracranial structures (extended cognition) [5]. Among these theories, we embrace the enactive approach to cognition. Enaction is the idea that individuals create their own experience through their actions;

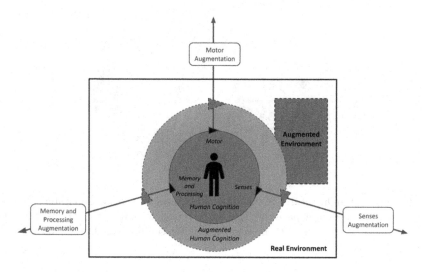

Fig. 1. Enative Perspective of a HA system: In green, human cognition arises from the three dimensions "senses", "motor" and "memory and processing". In blue, an augmented human cognition results from the enhancement along the three dimensions. An augmentation of the three dimensions allows the user to perceive and interact with elements embedded in the augmented environment. (Color figure online)

experience is the result of the reciprocal interaction between the organism's sensorimotor capacities and its environment, by means of transformative and not merely informational interactions [10]. Cognitive processes belong to the relational domain of the living body coupled to its environment [28]. Therefore, if cognition depends on the kind of experience that results from having a body with various sensorimotor capabilities [25], we can assume that a system that increases sensorimotor capabilities introduces radical changes in the interaction between the user and the environment that, according to an enactive view, can affect their cognitive processes. When we introduce new sensors and new modes of actions, we are augmenting the user's embodiment. A change in the embodiment leads to different interactions with the environment and consequently leads to changes at a level of cognitive processes [14, 25].

A schema illustrating our vision of a human augmentation system is depicted in Fig. 1. In the schema, we consider human cognition as the result of the individual's interaction with the environment through their sensorimotor, memory and processing capabilities. An augmentation can be therefore introduced on three dimensions named "senses", "motor" and "memory and processing". Such an augmentation allows the individual to interact in an augmented way with a hybrid real-virtual environment and can lead to an augmented cognition. Figure 2 shows a blueprint architecture for the design of HA systems. In the proposed architecture, a human-system coupling of the dimensions mentioned above enables new sensorimotor patterns, leading to new possibilities for actions and, therefore, cognition and experience. Augmenting the sensory dimension means

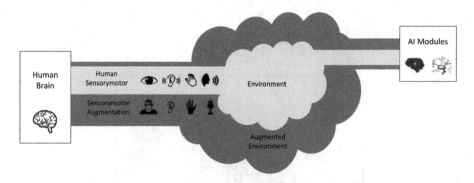

Fig. 2. Blueprint architecture for the design of HA systems. A human-system coupling enables new sensorimotor patterns, leading to new possibilities for actions, cognition and experience. Memory and processing capabilities can be extended by exploiting the system AI modules.

expanding the user's sensory possibilities by introducing devices equipped with sensors, such as visors, glasses, and haptic sensors. The motor dimension can be augmented by extending the physical capabilities of the human with artificial limbs, external tools or devices that capture user actions making them exploitable in a mixed environment, such as controllers, gloves, exoskeletons and tracking sensors. Human memory and processing capabilities can be supported and extended by exploiting the system processing and storage resources. The augmentation on this dimension can span from introducing simple modules and links to external resources to the integration in the system of advanced AI modules. In this context, both symbolic (ontologies and reasoners) and sub-symbolic modules (deep approaches, data-driven modules for the creation of semantic spaces) can be considered to analyse, classify and interpret information related to the interaction between humans and the environment, such as information perceived through sensory modalities, or concerning the performed actions.

In Sects. 2.1, 2.2 and 2.3 we will analyse, using non-exhaustive examples, how a partial augmentation can be achieved focusing mainly on a few of the identified dimensions. To analyse these systems in our perspective and along the defined dimensions, we interpret them as more situated on augmentation planes. The plans are partial views of the entire envisioned HA space; in our interpretation, they increase mainly perceptual, action or multimodal interaction capabilities. In Sect. 2.4 we'll describe some systems more in line with our holistic vision, since they cover the whole space and consider the effects on cognitive processes. In the final discussion, we will re-examine the proposed architecture, outlining possible approaches and risks to avoid in implementing our vision of HA.

2.1 Augmented Perception Plane

The augmentation on the perceptual level occurs by intervening mainly on the sensory and the memory and processing dimensions. The introduction of devices such as visors, glasses, haptic sensors, leads to an augmentation of the "senses" dimension. Combining this dimension with the introduction of methods of analysis, representation and understanding of what is observed, heard or touched in the environment, can enhance the user's perception. The two dimensions allows for an analysis and reasoning about data perceived through the added sensors.

Systems that rely mainly on this plane are those introduced to ensure greater accessibility, often to compensate a sensory gap by introducing elements to obtain a stimulus through other senses. This plane includes, for example, systems to assist indoor and outdoor navigation of visually impaired people, as in the case of the ARIANNA framework [9]. The possibility of replacing one sensory modality with another is also essential when it is impossible to get close to something, or even more, to touch it for people's safety or artefact protection purposes. By exploiting the touch sensory channel, some systems exploit 3D printed models that can be felt to compensate for vision. An augmentation on the "memory and processing" dimension allows the introduction of augmented information which can then be provided back to the user through audio, visual or tactile channels, which are activated by touching a model or moving along a path [13].

The senses can also be enhanced through the use of augmented reality devices. In this case, virtual elements can be introduced into the observed scene, increasing perception and knowledge, allowing the user to obtain information about something that is not accessible or no longer exists. As an example the MR game proposed in [8], recreates the setting of the archaeological excavations of the ancient Roman port of Naples. The game's mission is to spatially explore the augmented archaeological site, deepening understanding of the past artefacts' functions. The visualization of the excavation reconstruction is mediated by a sphere-shaped widget, which has a double function: allowing to explore the virtual environment and mitigate the FOV limitation of the device by adapting dynamically to it.

2.2 Augmented Action Plane

A contribution of augmentation mainly targeted on the "motor" and "memory and processing" dimensions define an Augmented Action plane, enabling new action possibilities. Extending the physical capabilities of human beings with external tools or devices, allows people to perform actions even in case of impairments or lower capacities due to age or illness. The use of specific devices allows for interaction in mixed reality. Technology becomes a support tool to maintain and promote wellness. It ensures that a limitation or deterioration of motor skills does not affect the individual's social life. Socially assistive technologies can work alongside people to fill in and complement human abilities enhancing their performances [21]. An example is the system proposed in [4], dedicated to patients needing rehabilitation from a stroke. This type of patient shows limitations in physical movements and, at the same time, requires monitoring of cognitive activities. The patients' motor abilities are mapped on virtual world dimensionalities, where they can perform simple cognitive games and exercises aimed at recovering the degrees of movement of the limbs with the supervision of a therapist. The adaptation of the game to the specific physical condition of the users augments their action possibilities as if in the virtual world they do not have physical limitations. Motor augmentation can also be obtained including in the environment actuators that can lead to a change in the state of the environment mediated by the system, which can also be accomplished by teleoperation or remote presence [27].

Combining the "motor" dimension with the "memory and processing" dimension, where the last dimension is augmented by modules for analyzing verbal and non-verbal signals leads to an extension of the possibilities of actions and their associated meanings. The system's ability to interpret a gesture, a gaze, or a speech signal in order to elicit a particular effect (in the real or virtual world) extends the meanings that simple actions could convey and increases the chances of communicating a specific intention or of changing the state of the environment. For example, let us consider the spontaneous movement of the eyes: it can be analyzed by the system to understand information related to users, for example their level of attention towards what they are looking at. In addition to this implicit augmentation mode, the user can employ this nonverbal communication modality to convey an intention explicitly. For this reason, the gaze is proposed and studied as a mode of interaction in place of other modalities, for example to trigger the selection of objects [23]. Similarly, also gesturing can be in a sense augmented by introducing modules that provide them a meaning or allow their use beyond the boundaries of physical reality [16].

2.3 Augmented Multimodal Plane

The systems that focus more on the "senses" and "motor" dimensions are often designed to offer multimodal experiences to users. The multimodal spaces ADA, Pulse and Dune offer an immersive and interactive experience. ADA is an intelligent room [7] which locates and identifies people by using vision, audition and touch senses and reacts with sound effects, images and games screened on a 360° ring of LCD projectors. Dune [1] is a light landscape where sensors and microphones capture participants' footsteps and sounds: the installation expresses a sort of mood; when is alone it is sleeping, while in the presence of people reacts with lights and sounds.

An engaging multimodal experience is provided by Sirena Digitale [3], a hologram impersonating a Parthenopean mermaid, performing the repertoire of traditional Neapolitan songs. The system, accessible as a permanent exhibition in Napoli, allows for a multimodal fruition of cultural and musical heritage. The visitors do not passively listen the songs proposed by the system, but they can interact with the system to choose a song and its language version. The interaction modality, based on sensors to track users' hands, was designed to exploit a set of intuitive gestures. The installation allowed to experiment with the haptic interaction providing the visitors with sensations in agreement with what they were observing. For instance, the user could perceive touching water while the hologram showed the mermaid immersed in the sea and getting feedback regarding interaction with the interface. The system shows the users the processed cultural information through the hologram, augmenting their visual sense and, at the same time, the visitors' touch employing the haptic device. Augmented multimodal experiences are often proposed for learning purposes. As an example, the Block Talks toolkit combines tangible computing and augmented reality (AR) technologies to foster sentence construction abilities [12].

2.4 Human Augmentation Space

In our enactive vision of human augmentation, we include more systems that address and combine all the aforementioned dimensions to support the user in performing a task and monitor how augmentation impacts the user's cognitive processes. An example is the use of AR in industrial settings to enable users to perform the task more efficiently. It has been proven that AR facilitates adequate working conditions and many perceptual/cognitively demanding tasks can be done better, easier, and faster compared with traditional methods. Ariansyah et al. [6] investigate the impact of different AR modalities in terms of information mode and interaction modality on user performance, workload and usability during a maintenance assembly task. The study found that the use of AR can reduce task-related workload but at the same time can induce non-task related workload.

In the context of the E-Brewery project [2] has been developed a system for industrial plants management. The system allows the user to analyze the overall production trend through specific information panels and intervene by modifying the settings of the industrial machines. The situated visualization of those panels permits to show the information in their spatial and semantic context just where the information is needed. The objective is to reduce the cognitive load due to information search and parameters control. The system continuously monitors such parameters and directly notifies them in the employee's headset. The system also aims to reduce interaction friction by employing some expedients, such as orienting the panels towards the user and allowing close and far interaction with its components.

Another scenario is the design of systems supporting users in daily activities, augmenting their abilities to complete everyday tasks. The aim of the study proposed in [17] was to introduce an intelligent assistant for individuals with mild cognitive impairment. The system exploits a serious game, adaptive fuzzy decision-making methods and IoT to augment the interaction possibilities of the users with the environment (enriched with AR objects) and help them in taking decisions more independently. The user's cognitive state is assessed according to the serious game scores.

An appealing context for human augmentation is the surgical environment. Technology is increasingly being employed in surgery [11], augmented reality for example is exploited for different purposes: to deepen the patient's condition and conduct simulations in a preoperative phase, for training or reexamination purposes, but also during the surgical procedure. It represents a challenging scenario to study and experiment human augmentation according to our enactive approach; the introduction of innovative devices and AI methodologies can strongly influence the possibilities of perception and actions of surgeons and their situations understanding and decision processes [14,15,22].

3 Concluding Remarks and Future Works

In this work we discussed an enactive perspective of HA. We have proposed a blueprint architecture for the design and implementation of systems that, by augmenting sensorimotor and mental dimensions in a synergic way, can expand the normal capabilities of users. We conceive such a HA system as somehow transparently intertwining with humans, i.e., the perception of the system should move to the background with respect to the offered opportunities, leading instead to the impression of an immersive, unmediated presence. It is therefore necessary to understand how the increase on the different dimensions and their combination may impact the user. Indeed, although different technologies used for human augmentation can lead to various advantages, adverse effects may be achieved. For example, the information to process may become excessive, resulting in a "negative effect" on the "memory and processing" dimension. XR technologies can support perception, search, memory and mental processing, providing visual cues that are lacking in the physical environment [20]. In some cases they can release mental resources, allowing users to focus more on accomplishing the task. In other cases the effect can be quite the opposite because introduced details in the observed objects can produce an information overload and force the user to perform additional interactions to select the information of interest [19]. In addition, allowing users to expand and increase their sensorimotor dimensions in an augmented environment may result in an increased mental workload due to the limited ability of humans to handle multiple sources of attention simultaneously and interpret both real and augmented information [20]. Another risk is that the access to information may not be transparent and introduce considerable friction. Some technologies could involve too many movements [29], leading to a "negative effect" on the "motor" dimension. The used devices should have an adequate resolution and FOV [19], to avoid a "negative effect" on the "senses" dimension.

Starting from these considerations, in future works, the proposed architecture will be deepened and exploited to design HA systems that, by introducing XR solutions and AI methodologies, can effectively expand the possibilities of human beings, pursuing and monitoring two important outcomes:

- Enactive augmentation outcome: an effective increase of user possibilities and abilities in the accomplishment of the task;
- Usability outcome: an high usability deriving from a high human-system coupleness level, characterized by low friction and a high transparency in information access.

As concrete example, let us consider as applicative scenario the laparoscopic surgery practice. An HA system can augment the sensorimotor abilities of surgeons during a preoperative or a operative task and as consequence, in the enactive perspective can influence their cognitive processes. This important aspect will drive the design and implementation of the HA system, to pursue an effective augmentation on the overall HA space. To implement the architecture modules for the specific scenario, it will be necessary to proceed from a cognitive analysis of the surgery practices, the involved cognitive processes and the required knowledge structures. As an example, usually surgeons analyze 2D computed tomography and magnetic resonance images to study the specific situation of a patient and define the best surgical strategy. The possibility to visualize a 3D model reconstructing the patient's organ, reduce the need to mentally reconstruct in 3D the patient's situation and perform visual imaginary processes. The possibility to manipulate such a 3D reconstruction of the organ, enable the ability to perform so-called epistemic actions, performed to obtain information that is difficult to obtain mentally. Therefore, starting from a cognitive analysis of surgical practices, in future works will be identified the more appropriate technologies and methodologies as well as evaluation procedures to accomplish such a HA vision.

References

1. Dune installation. https://archello.com/project/interactive-landscape-of-light-dune-40. Accessed 8 Mar 2022
2. E-brewery project. https://www.cerict.it/it/progetti-nazionali-in-corso/532-e-brewery.html. Accessed 08 Mar 2022
3. Sirena Digitale project. https://databenc.it/sirenadigitale/. Accessed 8 Mar 2022
4. Adinolfi, F., et al.: SmartCARE—an ICT platform in the domain of stroke pathology to manage rehabilitation treatment and telemonitoring at home. In: De Pietro, G., Gallo, L., Howlett, R.J., Jain, L.C. (eds.) Intelligent Interactive Multimedia Systems and Services 2016. SIST, vol. 55, pp. 39–49. Springer, Cham (2016). https://doi.org/10.1007/978-3-319-39345-2_4
5. Andrada, G.: Transparency and the phenomenology of extended cognition. LÍMITE Revista Interdisciplinaria de Filosofía y Psicología (2020)
6. Ariansyah, D., et al.: A head mounted augmented reality design practice for maintenance assembly: toward meeting perceptual and cognitive needs of AR users. Appl. Ergon. **98**, 103597 (2022)
7. Bullivant, L.: Ada: the intelligent room. Archit. Des. **75**(1), 86–90 (2005)
8. Caggianese, G., Gallo, L.: Field of view limitation-driven design of a mixed reality game for heritage sites. In: Ardito, C., et al. (eds.) INTERACT 2021, Part V. LNCS, vol. 12936, pp. 426–430. Springer, Cham (2021). https://doi.org/10.1007/978-3-030-85607-6_51
9. Croce, D., et al.: Supporting autonomous navigation of visually impaired people for experiencing cultural heritage. In: Seychell, D., Dingli, A. (eds.) Rediscovering Heritage Through Technology. SCI, vol. 859, pp. 25–46. Springer, Cham (2020). https://doi.org/10.1007/978-3-030-36107-5_2
10. Di Paolo, E., Rohde, M., De Jaegher, H.: Horizons for the enactive mind: values, social interaction, and play. In: Enaction: Towards a New Paradigm for Cognitive Science (2010)

11. Dias, R.D., Yule, S.J., Zenati, M.A.: Augmented cognition in the operating room. In: Atallah, S. (ed.) Digital Surgery, pp. 261–268. Springer, Cham (2021). https://doi.org/10.1007/978-3-030-49100-0_19

12. Fan, M., Baishya, U., Mclaren, E.S., Antle, A.N., Sarker, S., Vincent, A.: Block talks: a tangible and augmented reality toolkit for children to learn sentence construction. In: Extended Abstracts of the 2018 CHI Conference on Human Factors in Computing Systems, pp. 1–6 (2018)

13. Fitzgerald, D., Ishii, H.: Mediate: a spatial tangible interface for mixed reality. In: Extended Abstracts of the 2018 CHI Conference on Human Factors in Computing Systems, CHI EA 2018, pp. 1–6. Association for Computing Machinery, New York (2018)

14. Gatti, A.: On distinguishing sensorial and eliciting epistemic actions and on the relationship between perceptive structure of body and cognitive processes. In: Proceedings of the Annual Meeting of the Cognitive Science Society, vol. 27 (2005)

15. Gavriilidis, P., et al.: Navigated liver surgery: state of the art and future perspectives. Hepatobiliary Pancreat. Dis. Int. 21(3), 226–233 (2021)

16. Gentile, V., Milazzo, F., Sorce, S., Gentile, A., Augello, A., Pilato, G.: Body gestures and spoken sentences: a novel approach for revealing user's emotions. In: 2017 IEEE 11th International Conference on Semantic Computing (ICSC), pp. 69–72. IEEE (2017)

17. Ghorbani, F., Taghavi, M.F., Delrobaei, M.: Towards an intelligent assistive system based on augmented reality and serious games. Entertain. Comput. 40, 100458 (2022)

18. Guerrero, G., da Silva, F.J.M., Fernández-Caballero, A., Pereira, A.: Augmented humanity: a systematic mapping review. Sensors 22(2), 514 (2022)

19. Jeffri, N.F.S., Rambli, D.R.A.: A review of augmented reality systems and their effects on mental workload and task performance. Heliyon 7(3), e06277 (2021)

20. Klein, G.: Using cognitive task analysis to build a cognitive model. In: Proceedings of the Human Factors and Ergonomics Society Annual Meeting, vol. 44, pp. 596–599. SAGE Publications, Los Angeles(2000)

21. Matarić, M.J.: Socially assistive robotics: human augmentation versus automation. Sci. Robot. 2(4), eaam5410 (2017)

22. Menon, S.S.: ARiSE-Augmented Reality in Surgery and Education. Ph.D. thesis, Wright State University (2021)

23. Pfeuffer, K., et al.: ARtention: a design space for gaze-adaptive user interfaces in augmented reality. Comput. Graph. 95, 1–12 (2021)

24. Raisamo, R., Rakkolainen, I., Majaranta, P., Salminen, K., Rantala, J., Farooq, A.: Human augmentation: past, present and future. Int. J. Hum. Comput. Stud. 131, 131–143 (2019)

25. Scarinzi, A.: Why enactive world-making does not need the extended mind thesis. JOLMA 1(2), 237–254 (2020). e-ISSN 2723-9640

26. Schmidt, A.: Augmenting human intellect and amplifying perception and cognition. IEEE Pervasive Comput. 16(1), 6–10 (2017)

27. Stotko, P., et al.: A VR system for immersive teleoperation and live exploration with a mobile robot. In: 2019 IROS, pp. 3630–3637. IEEE (2019)

28. Varela, F.J., Thompson, E., Rosch, E.: The Embodied Mind, Revised Edition: Cognitive Science and Human Experience. MIT Press, Cambridge (2017)

29. Xi, N., Chen, J., Gama, F. et al.: The challenges of entering the metaverse: an experiment on the effect of extended reality on workload. Inf. Syst. Front. (2022). https://doi.org/10.1007/s10796-022-10244-x

XRShip: Augmented Reality for Ship Familiarizations

Yogi Udjaja[1]([✉]), Muhamad Fajar[1], Karen Etania Saputra[1], and Samsul Arifin[2]

[1] Computer Science Department, School of Computer Science, Bina Nusantara University, 11480 Jakarta, Indonesia
`yogi.udjaja@binus.ac.id`, {`muhamad.fajar,karen.saputra`}`@binus.edu`
[2] Statistic Department, School of Computer Science, Bina Nusantara University, 11480 Jakarta, Indonesia
`samsul.arifin@binus.edu`

Abstract. PT Pertamina Trans Kontinental (PTK) is a state-owned maritime company in Indonesia. PTK's vision and mission are to combine innovation with a dedication to digitization. As a result, we created the ShipXR Augmented Reality (AR) application to carry out that commitment and support business activities. The applications have been tested on a variety of devices. Metafrate Tools are evaluative measurement tools that we have created ourselves. The evaluation found that the program functions normally on both devices or that any serious difficulties were discovered. Furthermore, the result reveals that the application is very stable as a result of Metafrate Tools' output.

Keywords: Metaverse · Extended reality · Augmented reality · Vufora · State-owned enterprise · Frame rate evaluation · Frame rate tools · FPS measurement · FPS evaluation · FPS performance

1 Introduction

The Indonesian maritime sector now relies on narrow and ineffective traditional approaches for ship marketing. As a result, a more modern and coordinated alternative strategy is needed to improve the transportation sector's efficiency (Armanda et al. 2019). As a result, an alternative form of ship or vessel familiarization is required. Ship familiarization offers benefits to ship owners such as ease of familiarization and ship operational efficiency, as well as an introduction to the types and sizes of ships available for chartering (Surjandari et al. 2011). PT Pertamina Trans Kontinental (PTK) a subsidiary of PT Pertamina (Persero), is a state-owned enterprise that works in the maritime business. PTK's main business is to assist PT Pertamina (Persero) with everything from petroleum distribution to marine transportation, as well as acting as a General Agent and Handling Agent (Kontinental 2019). In keeping with Pertamina's purpose, PT. Pertamina (Persero) has committed to implementing a number of technology digitalization initiatives (Yudistiro et al. 2020).

One strategy of digitization is utilized to develop a ship familiarization or introduce ships and ease the charter ship procedure for the firm and vendor in order to meet

L. T. De Paolis et al. (Eds.): XR Salento 2022, LNCS 13445, pp. 229–238, 2022.
https://doi.org/10.1007/978-3-031-15546-8_20

the company's objective. Traditional Familiarization refers to the practice of familiarizing oneself with the ship by wandering around it (Tvedt et al. 2018). On the other hand, academics in the Human-Computer Interaction (HCI) and other study groups are increasingly researching and employing Extended Reality (XR) technology such as virtual, augmented, and mixed reality because of its potential for creativity, social, and psychological studies (Kristiadi et al., 2017; Sasmoko et al., 2019; Udjaja and Lailany, 2022). Augmented Reality (AR) is one of the XR technologies used in the application (Çöltekin et al. 2020; Fast-Berglund et al. 2018; Kwok and Koh 2021). AR is a technology that allows computer-generated virtual picture data to be projected in real time onto a live direct or indirect real-world environment (Fajar et al. 2021; Shi et al. 2019).

However, just a few studies have been conducted to determine how successful these are in the maritime industry (Chae et al. 2021; Renganayagalu et al. 2019). This application is expected to become one of the sector's marketing tools that can work in a metaverse environment, according to the findings of this study. Virtual reality (VR) and augmented reality (AR) environments are related to the metaverse (Mystakidis 2022). This environment combines physical reality with digital virtuality to enable multimodal, real-time interactions with virtual surroundings as well as dynamic interactions with digital artifacts, objects, and people (Lee 2021; Mystakidis 2022). We propose constructing a ship familiarization process using a familiarization approach employing Augmented Reality, due to the emergence of XR Technology and the public recognition of the terms metaverse. There is no significant difference between the virtual environment approach to familiarization and traditional familiarization, according to the previous study (Tvedt et al. 2018). The major suggestion of the Augmented Reality familiarization strategy is to introduce ship models to stakeholders including investors, vendors, companies, and others.

In this paper, we create and present XR Apps, an Augmented Reality application. We evaluate the application in terms of performance because there is no significant difference between virtual and traditional familiarization overall (Tvedt et al. 2018). Frame rates have been shown to be helpful in evaluating augmented reality applications from a performance standpoint in earlier studies (Fajar et al. 2021). We introduce Metafrate, a performance evaluation measure for applications such as Augmented Reality. As a result, we created Metafrate Tools to do a Metafrate-based evaluation. This paper is divided into six sections. The first section (Introduction) covers the research's origins and context. The second section (Related Research) goes over similar applications, studies, and evaluation metrics based on prior research. The third section (XRApps) describes and discusses the built Augmented Reality application. The evaluation and techniques utilized in this study are described in the fourth section (Method). The fifth section, titled " Result," describes and discusses the findings of the evaluation.

2 Related Research

AR in education and training is now considered to offer a more simplified method with more user adoption than ever before, thanks to technological advancements. AR offers a lot of potential in the real world for sophisticated learning experiences and information discovery (Azuma 1997; Lytridis and Tsinakos 2018; Shi et al. 2019). The future of

AR as a visualization tool is discussed in several research publications in the sectors of education and training. The interaction will undoubtedly be a part of education. Learning settings with augmented reality have the potential to be more productive, engaging, and dynamic than they have ever been. AR has the potential to not only engage students in a number of ways, but also to provide new content for everyone based on computer-generated three-dimensional environments and models. (Elmqaddem 2019; Lee 2012). Previous research, such as (Wimatra et al. 2019), created an Android-based AR application with 3D objects in the shape of a plane and its parts created using 3Dsmax and Blender applications, Unity as a game engine, and Vuforia as a library, with the goal of learning to recognize the shape and interior of the aircraft. Other research (Yudiantika et al. 2013) uses augmented reality to track objects with markers in museums and display real-time data. Because there are few studies on ship familiarization, one of the research projects (Armanda et al. 2019) focuses on developing PHP-based marketing website applications for ship products.

Previous research has shown that the performance of an XR-based application can be used to evaluate it (Louis et al. 2019; Roy and Kanjilal 2021). The frame rate can be used to determine the performance of Extended Reality-based applications such as Augmented Reality (Roy and Kanjilal 2021). In technologies like augmented reality, the frame rate is very crucial in presenting a presence (Louis et al. 2019). The frame rate has numerous levels that describe how well an application using XR technology performs (Rahman 2020). According to previous research, mobile applications should run at a frame rate of 24 to 30 Frames Per Second (FPS) in Normal Performance mode (Rahman 2020). If an application's frame rate is between 30 and 60 FPS, it is considered "Acceptable Performance" (Fajar et al. 2021; Roy and Kanjilal 2021). Meanwhile, if the application can run above 60 FPS, it is considered "Good Performance" (Fajar et al. 2021; Roy and Kanjilal 2021). They evaluated by comparing the frame rate in numerous situations on different devices, as they had done in earlier Augmented Reality experiments (Fajar et al. 2021).

3 XRShip

XRShip features a function that introduces the names of places and provides additional explanation on board (vessel); this feature is useful for new crew member introductions in education (see Fig. 2B). Original ships from PT Pertamina Trans Kontinental, such as the Transco Antasena and Patra Tanker II, are available (see Fig. 1B). We supply ship information specifications, such as Call Sign, Ship Type, Ship Status, and others, to suit the needs of our stakeholders (see Fig. 1C). This specification's information is required for presentation to stakeholders. On the other side, we're working on a performance assessment application for evaluation reasons called The Metafrate Tools, which can be utilized in an augmented reality application. (see Fig. 3).

XRShip application was created based on Augmented Reality (AR) using the Unity game engine and the Vuforia SDK (Software Development Kit). Vuforia SDK has been utilized in earlier research and can run on both mobile and desktop computers (PCs). Image Target is the foundation of our Augmented Reality application in XRShip. The Picture Target scans an image from a preset image target. Once the image has been scanned

Fig. 1. (A) Splash screen scene. (B) Home scene. (C) Main scene before scanning image target.

Fig. 2. (A) Main scene after scanning Image target and displaying some world canvas-based button to display information. (B) The main scene when displaying detail Information based on screen canvas. (C) The main scene when displaying specification information based on screen canvas.

by the camera, the selected ship object will appear. Users can move the smartphone in degrees-of-freedom (rotational movement) using the Augmented Reality visualization. These rotation movements include Looks Left and Right (LLR) from AR object, Pivots Left or Right (PLR) from AR object and Up Rotational and Down Rotational from AR object (RUD).

Three sceneries were created for XRShip, each with its unique collection of 2D and 3D assets. The first scene is the Splash Screen Scene (see Fig. 1A), which comprises 2D UnityUI (uGUI) components and displays the company and application logos. After twelve seconds, the Splash Screen Scene now has the option to automatically transition to the next scene. The second scene features The Home Scene (see Fig. 1B), which features a menu where the user can choose the type of ship they want to see. The digital ships Transko Antasena and Patra Tanker II are designed to look like real ships. The user will then move to the Main Scene after deciding (see Fig. 1C). The user can scan images with their smartphone camera to bring up the ship object in AR in the main scene.

After the image has been scanned, the ship appears in the Main Scene as AR. Many UnityUI canvases are used to display information. World Canvas, which is used as a button to trigger information, and Screen Canvas, which is used to display information, are the two types of canvas used. The data displayed is separated into two categories: Specs Information (Specification), which seeks to make the specifications of the presented ship as apparent as possible. The second section is Detail information (Detail), which depicts the term ship in relation to naval architecture. Among the details presented are the main deck, poop deck, forecastle, and explanations. The typewrite animation function is also utilized in the Details section to display an explanation and make it more interactive. The Specifications and Detail section of the information section seeks to educate or advertise the ship to various people who are interested in the ship's capabilities within the company's scope.

Ship details are provided to produce diverse 3D qualities in order to assist information that is more clearly given. The ship is a type of tanker with various features and uses. By including an interaction function, the user can see the property from a different angle. The three types of interactions offered are movement, zoom, and rotation. Because the movement is useful for changing the ship, the user does not have to manually move the Image Target on the touch screen with numerous fingers. The user can zoom in and out of the ship displayed in AR by pinching the touchscreen on the smartphone screen. Finally, rotating the image target or the shown ship in the real world eliminates the necessity for users to rotate the image target or the displayed ship.

4 Method

In order to demonstrate that the application works, we examine the XRShip application's performance based on frame rate, as we have done in earlier trials. Furthermore, Android-based smartphones are used on two different devices. The devices used for testing have the following configurations: (i) Device 1 Huawei Matepad R with 3 GB RAM, CPU 2×2.27 GHz Cortex-A76 and 6×1.88 GHz Cortex-A55, GPU Mali-G52 M5 (ii) Device 2 is the Samsung A80, which has 8 GB of RAM, a CPU with 2×2.2 GHz Kryo 470 Gold and 6×1.8 GHz Kryo 470 Silver cores, and a GPU with Adreno 618 graphics. We suggest the Metafrate (Measure the Action by Frame Rate) performance measuring evaluation for the evaluation. Metafrate is made up of four variables, each of which has a number of pieces or items that are determined by the custom action that can be performed in XRShip. The action is finished in a specific amount of time, which is measured in seconds (N) (see Table 1).

To obtain precise data, The Metafrate Tools is a tool (asset) that may capture the FPS over a defined time period. By writing a script that captures the FPS value in a specific time period to measure an action, we constructed a function (tool) to support an evaluation in Metafrate. This tool aims to aid Frame Rate recording while conducting custom actions. The user can give an action (item) a unique name and set a time range or interval (e.g., 10 s). When the user-activated Capture FPS button is pressed, the tools are able to begin recording frame rates in that time interval (see Fig. 3). Finally, the Metafrate Tools will capture, record, and save the action name along with the frame rate into Metafrate Tools Text in application storage at specific time intervals.

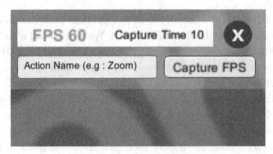

Fig. 3. The Metafrate Tools

Table 1. Metafrate

Variable	Explanation
Interface	During the application displays some uGUI interface components in several scenes, there are three diverse types of elements in the scene, namely Splash Screen Scene (Splash) in Fig. 1A, Home Scene, which displays the menu (Home) in Fig. 1B, and the Main Scene in the condition since the camera is turned on with target image has not been scanned or without AR object displays (Main) in Fig. 1C
Visualization	The Main Scene displays a ship object in AR, it is observed from the Degree of Freedom based on 3-DoF (rotational movement). The rotational movement is based on three items, namely Looks Left and Right (LLR) from ship object in AR, Rotate Up and Down (RUD) from ship object in AR, and Pivots Left and Right (PLR) from ship object in AR
Interaction	During the user interacts with the ship object to shift it (Movement), enlarge or minimize it (Zoom), change the rotation to visualize (Rotation)
Information	During the Main Scene displays the uGUI based on Canvas that is attached in the ship object in AR. That Interface consists of two components: namely specifications which are ship object information (Specification) and detailed items that describe the ship's parts (Details)

5 Result

N is a 10-s time interval (N = 10 s) between each action (Item) in Table 2. According to prior tests, each of these things could run at a regular frame rate of 24 to 30 frames per second. On Device 1, the lowest value (Avg = 24.2) is found in the Splash item in the Variable interface. Because the amount of frames during the Splash Screen is not large, the impact does not pose a significant problem after analysis. On Device 2, the average frame rate for Splash elements was normal for mobile devices (Avg = 29). On both the Home and Main items, the value is close to 30 FPS, with a low Standard Deviation number (Std < 0.5). When both the Home Scene and the Main Scene are active, the Frame Rate remains constant (see Table 2).

Table 2. Frame rate data tabulation

Variable	Item	N	Device 1				Device 2			
			Min	Max	Avg	Std	Min	Max	Avg	Std
Interface	Splash	10	11	30	24.2	7.83	23	29	28	2.16
	Home	10	29	30	29.2	0.42	29	29	29	0.00
	Main	10	29	30	29.2	0.42	29	29	29	0.00
Visualization	LLR	10	29	30	29.3	0.48	29	29	29	0.00
	RUD	10	30	30	30	0.00	29	29	29	0.00
	PLR	10	29	30	29.1	0.32	29	29	29	0.00
Interaction	Movement	10	29	30	29.5	0.53	29	29	29	0.00
	Zoom	10	29	30	29.6	0.52	29	29	29	0.00
	Rotation	10	29	30	29.1	0.32	29	29	29	0.00
Information	Specification	10	29	30	29.3	0.48	29	29	29	0.00
	Details	10	29	30	29.5	0.53	29	29	29	0.00

Note: (Min) The smallest frame rate value in the time range. (Max) the highest frame rate value in the time range. (Std) Value of standard deviation in the time range. (Avg) Average score over time

In the variable visualization part, the frame rate of the Transko Antasena ship object is explored. According to facts gathered during development, the Transko Antasena is more complicated and has a higher vertex level than the Patra Tanker II. The results of the Looks Left and Right from the Side of Ship Object (LLR) and Pivot Left and Right from the Top of Ship Object (PLR) tests on Device 1 indicated that the FPS value had changed (Frame Rate). However, the changes are minor, and the average ($0.32 < 0.48 < 1.00$) is expected to remain constant. Meanwhile, while rotating up and down from a ship object (RUD), steady results (Std < 0.01) are obtained. In the meantime, all objects on Device 2's visualization variable were normal (Avg $= 29$) and steady (Std < 0.01), with an average of 29 FPS (see Table 2). This means there will be no significant issues while the software visualizes shipping things in augmented reality on both devices (see Table 2).

In the interaction section, we discovered that Device 1 performs admirably on all items, averaging around 29 FPS and a Std value of ($0.6 < 1.00$), that movement and scale items utilizing pinch interaction are stable, and that rotating with the touchscreen produces a value of Std ($0.32 < 1.00$). On the other hand, on Device 2, all elements in the Interaction variable are very steady (Std < 0.01), and the average frame rate in every item is typical (Avg $= 29$). This shows that there are no serious issues when using the touchscreen technique in the program. As a result, this interaction has no impact on the application's performance (see Table 2).

Furthermore, the Information variable which consists of Specification items also shows results that tend to be stable with Std values ($0.48 < 1.00$) and indicates normal frame rate values (Avg 29.5) in Device 1. A slightly lower frame rate result was obtained in the Details item (Avg 29.3) while performing on Device 1. We suspect this is due to the implementation of the typewriter animation in Details Interface (Details item). However, the result tends to be stable with an Std value (0.53 < 1.00). Moreover, In Device 2 is very stable (Std < 0.01), and the average frame rate is normal in every item (Avg = 29) (see Table 2).

6 Conclusion

We construct an application named XRShip in this study, with the goal of supporting different business operations in the organization. Then, using Metafrate, we run a performance review. The outcome demonstrates that the program functions normally across all parts or items. Furthermore, the results show that the application runs are generally stable across all aspects. This also means that the application can be installed or moved on to the second level of review with responses. We also demonstrate through the Metafrate evaluation results that Metafrate tools can be used in different applications. This is also because the Metafrate measurement findings can be used to establish or examine the absence of a major problem in the ShipXR application. Furthermore, Metafrate Tools will focus on delivering other optional options, such as adding response time in the future. In addition, the SDK is being developed for public distribution in the form of Unity Packages, Assets, Sample Projects, and Documentation. As a result, the development of ShipXR will include the use of virtual reality glasses such as Google Cardboard to create more visualization options. Metafrate and Metafrate tools will also be employed in additional XR applications in future research and development.

Acknowledgment. As developers, we thank Mr. Hirau Akhmad Kekal and Mr. Irfan Aditya for their contributions to the project. We also want to express our gratitude to Mr. Yoga Keswara for his invaluable assistance during the development and evaluation process. We also want to thank Mr. Reza Ilham for providing us with a fantastic opportunity to start implementing extended reality applications in state-owned enterprises. Bina Nusantara University was also thanked. This research was made possible thanks to the Binus Initiative Project grant's facilities, finances, and infrastructure.

References

Armanda, R., Supomo, H., Baihaqi, I.: Desain Aplikasi website HUB marketing Berbasis E-Marketplace untuk Pemasaran Produk Kapal dan Komponennya. Jurnal Teknik ITS **8**(1), G1–G5 (2019)

Azuma, R T.: A survey of augmented reality. Presence Teleoperat. Virtual Environ. **6**(4), 355–385 (1997. https://doi.org/10.1162/pres.1997.6.4.355

Chae, C.-J., Kim, D., Lee, H.-T.: A study on the analysis of the effects of passenger ship abandonment training using VR. Appl. Sci. **11**(13), 5919 (2021)

Çöltekin, A., et al.: Extended reality in spatial sciences: a review of research challenges and future directions. ISPRS Int. J. Geo Inf. **9**(7), 439 (2020)

Elmqaddem, N.: Augmented reality and virtual reality in education. myth or reality? Int. J. Emerg. Technol. Learn. **14**(3), 234–242 (2019). https://doi.org/10.3991/ijet.v14i03.9289

Fajar, M., Udjaja, Y., Purwanto, E.S.: RTR AR photo booth: the real-time rendering augmented reality photo booth. In: 2021 1st International Conference on Computer Science and Artificial Intelligence (ICCSAI), vol. 1, pp. 289–294 (2021)

Fast-Berglund, Å., Gong, L., Li, D.: Testing and validating extended reality (xR) technologies in manufacturing. Procedia Manuf. **25**, 31–38 (2018)

Kristiadi, D.P., et al.: The effect of UI, UX and GX on video games. In: 2017 IEEE International Conference on Cybernetics and Computational Intelligence (CyberneticsCom), pp. 158–163. IEEE, November 2017

Kontinental, P.T.: Digitalization of Businesses Process and Strengthening HR (2019)

Kwok, A.O.J., Koh, S.G.M.: COVID-19 and extended reality (XR). Curr. Issue Tour. **24**(14), 1935–1940 (2021)

Lee, J.Y.: A study on metaverse hype for sustainable growth. Int. J. Adv. Smart Converg. **10**(3), 72–80 (2021)

Lee, K.: Augmented reality in education and training. TechTrends **56**(2), 13–21 (2012)

Louis, T., Troccaz, J., Rochet-Capellan, A., Bérard, F.: Is it real? Measuring the effect of resolution, latency, frame rate and jitter on the presence of virtual entities. In: ISS 2019 - Proceedings of the 2019 ACM International Conference on Interactive Surfaces and Spaces, pp. 5–16 (2019). https://doi.org/10.1145/3343055.3359710

Lytridis, C., Tsinakos, A.: Evaluation of the ARTutor augmented reality educational platform in tertiary education. Smart Learn. Environ. **5**(1), 1–15 (2018). https://doi.org/10.1186/s40561-018-0058-x

Mystakidis, S.: Metaverse. Encyclopedia **2**(1), 486–497 (2022)

Rahman, F.: Pengenalan Gedung Kampus Politeknik Negeri Lhokseumawe Menggunakan Voice Information Berbasis Virtual Reality. J. Infomedia **5**(1), 1–6 (2020)

Renganayagalu, S.K., Mallam, S.C., Nazir, S., Ernstsen, J., Haavardtun, P.: Impact of simulation fidelity on student self-efficacy and perceived skill development in maritime training. TransNav **13**(3), 663–669 (2019). https://doi.org/10.12716/1001.13.03.25

Roy, S.G., Kanjilal, U.: Web-based augmented reality for information delivery services: a performance study. DESIDOC J. Libr. Inf. Technol. **41**(3), 167–174 (2021). https://doi.org/10.14429/djlit.41.3.16428

Sasmoko, H.J., Udjaja, Y., Indrianti, Y., Moniaga, J.: The effect of game experience from counter-strike: global offensive. In: 2019 International Conference of Artificial Intelligence and Information Technology (ICAIIT), pp. 374–378. IEEE, March 2019

Shi, A., Wang, Y., Ding, N.: The effect of game–based immersive virtual reality learning environment on learning outcomes: designing an intrinsic integrated educational game for pre–class learning. Interact. Learn. Environ. **30**, 1–14 (2019). https://doi.org/10.1080/10494820.2019.1681467

Surjandari, I., Rachman, A., Dianawati, F., Wibowo, R.P.: Oil fuel delivery optimization for multi product and multi depot: the case of petrol station replenishment problem (PSRP). In: International Conference on Graphic and Image Processing (ICGIP 2011), 8285(Icgip), 82853Q (2011). https://doi.org/10.1117/12.914444

Tvedt, S., Oltedal, H., Batalden, B.M., Oliveira, M.: Way-finding on-board training for maritime vessels. Entertain. Comput. **26**, 30–40 (2018). https://doi.org/10.1016/j.entcom.2018.01.002

Udjaja, Y., Lailany, S.: Wacana Bencana: Android-Based Natural Disaster Simulation Game (2022)

Wimatra, A., Sunardi, S., Khair, R., Idris, I., Santosa, A.: Aplikasi augmented reality (AR) sebagai media edukasi pengenalan bentuk dan bagian pesawat berbasis Android. JurTI (Jurnal Teknologi Informasi) **3**(2), 212–221 (2019)

Yudiantika, A.R., Pasinggi, E.S., Sari, I.P., Hantono, B.S.: Implementasi augmented reality Di Museum: Studi Awal Perancangan Aplikasi Edukasi Untuk Pengunjung Museum. Yogyakarta: Konferensi Nasional Teknologi Informasi Dan Komunikasi (KNASTIK), Fakultas Teknologi Informasi, Universitas Kristen Duta Wacana (2013)

Yudistiro, M.R., Handayani, P.W., Hammi, M.K. (2020). Assessment of information technology governance capability levels and recommendations based on COBIT 5 framework in PT pertamina geothermal energy. In: Proceedings of 2020 International Conference on Information Management and Technology, ICIMTech 2020, August, pp. 103–107. https://doi.org/10.1109/ICIMTech50083.2020.9211144

Coupling Mobile AR with a Virtual Agent for End-User Engagement

Tina Katika$^{(\boxtimes)}$, Ioannis Karaseitanidis, and Angelos Amditis

Institute of Communication and Computer Systems, Athens, Greece
tina.katika@iccs.gr

Abstract. Virtual agents are introduced in our daily lives to guide end-users in a variety of tasks, contributing to a convenient user experience and boosting motivation and productivity. Along with the high data availability and modern algorithms, they contribute to the changing way end-users interact with their environment to obtain information, train, and socialize. In this study, we leverage the ability of mobile Augmented Reality (AR) technology to engage end-users to an immersive environment. Given the deep penetration of mobile phones in daily lives, we developed a mobile AR application that offers unique user-environment interaction. The AR application allows media visualizations, content manipulation, educational and gamification functionalities, and a virtual agent ensuring seamless interaction with the technology. The app aims to foster end-user engagement in sustainable practices (i.e., circular economy, water management, etc.) with a great potential to be applied in touristic and cultural appreciation, art and heritage promotion, etc. The purpose and functioning of the AR app, along with the system design and architecture, implementation challenges, and the end-users' feedback on the interactions with a virtual agent are thoroughly presented.

Keywords: Augmented reality · Mobile AR · User-engagement · Virtual agent

1 Introduction

Our experience of the surroundings and the environment we live in is as passive observers limiting the engagement potential to understand sustainable processes and how specific transformations and behaviors may impact our everyday lives. AR offers an interface between reality and the perception of reality, bridging the gap between the real and virtual worlds. AR provides experiences enabling end-users to move from observation to immersion which is often associated with the encouragement they experience in the digitally enhanced setting [1]. AR's immersive nature helps the audience see details, believe in actions, and connect events in a virtual story and their own lives.

For a seamless interaction between the physical and virtual environment of the end-user, a virtual agent can be employed for performing tasks supported by AR but also improve social interactions and motivation [2]. AR typically involves providing augmented capabilities related to objects and locations recognized in images or videos of the real world captured by an AR device. The presence of an agent can significantly

© Springer Nature Switzerland AG 2022
L. T. De Paolis et al. (Eds.): XR Salento 2022, LNCS 13445, pp. 239–248, 2022.
https://doi.org/10.1007/978-3-031-15546-8_21

improve the tasks involved with these processes. At the same time, the thoughts, feelings, and behaviors of end-users may be positively influenced. Related to user engagement, embodied agents can achieve higher social presence (as measured by self-report or behavioral data) by successfully integrating virtual content with the real world [3].

However good AR may be, adoption from the end-users is one of the most common issues this technology faces. People have demonstrated attraction to new ways of interaction as they like to communicate and share information as freely as possible. Still, at the same time, they judge harshly projects not well-executed, with poor usability, and not interesting content [4, 5].

The proposed mobile AR application fosters an environment of understanding and addressing the specific needs of each end-user, providing alternative representations and meta-data, fostering interactivity, and offering personalized information and guidelines. Attraction to content, acceptance of the technology, as well as usability and novelty of the proposed solution have been validated in Katika et al. [4, 6]. The present study emphasizes the adoption of the virtual agent supporting the AR functionalities and is organized as follows. First, work related to AR and virtual agents is presented. Then, the system design, the most dominant features (i.e., virtual agent), and the evaluation methodology are described. Before concluding and elaborating on the future research efforts, we present the results from our analysis.

2 Related Work

AR is currently being utilized across disciplines for end-user engagement and has been described to amplify educational success and motivation. Related to end-user engagement that is often associated with these parameters, mobile AR's adaptable nature can comfort the limitations that other engagement tools face. Immersive technologies have demonstrated a significant effect in educating end-users and offering an inclusive environment for people having a wide range of specificities [6].

Many researchers have elaborated on the use of AR in citizen participatory practices emphasizing the design and technical features but failing to communicate the adoption of their tools (e.g., [7, 8]). To bridge this gap, Katika et al. [4, 6] investigated the acceptance of AR as a citizen engagement tool aiming to empower and educate towards sustainability and circular economy practices. The results were promising, demonstrating that external variables, such as the end-user's tech-savviness, age, education level, and gender, did not impact the acceptance of AR technology.

To contribute to the research activity performed in end-user engagement utilizing AR technology and further define its acceptance, we propose the enhancement of gamification and educational mechanisms to improve interaction with AR. In this course of action, building a system with a virtual agent can influence how end-users view and use a system as the system can take on a more social role [9]. The agent's role is to influence users' perceptions and interactions as they treat the system more as another person and less as an impersonal tool. At the same time, the presence of an agent can leverage both verbal and non-verbal communication to achieve higher engagement levels and change users' perceptions and behaviors.

Barakonyi and Schmalstieg, [10], claimed that agents in mobile applications enrich interactions in AR. The authors detailed the design and implementation of agents in AR but did not elaborate on understanding users' reactions to them. Studying the user agent interaction, Kim and Welch, [11], described how an AR agent is situated in, and interacts with, the world affecting user's experience increasing a user's sense of presence.

Therefore, it is apparent that one of the main properties that have been proven to enable the adoption of virtual agents is the feeling of being with another person (co-presence). As Bevacqua et al., [12], reported this element should always be evaluated using a combination of objective and subjective measures (such as questionnaires or physiological responses, respectively).

3   Methodology

In this study, we present the design and development efforts of an AR agent as well as the results from its demonstration to investigate its adoption and effect on end-user engagement and motivation towards sustainability practices. We built a generic model for end-user engagement and customized the augmented content to sustainability and circular economy practices to make it more relatable to the participants involved. The evaluation process took place through active demonstrations and web surveys.

The mobile AR application presented in this section supports triggered AR content in three ways [13]. The supported marker-based function requires a marker (QR) to activate an augmentation related to media. Second, the location-based AR functionality uses the device's GPS location as a trigger to pair dynamic location with Points of Interest to augment relevant content. Finally, object recognition is a dynamic augmentation process based on trained Deep Learning Models.

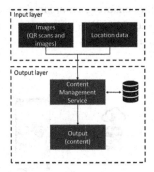

Fig. 1. The overall architecture of the mobile AR application.

Figure 1 shows the architecture of the mobile AR application (Circular) that contains three major components, including input, database, and an output engine. The app accesses the location of the device. In marker and object-based augmentations, both location and images are imported into the Content Management System to compare with the database. Then the output engine outputs the matching content on the screen of mobile devices.

3.1 Main Functionality and Use

The developed AR app acts as an engagement tool aiming to engage citizens in sustainability principles and practices, while empowering a sense of action towards this adoption. The main goal is to motivate and educate end-users around the notions of a living model supporting sustainability. Virtual content, consisting of 2D and 3D items, textual information, graphs, and quizzes, targets a wide range of end-users, aiming to motivate and engage them while improving their self-efficacy.

So far, the AR app has been used in Katika et al., [4, 6] to inform and engage the end-users on integrated sustainability frameworks that can be applied to our daily lives, in order for them to be able to: (a) identify their role in the water and waste value chain, (b) reflect on their part in the general picture of integrated water and waste management; (c) and to promote the idea of sustainability interventions as part of a broader awareness policy to ensure efficient and long-term viability of the resources.

3.2 System Design

The overall system architecture shown in Fig. 2 is designed to support two different users: the AR Content Management System (AR CMS) administrators and the mobile application users (CirculAR). The administrators produce and add content in the platform to create meaningful and educational experiences, so-called AR campaigns, that will be later enhanced with various gamification aspects and visualized by the mobile application end-users [4, 6].

The mobile AR application has undergone further improvements to support GPS localization and QR scanning for content attachment, but also has enabled object and image recognition functionalities ensuring a more in-depth penetration of the end-user to their environment. The virtual agent (ARis) is present in most functionalities and offers helpful tips and comments upon execution.

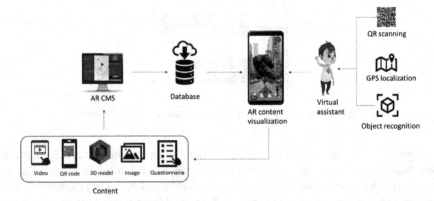

Fig. 2. The system design of the AR app supporting three means of interaction of the end-user with their environment through the virtual agent shown to the right side of the image.

Figure 3 summarizes the main functionalities of the mobile AR app, starting from registration, following with tutorial and help functions, selection of content, navigation to the nearest AR experience, interaction with the environment through the camera and object manipulation, object recognition, and the gamification and educative features [4, 6]. The functional features, describe the main services that the mobile application offers to the end-users as well as the main AR capabilities of our design. The gamification features, describe the features aiming to improve the user engagement, learning effectiveness and the educative character of the AR app.

3.3 Virtual Agent in AR

The virtual agent is introduced upon logging in to the mobile AR app where the agent presents the mission to the end-user. A tutorial page describes his name (ARis) and the places in the app where he is expected to guide the end-user to ensure that they benefit from his presence. Figure 4 shows four UIs where ARis provides helpful tips to the end-users, urging them to interact with their environment in three ways (GPS tracking, QR scanning, and object recognition).

The virtual agent is activated along with the AR features of the mobile application (e.g., camera activation for content visualization and manipulation). ARis uses textual communication to communicate with the end-user. Upon introducing ARis, it becomes apparent to the end-user that even if the interaction with the app becomes ambiguous, interaction with ARis will enable further steps. The virtual agent is programmed to react differently in all three user-environment interactions (GPS tracking, QR scanning, and object recognition), shedding light on follow-up activities to unlock the attached media.

4 Evaluation

There are challenges in performing usability evaluations on AR systems considering that they cannot rely on design guidelines for traditional UIs [14]. Evaluation is heavily dependent on the characteristics of the end-users (such as, novices, experts, casual users, frequent users, children, adults, elderly, etc.). We chose to pursue one of the proposed AR user evaluations to assess the effectiveness of the presence of the virtual agent [14]. Following the recruitment and demonstration from Katika et al., [4], we assessed how the presence of a virtual agent affected several engagement attributes of the participants involved. Information regarding the demographics and validation of measures can be found in the same paper. The AR virtual agent survey consisted of 6 items presented in Table 1. The Likert Scale was used to demonstrate the agreement of the participant with statements from "strongly agree" to "strongly disagree". At the same time, we assessed how the exposure of the participants to similar AR tools and mobile games, affected the virtual agent attributes (Table 2).

Fig. 3. The functional and gamification features of the AR engaging tool demonstrated through the user interfaces (UIs). a) the registration page (also available through Facebook), b) the profile editing (avatars are provided for further customization), c) the tutorial explaining all functionalities, d) the available campaigns with AR experiences and the distance from the end-user (the same UI displays the badges earned for each campaign as well as the overall score earned), e) the in-app map that navigates the end-user to the content of their selection (the camera button is activated as soon as the end-user reaches the AR experience), f) the camera activation from a GPS-enabled AR experience, g) the camera activation from a QR-enabled AR experience, h) the camera activation for object recognition, i) content visualization and j) content manipulation, k) a quiz and l) the user's leaderboard setting.

Fig. 4. a) The agent after login, and b) its functionality shown through tutorial. c) Prompting the end-user to assess an AR experience through QR scanning, and d) object recognition.

The participants were exposed to two functionalities of the virtual agent: a) helpful tips during GPS-enabled experiences, and b) guidance to scan a QR code.

The demographics and other characteristics of the participants, as well as the recruitment and survey process, can be found in Katika et al., [6]. Based on the feedback of 127 participants, we assessed that the engagement attributes under investigation were positively affected by the presence of ARis during the entire AR demonstration. Figure 5 shows all the trends in the engagement attributes.

Table 1. Survey items assessing how the virtual agent (ARis) affected the AR experience.

Nr	Statement
1	I will enjoy AR more due to the presence of ARis
2	ARis will improve my dedication to AR
3	The gender of the virtual agent will make an impression to me
4	The virtual agent will improve my dedication to AR
5	I will enjoy AR more due to the presence of the virtual agent
6	I would prefer a human like agent

Table 2. Summary of survey items assessing the tech-savviness and the educational level of the participants.

Item	Measure
Playing mobile games using AR	Everyday/Sometimes per week/Sometimes per month/Never

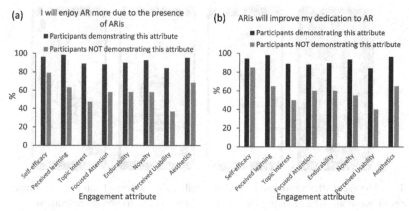

Fig. 5. The effects of the presence of ARis on the a) enjoyment and b) dedication to AR related to the user engagement attributes.

As demonstrated in Fig. 5, end-users scoring high on the engagement attributes (mentioned at the y-axis of each graph) declared that ARis made the AR experience more enjoyable and improved their dedication. End-users who scored low on the engagement attributes did not demonstrate the same acceptance of the virtual agent. The most dominant fluctuations are noticeable in terms of usability and topic interest. For end-users failing to understand the usability of the AR app and the sustainability practices presented, ARis did not improve their experience and dedication. Considering the novelty of the AR tool aiming to improve engagement in sustainable and circular practices, its acceptance has been identified before this study and reached more than 80% during the demonstration [4]. Therefore, it is apparent that evaluating the acceptance of such a novel technology prior to building upon more features and reaching a broader audience is crucial.

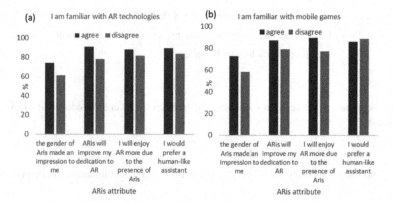

Fig. 6. The effects of AR and mobile game familiarity on the attributes of the virtual agent.

We proceeded by further showcasing the impact that familiarity with AR and mobile games had on the perception of the virtual agent. From the analysis presented in Fig. 6, it is shown that end-users more confident in both AR and mobile gaming were affected by the gender of the male-like virtual agent but also demonstrated higher dedication and enjoyment due to his presence. The preference towards a more human-like virtual agent did not show any significant fluctuation.

5 Conclusions and Future Studies

In this work, we reported designing and developing a user engagement mobile AR application coupled with a virtual agent supporting AR functionalities. End-user evaluation on the virtual agent reported an increase in the dedication and enjoyment of the AR app and demonstrated an increase in engagement attributes.

The contextually relevant tasks are recommended from the virtual agent to the user as an augmented message via text. Further implementation is required to enhance accessibility and inclusiveness in this field, as audio or other interfaces may allow the end-user to experience more virtual agent capabilities. Additionally, further research is required to understand whether the gender of the agent and the physical characteristics influence performance, as has been reported in VR from Makransky et al. [15].

Finally, leveraging AI functionalities and semantic understanding technology, the agent can transform into a virtual assistant to better understand user input, locate the required resource, and respond in an accurate, timely manner.

Funding. This research is based upon Work Supported by Funding from the EU Horizon 2020 project under grant agreement no. 869474 (water-mining).

References

1. Dede, C.: Immersive interfaces for engagement and learning. Science **323**(5910), 66–69 (2009). https://doi.org/10.1126/science.1167311
2. Miller, M.R., Jun, H., Herrera, F., Yu Villa, J., Welch, G., Bailenson, J.N.: Social interaction in augmented reality. PLoS ONE **14**(5), e0216290 (2019)
3. Kim, K., Maloney, D., Bruder, G., Bailenson, J.N., Welch, G.F.: The effects of virtual human's spatial and behavioral coherence with physical objects on social presence in AR. Comput. Anim. Virtual Worlds **28**, 1–9 (2017)
4. Katika, T., Bolierakis, S.N., Tousert, N., Karaseitanidis, I., Amditis, A.: Building a mobile AR engagement tool: evaluation of citizens attitude towards a sustainable future. In: Bourdot, P., Alcañiz Raya, M., Figueroa, P., Interrante, V., Kuhlen, T.W., Reiners, D. (eds.) EuroXR 2021. LNCS, vol. 13105, pp. 109–125. Springer, Cham (2021). https://doi.org/10.1007/978-3-030-90739-6_7
5. Mihai, D., Briciu, V., Duduman, I., Machidon, O.M.: A virtual assistant for natural interactions in museums. Sustainability **12**(17), 6958 (2020). https://doi.org/10.3390/su12176958
6. Katika, K., Karaseitanidis, I., Tsiakou, D., Makropoulos, C., Amditis, A.: Augmented reality (AR) supporting citizen engagement in circular economy. Circ. Econ. Sustain. (2022). https://doi.org/10.1007/s43615-021-00137-7

7. Pokrić, B., Krčo, S., Pokrić, M., Knežević, P., Jovanović, D.: Engaging citizen communities in smart cities using IoT, serious gaming and fast markerless Augmented Reality. In: International Conference on Recent Advances in Internet of Things, pp. 1–6. IEEE (2015)

8. Sanaeipoor, S., Emami, K.H.:. Smart city: exploring the role of augmented reality in placemaking. In: 2020 4th International Conference on Smart City, Internet of Things and Applications (SCIOT), pp. 91–98. IEEE (2020)

9. Lu, A., Wong, C.S., Cheung, R.Y., Im, T.S.: Supporting flipped and gamified learning with augmented reality in higher education. Front. Educ. **6**, 110 (2021)

10. Barakonyi, I., Schmalstieg, D.: Ubiquitous animated agents for augmented reality. In: 2006 IEEE/ACM International Symposium on Mixed and Augmented Reality, pp. 145–154. IEEE, October 2006

11. Kim, K., Welch, G.: Maintaining and enhancing human-surrogate presence in augmented reality. In: 2015 IEEE International Symposium on Mixed and Augmented Reality Workshops, pp. 15–19. IEEE (2015)

12. Bevacqua, E., Richard, R., De Loor, P.: Believability and co-presence in human-virtual character interaction. IEEE Comput. Graph. Appl. **37**(4), 17–29 (2017)

13. Edwards-Stewart, A., Hoyt, T., Reger, G.: Classifying different types of augmented reality technology. Annu. Rev. Cyberther. Telemed. **14**, 199–202 (2016)

14. Dünser, A., Billinghurst, M.: Evaluating augmented reality systems. In: Furht, B. (eds.) Handbook of Augmented Reality. Springer, New York (2011). https://doi.org/10.1007/978-1-4614-0064-6_13

15. Makransky, G., Wismer, P., Mayer, R.E.: A gender matching effect in learning with pedagogical agents in an immersive virtual reality science simulation. J. Comput. Assist. Learn. **35**(3), 349–358 (2019)

3D Audio + Augmented Reality + AI Chatbots + IoT: An Immersive Conversational Cultural Guide

Michalis Tsepapadakis[1], Damianos Gavalas[2](✉), and Panayiotis Koutsabasis[2]

[1] School of Science and Technology, Hellenic Open University, Patras, Greece
[2] Department of Product and Systems Design Engineering, University of the Aegean, Syros, Greece
{dgavalas,kgp}@aegean.gr

Abstract. Typical Augmented Reality (AR) cultural heritage (CH) guides adopt a visuo-centric approach, wherein visual virtual elements are superimposed onto the physical world. Recent research has investigated the use of Audio AR to evoke multisensory immersive experiences to visitors of CH sites adopting screen-free interfaces to ensure that user attention is not distracted from the physical exhibits. A parallel trend in the audience engagement programs of cultural institutions involves the employment of AI chatbots which are engaged in dialogues with visitors to provide meaningful responses to user questions. Herein, we present Exhibot, an intelligent audio guide system aiming at enhancing the user experience of CH site visitors. Exhibot represents the first-ever approach to combine Audio AR and chatbot technologies to enable natural visitor-exhibit interaction, while also leveraging IoT devices to contextualize the delivered information. The usability and utility of Exhibot has been tested in a case study in outdoors environment with the preliminary results indicating a very positive user experience.

Keywords: 3D audio · Audio augmented reality · Conversational audio guide · Chatbot · IoT · Context-awareness · Cultural heritage · Digital storytelling

1 Introduction

The use of audio guides has been long established as a tool to provide interpretive information to visitors of cultural heritage (CH) sites [13]. Later, the use of mobile multimedia guides, which complement audio content with visual information, has become widespread. A more recent development involves the use of augmented reality (AR) technologies as a means to inducing immersive experiences to cultural site visitors, mainly through the visual superimposition of interactive digital elements in the physical world [1].

Although AR tour guides have been shown to enhance users' learning in cultural contexts [1, 10] field research has highlighted the problem of technology interference, where users are distracted from the main purpose of their visit and mobile screens become the object of their attention even more than the exhibits [2]. Besides, the visitor becomes,

L. T. De Paolis et al. (Eds.): XR Salento 2022, LNCS 13445, pp. 249–260, 2022.
https://doi.org/10.1007/978-3-031-15546-8_22

for the most part, a passive recipient of the information. S/he is not given the opportunity or incentive to actively seek information and pursue exploratory learning, thus limiting the achievement of educational goals during the visit. Last, the guided tour experience does not offer interaction affordances similar to those offered in human guided tours; the information flow is essentially one-way (application → user) with the user being bound to predefined options for retrieving -static- content.

Audio Augmented Reality (AAR) represents a promising technological paradigm to address the challenge of producing distraction-free multisensory visiting experiences enabled by audio interfaces. AAR allows extending the real auditory environment with virtual audio entities [3, 11]. Taking into account the position and orientation of a user, an AAR system can create spatially registered sounds giving the illusion that the sound source is located at a specific point in the 3D space. In the context of CH applications, visitors may listen to 3D sound attributed either to 'talking' physical artefacts or invisible virtual characters [5, 6, 9, 16].

Recent developments in AI-powered chatbots create opportunities for the CH industry to address the problem of one-way flow of static information and provide a suitable tool to engage visitors in conversational interactions, where the chatbot provides meaningful responses to a number of user questions [14, 17]. In fact, a growing number of cultural institutions pursues this route, using bots as part of their audience engagement programs (e.g., to interact with their visitors through their websites, social media channels and mobile guides) [14].

This article introduces *Exhibot* (*exhi*bit+chat*bot*), a research prototype comprising an innovative combination of state-of-the-art technologies and tools to implement a pervasive personalized guide system for heritage sites. Exhibot utilizes AAR as a means of stimulating immersive experiences to CH site visitors. The latter engage in oral conversations with AI chatbots (powered by the IBM Watson Assistant cloud-based engine) impersonating selected 'talking' exhibits and artefacts. The adopted approach not only motivates visitors to undertake an exploratory role in information seeking but also suggests a natural and unobtrusive means of visitor-exhibit interaction thus minimizing the perceived technology interference and enhancing the overall cultural user experience. Besides AAR and AI chatbots, Exhibot also employs IoT technologies, in particular Bluetooth beacons and a small-factor wearable IMU device. The IoT devices are utilized to facilitate the extraction of contextual data (location and head orientation) so as to enable the provisioning of context-aware narratives. The Exhibot mobile application (executed on the visitors' Android phones) comprises the main user interface; the application interacts with the chatbot cloud service through forwarding user (vocal) input along with contextual data captured by the IoT devices and reproducing the received spatial sound (chatbot's response). The usability and utility of Exhibot has been tested in a case study in outdoors environment, with the preliminary results indicating a very positive attitude of users.

In the most typical use case, a user wearing a hat with a sewn wearable (BLE-enabled IMU) and carrying a smartphone with the Exhibot application approaches a 'talking' exhibit. The chatbot welcomes the visitor and engages her in a dialogue prompting her to ask questions so as to unlock information based on her interests. Notably, the chatbot uses first-person singular pronouns to signal an identity and increase its likeability and anthropomorphic perception by the user. Exhibot applies real-time binaural rendering of the chatbot's responses so as to match the relative position of the visitor's head to the sound source (i.e. the exhibit's location).

The remainder of the article is structured as follows: Sect. 2 reviews related work. Sections 3 and 4 present the design considerations and implementation aspects of the Exhibot system, respectively. Section 5 reports the key findings from the execution of the field trials. Last, Sect. 6 concludes our work.

2 Relevant Research

The use of audio guides has been long practiced in heritage sites providing screen-free guided tours [13]; thus, audio guides effectively address the problem of user distraction often reported for multimedia (including AR) guides which adopt a visuo-centric approach. Audio AR (AAR) represents a major step forward to generating immersive audio experiences; AAR technologies augment the user's auditory perception by embedding spatially registered virtual audio content into the physical environment. While conventional audio guides may be regarded as analogous to human guides, the AAR applications involve the exhibits themselves as storytellers that produce sounds or narrate stories in the first person, revealing sounds "hidden" in the environment and creating emotive visiting experiences.

Cliffe et al. [5] introduce two museum guide projects and investigate the challenges and opportunities of AAR as a means for promoting visitor exploration and engagement with cultural institutions, collections and exhibitions. In those projects, the spatial positions of virtual sound sources are set based on the estimation of the angle and distance of the listener as to real-world exhibits, where the estimation based on image tracking techniques. Thus, visitors are required to continuously 'scan' the environment with their camera to detect objects placed within line-of-sight; besides, the object tracking accuracy is prone to varying lighting conditions. These problems are addressed by an AAR guide system which estimates the user's location via her smartphone's GPS readings and her head orientation from an IMU mounted to a pair of headphones [6]. A similar AAR system configuration has been employed by users pursuing the exploration of a sound garden, i.e., a real urban park featuring a set of spatially situated sounds [16]. The authors found that the spatial audio encouraged a more exploratory and playful response to the environment. It is noted that in some of the above discussed implementations the user is only enrolled as a passive listener of automatically played 3D sounds [5, 16], while others account for users to control the audio scene either through voice commands [6] or head gestures [9].

The proliferation of open chatbot solutions unlocks opportunities for cultural organizations to incorporate chatbot technologies without committing human or computing resources. The adoption of chatbots in cultural sites has shown a positive effect on user engagement while offering an interactive, fun and always-on experience compared to traditional museum guides or organized visits [14]. AI chatbots inherently support personalized learning, helping to reduce intrinsic cognitive load and improve visitors' learning achievements [17].

Many of the museum chatbot examples are digital tour guides which respond to user questions or provide hints and information on how to make the most of the museum visit

[8]. Most of them offer text-based interaction where the chatbot undertakes a role analogous to human guides [8, 17]. Very few examples of voice-based interaction with chatbots exist. Such systems represent a significant step forward compared to conventional audio tours, as they do not rely on pre-prepared audio clips, but instead use cognitive chatbots to answers questions with broad conversational scope in real time.

For example, the Vocal Museum system [15] enables UWB-based indoors user localization while she moves through the exhibition space. Thus, it delivers relevant information (i.e., about the nearest artwork) via vocal or written interactions with a Google-powered chatbot. The visitor's app may also proactively invite her to request information about specific artworks. Besides utilizing location alone to infer context (thus having limited scene perception), the above presented system does not employ spatially registered sound. Therefore, it fails to unleash the full potential of conversational chatbots to bring subjects to life through experiential storytelling and support unmediated interaction between artworks and the visitors.

3   Exhibot: Objectives, Concept and Design Aspects

Exhibot has been developed following an agile user-centered system development methodology which comprised the following phases: domain analysis; requirements analysis; design; prototype development & testing; user evaluation. Domain analysis involved interviews with the identified stakeholders: curators from local cultural heritage institutions, local development and cultural agencies, professional guides, educators, general public.

The broad system design objective has been to create immersive experiences for *autonomous* guided tours of CH site visitors. We have opted for solutions of low-technological intensity to let the exhibits themselves (rather than the guide system) stand out as the protagonists of the tour.

The specific objectives included: the cultural guide system should not distract the user from his/her main visiting purpose, namely the experiential exploration of the site; users should be able to actively unlock information about points of interest (POIs)/landmarks based on their personal interests at their own pace through audio interaction; narratives must come from the exhibits/landmarks themselves in first-person so as to emotionally engage users; the system should provide guidance in a conversational manner to increase user engagement; narratives should be enriched with contextual parameters in order to be more meaningful and useful; the supportive technological infrastructure should be cost-effective, and easy to deploy.

The final concept dictated the combined use of AAR and AI chatbot technologies. The former unleashes the power of AR to create immersive experiences, yet, adopting eyes-free interaction and minimal user distraction. As regards the application domain of Exhibot, we target guided visits in large scale (preferable open-air) heritage sites as well as in public urban environments where the presence of visitors is relatively sparse, thus voice interaction is less likely to interfere with (or even disturb the experience of) other visitors.

We argue that Exhibot mostly suits guided visits to any kind of monuments, exhibits and artworks which legitimize AI chatbots to interact with the visitors using first-person narratives. For instance, the chatbot could effectively impersonate statues (e.g. to narrate a story from the depicted figure's perspective), artwork creators or historical figures associated with monuments (e.g., individuals who once lived or worked in monumental buildings).

The most typical use case supported by Exhibot involves a user approaching an exhibit. As soon as she enters a predefined zone around the exhibit (determined by the transmission range of a beacon), the chatbot which impersonates the exhibit narrates its story and invites the user to ask questions to unlock information. Though employing AAR techniques, users are immersed in storytelling as if the story was told by the exhibit itself, while still being able to control the narration flow by addressing questions for topics of their own interest. Another important feature of Exhibot aims at enhancing the whole experience enabling users to receive location and orientation-aware information. For instance, users could be prompted by the 'talking exhibit' to approach further in order to appreciate hidden details, receive different information depending on which side of the exhibit they look at or even obtain information for nearby attractions depending on their gaze direction.

4 Exhibot System: Implementation Aspects

4.1 Hardware Utilized in Exhibot

Exhibot's operation is based on off-the-self hardware employed to support the provisioning of context-aware services.

- A BlueBeacon Mini[1] sensor, a small form-factor BLE proximity beacon, is attached on selected exhibits. The beacon is powered by a replaceable battery with an estimated life of 18 months (see Fig. 1a, b). The application estimates the smartphone's distance from the beacon through measuring the signal strength (RSSI) of the received frames.
- A MetaMotionC[2] IMU (Inertial Measurement Unit), a wearable device that captures and streams activity measurements (taken from 3-axis gyroscope, magnetometer and accelerometer), utilized to infer user orientation data (see Fig. 1c). Its small form-factor makes it appropriate to sew on a standard hat worn by the user to estimate head orientation (see Fig. 1d). JSON-formatted activity data are streamed to the Exhibot mobile application via Bluetooth using the IMU's developers API.

In addition to collecting proximity and head orientation data, the mobile application also records the exact user's absolute position, taken from the smartphone's GPS receiver. Last, the user is required to use standard headphones with built-in microphone to enable hearing the spatial (3D) sound.

4.2 Exhibot's Architecture

The Exhibot system adopts a modular software design approach. The visitor uses a smartphone (Android) application and interacts with the system via an audio interface.

---

[1] https://blueup.myshopify.com/products/bluebeacon-mini.

[2] https://mbientlab.com/store/metamotionc/.

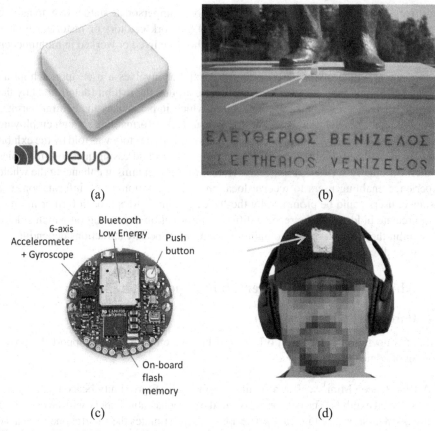

Fig. 1. (a) The BlueBeacon Mini beacon; (b) the beacon attached to a statue's base (c) the MetaMotionC wearable; (d) a user wearing a standard headset and a hat with the wearable device.

The key functions of the mobile application are: retrieval of raw sensor data from external sensors (i.e., the beacon device and the IMU) to infer user context (relative position of the user with reference to the exhibit's position and user head orientation); interaction with the chatbot, implementing a finite-state machine, which allows to monitor the state of the dialogue between the user and the chatbot.

The mobile app incorporates external software libraries, to enable local storage (in an SQLite database) of the identifying codes (UUIDs) of the registered beacons and also to configure spatial sound features. The spatialization of 3D audio is undertaken by the OpenAL software library[3] to. OpenAL is a cross-platform audio API, designed for efficient rendering of multichannel three-dimensional positional audio. OpenAL enables the adjustment of sound volume inversely with the user's distance from the beacon and the delivery of different sound volume to the left/right headphones depending on the user's orientation and relative position with reference to the beacon. In this way, it

---

[3] https://www.openal.org/.

becomes possible to create sounds giving the illusion that the sound source is located at a specific point in the 3D space (e.g., at a statue's mouth).

The implementation of the AI chatbot, which enables natural human-like conversations in Exhibot is based on the IBM Watson[4] engine. IBM Watson is built on deep learning and natural language processing (NLP) models to understand questions, find or search for the best answers, and react to the user's intended action. Watson also uses intent[5] classification to better understand the end-user statements context. The central component in the chatbot architecture is Watson Assistant which, given with a certain user-provided text statement (question), generates an appropriate response. Having interpreted the user intent, the chatbot follows a specified dialogue branch. In the Exhibot's implementation, the dialogue branch pursued by the chatbot is context-dependent, in the sense that it is conditioned on the contextual data (user's relative position and orientation) collected by the mobile app. For instance, the statement "I'd like to know what I am looking at" may generate different responses, depending on the user's position and head orientation.

The IBM cloud service ecosystem features a variety of complementary RESTful services utilized by Exhibot. In particular, the IBM's Speech-to-Text (STT) service enables fast and accurate speech transcription for the user's voice commands; likewise, the IBM's Text-to-Speech (TTS) service enables the conversion of written text (i.e., the chatbot's responses) into natural-sounding speech. For the purposes of Exhibot, we have exclusively used the English language to address voice messages to the user.

4.3 User-Exhibit Interaction in Exhibot

The user-exhibit interaction comprises the following steps (see Fig. 2):

1. The user issues a voice command captured by her headset's microphone.
2. The user's speech is streamed to the IBM Watson STT service which converts speech to a text transcript and returns it to the mobile app.
3. The app calculates the user's relative position (with reference to the exhibit) and head orientation.
4. A data tuple encompassing the text transcript of the user's statement along with the position/orientation data is forwarded to Watson Assistant, which returns the chatbot-generated reply in text. Watson Assistant may retrieve content from external providers, when the user's statement relates to seeking information about specific topics that do not match any of the predefined intents.
5. The chatbot's response is submitted to IBM Watson TTS service which converts the written text to audio.
6. The audio is passed to the OpenAL library which configures the spatial aspects of the chatbot's vocal response (based on the user's spatial context) and delivers it to the user's headphones.

---

[4] https://www.ibm.com/products/watson-assistant.

[5] An intent is a collection of user statements carrying the same meaning. For instance, the questions "How old are you?" and "When have you been born?" are classified under the same intent.

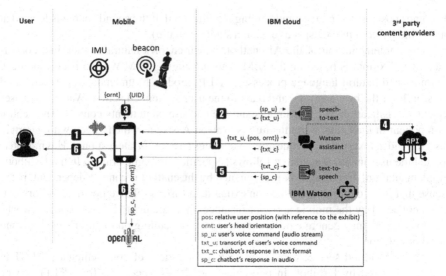

Fig. 2. Information exchange among the Exhibot system components.

The typical user-exhibit dialogue session starts with the exhibit greeting the user and then narrating an introductory story (around 90"). Unless the user formulates a question within short time after the end of the narration, the chatbot repeatedly suggests topics for further narratives to maintain user's engagement and motivate her in actively exploring available content. Then, it proposes the user to receive information about nearby POIs towards the direction she currently looks at (unless the user requests such information on her own initiative). The session is terminated when the user either declines listening to other narratives or exits the exhibit's surrounding zone. It is noted that the Exhibot's dialogue session management adopts well-established principles for effective voice user interface design [7] so as to provide a satisfying conversational experience.

5   Field Trials

Exhibot has undergone user evaluation trials for three days in November 2021. As a case study, we have chosen the statue of Eleftherios Venizelos (a prominent Greek politician of the early 20th century) in Heraklion, Greece. The statue is situated in the city center, close to several other tourist attractions.

Overall, we have edited 34 different intents representing different conversation topics (e.g. short greeting dialogues, narratives relevant to the history of the statue and selected episodes of his life and/or details of the historical context, information about nearby attractions and the city, weather reports, 'non-match' statements, etc.). The overall objective of dialogue management has been to simulate a natural human-to-human conversation[6]. The TTS service has been configured to utilize a male voice impersonating the statue's character.

---

[6] Exhibot demonstration: https://youtu.be/alW3RU41aZo.

Fig. 3. Users evaluating Exhibot during the field trials.

Exhibot has been evaluated by 16 individuals (7 F) 22–58 years old (median 31). Experimental sessions lasted 4′ 15″ on average. Initially, the evaluators were briefed by the developers about the main functional elements of Exhibot; then, they were asked to wear a hat with the IMU attached (see Fig. 1d). Afterwards, they were invited to install and start the application in their smartphone, to approach the statue and freely interact with the system (see Fig. 3).

Upon the termination of the experimental session, the evaluators were invited to answer a standard SUS (System Usability Scale) questionnaire [3]. The average received SUS score has been 82.1 (grade: A/Excellent). Figure 4 illustrates the SUS questionnaire results with respect to the average scores and the coefficient of variation (i.e. the ratio of standard deviation to mean value). Interestingly, the mean coefficient of variation for questions #4 and #10, which assess the learnability of the system [11], has been 52.8% while for the remainder questions, which assess the usability of the system, has been 24.4%. This result indicates a relatively high level of variability between users' opinions with regards to the perceived learnability of the system.

Then, the participants have been interviewed to allow the technical team collecting feedback about specific system aspects as well as about their overall perceived UX. The participants reported that the speech generated by the IBMs TTS service was reasonably realistic and that the pauses experienced in the dialogues resembled those of a normal conversation. The spatial sound was found accurately registered as to the user's standpoint. They also reported positive impressions both with respect to the relevance of the chatbot responses and the sense of participating in a human-like communication. Overall, the system was found easy to use, mainly due to the adopted natural means of

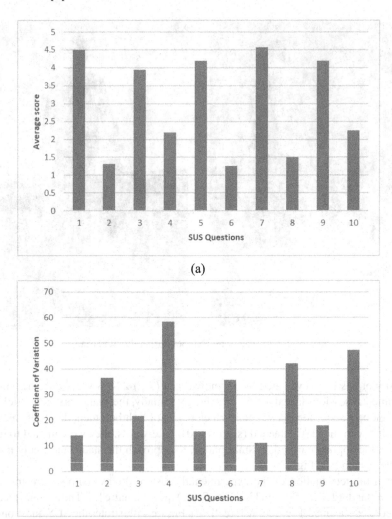

(a)

(b)

Fig. 4. SUS questionnaire results per question: (a) average scores; (b) coefficient of variation.

interaction. The participants also reported a sense of immersion (it felt like they really engaged in a dialogue with the statue's character, while the voice sounded like being spoken by the statue. Last, Exhibot was found to incite participants to learn by guided discovery (i.e., to seek information about topics relevant to the narrative, which they would not be interested to learn otherwise).

On the other hand, some participants reported a feeling of awkwardness when observed by bystanders, while other expressed privacy concerns (i.e., potential privacy violations due to streaming their voice to a cloud service).

6   Conclusion

This article introduced Exhibot, a conversational cultural heritage audio guide system. Exhibot provides visitors of heritage sites with a tool that enables autonomous guided tours and encourages active user involvement and discovery learning. The main design objective has been to evoke multisensory immersive experiences minimizing the perceived technology interference and enabling natural and unobtrusive means of interaction. Exhibot suggests a conceptual model wherein the exhibit or monument is not overshadowed by technology and visitors undertake an exploratory role in information seeking.

The key technological means utilized to pursue the above stated objectives have been: (a) Use of AAR to avoid the visuo-centric bias of 'traditional' AR guides and minimize the distraction coming from the interaction with mobile devices; besides, AAR offers far more than conventional audio guides as it enables the delivery of 3D sound (where the sound source is spatially registered at the exhibit), thus bringing subjects to life through experiential storytelling supporting unmediated interaction with visitors. (b) Use of AI chatbots as a means to engaging visitors in natural human-like dialogues with conversational agents which impersonate 'talking exhibits' and prompt users to unlock information, thus supporting personalized learning. (c) Use of IoT devices to capture contextual data (proximity and orientation) to enable the provisioning of context-aware narratives. Evidently, Exhibot achieves far more than a mere combination of state-of-the-art technologies; it makes a solid contribution in cultural guides research, on a conceptual, software engineering, technical and user experience level. It represents the first-ever attempt to synthesize the power of AAR, chatbot and IoT technologies to create immersive learning experiences and to generate added value out of the creative interplay among the involved technologies.

The field trials of the Exhibot system indicated a very positive attitude of evaluators with respect to usability, engagement, fun element, learning effectiveness, immersion, utility.

Acknowledgement. This research was funded by the Research e-Infrastructure "Interregional Digital Transformation for Culture and Tourism in Aegean Archipelagos" {Code Number MIS 5047046} which is implemented within the framework of the "Regional Excellence" Action of the Operational Program "Competitiveness, Entrepreneurship and Innovation". The action was co-funded by the European Regional Development Fund (ERDF) and the Greek State [Partnership Agreement 2014–2020].

References

1. Aliprantis, J., Caridakis, G.: A survey of augmented reality applications in cultural heritage. Int. J. Comput. Methods Herit. Sci. **3**(2), 118–147 (2019)
2. Aitamurto, T., Boin, J.B., Chen, K., Cherif, A., Shridhar, S.: The impact of augmented reality on art engagement: liking, impression of learning, and distraction. In: International Conference on Virtual, Augmented and Mixed Reality, pp. 153–171 (2018)
3. Brooke, J.: Sus: a "quick and dirty" usability. Usab. Eval. Ind. **189**(3) (1996)

4. Chatzidimitris, T., Gavalas, D., Michael, D.: SoundPacman: audio augmented reality in location-based games. In: 2016 18th Mediterranean Electrotechnical Conference (MELE-CON), pp. 1–6 (2016)
5. Cliffe, L., Mansell, J., Cormac, J., Greenhalgh, C., Hazzard, A.: The audible artefact: promoting cultural exploration and engagement with audio augmented reality. In: Proceedings of the 14th International Audio Mostly Conference: A Journey in Sound, pp. 176–182 (2019)
6. D'Auria, D., Di Mauro, D., Calandra, D.M., Cutugno, F.: A 3D audio augmented reality system for a cultural heritage management and fruition. J. Digit. Inf. Manag. **13**(4) (2015)
7. Fischer, J.E., Reeves, S., Porcheron, M., Sikveland, R.O.: Progressivity for voice interface design. In: Proceedings of the 1st International Conference on Conversational User Interfaces, pp. 1–8 (2019)
8. Gaia, G., Boiano, S., Borda, A.: Engaging museum visitors with AI: the case of Chatbots. In: Giannini, T., Bowen, J. (eds.) Museums and Digital Culture. Springer Series on Cultural Computing. Springer, Cham (2019). https://doi.org/10.1007/978-3-319-97457-6_15
9. Kaghat, F.Z., Azough, A., Fakhour, M.: SARIM: a gesture-based sound augmented reality interface for visiting museums. In: 2018 International Conference on Intelligent Systems and Computer Vision (ISCV), pp. 1–9 (2018)
10. Kasapakis, V., Gavalas, D., Galatis, P.: Augmented reality in cultural heritage: field of view awareness in an archaeological site mobile guide. J. Amb. Intell. Smart Environ. **8**(5), 501–514 (2016)
11. Lewis, J.R., Sauro, J.: The factor structure of the system usability scale. In: International Conference on Human Centered Design, pp. 94–103 (2009)
12. Nagele, A.N., et al.: Interactive audio augmented reality in participatory performance. Front. Virtual Real. **46** (2021)
13. Nikolarakis, A., Koutsabasis, P., Gavalas, D.: A location-based mobile guide for gamified exploration, audio narrative and visitor social interaction in cultural exhibitions. In: 24th International Conference on Human-Computer Interaction (HCI International 2022)
14. Schaffer, S., Gustke, O., Oldemeier, J., Reithinger, N.: Towards chatbots in the museum. In: mobileCH@ Mobile HCI (2018)
15. Sernani, P., Vagni, S., Falcionelli, N., Mekuria, D.N., Tomassini, S., Dragoni, A F.: Voice interaction with artworks via indoor localization: a vocal museum. In: International Conference on Augmented Reality, Virtual Reality and Computer Graphics, pp. 66–78 (2020)
16. Vazquez-Alvarez, Y., Oakley, I., Brewster, S.A.: Auditory display design for exploration in mobile audio-augmented reality. Pers. Ubiquit. Comput. **16**(8), 987–999 (2012)
17. Varitimiadis, S., Kotis, K., Pittou, D., Konstantakis, G.: Graph-based conversational AI: towards a distributed and collaborative multi-chatbot approach for museums. Appl. Sci. **11**(19), 9160 (2021)

eXtended Reality

Regulating the Metaverse, a Blueprint for the Future

Louis B. Rosenberg[✉]

Unanimous AI, San Francisco, CA, USA
Louis@Unanimous.ai

Abstract. The core Immersive Media (IM) technologies of Virtual Reality (VR) and Augmented Reality (AR) have steadily advanced over the last thirty years, enabling high fidelity experiences at consumer prices. Over the same period, networking speeds have increased dramatically, culminating in the deployment of 5G networks. Combined, these advancements greatly increase the prospects for widespread adoption of virtual and augmented worlds. Recently branded "the metaverse" by Meta and other large platforms, major corporations are currently investing billions to deploy immersive worlds that target mainstream activities from socializing and shopping to education and business. With the prospect that corporate-controlled metaverse environments proliferate society over the next decade, it is important to consider the risks to consumers and plan for meaningful regulation. This is especially true in light of the unexpected negative impact that social media platforms have had on society in recent years. The dangers of the metaverse are outlined herein along with proposals for sensible regulation.

Keywords: Metaverse · Augmented reality · Virtual reality · Extended reality · Mixed reality · XR · VR · AR · MR · Technology policy · Regulation

1 Background: Regulating Media

To provide a legal and philosophical basis for regulating the metaverse, it is helpful to first consider the arguments made for regulating social media, as the metaverse can be viewed as an evolution of the same industry. Assessing media regulation, Yale Law professor Jack Balkin describes social media companies as "key institutions in the twenty-first century digital public sphere," and explains that the public sphere "doesn't work properly without trusted and trustworthy institutions." He further argues the public sphere created by social media is a successor to the public sphere created by print and broadcast media, which has been regulated by industry norms and government oversight for generations [1]. At the same time, Balkin and other scholars express caution about government overreach, as aggressive regulation could be damaging to free speech and other rights, with some experts pushing for industrywide self-regulation as a means of reducing the level of necessary government oversight [2, 3].

As we look beyond social media to emerging technologies such as virtual reality and augmented reality, similar principals apply. In fact, the impact of the metaverse on the

L. T. De Paolis et al. (Eds.): XR Salento 2022, LNCS 13445, pp. 263–272, 2022.
https://doi.org/10.1007/978-3-031-15546-8_23

public sphere is likely to be far more encompassing. In October of 2021, Meta CEO, Mark Zuckerberg, wrote that *"in the metaverse, you'll be able to do almost anything you can imagine — get together with friends and family, work, learn, play, shop, create."* Clearly the metaverse, when broadly deployed by major corporations, aims to take on the role of "a public sphere" as much if not more than today's social media [4]. This transition may happen very quickly, as Meta is currently investing $10B per year with the stated goal that *"within the next decade, the metaverse will reach a billion people, host hundreds of billions of dollars of digital commerce, and support jobs for millions of creators and developers."* And Meta is not the only major corporation aggressively pursuing this vision – Apple, Microsoft, Google, Sony, Samsung, and Snap are just a few of the major players that have announced significant efforts [5, 6].

With Big Tech investing hundreds of billions of dollars in VR and AR products and services, it is reasonable to predict that the metaverse will impact the lives of billions of people within the next decade, driving a global transition from flat media to immersive media as the primary means by which users access digital content [7]. This will greatly impact the public sphere, giving even more control to platform providers than current technologies. With the industry heading in this direction, it's prudent to assess the potential dangers of the metaverse and propose viable regulatory solutions [8].

2   The Metaverse: Potential Dangers

At the highest level, "the metaverse" can be described as the societal transition from the current information ecosystem based on flat media viewed in the <u>third person</u> to a new ecosystem rooted in immersive media experienced in the <u>first person</u>. It is not the technology itself that is dangerous to consumers, but the fact that metaverse platforms are likely to be controlled by large corporations that implement aggressive business tactics similar to those used in social media. Before describing the potential dangers of corporate controlled metaverse platforms, it's worth defining "metaverse" along with the two primary forms of immersive media, "virtual reality" and "augmented reality":

> **Virtual Reality** *(VR) is an immersive and interactive simulated environment that is experienced in the first person and provides a strong sense of presence to the user* [27].

> **Augmented Reality** *(AR) is an immersive and interactive environment in which virtual content is spatially registered to the real world and experienced in the first person, providing a strong sense of presence in a combined real/virtual space* [9, 28].

> **Mixed Reality** *(MR) is commonly used as a synonym for augmented reality, referring to mixed environments of real/virtual content.* **Extended Reality** *(XR) is commonly used as a catch-all for all forms of immersive media* [9, 28].

> **Metaverse** *is a persistent and immersive simulated world that is experienced in the first person by large groups of simultaneous users who share a strong sense of mutual presence. It can be fully virtual (i.e. a* **Virtual Metaverse***) or it can be layers of virtual content overlaid on the real world (i.e. an* **Augmented Metaverse***)* [9, 27, 28].

With these definitions in place, we can express that a virtual metaverse is a fully simulated world in which users are represented by graphical avatars under their own individual control (see Fig. 1). Conversely, in an augmented metaverse the human participants are generally not avatar-based but interact directly with a real world that is embellished with virtual content (see Fig. 2).

Fig. 1. Virtual Metaverse example – The Nth Floor (Accenture)

Fig. 2. Augmented Metaverse example - (Keiichi Matsuda)

Some say a metaverse must also include rules of conduct and a fully functional economic system, but that is still open for debate [10]. In addition, some say that a metaverse must also be interoperable, enabling items and transactions to be exchanged among multiple virtual worlds. While it is likely that many virtual and augmented worlds will enable such interoperability, the definition of metaverse should allow for self-contained worlds, as it is likely that many platforms will be independent.

Whether a virtual metaverse or an augmented metaverse, it's not the technology itself that poses a risk to society, but the fact that the infrastructure required to enable immersive worlds will give powerful corporations the ability to monitor and mediate intimate aspects of our lives, from what products, services, and information consumers are exposed to, to what experiences they have throughout their day and who they are having those experiences with. On the surface, this may sound similar to the impact of today's social media, which also monitors and mediates user experiences, but in the metaverse the corporate intrusion could be far more extensive.

To explore the potential dangers in a structured way, it is helpful to describe what has been called *The Three M's of the Metaverse,* for the core social problems relate to the inherent ability of metaverse platforms to monitor users, manipulate users, and monetize users [11, 27]. These three risk-categories are outlined as follows:

(1) Monitoring Consumers in the Metaverse: Over the last two decades, technology companies have made a science of tracking and characterizing users on their platforms, as it enables the sale of targeted advertising [12]. Such targeting has been a boon for advertisers and a windfall for media platforms, resulting in some of the most valuable corporations in history. Unfortunately, such targeting has exploited consumers, reduced personal privacy, and has made social media a polarizing force by allowing third-parties to deploy customize messaging that is skillfully aimed at very specific demographic groups. This tactic has had the widespread effect of amplifying existing biases and preconceptions in populations, radicalizing political views and spreading misinformation [13].

In the metaverse, these problems are likely to get significantly worse [14]. That's because the technology will not just track where users click, but where they go, who they're with, what they do, what they look at, even how long their gaze lingers. Immersive platforms will also track facial expressions, vocal inflections, and vital signs, while intelligent algorithms use such data to predict each person's real-time emotional state [15–17]. Tracking will also include real-time monitoring of user gait and posture, assessing when users slow down to browse products or services. Metaverse platforms will even monitor manual reach, assessing when users grab for objects (both real and virtual) and tracking how long they hold the objects to investigate. This will be especially invasive in the *augmented metaverse* in which user gaze, gait, and reach will be monitored in the real world, for example while shopping in augmented physical stores. This may sound extreme, but real-time tracking of manual interactions with real objects goes back to the first interactive augmented reality system developed in 1992 at Air Force Research Laboratory (Virtual Fixtures platform) [7, 24, 26].

These various forms of tracking, when taken together, suggest that the platform providers controlling the metaverse will not just monitor how their users act, but how they react and interact, profiling their behaviors and responses at far deeper levels than has been possible in traditional media platforms. Of course, the danger is not merely that these personal parameters can be tracked and stored, but that advertisers and other paying third parties will be able to use this invasive data to manipulate consumers with targeted content more effectively than ever before.

(2) Manipulating Experiences in the Metaverse: From the early days of radio and television, advertisers have skillfully influenced public opinion on topics ranging from consumer products to political beliefs. With the advent of social media, custom targeted advertising has greatly increased the persuasive ability of promotional messaging [18, 19]. In the metaverse, such targeting will get far more personal and the content will get much harder to resist [20]. That's because in today's flat media environments like Facebook, Instagram, TikTok and Twitter, consumers are generally aware when they are being targeted by an advertisement and can muster a healthy dose of skepticism [21]. But in the metaverse, consumers won't be targeted with simple pop-up ads or promo-videos. Instead, consumers will have immersive content injected into their world such as virtual people, products, and activities that seem as real as everything else around them.

Virtual Product Placements (VPPs) are likely to become a widespread advertising tactic within the metaverse, being applied in both virtual and augmented worlds. We can define a VPP as *a simulated product, service, or activity injected into a virtual or augmented world on behalf of a paying sponsor such that it appears as a natural element of the ambient environment.* Such advertising can be quite effective because users can easily mistake a VPP for an organic part of the world that was serendipitously encountered rather than a targeted piece of promotional material that was deliberately inserted into the world for that specific user to experience.

For example, imagine walking down the street in a virtual or augmented world. In both cases, the platform provider will be able to track where you are in real-time, how fast you are moving, and what your gaze is aimed at. The platform provider will also have access to a database about your behaviors and interests, values and affiliations, and of course, your shopping history. In social media, this personal information would be used to target you with traditional advertising. In the metaverse, platform providers will be able to manipulate your real-time experiences. This might include seeing particular cars on the virtual streets, particular brands in store windows, or even include simulated people drinking a particular soft drink as they walk past you on the sidewalk. You might assume that everyone around you is seeing the same thing, but that is not the case – these promotional experiences could have been injected exclusively for you by the platform provider on behalf of a paying third party.

Virtual People *(Veeple)*: In the metaverse, immersive promotional content will go beyond inanimate objects to AI-driven simulated people that look and act like any other user but are computer generated spokespeople controlled by AI engines programmed to pursue a persuasive agenda. These virtual people will be placed in the metaverse, targeting specific users for either (i) passive observation or (ii) direct engagement. As a passive example, a targeted user might observe two people having a conversation about a product, service, or idea. The targeted user may assume that the people are other metaverse users like themselves, not realizing that a third party injected those virtual people into their world as a subtle form of targeted advertising. As an active example, a targeted user may be approached by a virtual person that engages them in promotional conversation. The interaction could be so authentic, the targeted user would not realize it's an AI-driven avatar with a persuasive agenda.

For both active and passive uses, these AI agents will have access to profile data collected about the targeted user, including their preferences, interests, and a historical record of their reactions to prior promotional engagements. These AI agents will also have access to real-time emotional data generated by capturing facial expressions, vocal inflections, and vital signs of the targeted users. This will enable the AI agent to adjust conversational tactics in real-time for optimal persuasion. Even the manner in which these simulated people appear will be crafted for maximum persuasion—their gender, hair color, eye color, clothing style, voice and mannerisms—will be custom generated by algorithms that predict which sets of features are most likely to influence the targeted user based on previous interactions and behaviors (see Fig. 3) [11, 23, 27].

Fig. 3. Virtual human used in social trust research (2019) [23]

In the past, researchers have expressed doubt that computer generated avatars could successfully fool consumers, but recent research suggests otherwise. In a 2022 study, researchers from Lancaster University and UC Berkeley demonstrated that when virtual people are created using generative adversarial networks (GANs), the resulting faces are indistinguishable from real humans to average consumers. Even more surprising, they determined that average consumers perceive virtual people as "more trustworthy" than real people [29]. This suggests that in the not so distant future, advertisers will prefer AI-driven artificial humans as their promotional representatives.

(3) Monetizing Users in the Metaverse: It is worth acknowledging that platform providers are not charities but commercial entities that require substantial revenue to support the interests of their employees and shareholders. And because the public has resisted paying subscriptions for access to online platforms, the most common industry model is to provide free access in exchange for widespread advertising, focusing largely on "targeted ads" that can be precisely delivered based on the unique behaviors and interests of individual users. It is the business model of targeted advertising that has driven platform providers to pursue extensive tracking and profiling of their users. This suggests that one way to reduce these risks in future metaverse platforms is to shift from ad-based to subscription-based business models [11, 27].

3   The Metaverse: Non-regulatory Solutions

As described above, shifting from ad-based to subscription-based models could reduce the motivation that platform providers have to profile and target their userbase. This is only viable if consumers are willing to pay for access in other ways. Therefore we cannot assume this approach will become widespread anytime soon. We also can't assume that the industry will adopt trusted norms and practices that eliminate abuses without government oversight. And finally, we can't expect consumers to simply opt-out of the metaverse if they are uncomfortable with extensive tracking and targeting. This is because metaverse platforms will become a primary access point to digital content. Similar to how consumers cannot opt out of using the internet, opting out of the metaverse would mean missing out on critical information and services [8, 11, 27].

4   The Metaverse: Regulatory Solutions

Assuming the problems are not solved by industry norms or by changes in business models, we will need some level of government regulation of the metaverse to prevent exploitation of consumers. Of course, the question is – *what needs to be regulated?* A number of ideas are presented below for consideration:

4a – Restrict User Monitoring: As described above, platform providers will have access to everything their users do, say, touch and see inside the metaverse. It may be impossible to prevent this, as tracking is required for real-time simulation of virtual interactions. That said, platform providers should not be allowed to store this data for more than the short periods of time required to mediate whatever virtual experience is being generated. This would greatly reduce the degree to which providers can profile user behaviors over time. In addition, providers should be required to inform the public as to what is being tracked and how long it is retained. For example, if a platform is monitoring the direction and duration of a user's gaze as you walk through a virtual or augmented world, that user should be overtly notified at the time of tracking.

4b – Restrict Emotional Analysis: As outlined above, the metaverse will likely use advertising algorithms that monitor personal features such as facial expressions, vocal inflections, posture, and vital signs including heart rate, respiration rate, blood pressure, and galvanic skin response captured through smart-watches and other wearable devices such as earbuds. Unless regulated, these invasive physiological reactions will be used to generate emotional profiles and optimize marketing messages, enabling AI agents to adjust their conversational strategy in real time. Regulation should be crafted to limit the scope of such advertising. In addition, users should be overtly informed whenever these personal qualities are being tracked and stored for promotional purposes.

4c – Regulate Virtual Product Placements: inside the metaverse, advertisers will move away from traditional marketing methods like pop-up ads and promo-videos, instead leveraging the immersive features of the technology. This will include targeting users with promotional artifacts and activities injected into their environment that seem authentic. In the metaverse, a targeted user might observe a person walking down the street drinking a particular brand of soft drink. That observation will influence the targeted user, consciously or subconsciously, especially if they notice many people drinking that same product throughout their day. Users could easily believe such virtual experiences were authentic serendipitous encounters that reflect popularity of the particular drink in their community, when really, it was a targeted experience, injected into their world for an unknown third-party. And this type of manipulation can extend beyond soft drinks to biased political messaging, disinformation, and other socially destabilizing forms of agenda-driven promotion.

Because it may be impossible to distinguish between authentic and manufactured experiences in the metaverse, regulation is needed to protect consumers. At a minimum, platform providers should be required to inform users of all product placement in virtual or augmented worlds, ensuring that targeted promotional content is not misinterpreted as natural serendipitous encounters. In fact, product placements should be *visually distinct* from other items in the metaverse, enabling users to easily identify when an artifact has been placed in the world for promotional purposes versus organic content. In addition, platform providers should be required to inform users who sponsored each virtual product placement. Such transparency will greatly protect consumers.

4d – Regulate Virtual People: as described above, the most manipulative form of persuasion in the metaverse is likely to be through agenda-driven artificial agents that engage users in promotional conversation. These virtual people will look and sound like other users in the metaverse, whether the virtual world uses cartoon avatars or photorealistic human representations [14, 22]. Regardless of fidelity, if consumers can't distinguish between real users and artificial agents, they can be misled into believing they are having a natural encounter when really, it's a targeted promotional interaction.

To protect consumers, platform providers should be required to overtly inform users whenever they are engaged by conversational agents controlled by AI engines. This becomes even more important when the algorithms have access to user behavioral profiles and real-time emotional data. At a minimum, platforms should be required to distinguish, through overt visual and audio cues, that a user is interacting with an artificial agent and further indicate if the agent can perform emotional analysis. In addition, the use of vital signs such as blood pressure and heart rate should be banned for use in AI-driven conversational advertising.

5   The Metaverse: Is It Worth It?

In 2021, the Aspen Institute published an 80 pages report indicating that social media platforms have become a "force multiplier for exacerbating our worst problems as a society."[25] As described above, metaverse platforms could create similar but more extreme problems, enabling more invasive forms of profiling and more persuasive methods of targeting.[27] Despite these risks, the metaverse has enormous potential to unleash creativity and productivity, expanding what it means to be human. To enable these benefits while protecting consumers, government and industry actors should push quickly for meaningful and aggressive regulation.

References

1. Balkin, J.: How to regulate (and not regulate) social media. J. Free Speech Law **71**, 1–31 (2021). (Knight Institute Occasional Paper Series, No. 1, 25 March 2020, Yale Law School, Public Law Research Paper)
2. Weissmann, S.: How not to regulate social media. The New Atlantis. **58**, 58–64 (2019). https://www.jstor.org/stable/26609117
3. Cusumano, M., Gawer, A., Yoffie, D.: Social media companies should self-regulate. Now. Harvard Business Review (2021)
4. Letter, F., Zuckerberg, M. 28 October 2021. https://about.fb.com/news/2021/10/founders-letter/
5. Strange, A.: Facebook planted the idea of the metaverse but Apple can actually populate it. Quartz, 29 November 2021. https://qz.com/2095986/facebook-is-marketing-the-metaverse-but-apple-can-make-it-real/
6. Burke, E.: Tim Cook, AR will pervade our entire lives. Silicon Republic, January 2020
7. Rosenberg, L.B.: Augmented reality: reflections at thirty years. In: Arai, K. (ed.) FTC 2021. LNNS, vol. 358, pp. 1–11. Springer, Cham (2022). https://doi.org/10.1007/978-3-030-89906-6_1
8. Rosenberg, L.: The Metaverse needs Aggressive Regulation. VentureBeat Magazine, 4 December 2021. https://venturebeat.com/2021/11/30/the-power-of-community-3-ways-scopely-keeps-players-engaged-entertained-and-connected/
9. Rosenberg, L.: VR vs. AR vs. MR vs. XR: What's the difference? Big Think. 18 January 2022. https://bigthink.com/the-future/vr-ar-mr-xr-metaverse/
10. Park, G.: Silicon Valley is racing to build the next version of the Internet. The Washington Post, 17 April 2020. https://www.washingtonpost.com/video-games/2020/04/17/fortnite-metaverse-new-internet/
11. Rosenberg, L.: Fixing the Metaverse: Augmented reality pioneer shares ideas for avoiding dystopia. Big Think; 9 December 2021. https://bigthink.com/the-future/metaverse-dystopia/
12. Tucker, C.: The economics of advertising and privacy. Int. J. Indust. Organiz. **30**(3), 326–329 (2012). ISSN 0167–7187
13. Crain, M., Nadler, A.: Political Manipulation and Internet Advertising Infrastructure. J. Inf. Policy. **9**, 370–410 (2019). https://doi.org/10.5325/jinfopoli.9.2019.0370
14. Rosenberg, L.: Metaverse: Augmented reality pioneer warns it could be far worse than social media. Big Think. 6 November 2021. https://bigthink.com/the-future/metaverse-augmented-reality-danger/
15. Ivanova, E., Borzunov, G.: Optimization of machine learning algorithm of emotion recognition in terms of human facial expressions. Proc. Comput. Sci. **169**, 244–248 (2020)
16. van den Broek, E.L., Lisý, V., Janssen, J.H., Westerink, J.H.D.M., Schut, M.H., Tuinenbreijer, K.: affective man-machine interface: unveiling human emotions through biosignals. In: Fred, A., Filipe, J., Gamboa, H. (eds.) Biomedical Engineering Systems and Technologies. CCIS, vol. 52, pp. 21–47. Springer, Heidelberg (2010). https://doi.org/10.1007/978-3-642-11721-3_2
17. Boz, H., Kose, U.: Emotion extraction from facial expressions by using artificial intelligence techniques. BRAIN. Broad Res. Artif. Intell. Neurosci. **9**(1), 5–16 (2018). ISSN 2067–3957
18. Zarouali, B., et al.: Using a personality-profiling algorithm to investigate political microtargeting: assessing the persuasion effects of personality-tailored ads on social media. Commun. Res. 0093650220961965 (2020)
19. Van Reijmersdal, E.A., et al.: Processes and effects of targeted online advertising among children. Int. J. Advert. **36**(3), 396–414 (2017)

20. Hirsh, J.B., Kang, S.K., Bodenhausen, G.V.: Personalized persuasion: tailoring persuasive appeals to recipients' personality traits. Psychol. Sci. **23**(6), 578–581 (2012)

21. Wojdynski, B.W., Evans, N.J.: The covert advertising recognition and effects (CARE) model: processes of persuasion in native advertising and other masked formats. Int. J. Advert. **39**(1), 4–31 (2020)

22. Rosenberg, L.: The Metaverse will be filled with Elves. TechCrunch, 12 January 2022. https://techcrunch.com/2022/01/12/the-metaverse-will-be-filled-with-elves/

23. Zibrek, K., Martin, S., McDonnell, R.: Is Photorealism Important for Perception of Expressive Virtual Humans in Virtual Reality? ACM Trans. Appl. Percept. **16**(3), 19 (2019). https://doi.org/10.1145/3349609

24. Rosenberg, L.: The Use of Virtual Fixtures as Perceptual Overlays to Enhance Operator Performance in Remote Environments. Technical report AL-TR-0089, USAF Armstrong Laboratory, Wright-Patterson AFB OH (1992)

25. Commission on Information Disorder Final Report, Aspen Institute, November 2021. https://www.aspeninstitute.org/publications/commission-on-information-disorder-final-report/AspenDigital

26. Rosenberg, L.: How a Parachute Accident Helped Jump-start Augmented Reality. IEEE Spectrum, 7 April 2022. https://spectrum.ieee.org/history-of-augmented-reality

27. Rosenberg, L.: Regulation of the metaverse: a roadmap. In: The 6th International Conference on Virtual and Augmented Reality Simulations (ICVARS 2022), 25–27 March 2022, Brisbane Australia (2022)

28. Metaverse 101: Defining the Key Components. VentureBeat, 5 February 2022. https://venturebeat.com/2022/02/05/metaverse-101-defining-the-key-components/

29. Nightingale, S., Hany, J.F.: AI-synthesized faces are indistinguishable from real faces and more trustworthy. In: Proceedings of the National Academy of Sciences, 22 February 2022. https://doi.org/10.1073/pnas.2120481119

Do Presence Questionnaires Actually Measure Presence? A Content Analysis of Presence Measurement Scales

Olivier Nannipieri[✉]

IMSIC, University of Toulon, Toulon, France
`olivier.nannipieri@univ-tln.fr`

Abstract. Il the field of virtual and augmented reality environments, presence is usually defined as the feeling of being in one place or environment even when you are physically located in another. The main question of this contribution is: do presence questionnaires actually measure presence? This article proposes a critical analysis of measuring the experience of presence in immersive environments on the basis of a content analysis of the items of 38 presence measurement scales. This contribution is based on a literature review of original presence questionnaires. The aim is to conduct an analysis of academic publications proposing the creation of a scale for measuring presence funded on an examination of the validity of content of the items of the questionnaires. In conclusion, this article highlights the lack of relevant presence conceptualization and appropriate items in presence questionnaires because of several inconsistencies existing between the definition of this concept and the dimensions and items used in the literature.

Keywords: Presence · Questionnaire · Measurement · Scales

1 Introduction[1]

Frederick Brooks, professor of computing science at the University of North Carolina, had tested a flight on a simulator of 747. He said: «Within a very few minutes I was not in a simulator, I was flying the airplane: taxiing, taking off, climbing out, circling the airport, and trying to keep the plane at constant altitude.» (Brooks 1999).

Strange testimony: F. Brooks is (really) in a flight simulator and, at the same time, he is (virtually) in a plane. Even if this virtual flight is created artificially by a machine, F. Brooks lives this experience as if he was really present in this plane. Which is the meaning of this paradox?

Assert that this is a sensory illusion is simplistic because this answer is based on a prejudice: only the objective reality has a value and is authentically true. The virtual reality is an illusion of the senses.

Yet, the objective reality, understood as the existence of an environment independent from the observer, is inaccessible by definition (Kant 1787). We have access only

---

[1] The author would like to thank the CARTT of the University Institute of Technology of the University of Toulon.

L. T. De Paolis et al. (Eds.): XR Salento 2022, LNCS 13445, pp. 273–295, 2022.
https://doi.org/10.1007/978-3-031-15546-8_24

to our representation of the reality (Hume 1748). Because the reality which we objectify is already a construction produced by our faculties (Kant 1787), besides, a social construction (Berger and Luckmann 1966).

Besides, if only the objective reality has a value, why do we dive us into a novel, why are we captivated by a movie, why can we be immersed in a virtual environment? And why, in these situations, do we feel to be in a place in which we are not really? This feeling has a name: the presence.

Defined as the feeling to be in an environment in which we are not really, the presence is a kind of experience of no-mediation (Lombard and Ditton 1997), of transparency (Marsh 2003) or of pseudo-natural immersion (Arnaldi et al. 2003). So, to be present, it seems necessary, for the human being, to forget that he lives this experience through a medium (immediacy). That is why when immersed in a virtual environment, humans can have a paradoxical experience: the feeling of presence or the sense of "being there" in the virtual environment (He et al. 2018). The user is physically in a real environment but could feel or believe that he/she is in another environment (virtual). Several measurement tools are used in the scientific literature to estimate this experience.

Presence can be estimated based on behavioral measures such as performance and postural reactions (*e.g.* Freeman et al. 2000; Lepecq et al. 2009; Ohmi 1998) and physiological or neurophysiological measures such as heart rate and skin conductance (*e.g.* Alcaniz et al. 2009; Gandy et al. 2010; Nacke and Lindley 2008; Peperkorn et al. 2015; Villani et al. 2012; Wiederhold et al. 2003). But the widely used measurement tools were post-rated questionnaires (or sometimes questionnaires rated during exposure: IJsselsteijn et al. 1998). Except for a few qualitative studies (Freeman and Avons 2000; Muratore and Nannipieri 2016; Wissmath et al. 2009), post-rated questionnaires were analyzed based on quantitative methods (means, internal consistency, and exploratory factor analyses).

This article proposes a critical analysis of measuring "presence" in immersive environments (i.e., the feeling of being in one place or environment even when you are physically located in another). The aim of this contribution is to conduct an analysis of academic publications proposing the creation of a scale for measuring presence based on an examination of the validity of content of the items of the questionnaires. In conclusion, this article highlights the lack of relevant presence conceptualization, several inconsistencies in the definition and structure of presence and inappropriate items in presence questionnaires.

2   Methodology: Criteria for Including and Excluding Publications

The inclusion and exclusion criteria for publications applied to the measurement collection procedure were based on three types of sources.

The first source was a literature review based on a search of measurements in the Google Scholar database using the following keywords (in English and French): presence + measure + virtual reality; presence + measure + augmented reality; presence + measure + video game; presence + measurement + virtual reality; presence + measurement + augmented reality; presence + measurement + video game; presence + questionnaire + virtual reality; presence + questionnaire + augmented reality; and presence + questionnaire + video game. The analysis of the relevance of the results was limited to the first 100 results for each query. The second source was based on a search of a review of bibliographic references of the selected contributions to identify the original measure. The third source was based on a review of publications offering a literature review of presence measures (Grassini and Laumann 2020; IJsselsteijn et al. 2000; Schuemie et al. 2001; Van Baren and IJsselsteijn 2004; Youngblut 2003).

Only contributions proposing one or more original measures were analyzed. Even if these measures did not have the same epistemological and methodological values, the analysis was based on the assumption that the publication of an empirical study in an academic journal in workshops on presence or in IEEE proceedings guaranteeing a scientific value.

Contributions using measures already mobilized in previous contributions were excluded (*e.g.* Shubber 1998; Bystrom and Barfield 1999; Murray et al. 2000; Biocca et al. 2001; Schubert et al. 2001; Krauss et al. 2001; Lin et al. 2002; Price et al. 2011; Villani et al. 2012; Chicchi Giglioli et al. 2016; Deniaud 2017; Makransky et al. 2017; Buttussi and Chittaro 2018; Gorisse et al. 2018; Tcha-Tokey et al. 2018; Prévost, 2019; Schwind et al. 2019).

A total of 38 academic publications that proposed an original presence questionnaire were included in the following analysis.

3 Analysis of the Contributions

Regarding the construct's structure, among the 38 questionnaires, 21 proposed a measure based on a single dimension and 17 on a multidimensional scale. A content analysis of the items emphasized that there were three main types of items or themes (see Table 1).

Theme 1: Constructs that are close to presence

- Personal presence: The sense or feeling of being in a virtual environment
- Environmental presence: The extent to which the (virtual) environment exists for the user during exposure
- Co-personal presence with virtual objects or avatars: The sense or feeling of being close to virtual objects or avatars (relevant construct in augmented reality)
- Behavioral presence or agency: Behavioral presence is the extent to which the user interacts with virtual objects in environments and agency is the extent to which the user assigns to himself/herself the effects of his/her own actions

Theme 2: User experience characteristics

- Experience credibility level: The extent to which the user believes that the experience is credible
- Focus attention: The extent to which the user focuses his/her attention on the virtual environment and assigned task
- Disappearance of the reality: The extent to which the user forgets the real environment during exposure
- Device transparency: The extent to which the user forgets the device (e.g., HMD and sensorimotor interfaces)

- Emotion level: The emotions felt during the exposure phase
- Enjoyment: The enjoyment or pleasure felt during the exposure phase
- Involvement: The extent to which the user participates in actions or tasks during exposure
- Mental effort: The allocation level of cognitive resources
- Sense engagement: The extent to which the user's senses are completely engaged during the experience

Theme 3: Device or virtual environment characteristics

- Realism: The extent to which the virtual objects/environments resemble real objects/environments
- Ease of use: The extent to which the device is easy to use
- Display quality: The stimuli's sensory quality (e.g., sight and hearing)

The following table proposes for each contribution the definition of presence, the construct's dimensions, significant examples of items for each theme, and themes.

Table 1. Presence: definitions, dimensions, items, and themes.

Authors	Definitions device tasks/environment sample (N)	Dimensions	Items (one example for each related theme)	Themes
Axelsson et al. (2001)	No definition Cave, Desktop Puzzle problem solving N = 44	1 dimension	To what extent did you have a sense of being in the same room as the cubes?	Co-personal presence with virtual objects or avatars
Bailey et al. (2012)	Physical presence measures how real the virtual space and the objects within it seem to users HMD Memory task N = 33	1 dimension	To what extent did you feel: That you were really inside the virtual shower? That the virtual shower seemed like the real world? That you could reach out and touch the objects in the virtual shower?	Personal presence Realism Behavioral presence or agency
Baños et al. (2000)	The experience a person has when in a virtual environment of "being there" or the subjective experience of being in one place or environment even when you are physically located in another HMD Claustrophobic scenarios, body image scenarios, Interactions with a spider N = 124	Reality judgment	In your opinion, how was the quality of the images in the virtual world? To what extent was what you saw in the virtual world similar to reality? To what extent was what you experienced in the virtual world congruent to other experiences in the real world? To what extent did you feel you "went into" the virtual world?	Display quality Realism Experience credibility level Personal presence

(continued)

Table 1. (*continued*)

Authors	Definitions device tasks/environment sample (N)	Dimensions	Items (one example for each related theme)	Themes
		Internal/external correspondence	To what extent did the virtual world respond to your actions?	Behavioral presence or agency
		Attention/absorption	To what extent did you feel like you "went into" the virtual world and you almost forgot about the world outside? To what extent did you have to pay excessive attention to what was going on in the virtual world?	Personal presence/Disappearance of the reality Focus attention/Mental effort
Barfield et al. (1998)	A subset of our questions logically relates to a construct that appears to represent "presence" as defined by numerous authors HMD A virtual representation of Stonehenge with a night setting N = 8	1 dimension	How strong was your sense of presence (i.e., feeling like you were there) in the virtual environment? How aware were you of the other person(s) in the real world with you? How aware were you of the real-world surroundings while navigating the virtual pathway (i.e., curtains, table, chair, room temperature, noise, etc.)? How completely were your visual senses engaged by the virtual environment? Did the input device used to navigate the virtual environment affect your sense of presence? With what degree of ease were you able to navigate within the virtual environment? How well did the movements of the input device correspond with the movements in the virtual world? How would you rate the fidelity (i.e., the goodness) of the display? To what degree did the virtual world appear to have realistic depth/volume? What was your overall enjoyment in navigating throughout this environment?	Personal presence Co-personal presence with virtual objects or avatars Disappearance of the reality Sense engagement Device transparency Ease of use Experience credibility level Display quality Realism Enjoyment
Baus and Bouchard (2016)	No definition, but the contribution was based on Heeter's (1992) distinction (personal presence and environmental presence) Stereoscopic screen Crime scene N = 60	Sense of presence	On a scale of 0% to 100%, to what extent do you feel present here in the …?	Personal presence
		Sense of reality	On a scale of 0% to 100%, to what extent does your experience here in the … seem real?	Experience credibility level

(*continued*)

Table 1. (*continued*)

Authors	Definitions device tasks/environment sample (N)	Dimensions	Items (one example for each related theme)	Themes
Bouvier (2009)	The authentic feeling of being in a world other than the physical world where the body is Stereoscopic screen Video game N = 48	Global presence	I felt I existed in the environment The emotions I felt were almost as strong as if the situation were real	Personal presence Experience credibility level / Emotion level
		Environmental presence	During the experience, what was your strongest feeling of being in a virtual reality lab or being on the planet?	Environmental presence
		Presence of self	Specific items related to user/avatar relationship	
		Social presence	I felt like I was interacting with other humans	Co-personal presence with virtual objects or avatars
		Behavioral presence	I had the feeling of acting in virtual space rather than acting on any mechanism outside it	Behavioral presence or agency
Cho et al. (2003)	The user in the environment believing that one is or is doing something "in" the synthetic environment 50 inch. screen Virtual undersea world	1 dimension	Rate on a scale from 0 to 100: The visual realism of the objects The feeling of being in the environment	Realism Personal presence
Choi et al. (2019)	The user's sense of feeling inside the virtual world different from the real world that the user is in Smartphone AR app Visualization of AR objects N = 12	User immersion and presence	How well did the overall AR environment attract your attention? How much effort (mental fatigue) did you have to put into viewing the overall AR environment? How naturally did the overall AR environment look and feel? To what extent did the lighting condition influence the degree of immersion in the AR environment? How much did you think you were immersed in AR environment?	Focus attention Mental engagement Realism / Experience credibility level Display quality Personal presence
		Object presence	To what extent did the augmented information hold your attention? How much mental effort did you put into watching the augmented object? How natural and harmonious (to the real world) did the augmented information look and feel? To what extent did feel like you were in the real space with the augmented object(s)? To what extent did the augmented objects felt realistic?	Focus attention Mental engagement Realism / Experience credibility level Co-personal presence with virtual objects or avatars Realism

(*continued*)

Table 1. (*continued*)

Authors	Definitions device tasks/environment sample (N)	Dimensions	Items (one example for each related theme)	Themes
Dinh et al. (1999)	No definition HMD +olfactory stimulation +ambient auditory stimulation +tactile stimulation Corporate office suite N = 322	1 dimension	How strong was your sense of presence in the virtual environment? How aware were you of the real-world surroundings while moving through the virtual world (i.e., sounds, room temperature, other people, etc.)? In general, how realistic did the virtual world appear to you? With what degree of ease were you able to look around the virtual environment? Do you feel that you could have reached into the virtual world and grasped an object? What was your overall enjoyment level in the virtual environment? To what extent were there times during the experience when the computer-generated world became the reality for you and you almost forgot about the "real world" outside? What was the quality of the visual display?	Personal presence Disappearance of the reality Realism Ease of use Behavioral presence or agency Enjoyment Environmental presence/Disappearance of the reality Display quality
Fornerino et al. (2008)	An affective, cognitive, and sensory process that is the means of accessing a particular goal, the experience of a subjective experience that, combined with other subjective experiences, contributes in particular to the achievement of a global goal of constructing the individual's identity Rock concert N = 15	1 dimension	The show created a new world that suddenly disappeared at the end of the show At times I lost consciousness of what was around me	Environmental presence Disappearance of the reality
Gackenbach and Rosie (2011)	No definition TV screen VR Google glasses First person adventure/action game N = 40	1 dimension	How involving was the media experience? How completely were your senses engaged? How much of a sense of physical movement did you feel during the media experience? The experience caused real feelings and emotions for me Did they look like they would if you had experienced them directly? To what extent did you experience a sense of "being there" inside the environment you saw/heard?	Involvement Sense engagement Behavioral presence or agency Emotion level Device transparency Personal presence

(*continued*)

Table 1. (*continued*)

Authors	Definitions device tasks/environment sample (N)	Dimensions	Items (one example for each related theme)	Themes
Gerhard et al. (2001)	The possible result of the cognitive immersion process Website Collaborative virtual environment N = 27	Involvement	Were you involved in communication and the experimental task to the extent that you lost track of time? To what extent did events occurring outside the virtual gallery distract from your experience in the virtual environment? I was an active participant in the meeting I enjoyed the virtual gallery experience	Involvement Disappearance of the reality Behavioral presence or agency Enjoyment
		Immersion	My senses were completely engaged during the experience	Sense engagement
		Awareness	I was immediately aware of the existence of other participants	Co-personal presence with virtual objects or avatars
		Communication	How responsive were the avatars of other participants to verbal communication that you initiated?	Co-personal presence with virtual objects or avatars
Georgiou and Kyza (2017)	A suboptimal psychological process of becoming engaged in the game-playing experience Tablet AR app. for learning science N = 176	1 dimension	The activity felt so authentic that it made me think that the virtual characters/objects existed for real I so was involved that I felt that my actions could affect the activity	Experience credibility level Involvement/Behavioral presence or agency
Hartmann et al. (2016)	Definitions of Lee (2004) and Draper et al. (1998) Text book, film, hypertext screen, 3D glasses Various environments N = 695	Spatial presence: Self location	I felt like I was actually there in the presentation's environment It seemed as though I actually participated in the presentation's action	Personal presence Behavioral presence or agency
		Spatial presence: Possible actions	The objects in the presentation gave me the feeling that I could do things with them	Behavioral presence or agency
He et al. (2018)	The sense of "being there" in the virtual environment AR video Visit a museum N = 225	1 dimension	The environment the painting describes became a place rather than just images I felt "being there" in the environment the painting describes The environment the painting describes seemed realistic	Environmental presence Personal presence Realism
Hendrix and Barfield (1996)	The feeling of being immersed in a virtual environment Projection screen A room with chairs and tables N = 16	1 dimension	How strong was your sense of presence, "being there," in the virtual environment? How realistic did the virtual world appear to you?	Personal presence Realism

(*continued*)

Table 1. (*continued*)

Authors	Definitions device tasks/environment sample (N)	Dimensions	Items (one example for each related theme)	Themes
Jennett et al. (2008)	Immersion is the prosaic experience of engaging with a video game Desktop screen Attention tasks N = 244	1 dimension	It was as if I could interact with the game's world as if I was in the real world I was unaware of what was happening around me I did not feel like I was in the real world but in the game's world	Experience credibility level / Behavioral presence or agency Disappearance of the reality Environmental presence
Kan et al. (2014)	No definition Video & HMD Comparison between AR objects and real objects N = 30	1 dimension	Watching the virtual object was just as natural as watching the real world The virtual element seemed real for me	Experience credibility level Environmental presence
Kim and Biocca (1997)	A person's perception of being at a specified or understood place TV screen Infomercial N = 96	Arrival: Being present in the mediated environment)	The TV created a new world for me, and the world suddenly disappeared when the broadcast ended During the broadcast, I felt I was in the world that the television created During the broadcast, my body was in the room, but my mind was inside the world created by the TV	Environmental presence/Disappearance of the reality Environmental presence Personal presence
		Departure: Not being present in the unmediated environment	The TV-generated world seemed to be only "something I saw" rather than "somewhere I visited." During the broadcast, my mind was in the room, not in the world created by TV	Environmental presence Personal presence
Lao et al. (2019)	User is "elsewhere" than where he/she is physically Tablet Apartment visit N = 300	1 dimension	I did not just "see" the place, I actually "visited" it	Personal presence
Larsson et al. (2001)	Presence can best be defined as "being there" HMD Simple tasks to achieve in a church N = 32	Presence	How natural was the interaction with the environment? To what extent did you feel that you were present in the virtual environment? How involved were you in the experience? To what extent did you think that the things you did and saw happened naturally and without much mental effort?	Experience credibility level/Device transparency Personal presence Involvement Mental effort
		External awareness	To what extent were you aware of things happening around you outside the virtual environment? To what extent did you focus your attention on the situation rather than other things?	Disappearance of the reality Focus attention
		Enjoyment	To what extent did you find the virtual environment fascinating?	Enjoyment/Emotion level

(*continued*)

Table 1. (*continued*)

Authors	Definitions device tasks/environment sample (N)	Dimensions	Items (one example for each related theme)	Themes
Lessiter et al. (2001)	A subjective sensation of "being there" Films, videos, Racing video game, IMAX (2D & 3D), Cinema Chain film, Films onto 2X3m display screen, Short video (28 inches TV) & Videogame console (28 inches TV) N = 604		Items are confidential	
Lombard et al. (2009)	No definition (but several definitions/dimensions of presence) IMAX, Small, black & white images and monaural sound IMAX T-Rex film, old episode of an American comedy, Science fiction clip, Comedy show, Civil war documentary N = 515	Spatial presence	How much did it seem as if the objects and people you saw/heard had come to the place you were? To what extent did you experience a sense of being there inside the environment you saw/heard? How often did you want to or try to touch something you saw/heard? Did the experience seem more like looking at the events/people on a movie screen or more like looking at the events/people through a window?	Co-personal presence with virtual objects or avatars Personal presence Behavioral presence or agency Environmental presence
		Social presence: Actor within medium	Specific items measuring social presence	
		Social presence: Passive interpersonal	Specific items measuring social presence	
		Social presence: Active interpersonal	Specific items measuring social presence	
		Engagement (mental immersion)	To what extent did you feel mentally immersed in the experience? How involving was the experience? How completely were your senses engaged? To what extent did you experience a sensation of reality?	Personal presence Involvement Sense engagement Experience credibility level
		Social richness	Specific items measuring social presence	
		Social realism	The events I saw/heard would occur in the real world	Experience credibility level
		Perceptual realism	Overall, how much did touching the things and people in the environment you saw/heard feel like it would if you had experienced them directly?	Experience credibility level / Device transparency

(*continued*)

Table 1. (*continued*)

Authors	Definitions device tasks/environment sample (N)	Dimensions	Items (one example for each related theme)	Themes
Nannipieri et al. (2015)	The feeling of being in the virtual environment (personal presence) and the feeling that the virtual environment exists (environmental presence) Dream, imagination, novel, film, videogame, virtual world, virtual environment N = 180	Personal presence	I was immersed in this environment	Personal presence
		Environmental presence	This environment was the reality for me	Environmental presence
Nichols et al. (2000)	No definition HMD & Computer screen Shooting ducks N = 24	1 dimension	In the computer-generated world, I had the sense of "being there." Do you think of the computer-generated world as something I saw/somewhere I visited? The computer-generated world became more real or present to me than the "real world."	Personal presence Environmental presence Experience credibility level
Nowak and Biocca (2003)	The sensation of "being there" in the virtual or mediated environment Computer screen with headphones, microphone & keyboard Meeting room N = 134	One dimension	How involving was the experience? How intense was the experience? To what extent did you feel like you were inside the environment you saw/heard?	Involvement Emotion level Personal presence
Persky and Blascovich (2008)	The subjective experience of being in one place or environment even when one is physically situated in another HMD & Computer screen First person shooter N = 62	1 dimension	I forgot about my immediate physical surroundings (i.e., the lab room) when I was in the game environment I wanted/tried to reach out and touch things in the game environment The game environment became "reality" for me	Disappearance of the reality Behavioral presence or agency Environmental presence / Experience credibility level

(*continued*)

Table 1. (*continued*)

Authors	Definitions device tasks/environment sample (N)	Dimensions	Items (one example for each related theme)	Themes
Prothero et al. (1995)	"Being in" a virtual environment HMD Shark fishing N = 39	1 dimension	In sharkworld, I felt like I was standing in the laboratory wearing a virtual reality helmet/I was in some sort of ocean near a shark-infested shipwreck How real did the virtual world seem to you? To what extent were there times when you felt that the virtual world became the "reality" for you and you almost forgot about the real world outside? Did the virtual world seem more like something you saw or someplace you visited?	Environmental presence Experience credibility level Environmental presence / Disappearance of the reality Environmental presence
Psotka and Davison (1993)	The feeling of really being there HMD Unspecified task N = 15	1 dimension	How much more enjoyable would it have been to have the immersion experience with no one else in the room? How completely did you believe you were part of the virtual environment? How realistic was this experience visually? How completely were all of your senses engaged by the VR world?	Enjoyment Personal presence Realism Sense engagement
Ratan and Hasler (2009)	Proto self-presence: The extent to which a media tool and corresponding virtual self-representation are integrated into the body schema Core self-presence: The extent to which mediated interactions between a virtual self-representation and virtual objects cause emotional responses Extended self-presence: The extent to which some mediated identity is important to the individual Video-conference environement Collaborative work meeting N = 31	Proto self-presence	When using your avatar, do you feel physically close to the objects and other avatars in the game/virtual environment? When using your avatar, to what extent do you feel like you can reach into the game/virtual environment through your avatar? When playing the game/using the virtual environment, to what extent do you feel like your hand is inside of the game/virtual environment?	Co-personal presence with virtual objects or avatars Behavioral presence or agency Personal presence
		Core self-presence	When happy events happen to your avatar, to what extent do you feel happy?	Emotion level / Enjoyment
		Extended self-presence	Specific items measuring the relationships between the user and his/her avatar	

(*continued*)

Table 1. (*continued*)

Authors	Definitions device tasks/environment sample (N)	Dimensions	Items (one example for each related theme)	Themes
Roy (2014)	The feeling of "being there" in the virtual environment although the body is in the real world Website Set up a sales area N = 60	Presence of self	It was like I was in the store/It was like I saw pictures of a store without feeling inside I put away the objects for the store tutor/I put away the objects to pass the simulation	Personal presence Behavioral presence or agency
		Social presence	It was like the tutor was with me/It was like I was alone The tutor's voice was clear and easy to understand/The tutor's voice was not clear and not easy to hear	Co-personal presence with virtual objects or avatars Display quality
		Spatial presence	Objects and furniture were neat and easy to see/Objects and furniture were not neat and not easy to see When I moved objects, it was what I expected/When I moved objects, I was surprised by what was happening	Display quality Behavioral presence or agency
		Behavioral presence	My movements to move objects seemed easy/Using joysticks to move objects seemed difficult I was active/I was a spectator	Ease of use Behavioral presence or agency
Schroeder et al. (2001)	The experience of being in a place other than the one in which you are physically present Cave Rubik's cube collaborative problem solving N = 132		To what extent did you have the experience of being in the same room as the cubes?	Co-personal presence with virtual objects or avatars
Schubert et al. (1999)	Presence means the experience of being in a virtual environment Computer screen & HMD Videogame N = 542	Global presence	In the computer-generated world, I had a sense of "being there."	Personal presence
		Spatial presence	I did not feel present in the virtual space I had a sense of acting in the virtual space rather than operating something from outside	Personal presence Behavioral presence or agency
		Involvement	How aware were you of the real-world surroundings while navigating in the virtual world? I was completely captivated by the virtual world	Disappearance of the reality Involvement /Focus attention
		Experienced realism	How much did your experience in the virtual environment seem consistent with your real-world experience?	Experience credibility level

(*continued*)

Table 1. (*continued*)

Authors	Definitions device tasks/environment sample (N)	Dimensions	Items (one example for each related theme)	Themes
Slater et al. (1994)	The participant's sense of "being there" in the virtual environment HMD Subjects are in a room facing a precipice N = 34	1 dimension	To what extent were there times during the experience when the virtual environment was the reality for you? When you think back to the experience, do you think of the virtual environment more as images that you saw or more as somewhere that you visited? During the time of the experience, which was the strongest on the whole, your sense of being in the virtual environment or of being elsewhere?	Environmental presence / Experience credibility level Environmental presence Personal presence
Stevens et al. (2002)	The subjective experience that a particular object exists in a user's environment even when that object does not Projection-augmented models (visual and haptic) Drawing colors on a cell phone N = 16	1 dimension	Same items as PQ (Witmer and Singer, 1998) adapted: the user's presence is replaced by the object's presence	Co-personal presence with virtual objects or avatars
Vorderer et al. (2004)	No definition Text book, film, hypertext screen, 3D glasses Various environments N = 685	Spatial presence: Self location	I had the feeling that I was in the middle of the action rather than merely observing I felt like I was actually there in the presentation's environment	Behavioral presence or agency Personal presence
		Spatial presence: Possible actions	I had the impression that I could act in the presentation's environment It seemed to me that I could have some effect on things in the presentation as I do in real life	Behavioral presence or agency Experience credibility level
Welch et al. (1996)	The feeling that subjects were physically located in and surrounded by the portrayed visual world rather than in the laboratory in which they knew the experiment to be taking place HMD Driving task N = 20	1 dimension	In which world did you more strongly feel that you were surrounded by the car and outside world rather than being in the laboratory in which this experiment was taking place?	Personal presence

(*continued*)

Table 1. (*continued*)

Authors	Definitions device tasks/environment sample (N)	Dimensions	Items (one example for each related theme)	Themes
Witmer and Singer (1998)/Witmer et al. (2005)	The subjective experience of being in one place or environment even when one is physically situated in another HMD Several simple tasks N = 325	Involvement	How much were you able to control events? How much did the environment's visual aspects involve you? How compelling was your sense of objects moving through space? How much did your experiences in the virtual environment seem consistent with your real-world experiences?	Behavioral presence or agency Involvement Sense engagement Experience credibility level
		Sensory fidelity	How much did the environment's auditory aspects involve you? How closely were you able to examine objects?	Involvement Behavioral presence or agency
		Adaptation/immersion	How well could you concentrate on the assigned tasks or required activities rather than on the mechanisms used to perform those tasks or activities? How completely were your senses engaged in this experience? Were there moments during the virtual environment experience when you felt completely focused on the task or environment? How easily did you adjust to the control devices used to interact with the virtual environment? Was the information provided through different senses in the virtual environment (e.g., vision, hearing, and touch) consistent?	Focus attention / Mental effort Sense engagement Focus attention Ease of use Experience credibility level
		Interface quality	How much delay did you experience between your actions and expected outcomes? How much did the control devices interfere with the performance of assigned tasks or other activities?	Display quality Device transparency

Except for studies focused on a particular dimension of presence, presence was consensually defined. Nevertheless, all of the studies that used a consensual definition of presence as the feeling of being there also used items that did not only measure the feeling of being there, except the contribution of Barfield et al. (1998), which measured presence with a single item (How strong was your sense of presence [i.e., feeling like you were there] in the virtual environment?) but also measured other related constructs in the items' measurement scale. A content analysis showed that several constructs called "presence" but items did not measure presence as the feeling of being there. More precisely, some constructs and items did not measure presence but could have been antecedent variables influencing the presence. For example, some variables and items mentioned in the table had a positive effect on the level of presence: focus attention

(Witmer and Singer 1998), agency (Nannipieri 2018), weak latency (Sheridan 1992; Witmer and Singer 1998), the environment's realism (Dillon et al. 2001; Witmer and Singer 1998), the details' precision (Shim and Kim 2003), and the presence of avatars (Biocca et al. 2003). From a theoretical perspective, the content validities of the items in the scales were not satisfactory.

For example, the most used questionnaire (Witmer and Singer 1998, or the new version in Witmer et al. 2005) in various studies was based on a consensual definition (i.e., "The subjective experience of being in one place or environment even when one is physically situated in another," Witmer and Singer 1998, p. 225) but proposed items related to various constructs. The name of each dimension of presence underlined that, in fact, this questionnaire did not measure presence at all but involvement, sensory fidelity, adaptation/immersion, and interface quality. For example, interface quality did not measure presence, that is, a subjective feeling of being there, but the perceived quality of the device's interface. Indeed, the interface quality could have been a variable that influenced presence. More precisely, the item "How much did the visual display quality interfere or distract you from performing assigned tasks or required activities?" (interface quality dimension) could have influenced the level of presence: for example, the accuracy of details (Shim and Kim 2003) or the extent of colors (Barfield and Weghorst 1993) increased the level of presence. Moreover, the correlations between the dimension of the presence questionnaire were weak for two of them (sensory fidelity and adaptation/immersion; interface quality and adaptation/immersion) and raised two main questions: did the "presence questionnaire" measure a unified construct? Did the "presence questionnaire" measure presence?

That is why we agree with Slater's analysis proposed in a well-known publication: "Measuring Presence: A Response to the Witmer and Singer Presence Questionnaire" (Slater 1999). Indeed, Slater underlined that: "The overall score is the sum of the answers to all 32 questions. Note that none of the questions is directly about presence" (Slater 1999, p. 568). How can we measure presence in a questionnaire without asking questions about presence? Moreover, the fact that correlations exist between the construct have "nothing to do with any empirical relationships around the issue of presence" (Slater 1999, p. 570). Indeed, "I would rather attempt (even if not successful) to find a measure of presence based on a methodology that is directly concerned with the concept in itself, as usefully summarized in the earlier quote from Witmer and Singer." There was a gap between the definition of presence proposed by Witmer and Singer ("Presence is defined as the subjective experience of being in one place or environment even when one is physically situated in another," Witmer and Singer 1998, p. 225) and the measurement tool.

Other example: Even if Baños et al. (2000) defined presence as "the experience a person has when in a virtual environment of 'being there' or the subjective experience of being in one place or environment even when you are physically located in another" (Witmer and Singer's definition), the construct included three dimensions (reality judgment, internal/external correspondence, and attention/absorption). Regarding the reality judgment dimension (which included items directly linked to presence), even if the loading factors were correct (between .543 and .819), there were various constructs measured in this list of items (see Table 2).

Table 2. Presence: definitions, dimensions, items, and themes.

Items	Themes
To what extent did the experience seem real to you?	Experience credibility level
In your opinion, how was the quality of the images in the virtual world?	Display quality
To what extent was what you saw in the virtual world similar to reality?	Experience credibility level
How real did the virtual objects seem to you?	Environmental presence
To what extent was what you experienced in the virtual world congruent to other experiences in the real world?	Experience credibility level
To what extent did you feel you "went into" the virtual world?	Personal presence
To what extent did your interactions with the virtual world seem natural to you, like those in the real world?	Device transparency
To what extent did you feel you "were" physically in the virtual world?	Personal presence

The unique conclusion of this exploratory factor analysis was the following: the experience credibility level, display quality, environmental presence, device transparency, and personal presence might be more or less linked. Indeed, items were correlated or (but nothing proved it) had causal relationships, but it was impossible to deduce that these items measured a unified construct from a theoretical perspective.

For example, Georgiou and Kyza (2017) used these items: "The activity felt so authentic that it made me think that the virtual characters/objects existed for real," "I felt that what I was experiencing was something real instead of a fictional activity," "I was so involved in the activity that in some cases I wanted to interact with the virtual characters/objects directly," and "I was so involved that I felt that my actions could affect the activity." Indeed, the items did not measure stricto sensu the presence according to Georgiou and Kyza's definition ("Sense of feeling surrounded by a blended yet realistic physical/virtual environment," Georgiou and Kyza (2017 p. 28) but measured environmental presence, involvement, and behavioral presence that could have been variables that correlated or could influence the feeling of being there (personal presence).

A last example: Schubert et al. (2001) proposed a range of items closely related to presence. The authors called this construct "spatial presence," which was for them "the classic description of presence" (Schubert et al. 2001, p. 11) and measured it with the following items: "In the virtual environment I had a sense of being there," "I felt present in the virtual space," and "I had a sense of acting in the virtual space instead of operating something from the outside." Despite this scale's consistency from a theoretical perspective, the third item was closer to behavioral presence than personal presence: it measured a sense of acting, not a sense of being, but the sense of being present somewhere (in a real or virtual environment) was different from acting in this environment (e.g., "I could feel present without doing anything").

4 Conclusion

It is scientifically valid to create measurement tools reflecting a concept (i.e., its definition). Indeed, the analysis of the literature highlighted that there was confusion between the feeling of presence and the whole user experience. Presence might be a part (less or more important) of the whole user experience, similar to environmental presence, experience credibility, and involvement. The user experience could not be reduced or summarized to the sense of presence.

More conceptualization is necessary before measuring and a better understanding of the psychological, behavioral, and physiological levels involved in the feeling of presence based on a qualitative or interpretative approach of the user experience before building quantitative measurement tools.

Understanding presence requires more in-depth analyses to find the right items that are able to manifest, on a quantitative level, a qualitative phenomenon called "presence." Indeed, the measure of presence is not necessarily multidimensional: a single item or pair of items may be sufficient to reflect the consensual definition of presence as the feeling of being there. More consistent items also deal with personal presence.

Despite these conclusions, this analysis remains limited: it focused on presence measurement contributions in the literature review and not on presence in general. Further research must consider a larger range of studies.

Furthermore, to take into account a large range of presence manifestations (e.g., behavioral indicators, physiological indicators, and psychological indicators), future research could try to identify and, if any, correlate these various types of indicators.

References

Alcaniz, M., Rey, B., Tembl, J., Parkhutik, V.: A Neuroscience approach to virtual reality experience using transcranial Doppler monitoring. Presence **18**(2), 97–111 (2009). https://doi.org/10.1162/pres.18.2.97

Arnaldi, B., Fuchs, P., Tisseau, J.: Chapitre, 1, Le traité de la réalité virtuelle, Presses de l'Ecole des Mines de Paris, 2ème édn. Paris (2003)

Axelsson, A.-S., Abelin, A., Heldal, I., Schroeder, R., Wideström, J.: Cubes in the cube: a comparison of a puzzle-solving task in a virtual and a real environment. Cyberpsychol. Behav. **4**(2), 279–286 (2001). https://doi.org/10.1089/109493101300117956

Bailey, J., Bailenson, J.N., Won, A.S., Flora, J., Armel, K.C.: Presence and memory: immersive virtual reality effects on cued recall. In: Proceedings of the International Society for Presence Research Annual Conference, October 24–26, Philadelphia, Pennsylvania, USA (2012)

Baños, R.M., Botella, C., Garcia-Palacios, A., Villa, H., Perpiñá, C., Alcaniz, M.: Presence and reality judgment in virtual environments: A unitary construct? CyberPsychol. Behav. **3**(3), 327–335 (2000). https://doi.org/10.1089/10949310050078760

Barfield, W., Baird, K.M., Bjorneseth, O.J.: Presence in virtual environments as a function of type of input device and display update rate. Displays **19**, 91–98 (1999). https://doi.org/10.1016/S0141-9382(98)00041-9

Barfield, W., Weghorst, S.: The sense of presence within virtual environment: a conceptual framework. Proc. Int. Conf. Hum. Comput. Interact. **5**, 699–704 (1993)

Baus, O., Bouchard, S.: Exposure to an unpleasant Odour Increases the Sense of Presence in Virtual Reality. In: Baus, O.L. (ed.)'effet de l'exposition aux stimuli olfactifs sur le sentiment de présence en réalité virtuelle. Thèse de doctorat en psychologie expérimentale, Université d'Ottawa (2016). https://doi.org/10.20381/ruor-5220

Berger, P., Luckmann, T.: The Social Construction Of Reality: A Treatise in the Sociology of Knowledge, Anchor Books (1966)

Biocca, F., Harms, C., Burgoon, J.K.: Toward a more robust theory and measure of social presence: review and suggested criteria. Presence **12**(5), 456–480 (2003). https://doi.org/10.1162/105474 603322761270

Biocca, F., Kim, J., Choi, Y.: Visual touch in virtual environments: an exploratory study of presence multimodal interfaces, and cross-modal sensory illusions. Presence **10**(3), 247–265 (2001). https://doi.org/10.1162/105474601300343595

Bouvier, P.: La présence en réalité virtuelle, une approche centrée utilisateur. Thèse de doctorat en informatique, Université Paris Est. Corpus ID: 43898562 (2009)

Brooks, F.P.: What's real about virtual reality? IEEE Computer Graphics and Applications, Special Report, November-December (1999)

Buttussi, F., Chittaro, L.: Effects of different types of virtual reality display on presence and learning in a safety training scenario. IEEE Trans. Visual Comput. Graphics **24**(2), 1063–1076 (2018)

Bystrom, K.-E., Barfield, W.: Collaborative task performance for learning using a virtual environment. Presence **8**(4), 435–448 (1999). https://doi.org/10.1162/105474699566323

Chicchi Giglioli, I.A., et al.: Feeling ghost food as real one: psychometric assessment of presence engagement exposing to food in augmented reality. In: Serino, S., Matic, A., Giakoumis, D., Lopez, G., Cipresso, P. (eds.) MindCare 2015. CCIS, vol. 604, pp. 99–109. Springer, Cham (2016). https://doi.org/10.1007/978-3-319-32270-4_10

Cho, D., Park, J., Kim, G.J., Hong, S., Han, S., Lee, S.: The dichotomy of presence elements: The where and what. In: IEEE Virtual Reality Proceedings, pp. 273–274 (2003). https://doi.org/10.1109/VR.2003.1191155

Choi, H., Kim, Y.R., Kim, G.J.: Presence, immersion and usability of mobile augmented reality. In: Chen, J.Y.C., Fragomeni, G. (eds.) HCII 2019. LNCS, vol. 11574, pp. 3–15. Springer, Cham (2019). https://doi.org/10.1007/978-3-030-21607-8_1

Deniaud, D.: Optimiser la validité des comportements observés sur simulateur de conduite : Etude des interactions entre immersion, présence et comportement. Université Aix-Marseille II, Thèse de doctorat en sciences cognitives (2017)

Dillon, C., Keogh, E., Freeman, J., Davidoff, J.: Presence: Is your heart in it? In: 4th International Workshop on Presence (2021)

Dinh, H.Q., Walker, N., Song, C., Kobayashi, A., Hodges, L.F.: Evaluating the importance of multi-sensory input on memory and the sense of presence in virtual environments. In: Proceedings of the IEEE Virtual Reality, Washington, DC, USA (1999). https://doi.org/10.1109/VR.1999.756955

Fornerino, M., Helme-Guizon, A., Gotteland, D.: Expériences cinématographiques en état d'immersion : effets sur la satisfaction. Rech. Appl. Mark. **23**(3), 93–111 (2008). https://doi.org/10.1177/076737010802300304

Freeman, J., Avons, S.E.: Focus group exploration of presence through advanced broadcast services. In: Proceedings of the SPIE, Human Vision and Electronic Imaging, pp. 3959–3976 (2000). https://doi.org/10.1117/12.387207

Freeman, J., Avons, S.E., Meddis, R., Pearson, D.E., IJsselsteijn, W.A.: Using behavioural realism to estimate presence: a study of the utility of postural responses to motion stimuli. Presence **9**(2), 149–164 (2000). https://doi.org/10.1162/105474600566691

Gackenbach, J., Rosie, M.: Presence in video game play and nighttime dreams: an empirical inquiry. Int. J. Dream Res. **4**(2), 98–109 (2011). https://doi.org/10.11588/ijodr.2011.2.9059

Gandy, M., et al.: Experiences with an AR evaluation test bed: presence, performance, and physiological measurement. In: 2010 IEEE International Symposium on Mixed and Augmented Reality (2010). https://doi.org/10.1109/ISMAR.2010.5643560

Gerhard, M., Moore, D.J., Hobbs, D.J.: Continuous presence in collaborative virtual environments: towards a hybrid avatar-agent model for user representation. In: de Antonio, A., Aylett, R., Ballin, D. (eds.) IVA 2001. LNCS (LNAI), vol. 2190, pp. 137–155. Springer, Heidelberg (2001). https://doi.org/10.1007/3-540-44812-8_12

Georgiou, Y., Kyza, E.: The development and validation of the ARI questionnaire: an instrument for measuring immersion in location-based augmented reality settings. Int. J. Hum Comput Stud. **98**, 24–37 (2017). https://doi.org/10.1016/j.ijhcs.2016.09.014

Gorisse, G., Christmann, O., Richir, S.: De la présence à l'incarnation. Interf. Numériques **7**(1), 94–114 (2018)

Grassini, S. et Laumann, K.: Questionnaire measures and physiological correlates of presence: a systematic review. Front. Psychol. **11**, 349 (2020). https://doi.org/10.3389/fpsyg.2020.00349

Hartmann, T., et al.: The spatial presence experience scale (SPES). A short self-report measure for diverse media settings. J. Media Psychol. **28**(1), pp. 1–15 (2016). https://doi.org/10.1027/1864-1105/a000137

He, Z., Wu, L., Li, X.R.: When art meets tech: the role of augmented reality in enhancing museum experiences and purchase intentions. Tour. Manage. **68**, 127–139 (2018). https://doi.org/10.1016/j.tourman.2018.03.003

Hendrix, C., Barfield, W.: Presence within virtual environments as a function of visual display parameters. Presence **5**, 274–289 (1996). https://doi.org/10.1162/pres.1996.5.3.274

Hume D.: Philosophical Essays Concerning Human Understanding, A. Millar, London (1748)

IJsselsteijn, W.A., De Ridder, H., Freeman, J., Avons, S.E.: Presence: concept, determinants and measurement. In: Proceedings of SPIE - The International Society for Optical Engineering (2000). https://doi.org/10.1117/12.387188

IJsselsteijn, W.A., De Ridder, H., Hamberg, R., Bouwhuis, D., Freeman, J.: Perceived depth and the feèling of presence in 3DTV. Displays **18**, 207–214 (1998). https://doi.org/10.1016/S0141-9382(98)00022-5

Jennett, C., et al.: Measuring and defining the experience of immersion in games. Int. J. Hum. Comput. Stud. **66**, 641–661 (2008). https://doi.org/10.1016/j.ijhcs.2008.04.004

Kan, P., Dünser, A., Billinghurst, M., Schönauer, C., Kaufmann, H.: The effects of direct and global illumination on presence in augmented reality. In: Challenging Presence-Proceedings of 15th International Conference on Presence (2014)

Kant, E.: Kritik der reinen Vernunft, éd. J.F. Hartknoch, 2n édn. Riga (1787)

Kim, T., Biocca, F.: Telepresence via television: two dimensions of telepresence may have different connections to memory and persuasion. J. Comput. Mediat. Commun. **3**, 2 (1997). https://doi.org/10.1111/j.1083-6101.1997.tb00073.x

Krauss, M., Scheuchenpflug, R., Piechulla, W., Zimmer, A.: Measurement of presence in virtual environments, In: Zimmer, A., et al. (eds.) Experimentelle Psychologie. Pabst Science Publisher, Lengerich (2001)

Lao, A., Martin, A., Jeanpert, S.: Stimulation de la présence et des états affectifs par l'imagerie mentale. Une application aux visites en 3D versus 2D. Théoros **38**, 2 (2019)

Larsson, P., Västfjäll, D., Kleiner, M.: The actor-observer effect in virtual reality presentations. Cyberpsychol. Behav. **4**(2), 239–246 (2001). https://doi.org/10.7202/1065650AR

Lepecq, J.-C., Bringoux, L., Pergandi, J.-M., Coyle, T., Mestre, D.: Afforded actions as a behavioral assessment of physical presence in virtual environments. Virtual Real. **13**, 141–151 (2009). https://doi.org/10.1007/s10055-009-0118-1

Lessiter, J., Freeman, J., Keogh, E., Davidoff, J.: A cross-media presence questionnaire: the ITC-sense of presence inventory. Presence **10**(3), 282–297 (2001). https://doi.org/10.1162/105474601300343612

Lin, J.J.W., et al.: Effects of field of view on presence, enjoyment, memory, and simulator sickness in a virtual environment. In: Proceedings of Virtual Reality, IEEE, pp. 164–171 (2002)

Lombard, M., Ditton, T.: At the heart of it all: the concept of presence. J. Comput.Mediat. Commun. **3**, 2 (1997). https://doi.org/10.1111/j.1083-6101.1997.tb00072.x

Lombard, M., Ditton, T.B., Weinstein, L.: Measuring (tele) presence: the temple presence inventory. In: The Twelfth International Workshop on Presence, Los Angeles, California, USA (2009)

Makransky, G., Lilleholt, L., Aaby, A.: Development and validation of the multimodal presence scale for virtual reality environments: a confirmatory factor analysis and item response theory approach. Comput. Hum. Behav. **72**, 276–285 (2017). https://doi.org/10.1016/j.chb.2017.02.066

Marsh, T.: Staying there: an activity-based approach to narrative design and evaluation as an antidote to virtual corpsing. In: Riva, G., Davide, F., Ijsselsteijn, W. (eds.) Being there: concepts, effects and measurement of user presence in synthetic environments, pp. 86–95. Ios Press, Amsterdam, The Netherlands (2003)

Muratore, I., Nannipieri, O.: L'expérience immersive d'un jeu promotionnel en réalité augmentée destiné aux enfants. Décis. Mark. **81**, 2016 (2016). https://doi.org/10.7193/DM.081.27.40

Murray, C., Arnold, P., Thornton, B.: Presence accompanying induced hearing loss: implications for immersive virtual environments. Presence **9**, 137–148 (2000). https://doi.org/10.1162/105474600566682

Nacke, L., Lindley, C.A.: Flow and immersion in first-person shooters: measuring the player's gameplay experience. In: Proceedings of the 2008 Conference on Future Play: Research, Play, Share, November 3–5, Toronto, Canada (2008). https://doi.org/10.1145/1496984.1496998

Nannipieri, O.: Agentivité et présence dans les environnements virtuels. Interf. Num. **7**(1), 77–93 (2018). https://doi.org/10.25965/interfaces-numeriques.3289

Nannipieri, O., Muratore, I., Dumas, P., Renucci, F. : Immersion, subjectivité et communication. In : Technologies, Communication et société, Editions l'Harmattan (2015)

Nichols, S., Haldane, C., Wilson, J.R.: Measurement of presence and its consequences in virtual environments. Int. J. Hum. Comput. Stud. **52**(3), 471–491 (2000). https://doi.org/10.1006/ijhc.1999.0343

Nowak, K.L., Biocca, F.: The effect of the agency and anthropomorphism on users' sense of telepresence, copresence, and social presence in virtual environments. Presence **12**(5), 481–494 (2003). https://doi.org/10.1162/105474603322761289

Ohmi, M.: Sensation of self-motion induced by real-world stimuli. Selection and integration of visual information. In: Proceedings of the International Workshop on Advances in Research on Visual Cognition, Tsukuba, Japan, 8–11 December 1997, pp. 175–181 (1998)

Peperkorn, H.M., Diemer, J., Mühlberger, A.: Temporal dynamics in the relation between presence and fear in virtual reality. Comput. Hum. Behav. **48**, 542–547 (2015). https://doi.org/10.1016/j.chb.2015.02.028

Persky, S., Blascovich, J.: Immersive virtual video game play and presence: influences on aggressive feelings and behavior. Présence **17**(1), 57–72 (2008). https://doi.org/10.1162/pres.17.1.57

Prévost, R.: propension à l'immersion, les attitudes envers la technologie et l'anxiété ressentie durant l'immersion comme facteurs associés au sentiment de présence chez les aînés anxieux à propos de leur santé. Université de Montréal, Thèse de doctorat en psychologie (2019)

Price, M., Mehta, N., Tone, E.B., Anderson, P.L.: Does engagement with exposure yield better outcomes? Components of presence as a predictor of treatment response for virtual reality exposure therapy for social phobia. J. Anx. Disord. **25**(6), 763–770 (2011). https://doi.org/10.1016/j.janxdis.2011.03.004

Prothero, J.D., Hoffman, H.G., Parker, D.E., Furness T.A., Wells, M.J.: Foreground/background manipulations affect presence. In: Proceedings of Human Factors and Ergonomics Society 39th Annual Meeting, pp. 1410–1414 (195). https://doi.org/10.1177/154193129503902111

Psotka, J., Davison, S.: Cognitive factors associated with immersion in virtual environments. Rapport, U. S. Army Research Institute and Catholic University (unplublished paper) (1993)

Ratan, R.A., Hasler, B.: Self-presence standardized: Introducing the Self-Presence Questionnaire (SPQ) (2009). In: Proceedings of the 12th Annual International Workshop on Presence, vol. 81 (2009)

Roy, M.: Sentiment de présence et réalité virtuelle pour les langues – Une étude de l'émergence de la présence et de son influence sur la compréhension de l'oral en allemand langue étrangère », Alsic [On line], 17 (2014). https://doi.org/10.4000/alsic.2709

Schroeder, R., et al.: Collaborating in networked immersive spaces: as good as being together? Comput. Graph. **25**, 781–788 (2001). https://doi.org/10.1016/S0097-8493(01)00120-0

Schubert, T., Friedmann, F., Regenbrecht, H.: Embodied presence in virtual environments. In: Paton, R., Neilson, I. (eds.) Visual Representations and Interpretations, pp. 269–278. Springer, London (1999). https://doi.org/10.1007/978-1-4471-0563-3_30

Schubert, T., Friedmann, F., Regenbrecht, H.: The experience of presence: factor analytic insights. Presence **10**(3), 266–281 (2001). https://doi.org/10.1162/105474601300343603

Schuemie, M.J., Van Der Straaten, P., Krijn, M., Van Der Mast, C.A.P.G.: Research on presence in virtual reality: a survey. Cyberpsychol. Behav **4**(2) (2001), 183–202 (2001). https://doi.org/10.1089/109493101300117884

Schwind, V., Knierim, P., Haas, N., et Henze, N.: Using presence questionnaires in virtual reality. In: Proceedings of the 2019 CHI Conference on Human Factors in Computing Systems - CHI 2019 (2019)

Sheridan, T.B.: Musings on telepresence and virtual presence. Presence **1**(1), 120–125 (1992). https://doi.org/10.1162/pres.1992.1.1.120

Shim, W., Kim, G.J.: Designing for presence and performance: the case of the virtual fishtank. Presence **12**, 374–386 (2003). https://doi.org/10.1162/105474603322391613

Shubber, Y.: Les réalités virtuelles et la présence: de la conceptualisation à l'operationnalisation. Recherches en communication **10**(10), 161–185 (1998)

Slater, M.: Measuring presence: a response to the Witmer and singer presence questionnaire. Presence **8**(5), 560–565 (1999). https://doi.org/10.1162/105474699566477

Slater, M., Usoh, M., Steed, A.: Depth of presence in virtual environments. Presence **3**, 130–144 (1994). https://doi.org/10.1162/pres.1994.3.2.130

Stevens, B., Jerrams-Smith, J., Heathcote, D., Callear, D.: Putting the virtual into reality: assessing object-presence with projection-augmented models. Presence **11**(1), 79–92 (2002). https://doi.org/10.1162/105474602317343677

Tcha-Tokey, K., Richir, K., Loup, G., Loup-Escande, C.O.: Towards a model of user experience in immersive virtual environments. Adv. Hum. Comput. Interact. **2018**, 7827286 (2018). https://doi.org/10.1155/2018/7827286

Van Baren, J., IJsselsteijn, W.A.: Measuring presence: a guide to current measurement approaches. In: OmniPres project IST-2001-39237 (2004)

Villani, D., Repetto, C., Cipresso, P., Riva, G.: May I experience more presence in doing the same thing in virtual reality than in reality? An answer from a simulated job interview. Interact. Comput. **24**, 265–272 (2012). https://doi.org/10.1016/j.intcom.2012.04.008

Vorderer, P., et al.: MEC spatial presence questionnaire (MECSPQ): short documentation and instructions for application. Report to the European Community, Project Presence: MEC (IST-2001-37661) (2004). http://www.ijk.hmt-hannover.de/presence

Welch, R.B., Blackmon, T.T., Liu, A., Mellers, B., Stark, L.W.: The effects of pictoral realism, delay of visual feedback, and observer interactivity on the subjective sense of presence. Presence **5**, 263–273 (1996). https://doi.org/10.1162/pres.1996.5.3.263

Wiederhold, B. K., et al.: An investigation into physiological responses in virtual environments: an objective measurement of presence. In: Riva, G., Galimberti, C.: (eds.) Towards CyberPsychology: Mind, Cognitions and Society in the Internet Age, pp. 175–183. IOS Press, Amsterdam (2003). https://doi.org/10.1109/SAI.2015.7237225

Wissmath, B., Weibel, D., Mast, F.W.: Measuring presence with verbal versus pictorial scales: a comparison between online and ex post-ratings. Virtual Real. **14**(1), 43–53 (2009). https://doi.org/10.1007/s10055-009-0127-0

Witmer, B., G., & Singer, M., J.: Measuring presence in virtual environments: a presence questionnaire. Presence **7**(3), 225–240 (1998). https://doi.org/10.1162/105474698565686

Witmer, B.G., Jerome, C., G., Singer, M.J.: The factor structure of the presence questionnaire. Presence **14**(3), 298–231 (2005). https://doi.org/10.1162/105474605323384654

Youngblut, C.:Experience of presence in virtual environments. Institute for Defense Analyses, IDA Document D-2960 (2003). https://doi.org/10.21236/ada427495

Self Assessment Tool to Bridge the Gap Between XR Technology, SMEs, and HEIs

Ahmet Köse(✉) ⓘ, Aleksei Tepljakovⓘ, Saleh Alsalehⓘ,
and Eduard Petlenkovⓘ

Department of Computer Systems, Tallinn University of Technology,
Akadeemia tee 15a, 12618 Tallinn, Estonia
ahmet.kose@taltech.ee

Abstract. Extended reality (XR) is a cutting-edge technology. With the introduction of low-cost head-mounted display (HMD) devices and affordable mobile devices with augmented features, this technology has become widely available. However, due to concerns about applicability of XR technology in business-related activities, it has not reached its full potential for small and medium size businesses (SMEs) yet. In this paper, we present our novel approach to fill the gap between the technology and target groups, with a focus on identifying specific difficulties and challenges to overcome through the use of a novel self-assessment tool. Besides that, SME representatives are able to validate their experience towards XR technology with the solution. The tool also includes a separate module for higher education institutions (HEIs) to improve the curriculum, allowing graduates to be better prepared for business needs and to promote this technology. The implementation results with a report that suggests the level of understanding of XR technology based on the responses. The level groups are divided to receive individual coaching programs developed as part of a European level project. Preliminary results suggest that the developed tool is sufficient for both groups to recognize the advantages of XR technology and identify the gaps. At the same time, the results will give a better understanding to XR developers and experts towards the expectations and interests of SMEs in different sectors.

Keywords: Extended reality · Skills gap detector · Training gap detector · SMEs · HEI · Self assessment tool

1 Introduction

Virtual Reality (VR) is a high-end human computer interface that can be defined with four essential elements: virtual world, immersion, sensory feedback, and interactivity [8]. VR is a powerful medium allowing for an unprecedented level of human-machine and human-human interactions leveraging present day

Supported by organization Erasmus+ Project entitled "VAM Realities".

computing, visualization, and motion tracking technology, whereby the user is "transported" into an artificial reality from the visual and auditory perspective. Meanwhile, Augmented Reality (AR) is a close relative of VR but operates on a different principle. While VR completely replaces the environment perceived by the user and thus confines the user's motions to the confines of the surrounding real-life physical environment, AR actually augments the existing environment by adding artificial objects and subjects to it and allowing the user to interact with them. VR and AR-are combined into a single term known as Mixed Reality (MR), though there is some debate around misuse of at least the MR concept. On the other hand, as of 2022, the term *eXtended Reality* (XR) is mainly used as an umbrella term referring both to AR and VR.

The global XR market size was expected to be worth 31 billion U.S. dollars in 2021, rising to close to 300 billion U.S. dollars by 2024 [10]. One of main challenges to reach its expectations is to get acquainted with industrial stakeholders such as representatives of small- and medium-sized enterprises and persuading them of the benefits of XR technology.

What complicates matters even more, is that XR is a technology that requires a wide range of skills from developers. Even if the SME business model is not centered on development *per se*, a set of micro-skills and knowledge are still required to engage and succeed with this novel technology.

As a result, in this paper, we present a novel contribution—a skills and training assessment tool—that can assist relevant stakeholders in understanding gaps in their skills and knowledge related to the broad topic of XR. The assessment tool takes to form of a survey that must be completed online. Upon completion of the survey, the user is presented with a set of recommendations that are based on how the user answered the questions in the survey. The tool accommodates two individual modules. The skills gap detector is dedicated for SMEs and the training gap detector is for HEI representatives. The recommendations revolve around a set of additional materials tailored to each of the identified skills or knowledge gaps. The skills assessment tool and the materials are prepared under the same ERASMUS+ project entitled "VAM Realities"[1] and as such, the users of the skills assessment tool receive a comprehensive experience.

The structure of the paper is as follows. In Sect. 1.1, a brief overview of existing literature is presented and some research gaps are identified. In Sect. 2, the model of the proposed solution is discussed. Our novel materials to bridge the gaps towards XR technology are also explained in this section. The implementation and insights through the development are described in Sect. 3. Primary results of the developed tool and the planned use case is presented Sect. 4. Finally, conclusions are drawn in Sect. 5.

1.1 Related Work

There are certain application areas in which XR technologies have achieved tangible return on investment among which are manufacturing industry

---

[1] The official website for the project is located at https://vam-realities.eu/.

(automotive, avionics, heavy industrial products); power, energy, mining and utilities; media and telecommunications; healthcare and surgery; financial services; retail hospitality and leisure [9]. On the other hand, the rate of adoption of XR in manufacturing in general is still rather slow. Some recent studies were conducted to understand the current state of affairs concerning adoption of XR in small- and medium size enterprises [6]. The findings suggested that while SMEs are, in general, aware of XR technologies and their benefits, there are quite a few limiting factors that prohibit the incorporation of XR into relevant business models, whereas the technological factor—the need to deal with many aspects of implementing and adopting the technology that exist primarily due to the novel and multidisciplinary nature of XR—is considered one of the most important obstacles.

On the other side, there is academia. With the introduction of scalable XR solutions in the early 2010s, many research institutions established new XR laboratories or retrofitted existing ones with XR technology [15]. As a result, research and development capacity has increased in research institutions, but not in SMEs, which cannot typically afford a dedicated R&D department focused on emerging technology adoption. However, even in the case of HEIs there are various limiting factors related to skills and knowledge gaps that prohibit the efficient adoption of XR technology [11]. One can conclude that a holistic approach towards identifying these gaps and proposing the best possible scenarios for bridging them with relevant information.

One viable solution to this problem, namely, filling the knowledge and skills gap in XR technology for SMEs and HEIs, is to provide them with a wide range of optimized learning materials. This is one of the objective of the ERASMUS+ project "VAM Realities". If fact, one of the working packages of the project aims to address the idea of skills and knowledge transfer through the use of an automated skills assessment tool. The latter can assess the user's skill level and recommend specific materials with which the user should become acquainted in order to bridge gaps in XR technology knowledge. In this section, we review some existing literature that covers similar ideas and approaches.

Only a few papers dedicated to the design and implementation of a *skills gap detector* can be found in existing literature. One notable example is the paper dedicated to developing a method for preparing training courses based on a skills gap analysis [4]. The proposed solution does not generate specific suggestions to a given user, rather, it provides insights as to which courses the user must take to improve on the identified skills or knowledge gaps.

Research into skills gaps is typically focused on determining the expectations of businesses regarding graduates from educational institutions. For example, in [5] an automatic tool was proposed that examines the skills requirements in job postings and compares them to the syllabi of related educational courses to identify skills requirements for specific jobs in the industry. On the other hand, skills gap analyses in general are typically performed by analyzing survey results [1, 2, 7].

What concerns XR technologies specifically, no relevant research regarding the design of a tool for automatic skills gap detection has been identified. Existing research has been mostly dealing with similar issues as above—for example, a study investigating the skill requirements for AR and VR based on job advertisements was presented in [17]. Barriers toward AR adoption in manufacturing were discussed in [14]; loss of routie and loss of competence were listed among the contributing factors. The same study also emphasizes the importance of early worker involvement in AR adoption. An extended technology acceptance model (TAM) for AR in the retail industry was presented in [3]. In the paper, the authors present the results of research based on conducting a structured survey. The study confirms that technological knowledge was one of the key factors influencing the decision to use AR in the retail business. Lack of external support for technology adoption was also identified as a critical issue.

The reviewed literature hints at a research gap in terms of a solution for skills gap analysis for extended reality technologies suitable for automatically assessing the gaps in skills and knowledge in both SME and HEI representatives and generating a useful report with specific suggestions. It is also apparent that combining an automatic analysis approach based on collected survey data is the most reasonable way to proceed to make the suggestions specific enough. In what follows, we describe the model for the XR skills gap detector for SMEs and training gap detector for HEIs, provide information about the implementation, and discuss the resulting solution.

2   Identification Gaps and Modelling

The goals of our implementation are to investigate the desired set of knowledge, skills, and competencies for SME personnel in order to allow VR/AR/MR adoption, as well as to investigate necessary training features for educational activities to be offered by HEIs, and to assist SME in their VR/AR/MR adoption.

The modeled self-assessment tool accommodates two modules for each target group. The tool comprises around 21–24 questions in four sections to identify gaps that are also partially supported with visual materials. Each correct (or expected) response rewards the user with 1, 2 points respectively and they can achieve a maximum of 42 points. The participant can gain higher points with correct answers to technical questions. *XR Advisor Report* is created after the submission based on a unique rating system. The system divides individuals into three main categories based on the skills and knowledge assessments. We developed the scoring system to assist the coaching program that targets to SMEs is explained in Sect. 4.

The journey starts with a basic background check to map the current interest of the company and organization towards XR technology. The set of questions is classified depending on the availability of technical resources within the organization, the availability of XR experts in the surrounding area, and the motivation to incorporate XR technology into commercial activities.

1. Background check

2. XR Knowledge Inspection

3. Gap Identification

  a. Theoretical knowledge barrier

    1. General Overview
    2. Hardware
    3. Software
    4. Use cases
    5. Application areas

  b. Practical Challenges

    1. Feasibility
    2. Cost Analysis

  c. Specific issue to consult

4. XR Experience Validation

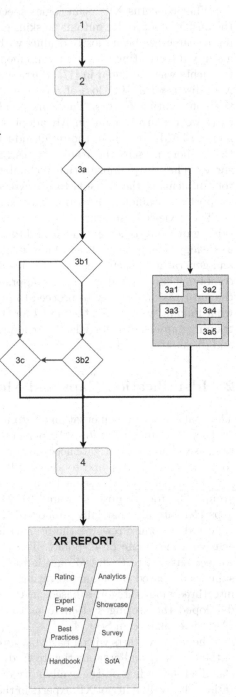

Fig. 1. Workflow of the self-assessment tool

The next section focuses on the accessibility of XR technology. In addition to multiple-choice alternatives, questions are constructed based on the extent of knowledge and experience. Because the cost analysis is an essential topic for target populations, the section also includes anticipated costs for establishing an XR project as well as expected prices for affordable XR equipment. Later in the report, readers are presented with an info-graphic that provides preliminary comparison analysis.

The viability of adapting XR technology is investigated in the following section. In other words, if it is clear what the obstacles and barriers to XR technology are, there are specific questions to advise users. This phase is also accompanied by a half-minute film to encourage and maintain concentration.

In the last step, we want to learn about people's XR experiences and skills. Because the ultimate purpose of VAMR's coaching program is to assist SMEs at all levels with XR technology, it is critical to examine existing knowledge and ideas on the subject.

Once the participants complete the journey, the advice with a 4–5 pages report is available immediately in PDF format. According to the user's input, relevant materials described below become available. If the tool identifies existing knowledge and experience, the report advises to study selected materials to advance business-related activities. The workflow to illustrate the complete self-assessment tool is depicted in Fig. 1.

In what follows, we present the content materials for a generated report that is prepared based on user's responses are convenient for the need and interest of participants.

2.1 Developed Materials to Bridge the Gap

We have developed a set of materials as part of this project to bridge the gap between XR technology, SMEs, and HEIs. One of goals for the developed tool is to help delivering those materials to the target groups. The set contains the State-of-the-Art (SotA) Report, Handbook, Experts Panel, Showcases, Survey. From the end-user perspective, such materials dedicated to the particular group will presumably engage much better. Data-driven decisions based on given answers are the primary keys to linking those materials that are described as follows:

- The SotA report has four chapters to include multiple aspects of XR technology that were updated at the beginning of 2022. Besides providing a basic understanding of XR technology, it serves as a catalog of VR/AR hardware and software are currently available on the market, with a price guide and independent reviews and ratings. The report also catalogs a range of use cases for the adoption of VR/AR into the industry to help one understand how this technology can be used in one's organization. The SotA report becomes available with instructions for participants who would need to gain theoretical knowledge or improve existing knowledge of hardware, software, and use cases of XR technology.

- The project showcase is composed of innovative projects across the EU show-cases best practice examples of developments in VR and AR and offer net-working opportunities for you to get involved. It is recommended for partici-pants who would like to discover practical examples and success stories.
- The expert panel maps a list of verified VR and AR experts right across Europe that aims to support adopting VR/AR in particular regions and spe-cific areas of business. The panel appears in the given report if the individuals have particular cases in which the developed materials are not relevant.
- The European SME Survey report provides an overview on Augmented Real-ity (AR), Mixed Reality (MR), and Virtual Reality (VR) adoption and uses in European manufacturing SMEs in 2020. The report is the result of inter-views and surveys with over 300 SMEs across Europe. The survey report gives an overall picture of the current state of AR and VR in European manufac-turing SMEs and identifies use cases of AR and VR as well as the current level of awareness and use of these technologies in SMEs. Finally, the report has a list of SMEs' recommendations and a 10-points action plan to follow to support the AR/VR adoption efforts. The survey report appears in recom-mendation list, if the assessment tool identifies that participants from SMEs may have various organizational, technological, and external issues that can act as barriers for AR/VR adoption.
- The handbook aims to address how Higher Education Institutes can support manufacturing SMEs to adopt and integrate XR technologies successfully into their business operations. The handbook is suggested for participants who are willing to develop XR applications or to consult and cooperate.

3   Implementation

Web-based applications can be built in a variety of ways. We sought a tool that was flexible enough to handle all of the project's needs while also having built-in methods that handled fundamental communication operations like user authentication, form management, and uploading content such as images and videos, therefore we chose Django [16] as the core framework for the development of our application.

Django is a Python-based web application framework that is free and open-source, due to its wide use it has a large number of community created appli-cations, one such application is the "Django survey application" [13] which was utilized as a foundation for the website's development. The survey application allows the creation of surveys with a variety of question types and generating reports based on the survey responses. Our proposed assessment tool necessitated the addition of another question type beyond the built-in types. As a result, a matrix-style question type as shown in Fig. 2 was developed and included to the application. A list of the built-in and additional question types developed for the purpose of the Skills Advisor in the survey application is shown in Table 1.

With the addition of the matrix question type the application had all of the question types that our tool required. Furthermore, the nature of XR content

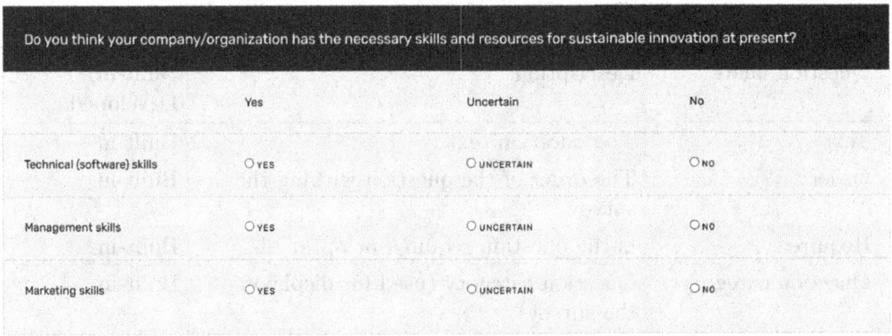

Fig. 2. Multiple radio question type (matrix-style).

Table 1. Built-in and developed question types in "Django survey application".

Question type	Used in the tool	Built-in/Developed
Text	Yes	Built-in
Short-text	No	Built-in
Radio	Yes	Built-in
Select	No	Built-in
Select image	No	Built-in
Select multiple	No	Built-in
Integer	Yes	Built-in
Float	No	Built-in
Date	No	Built-in
Multiple radio (matrix)	Yes	Developed

necessitates the inclusion of the possibility to attach images and video to the questions. This interactive content can be used for example to show a video or an image of a possible VR/AR solution before asking a related questions.

Another core feature of the application is the ability to save the user's responses to be retrieved later and used to report on their responses by displaying statistical data. The assessment tool, on the other hand, requires that the application be extended so that the answers may be evaluated in a way that allows us to make a final judgment based on the user's responses; as a result, we added a score field which will was subsequently used to reflect the user's score for each answer. Furthermore, a method for organizing the questions into several assessment categories was also implemented. Table 2 shows an overview of the question model fields including both the built-in and added fields.

Table 2. Overview of the question model fields.

Question fields	Description	Built-in/ Developed
Text	The question text	Built-in
Order	The order of the question withing the survey	Built-in
Required	Is the question required or optional	Built-in
Question category	Question category (used for displaying the survey)	Built-in
Assessment category	Assessment category (used for calculating the score)	Developed
Survey	The survey which the question belongs to	Built-in
Type	Type of the question (list of question types is shown in Table 1)	Built-in
Choices	A comma-separated list of options for this question	Developed
Scores	A comma-separated list of scores for each choice for this question	Developed
Image	Source image to be included with the question	Developed
Video	Source video to be included with the question	Developed

The following is a list of added features to the "survey application" to make it compatible with the requirements of the assessment tool:

– Multiple radio question type (matrix-style);
– Videos and images embedded questions;
– Scores and assessment category.

The tool uses the Django built-in framework to enable administration of the survey's content, such as providing the questions. Figure 3 shows how the question is displayed to the application user.

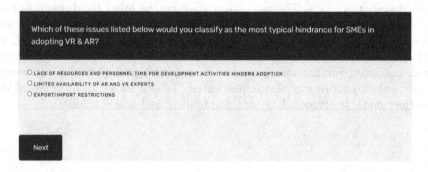

Fig. 3. An example of how a survey question is displayed to the user of the skills advisor application.

The first application allows creating survey that can be scored into different assessment categories and saving the answers and overall results in the database. A second application was developed to generate a report embedded with recommendations based on the users answers and scores collected in the first application. The final report has three main components: overall score, recommendations based on assessments category and comparison with other users for a predefined set of numerical questions.

First, the overall score is calculated based on the answers of all the questions within a given survey. The overall level is categorized into different categories. A scalable vector graphic based gauge is used to indicate the total score. An example of the total score is shown in Fig. 4. Furthermore a table is used to show the user's identified strengths and identified opportunities based on the calculated total score.

XR Training Advisor Report

Based on the information provided the Training Gap detector has assessed your skills and given you the following rating and list of recommendations.

This means that it is most likely that your level of skills and knowledge in XR is **Highly adaptable**.

Fig. 4. An example of the total score.

The recommendations in the second section of the report are based on the user's results in several assessment categories; the written recommendations are embedded with videos and links to the relevant VAMRs deliverables. An example of generated recommendations is shown in Fig. 5.

The final part of the report comprises a statistical and visual comparison of the user's answers to questions that require a numeric input. These questions are designed to assist users understand how their expectations compare to those of other users by asking them to assign a numerical figure to the cost of XR hardware or solutions. The report shows the users how their estimates compare to the average, minimum and maximum estimates given by other users. An example of the statistical and visual comparison is shown in Fig. 6 and the list of the numerical questions is shown in Table 3.

4 Grouping Results and Coaching Program

One of the most difficult challenges for XR technology is allowing consumers to discover the potential for business-related activities in many areas. XR apps

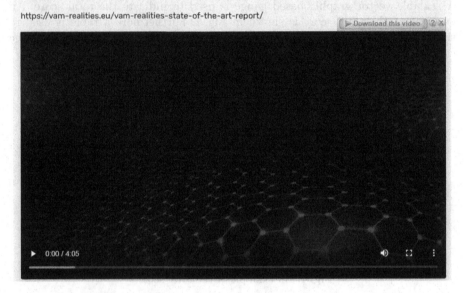

Fig. 5. An example of one of the generated recommendations based on the user's assessment results.

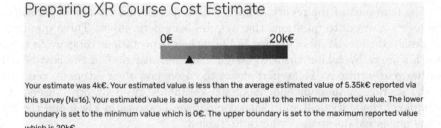

Fig. 6. An example of the statistical and visual comparison calculated based on the users estimates to the numerical questions.

Table 3. List of numerical question in the SME and HEI assessment tool.

Question	Survey (SME/HEI)	Minimum	Maximum	Average
Oculus quest price estimate	SME	4€	25k€	1.49k€
AR application solution cost estimate	SME	3€	50k	6.54k€
VR project cost estimate	SME	5€	20k	6.26k€
Oculus quest price estimate	HEI	0€	5k	755€
Preparing XR course cost estimate	HEI	€	20k€	5.35k€

are frequently supplied with interactivity, which may be one of the elements persuading SMEs to modify their processes, services, and products [12]. Based on the analysis of the data provided the VAMRS project recommends enrolling in the corresponding coaching program, particularly for SMEs that are willing to adapt to XR technology.

Furthermore, HEI will gain the necessary knowledge to equip themselves not only as competent consultants in XR adoption for SMEs, but also to develop relevant training and study courses for full-time and part-time students that meet the needs of industry and address the growing importance of VR/AR technology in order to become an exemplary XR center of excellence and set new standards for other European HEIs to follow.

On the whole, understanding the current status in XR technology might also encourage joyful learning approaches. Moreover, the collected data provides a basis for studies towards industrial applications in VR and AR for various purposes. The tool can be improved with experimental XR applications and devices as a part of the assessment.

4.1 Coaching Program for SMEs

In order to assist SMEs in learning more about VR/AR technology and supporting its adoption into the industry, a relevant coaching program was developed for SMEs. The program is structured to cater to the needs and requirements of organizations at every level of VR/AR adoption, regardless of the level of knowledge or experience that an organization has in this technology. Based on the answers and inputs through the developed tool, the SME coaching program is recommended for participants at different levels in which organizations can expect to learn the skills, improve the knowledge and gain experience and expand the network towards XR technology.

The coaching program contains three levels. The levels are determined based on collected points. SME will have obtained the necessary knowledge, skills and practical experience to adopt and integrate VR/AR technology in at least one area of its operations. With the knowledge obtained, the SME can competently continue to integrate the technology into other areas of the business. Main benefits for SMEs as follows:

- Access to XR Hardware and Software;
- Access to Expertise and XR providers;
- Hands-on Training in XR technology for SME staff;
- Create own XR content for SME;
- Opportunity to visit selected best practice use-cases around Europe;
- No consulting fee, no purchase obligation for participation.

Let us now recount the levels available in the coaching program.

Beginner XR Bootcamp program (0–14 points) is the first level of coaching program and it serves as an introduction to VR/AR and teaches basic concepts, with a selection of use-cases to help individuals to understand the technologies' potential for the industry. Furthermore, practical training in the latest VR and AR hardware is also part of the first level program. It might take up to 9 months depending on available resources for SMEs.

Advanced XR SME Launchpad (14–28 points) is dedicated to guide organizations in the adoption of both VR and AR in specific areas of business operation areas such as product design, collaboration, remote maintenance, enhancing work process, sales, and marketing. Hands-on coaching in a selected series of the latest VR/AR software applications and development of VR/AR products and applications is included in the second level program that may take up to 6 months.

Pro XR Business (28–42 points) program serves as a collaboration to mutually develop a customized VR/AR Solution for the needs of organizations that have existing knowledge and sufficient experience towards XR technology. The program enables also a potential engagement with leading VR/AR service providers to implement the concept into business related activities and site visits. The last level program may take approximately 3 months for participants (Table 4).

Table 4. VAMRS XR Coaching program for SMEs.

Level	Beginner	Intermediate	Advanced
Basic VR/AR training	✓	✓	✓
Access to AR/VR service providers	✓	✓	✓
Accessibility to online support systems	✓	✓	✓
Individual XR concept development		✓	✓
Individual XR concept deployment		✓	✓
Full integration of XR concept			✓
Maintenance and support			✓

The first page of a report that is created through the live application to illustrate the coaching program assessment is depicted in Fig. 7.

XR Skills Advisor Report

Based on the information provided the Skills Gap detector has assessed your skills and given you the following rating and list of recommendations.

This means that it is most likely that your level of skills and knowledge in XR is sufficient to proceed with our **Intermediate** level coaching program. Details are provided below.

Strengths identified	Opportunities identified
· Solid market understanding and XR potential	· Mitigation recommended meeting reluctance to invest resources in XR technology
· Solid understanding of AR/VR integration potential in own organization	· Familiar in dealing with XR service providers would be beneficial
· Practiced knowledge and experience of XR technology and use cases	· Experience in custom XR integration would be beneficial
· A clear Competitive Technology readiness factor	· Minimal investment in learning and support

Fig. 7. The first page of five pages automatically generated report

5   Conclusion and Future Work

While it may appear that AR and VR, in particular, have numerous obstacles in terms of large-scale adoption by SMEs, this is due to the fact that the technology is still relatively new and changing rapidly. At the same time, current concerns present great opportunities for those who can address them. HEIs may also benefit from the situation by improving their curricula, allowing graduates to be better equipped for current business needs, and assisting them in adapting to this technology and cooperating with SMEs.

Therefore, we developed a self-assessment tool aimed at bridging the gap between XR Technology, SMEs, and HEIs. We developed the tool as a web-based application to provide data-driven results and comparisons. Besides giving pertinent recommendations and ratings, the application allows participants to compare their financial perspectives with those of other people via an automated report. Since the current tool is intended to be used to adapt XR technology with coaching programs based on the assessment of given responses, additional development efforts should be exhibited to provide statistical conclusions in order to feed the output of collected information to the tool, as the estimated amount of participants from Europe is over 300 by the end of 2022. Furthermore, the approach given here may help other organizations that are having similar challenges adapting XR technology for corporate, educational, and training purposes. XR developers may also have a better understanding to support redirection strategies in XR-based applications in target groups. In the future, the assessment tool will have the calculation of ROI for industrial projects in order to stimulate interest.

References

1. Adepoju, O.O., Aigbavboa, C.O.: Assessing knowledge and skills gap for construction 4.0 in a developing economy. J. Public Aff. **21**(3) (2020). https://doi.org/10.1002/pa.2264
2. Akdur, D.: Skills gaps in the industry. ACM Trans. Embed. Comput. Syst. **20**(5), 1–39 (2021). https://doi.org/10.1145/3463340
3. Alam, S.S., Susmit, S., Lin, C.Y., Masukujjaman, M., Ho, Y.H.: Factors affecting augmented reality adoption in the retail industry. J. Open Innov. Technol. Market Complex. **7**(2), 142 (2021). https://doi.org/10.3390/joitmc7020142
4. Antonucci, L., d'Ovidio, F.D.: An informative system based on the skill gap analysis to planning training courses. Appl. Math. **03**(11), 1619–1626 (2012). https://doi.org/10.4236/am.2012.311224
5. Chang, X., Wang, B., Hui, B.: Towards an automatic approach for assessing program competencies. In: LAK22: 12th International Learning Analytics and Knowledge Conference. ACM, March 2022. https://doi.org/10.1145/3506860.3506875
6. Jalo, H., Pirkkalainen, H., Torro, O., et al.: Extended reality technologies in small and medium-sized European industrial companies: level of awareness, diffusion and enablers of adoption. Virtual Reality (2022). https://doi.org/10.1007/s10055-022-00662-2

7. Janssen, J., Stoyanov, S., Ferrari, A., Punie, Y., Pannekeet, K., Sloep, P.: Experts' views on digital competence: commonalities and differences. Comput. Educ. **68**, 473–481 (2013). https://doi.org/10.1016/j.compedu.2013.06.008

8. Jerald, J.: The VR Book. Association for Computing Machinery, October 2015. https://doi.org/10.1145/2792790

9. Kress, B.C.: Optical Architectures for Augmented-, Virtual-, and Mixed-Reality Headsets. SPIE (2020). https://doi.org/10.1117/3.2559304

10. Lee, J.J., Hu-Au, E.: E3XR: an analytical framework for ethical, educational and Eudaimonic XR design. Front. Virtual Real. **2** (2021). https://doi.org/10.3389/frvir.2021.697667. https://www.frontiersin.org/article/10.3389/frvir.2021.697667

11. Matsika, C., Zhou, M.: Factors affecting the adoption and use of AVR technology in higher and tertiary education. Technol. Soc **67**, 101694 (2021). https://doi.org/10.1016/j.techsoc.2021.101694

12. Merino, L., Ghafari, M., Anslow, C., Nierstrasz, O.: CityVR: gameful software visualization. In: 2017 IEEE International Conference on Software Maintenance and Evolution (ICSME). IEEE, September 2017. https://doi.org/10.1109/icsme.2017.70

13. Sassoulas, P.: Github repository of the Django survey app. https://github.com/Pierre-Sassoulas/django-survey. Accessed 18 Apr 2022

14. Schein, K., Rauschnabel, P.: Augmented reality in manufacturing: Exploring workers' perceptions of barriers. IEEE Trans. Eng. Manage. 1–14 (2021). https://doi.org/10.1109/tem.2021.3093833

15. Shippee, M., Lubinsky, J.: Training and learning in virtual reality: Designing for consistent, replicable, and scalable solutions. In: 2021 International Conference on Electrical, Computer and Energy Technologies (ICECET). IEEE, December 2021. https://doi.org/10.1109/icecet52533.2021.9698487

16. The Django Software Foundation: The official website of the Django project. https://www.djangoproject.com/. Accessed 18 Apr 2022

17. Verma, A., Purohit, P., Thornton, T., Lamsal, K.: An examination of skill requirements for augmented reality and virtual reality job advertisements, August 2021

An Overview on Technologies for the Distribution and Participation in Live Events

Vito Del Vecchio, Mariangela Lazoi[✉], and Marianna Lezzi

Dipartimento di Ingegneria dell'Innovazione, Università del Salento, Lecce, Italy
mariangela.lazoi@unisalento.it

Abstract. COVID-19 has impacted several sectors, designing news way of collaboration and interaction with customers and partners. The performing arts sector is one of the most affected; activities have been stopped for months and months but, at the same time, the sector has embarked on a systemic transition where old, unsustainable practices have been replaced with more sustainable and technology-based alternatives. Through a narrative literature review, the paper discusses needs, current studies based on immersive technologies, strengths and weakness to be managed, opportunities to be leveraged and threats to be overcome, in order to improve competitiveness and plan future actions. Academics and practitioners can benefit from the results to address their current research and activities.

Keywords: Performing arts · COVID-19 · Immersive technologies · Technological transformation · Narrative literature review

1 Introduction

The adoption of digital technologies and streaming methods arises in different domains of the performing arts industry, such as theatre [1–3], cinema [4, 5], dance [6–9], music [10–13], gaming [14–16]. Live streaming in the performing arts industry appears in the literature under different alternative labels, including "digital broadcast cinema" [17], "live-cast and recorded theatre" [18], "livecasting", "simulcasts", "cinema live-casts", "beamed live performances", "alternative content" [19], "live-broadcasting", "webcasting" [4].

While some domains, such as digital gaming, have found a rapid spread in the streaming market and an increasing interest from customers, in other cases, virtual environments have struggled, as in the domains of theatre and music [20]. This could be because people usually attend live events to validate their identities [21], to feel part of a community [22], to celebrate their shared values [23], and to build social commitment to construct the experience [24, 25]. In addition to the performers, the venue of live events contributes to the meaning of any performance, affecting it in physical (e.g., acoustic), but also symbolic and conceptual terms [26]. On the other side, the case of the digital gaming is completely different. The possibility to have a digital platform, such

L. T. De Paolis et al. (Eds.): XR Salento 2022, LNCS 13445, pp. 312–323, 2022.
https://doi.org/10.1007/978-3-031-15546-8_26

as Twitch, provides a virtual place recognised as a social environment where users feel a sense of shared identity and the community grows around a common passion [15]. Moreover, social virtual environments have the potential to provide a greater degree of social awareness within a virtual audience. This represents a great opportunity for improving the user experience of live streamed contents [27].

The aim of this paper is to provide an overview of the technological needs for performing arts organizations, highlighting the important role of immersive technologies in the (post-)Covid era. The current state of art is explored using a narrative approach that analyses different references to build a comprehensive analysis of technological needs and existing studies highlighting strengths, weakness, opportunities and threats. Specifically, Scopus (https://www.scopus.com) has been used as the main source of information. Indeed, as stated by [28], it is one of the most important electronic databases containing scientific dissemination articles recognised in the academic environment. Different keywords have been adopted for querying the database such as "performing art", "immersive technologies", "virtual reality", "augmented reality", "streaming", "live", "broadcast", and different combinations have been implemented. The keywords have been searched in title, abstract and keywords of each papers, which have been selected according to their relevance for this research. Furthermore, to improve the quality of the retrieved information, studies published on journals have been only considered.

In the next section, insights into the need for a technological transformation of the performing arts sector are provided. A detailed description of current studies treating immersive technologies for the performing arts follows, and the contribution in terms of strengths, weaknesses, opportunities and threats are summarized in a further section. Conclusions end the paper.

2 The Need for Technological Advancement

The performing arts industry, as most other industries and related organizations, have had to adopt innovative approaches over time to attract current and potential audience, also due to the COVID-19 pandemic [29]. The common choice of these companies was the launch of the online streaming platforms for virtually distributing entertainment contents [6]. In a new contactless era, the shift of businesses to the online stage is inevitable. Live streaming of the performing arts can not only catch new audiences, but can also offer new value by providing alternative experiences. This is a time of significant change, and the web connectivity and the quick rise of pervasive media are changing the ways in which people communicate, access information, experience news. Furthermore, in the content industries, technological progress brings with it the destruction of old business models and the creation of new ones [5].

The performing arts industry is facings an existential crisis, as it has historically been an artistic endeavour that required face-to-face interactions. However, in the last few years, there has been an increase in live-streaming of the performing arts, causing a successful transition to online platforms [1]. There are also several reasons for arts organizations to rely on these new approaches. Firstly, with the rise of smart devices, such as smartphones and tablet PCs, the online streaming market is expected to grow, and the rapid development of data transmission enables the content provision through streaming services. In this context, the introduction of innovative digital technologies facilitates this trend [6]. Secondly, the exploration of other technologies, such as the Internet of Things (IoT), Augmented Reality (AR) and Virtual Reality (VR) seems to be promising for the streaming platform market [30, 31]. Third, there is an increase of demand for streaming services, since contents can be available without time and space constraints [6]. Fourth, audience, particularly younger audience, tends to move from traditional to online channels, video-on-demand and online streaming services [32]. For these reasons, entertainment organizations are interested in using online platforms also in the post-pandemic period. Moreover, digital technologies can be exploited not only for streaming online contents, but also to improve the quality of live performances and events. Many other benefits arise in terms of additional revenue streams, audience reach, audience development and global cultural exchange [33, 34].

Nevertheless, the exploration of streaming solutions is not only due to COVID-19. In such cases, virtual contents appeared also before the pandemic period. For example, the first demonstration of live contents dates back to 1926 when, due to the prohibitive cost of videotapes, television contents were broadcast via radio channels [4]. In the case of music, the band Sever Tire Damage has been streaming their live performances online since 1993 [20]. In 2009, the UK's National Theatre experienced the cinematic live-streaming of Shakespeare from stage to screen, and in 2013 the Royal Shakespeare Company broadcast its production to cinemas and schools [1]. Most recently, Aebischer have explored the digital transformation of theatre to offer their successful productions online via Globe Player during the closure of theatres [1].

3   The Use of Immersive Technologies

Despite rapid and significant technological advances, relatively little academic attention has been paid to the challenges that new technologies pose to the performing art industry [4]. Among the different new digital solutions, immersive technologies, and in particular AR and VR, seem to be the most widely adopted in the arts industry. In fact, the last decade has seen significant advancements in these solutions and customer engagement [7, 10]. The following describes applications found in the literature based on content enhancement and streaming-enabling technologies.

3.1   Technologies Improving Content Participation

Chang and Shin [11] discussed the use of hologram technology in music concerts at K-Live (in Korea) used to control and direct the virtual experience of audience, to sustain their engagement and satisfaction with the performance, and to create virtual experience contents. 3D visual technology is central to virtual experience and enables consumers to have multisensory interactions with products in electronic commercial environments [35, 36]. Virtual experiences consist of visual, textual, and audio cues guiding consumers when they interact with a virtual product [37]. According to the authors, hologram technologies offer digital simulations of concerts that allow audience to interactively experience the virtual representation of contents as real and natural, rather than artificial and constructed. Moreover, the holographic concert allows people to feel a more intimate and physically comfortable experience, instead of standing among thousands of strangers in a typical concert hall.

On the other hand, Valbom and Marcos [10] presented a Virtual Audio Environment (WAVE) that embraces the implementation of an immersive musical instrument model that uses 3D sound techniques combined with visualisation and virtual reality technologies. The environment is designed to cope with different facets of music and sound, such as performing, playing, creating and composing, by generating new sounds or modifying existing musical and sound structures, while facilitating a wider access for the audiences. Moreover, this system combines traditional and new musical concepts that can also be configured for musical composition and performance situations, giving more possibilities to the users.

Furthermore, Yan et al. [38] designed an interactive brain-computer system for the measurement and analysis of audience engagement level through an interactive three-dimensional virtual theatre. The system monitors audience engagement in real time using electroencephalography (EEG) measurement and tries to improve it by applying content-related performing cues when the engagement level decreases. The audience engagement is recognised as the key measure of quality in live performance [39], and according to the authors, the audience response is an important indicator of the quality of performing arts. Psychophysiological measurements enable to perceive and understand audience response by collecting their bio-signals during a live performance. The system provides three main functionalities. First, it measures the audience engagement during a digital theatre performance and uses an algorithm to determine the decreasing threshold. Second, the content-related performing cues are triggered as an immediate stimulus when audience engagement reaches the decreasing threshold. Third, the system detects whether the performing cues re-engage the audience successfully and how they affect the engagement according to the various types of performance. The system architecture designed by the authors is based on different tiers. The user tier includes the input interface (an Emotiv EEG headset and a visualized graphical user interface) which displays audience engagement in real time, and the output interface that presents the rendered performance content on a 3D circular-screen. The logic level consists of parsing the EEG data and determining when to initiate the performing cues. It also includes the software module that renders and exports the virtual scenes of theatre performance under the design process. The engine level includes the main functions developed on the basis of CryENGINE, a highly advanced game engine, in which virtual scenes are created. The performing cues are created in the Flow Graph Editor, a visual scripting system embedded in CryENGINE Sandbox.

According to Cham [40] the concept of complex systems is associated with the art industry. In particular, the author defined digitally interactive media as a machine system, which reacts in the moment by virtue of automated reasoning based on data from its sensory apparatus [41]. Digital interaction through a graphic user interface (GUI) is a graphic model of interaction, and a digital interface can allow multiple authors and multiple readers to participate in a simultaneous and instantaneous reproduction and dissemination of their divergent interpretations of an artefact as part of a networked participatory process.

Some other important VR solutions appear in the reference market. As reported by [42], MelodyVR [43] arises in the field of creativity and live acoustic performances, festivals and concerts, as well as live music events using combinations of virtual and real stimuli. The application also provides 360-degree live video, on-demand contents, intimate and exclusive experiences. ConcertVR [44] is a VR application focused on the virtual concert experience. Both live and on-demand contents are available, by providing 360-degree videos on smartphones or VR cardboard which enable a stereoscopic experience. Furthermore, the application provides multiple camera angles for easily switching views. VRZONE project [45] also focuses on providing virtual contents leveraging both VR and AR technologies. The application develops specific virtual experiences for users' entertainment in different fields such as sport venues, conferences, theatres, education and training sessions.

Many other immersive applications have been developed in the cultural heritage sector, adopting augmented reality technology. For instance, leveraging a head mounted display, visitors of archaeological sites can directly see virtual reconstructions of temples and other monuments while running around in the real world [46]. Within museums, intuitive access to information enhances the impact of the exhibition on virtual visitors [47]. Moreover, Wojciechowski et al. [48] developed an AR-system composed of an authoring tool, which allows museum supervisors to design virtual and augmented reality exhibitions, and an AR-browser, through which visitors can see the representations of cultural objects overlaid on the video captured by a camera.

Finally, according to Brondi et al. [49], mixed reality (MR) applications, defined as the combination of AR and VR technologies, are gaining increasing consensus in the context of cultural heritage. This is due to of a variety of purposes, such as: digital conservation and the possibility to rebuild damaged or destroyed artwork [50, 51]; validation of scientific hypotheses in archaeological reconstructions [52]; and education [53]. The authors proposed a general architecture for MR systems that can be used to provide an immersive experience to cultural heritage visitors. The architecture is based on XVR technology, a flexible and general-purpose framework for complex virtual reality development, that includes support for 3D animation, 3D sound effects, audio and video streaming and advanced user interaction, on head mounted display (such as Oculus Rift and HTC Vive), and also on projection systems (such as CAVE displays).

3.2 Technologies Enabling Distribution

Mobile head-mounted display devices for virtual reality applications have become increasingly popular in streaming contents, and the immersive VR applications have started to gain traction in many video streaming scenarios. For instance, many events, such as NBA games, WWE, ICC soccer and concerts have been broadcasted via VR videos by using Oculus Venues [54] and NextVR [55]. Both solutions provide VR applications to attend entertainment events as if they were real. According to [56], NextVR is among the most important immersive applications that emerge as key commercial players in the generation of 3D user experience. Compared to other solutions, it allows for streaming videos in real time since it is based on a technique that requires almost no computation for data processing [57].

In the same way, Hudson [20] explored the user experience of live streaming using a social virtual environment called Janus VR. This is a multi-user virtual reality web-browser in which websites are rendered in 3D and can be used with either a VR head-mounted display (HMD) or a standard desktop display. This environment allows users to watch a 360-degree video stream of a live music concert within a multi-user virtual place, but also to interact via text chat and voice communication. In addition, this environment gives users a virtual representation in the form of an avatar that allows them to express themselves physically. According to the author, while streaming content cannot replace the experience of a live event, it has the potential to provide a similar valuable alternative experience to audiences who could not otherwise attend.

Moreover, Mees et al. [58] tried to increase the social presence of a remote audience by creating a system in which audience members can communicate directly with each other and the characters during the performance. Their aim was to create an event for a large online audience that combines digital connectivity and interactivity with the liveness and shared experience of theatre. In this context, two environments emerge: the physical venue that directly involves the performers, and the virtual environment in which the virtual audience experiences the stream. Their interaction creates a new kind of hybridised, digitally-driven storytelling and a play environment offering the opportunity to socialise and engage with each other.

On the other hand, Kim, Kim and Hong [6] discussed the distribution strategy of online performances through virtualization of dance contents and over-the-top (OTT) streaming. The authors focused on analysing the level of customer satisfaction by considering different attributes. First, "quality of the dance performance", "platform for OTT streaming" and "promotion for potential audience development" are presented as the most important elements that must be met to positively affect the viewing satisfaction with online dance contents. Second, "brand awareness of the choreographer or dance company", "services for online audiences" and "fee and price criteria" are introduced as attractive factors, although consumers do not expect much. Third, "new formats and curation", "convergence technology for field sense" and "services for online audiences" are factors that, if met, may have a positive effect on viewing satisfaction, but if not, do not have a significant negative impact. Fourth, "production and editing competency", "quality of videos and sounds", "copyright of performance creation" and "fandom and audience management" are considered essential elements expected by consumers that, if not met, may negatively impact on satisfaction.

Feng, Bao and Wei [59] analysed the streaming of virtual reality videos highlighting the need to face a significant bandwidth challenge due to the high volume of data for the 360-degree videos. The authors developed a live viewport prediction mechanism based on a learning algorithm in order to save significant bandwidth.

Finally, Bakhshi and Throsby [5] drew the attention to the potential cannibalisation of revenues streams due to the fact that digital broadcast technologies have expanded the virtual capacity of performing arts venues. Even if the new channels, by conveying cultural contents to consumers, have expanded the audience of companies, there is a fear that customers completely switch from venues access to the new digital formats. In their discussion the authors launched a challenging reflection: whether live broadcast can substitute or complement audiences of traditional theatre. By carrying out an empirical case study based on the UK's National Theatre, the authors concluded that, if their results can be representative of live broadcasts more generally, theatre companies can significantly expand their audience reach through digital broadcasts to the cinema without cannibalising their audiences in the theatre.

4 SWOT Analysis

SWOT (Strengths, Weaknesses, Opportunities, Threats) analysis is a popular strategic method used in business organizations to identify different elements of competition and to understand priorities and alternative solutions. In the era of digital ecosystems, it is also used for strategic planning, quality control and the design and promotion of new initiatives [60].

Table 1 summarises the most important strengths, weaknesses, opportunities and threats arising from the adoption of digital technologies and streaming solutions in the performing arts industry. While the first two elements highlight competition from the internal perspective, the other ones focus on the external environment.

The contributions available in the literature analysed the adoption of digital technologies for different purposes (such as to engage audience) to explore innovative contents, to provide virtual experience, to improve the quality of live performance, to enable new forms of entertainment, to improve the event participation and to provide alternative immersive contents. The analysis also revealed that the adoption of immersive technologies, and in particular virtual reality (VR), is the most predominant solution for exploiting virtual contents in a more interacting way. However, digital technologies could be the cause of some issues related to the low participations of live events and venues and the construction of a social environment where people can physically share their emotions.

Table 1. SWOT analysis of digital technologies adoption in the performing art industry

Strengths	Weaknesses
• Improved user experience of live streamed contents [20, 27] • Virtual and immersive interaction [10, 11, 20, 47–49] • Augmented perception of performing arts contents and performance [15, 23, 25, 27] • Alternative value for customers [20, 23, 38, 46, 47] • Feeling part of a community [20, 22] • Social sharing of emotions [15, 38, 58] • Reaching people who cannot physically attend the shows [20] • Overcoming time and space constraints [6, 11, 20] • Building a social experience [20, 24, 25]	• Reduced importance of venues and live performance [5, 26] • Resistance to use innovative technologies in common traditional environments [20] • Distortion of the real performance [20] • Reduction of social interactions [11, 58] • Similar scenes and outdated costumes for more shows over the time [61] • Faithfully reproducing of emotions of live events [20] • Recognising the attribute of reality of live events [11]

(continued)

Table 1. (*continued*)

Opportunities	Threats
• Exploring other technologies (e.g., VR) [7, 10, 11, 30, 31, 38, 48, 49] • Catching younger audience [32] • Increasing revenue streams [5, 33, 34] • Attracting current and potential audience [5, 32–34] • Exchanging culture at a global scale [33, 34] • Providing a virtual community where sharing common passion [15] • Digital conservation [50, 51] • Rebuilding artwork damaged or destroyed [50, 51] • Building an interactive environment [11, 58] • Developing alternative audience experience [11, 20, 41] • Enriching the quality of performance [6, 38]	• Consolidating the importance of physical venues [26] • Low attendance of live events and venues [5] • Substituting live performance [5] • Affecting performers [26] • Development of technologies [61] • Changes of modern art trends [61]

5   Conclusion

This paper wants to provide a preliminary knowledge for an open discussion on the use of immersive technologies for performing arts (such as concert, ballet and theater). The original contribution of the research is to study the application of immersive technology in the performing arts sector, in particular for the event participation. In the Covid era, the performing arts sector feels the need to combine the definitive adoption of technologies (such as streaming services), which bring added value to the fruition of live events. This trend can benefit from other previous studies to leverage opportunities overcome threats and to be aware of strengths and weaknesses of innovative digital solutions in the performing art industry. Therefore, a need emerges that goes against the authentic concept of the fruition of the live event.

It is important to highlight that some barriers can obstacle the diffusion of such technologies in the performing arts: a) economic sustainability (i.e., the investments required may not be sustainable by performing arts organizations that usually are micro or small enterprises or association); b) contents creation and distribution (i.e., the organizers are responsible for creating the content to be brought into the virtual space and need specific competences); c) problem of scalability (i.e., to reach many users, a strong promotional effort is needed, and in addition to creating a service, a community of users needs to be created).

Therefore, the main phases of a roadmap for leading future research in this field can be suggested:

1. Define the current and future needs of performing arts organization to play in the market and be resilient to any external changes.

2. Explore the cost-effective trade-off for evaluating the cost of deploying and using the solution by events' organizers and the benefits in terms of image, revenue and industry growth.
3. Design a logical and technical architecture defining the systems and functionalities to be used that satisfies constraints of costs, time and competencies.
4. Define an algorithm for calculating the best virtual ticket amount.
5. Define a competence management methodology and tools that monitor available competence and suggest training programs to be updated with new XR technologies.
6. Suggest policies at regional, national and international levels for supporting the digital transformation of the sector.

Furthermore, future research will use the findings of this study to address the design of innovative technological solutions and new business models for organizations operating in the performing arts industry. In these terms, digital technologies could be leveraged in different directions: i) improving audience interaction and participation in live events; ii) providing a means for broadcasting performing arts' contents with no limit of space and time; iii) developing a hybrid user experience for both physical and virtual attendance.

Acknowledgement. This project has received funding from the Italian Ministry of University and Research, programme "Avviso FISR 2020 – COVID – Prima Fase", under the SAFE (Safe Approach For Event management) project, grant agreement n∘ FISR2020IP_03837.

References

1. Cho, D.: Digitally mediated Shakespeare in South Korea. Shakespeare **17**, 344–358 (2021)
2. O'Dwyer, N.: The scenographic turn: the pharmacology of the digitisation of scenography. Theatre Perform. Des. **I**(1), 48–63 (2015)
3. Ferrari, R.: Architecture and/in theatre from the Bauhaus to Hong Kong: Mathias Woo's looking for Mies. New Theatre Q. **28**(1), 3–19 (2012)
4. Mueser, D., Vlachos, P.: Almost like being there? A conceptualisation of live-streaming theatre. Int. J. Event Festival Manag. **19**(2), 183–203 (2018)
5. Bakhshi, H., Throsby, D.: Digital complements or substitutes? A quasi-field experiment from the royal national theatre. J. Cult. Econ. **38**, 1–8 (2014)
6. Kim, J., Kim, E., Hong, A.: OTT streaming distribution strategies for dance performances in the post-COVID-19 age: a modified importance-performance analysis. Int. J. Environ. Res. Publ. Health. **19**(327), 1–11 (2022)
7. Lee, J., Kim, Y., Heo, M., Kim, D.S.B.: Real-time projection-based augmented reality system for dynamic objects in the performing arts. Symmetry **7**(1), 182–192 (2015)
8. Mandilian, L., Diefenbach, P., Kim, Y.: Information overload: a collaborative dance performance. IEEE Multimed. **17**(1), 8–13 (2010)
9. Nam, J., Kim, Y., In, N., Nam, S.: 360 VR content production based on the analysis of the movements in the korean traditional court dances, Cheoyongmu and Bosangmu. Int. J. Innov. Technol. Explor. Eng. **8**(1), 2334–2338 (2019)
10. Valbom, L., Marcos, A.: WAVE: sound and music in an immersive environment. Comput. Graph. **19**(6), 871–881 (2005)
11. Chang, W., Shin, H.: Virtual experience in the performing arts: K-live hologram music concerts. Popular Entertain. Stud. **10**(1), 34–50 (2019)

12. Wu, Y., Zhang, L., BryanKinns, N., Barthet, M.: Open symphony: creative participation for audiences of live music performances. IEEE Multimed. **25**(1), 48–62 (2017)

13. Lazar, L., Myers, C.: Desire to listen: one learning management, system-based solution to providing, copyright compliant streaming, audio reserves. Music Ref. Serv. Q. **14**(3), 149–172 (2012)

14. Kaytoue, M., Silva, A., Cerf, L., Meira, W., Jr., Raïssi, C.: Watch me playing, I am a professional: a first study on video game live streaming. In: 21st International Conference Companion on World Wide Web, Lyon, France (2012)

15. Smith, T., Obrist, M., Wright, P.: Live-streaming changes the (video) game. In: 11th European Conference on Interactive TV and Video, New York (2013)

16. Jung, H., Hong, S., Kim, H.: A study on the properties of the relation between digital computer games and media performance with a focus on the Kinect device. Int. J. Multimed. Ubiquit. Eng. **9**(7), 109–120 (2014)

17. Heyer, P.: Live from the met: medium theory and digital broadcast cinema. Candian J. Commun. **33**(4), 591–604 (2008)

18. MeyerDinkgräfe, D.: Liveness: Phelan, Auslander, and after. J. Dram. Theory. Crit. **29**(2), 69–79 (2015)

19. Barker, M.: Live to your Local Cinema: The Remarkable Rise of Livecasting. Springer, Palgrave Macmillan, London, New York (2012). https://doi.org/10.1057/9781137288691

20. Hudson, M.: Live streaming performing arts within a social virtual environment. Int. J. Arts Technol. 10(4), 271–284 (2018)

21. Frith, S.: Live music matters. Scott. Music Rev. **I**(1), 1–17 (2007)

22. Overell, R.: Affective Intensities in Extreme Music Scenes: Cases from Australia and Japan. Palgrave Macmillan, New York (2014)

23. Small, C.: Musicking: The Meanings of Performing and Listening. Wesleyan University Press, Hanover (2011)

24. Clark, H.: Social actions, social commitments. In: Roots of Human Sociality: Culture, Cognition and Interaction, New York, USA (2006)

25. Pitts, S.: What makes an audience? Investigating the roles and experiences of listeners at a chamber music festival. Music Lett. **86**(2), 257–269 (2005)

26. Pitts, S., Spencer, C.: Loyalty and longevity in audience listening: investigating experiences of attendance at a chamber music festival. Music Lett. **86**(2), 227–238 (2008)

27. Hudson, M., Cairns, P.: Measuring social presence in team-based digital games. In: Interacting with Presence: HCI and the Sense of Presence in Computer-mediated Environments, Warsaw, Poland, De Gruyter Open Polan, pp. 83–98 (2014)

28. Corallo, A., Crespino, A.M., Del Vecchio, V., Lazoi, M., Marra, M.: Understanding and defining dark data for the manufacturing industry. IEEE Trans. Eng. Manag. 1–13 (2021)

29. Kim, J., Lee, J.: The concept and systematic classification for the dance industry. Dance Res. J. Korea. **20**, 63–82 (2020)

30. Hutchins, B., Li, B., Rowe, D.: Over-the-top sport: live streaming services, changing coverage rights markets and the growth of media sport portals. Med. Cult. Soc. **61**(7), 975–994 (2019)

31. Liebowitz, S., Zentner, A.: Clash of the Titans: does internet use reduce television viewing? Rev. Econ. Statist. **94**(1), 234–245 (2012)

32. Liebowitz, S., Zentner, A.: Clash of the Titans: does internet use reduce television viewing? Rev. Econ. Statist. **94**(1), 234–245 (2012)

33. Cochrane, B., Bonner, F.: Screening from the met, the NT, or the house: what changes with the live relay. Adaption **7**(2), 121–133 (2014)

34. King, T.: Streaming from stage to screen. Its place in the cultural marketplace and the implication for UK arts policy. Int. J. Cult. Policy. **24**(2), 220–235 (2016)

35. Soukup, C.: Building a theory of multi-media CMC: an analysis, critique and integration of computer-mediated communication theory and research. New Med. Soc. **2**(4), 407–425 (2000)
36. Li, H., Daugherty, T., Biocca, F.: Characteristics of virtual experience in electronic commerce: a protocol analysis. J. Interact. Mark. **15**(3), 13–30 (2001)
37. Norman, D.A.: Affordances, conventions and design. Interactions **6**(3), 38–43 (1999)
38. Yan, S., et al.: Exploring audience response in performing arts with a brain-adaptive digital performance system. ACM Trans. Interact. Intell. Syst. **7**(4), 1–28 (2017)
39. Radbourne, J., Johanson, K., Glow, H., White, T.: The audience experience: measuring quality in the performing arts. Int. J. Arts Manag. **11**(3), 16–29 (2009)
40. Karen, C.: Reconstruction theory, designing the space of possibility in complex media. Int. J. Perform. Arts Digital Med. **3**(2), 253–267 (2007)
41. Penny, S.: From A to D and back again; the emerging aesthetics of interactive art. Leonardo Electron. Alm. **3**(4), 4–7 (1996)
42. Rajguru, C., Obrist, M., Memoli, G.: spatial soundscapes and virtual worlds: challenges and opportunities. Front. Psychol. **11**, 569056 (2020)
43. MelodyVR: MelodyVR (2022). https://melodyvr.com/. Accessed 1 Feb 2022
44. concertVR: concertVR (2022). https://concertvr.io/. Accessed 1 Feb 2022
45. VRZONE project: VRZONE project (2022). https://www.vrzone.it/. Accessed 1 Feb 2022
46. Vlahakis, V., et al.: ARCHEOGUIDE: first results of an augmented reality, mobile computing system in cultural heritage sites. In: Proceedings of the 2001 Conference on Virtual Reality, Archeology, and Cultural Heritage, Glyfada, Greece (2001)
47. Sylaiou, S., Liarokapis, F., Kotsakis, K., Patias, P.: Virtual museums, a survey and some issues for consideration. J. Cult. Herit. **10**(4), 520–528 (2009)
48. Wojciechowski, R., Walczak, K., White, M., Cellary, W.: Building virtual and augmented reality museum exhibitions. In: Proceeding of the Ninth International Conference on 3D Web Technology, Web3D, Monterey, California, USA (2004)
49. Brondi, R., Carrozzino, M., Lorenzini, C., Tecchia, F.: Using mixed reality and natural interaction in cultural heritage applications. Informatica. **60**(3), 311–316 (2016)
50. Carrozzino, M., Evangelista, C., Scucces, A., Tecchia, F., Tennirelli, G., Bergamasco, M.: The virtual museum of sculpture. In: Proceedings of the Third International Conference on Digital Interactive Media in Entertainment and Arts, Athens, Greece (2008)
51. Brondi, R., Carrozzino, M.: ARTworks: an augmented reality interface as an aid for restoration professionals. In: De Paolis, L.T., Mongelli, A. (eds.) AVR 2015. LNCS, vol. 9254, pp. 384–398. Springer, Cham (2015). https://doi.org/10.1007/978-3-319-22888-4_28
52. Barceló, J., Forte, M., Sanders, D.: Virtual Reality in Archaeology. Archaeo Press, Oxford (2000)
53. EconomouLaia, M., Pujol, P.: Educational tool or expensive toy? Evaluating VR evaluation and its relevance for virtual heritage. In: New Heritage: New Media and Cultural Heritage, Routledge (2008)
54. Meta Quest, Facebook Technologies, LLC (2022). https://www.oculus.com/experiences/quest/2464560730245504/?locale=it_IT. Accessed 1 Feb 2022
55. Meta Quest, Facebook Technologies, LLC (2022). https://www.oculus.com/experiences/go/858258597574484/?locale=it_IT. Accessed 1 Feb 2022
56. Bae, S., et al.: 2D reprojection of plenoptic 3D voxel data using Gaussian intensity spreading. In: International Conference on Information and Communication Technology Convergence (ICTC), Jeju, Korea (2020)
57. Xu, F., Zhao, T., Luo, B., Dai, Q.: Generating VR live videos with tripod panoramic rig. In: IEEE Conference on Virtual Reality and 3D User Interfaces (VR), Tuebingen/Reutlingen, Germany (2018)

58. Mees, A., Wright, T., Donald, N., Gillies, M., Prime, S., Milne, A.: Coney: Better Than Life. 10 (2015). https://research.gold.ac.uk/id/eprint/13925/1/Coney-project-report-1.pdf. Accessed 1 Feb 2022

59. Feng, X., Bao, Z., Wei, S.: LiveObj: object semantics-based viewport prediction for live mobile virtual reality streaming. IEEE Trans. Visualiz. Comput. Graph. **27**(5), 2736–2745 (2021)

60. Namugenyia, C., Nimmagadda, S.L., Reiners, T.: Design of a SWOT analysis model and its evaluation in diverse digital business ecosystem contexts. In: International Conference on Knowledge-Based and Intelligent Information & Engineering Systems, Budapest, Hungary (2019)

61. Sari, T., Subagyo, H.: SWOT analysis of art performance as city promotional strategy In Yogyakarta. J. Educ. Cult. Soc. **11**(1), 370–378 (2020)

How to Improve Vehicle Lateral Control: The Effect of Visual Feedback Luminance

Riccardo Rossi[1,2] , Giulia De Cet[2,3] , and Federico Orsini[1,2](✉)

[1] Department of Civil, Environmental and Architectural Engineering, University of Padua, Padua, Italy
riccardo.rossi@unipd.it, federico.orsini@dicea.unipd.it
[2] Mobility and Behavior Research Center – MoBe, University of Padua, Padua, Italy
giulia.decet@unipd.it
[3] Department of Industrial Engineering, University of Padua, Padua, Italy

Abstract. In previous driving simulator studies, the effectiveness of various precision teaching feedback systems on lateral vehicle control has been demonstrated. The aim of this work is to test the impact of the visual feedback luminance on the system's effectiveness. Seventeen participants were recruited to take part in the simulator experiment. Each participant drove for 4 consecutive trials on the same path; the first was a baseline trial, without feedback delivery. The feedback system monitored vehicle position, presenting an auditory stimulus and a visual stimulus with luminance change. To evaluate the feedback effect, repeated measure ANOVAs were performed on several lateral control variables. Results showed that the presence of feedback improved participants' lateral control of the vehicle, with drivers improving the investigated variables while maintaining a correct position within the lane. Furthermore, the multimodal feedback system of the present work was compared with auditory-only feedback, showing significant speed up in the performance enhancement, thanks to redundancy gain.

Keywords: Precision teaching · Driving simulator · Lateral control · Road safety · Driving assistance system

1 Introduction

Precision teaching (PT) refers to a teaching technique grounded in the theoretical framework of behavioral analysis [1]. The method aims to have the learner perform a given task with higher fluency [2, 3], i.e. to provide faster or more accurate responses. This teaching method aims to automatize the reaction of the learners, allowing them to automatically generate the appropriate pattern of responses to the stimulation specified and to minimize the involvement of conscious control processes.

PT is a flexible method that can be applied to a variety of qualitatively different tasks [4]. It is particularly well suited for structured tasks in which there is a clear connection between the stimuli and the response. It should be noted that the stimuli and the response need not be simple: the first can be a complex configuration of multimodal signals and the second can be the execution of a sequence of tasks. However, it is important that the

© Springer Nature Switzerland AG 2022
L. T. De Paolis et al. (Eds.): XR Salento 2022, LNCS 13445, pp. 324–334, 2022.
https://doi.org/10.1007/978-3-031-15546-8_27

rules that connect each configuration of stimuli to each response are clearly defined, for the model to work best.

PT has been formally introduced to road safety research by Biondi et al. [5], who applied both auditory and visual feedback systems to improve vehicle lateral control within a driving simulator experiment, with significant results. Previously, PT had been implicitly applied in several other works, in the context of eco-driving [6–8] and lane maintenance training [9].

As drivers are normally required to maintain their vehicle within lane boundaries, lane boundary encroachments and increased lane weaving are indicative of degraded directional control, which relates to increased risk of accidents (e.g., head-on collisions or road departures)[10]. In this sense, the development of techniques to improve drivers' lateral control represents a relevant challenge in road safety, and several advanced driver assistance systems (ADAS) have been developed to address this issue [11, 12].

Driving simulators present many unique features for the study of traffic safety [13]: virtual traffic behavior, road layout, and other characteristics can be manipulated according to research needs, in a standardized, controllable, and reproducible way. They can be used for experimental manipulations in order to study, among others, what-if scenarios in relation to new technologies. For these reasons, they are excellent tools for an interdisciplinary approach to road safety, which includes elements of engineering and psychology research.

The work presented in this paper further investigates, by means of a driving simulator experiment, the effects of PT on drivers lateral control, testing a new feedback system and comparing it with those presented in Biondi et al. [5]. In that study, two feedback systems were applied to inform drivers of the correctness of their position within the lane. The first was an auditory system, which provided negative feedback (represented by a low-frequency tone) when drivers veered out of the admitted area (see Fig. 2a) and positive feedback (in the form of a high-frequency tone) when they entered it. The second was a combination of the auditory system previously described and a visual one, in which a colored circle indicated the correctness of the lateral position, turning green when the vehicle was within the positive feedback zone and red when it moved outside of this zone. The circle was placed in the near-peripheral visual field to ensure detection without potentially distracting the driver. The second system was developed based on the assumption that simultaneous presentation of stimuli in different modes not only accelerates the process of learning, but also facilitates their detection [14, 15]; however, despite feedback redundancy, no further improvement was observed.

Here, a new feedback system was developed and tested. Similarly, to the second one of Biondi et al. [5], it consisted of a circle indicating the correctness of the lateral position of the drivers in a continuous way. In this case, instead of being green or red, it was white (positive feedback) or black (negative). This choice was motivated by the fact that human near-peripheral vision is more sensitive to changes in luminance than to changes in color tonality [16]. In addition to this, the positive and negative feedback zones of the system were divided into three subzones each, with the colored circle changing its luminance depending on the subzone in which the vehicle was located (more details in Sect. 2.4).

This work aims to determine whether the proposed visual feedback system that changes in luminance is capable of improving the effectiveness of PT for vehicle lateral control, with potentially relevant consequences for practical applications.

The paper is divided as follows: in Sect. 2 the methodology of the study is presented, Sect. 3 presents the analysis of results, and finally the discussion and conclusion are presented in the fourth and final section.

2 Methodology

A driving simulator experiment was developed and performed at the Transportation Laboratory of the University of Padua. Before carrying out the test, participants familiarized with the simulator for about 10 min. After checking the condition of the participants [17], each of them drove for 4 consecutive trials on the same path (the first was a baseline trial, without feedback delivery). Each trial consisted of driving along the scenario path described in Sect. 2.3. During the second, third, and fourth trials, a feedback system was presented. Participants were informed about the ability under evaluation by the feedback.

2.1 Participants

Seventeen participants were recruited to participate in the simulator experiment. They were students or staff of the University of Padua. All participants had never used the driving simulator before and had had a car driving license for at least one year. There were 7 women and 10 men, the age range was 19–28 years with an average of 23.8. In addition to the 17 participants, 2 other subjects took part in the study, but they were affected by simulator sickness, and therefore excluded from the analysis.

2.2 Driving Simulator

In this study, a fixed base driving simulator produced by STSoftware® was used (Fig. 1). The simulator had: a cockpit, composed of an adjustable car seat, a gaming dynamic force feedback steering wheel with a 900° turn angle and gas, brake and clutch pedals. Three networked computers and five full high-definition ($1,920 \times 1,080$ pixels) screens creating a 330° (horizontal) by 45° (vertical) field of view were included in the system. The simulator is equipped with a Dolby Surround® sound system, which produces realistic virtual views of the road and the surrounding environment. The simulator has previously been validated [18, 19] and used in several road safety experiments [20–25].

2.3 Scenario

The road scenario used for the experiment consisted of a bidirectional two-lane road designed in virtual reality with the 3D editing software of the driving simulator. The width of the lane was 2.95 m. The route was 10 km long and consisted of a sequence of alternating left and right turns. Each curve had a length of 174.53 m with a radius of 500 m. The route was divided into three sections according to the landscape and the speed limit in force: extra-urban (limit: 70 km/h; length 2 km), urban (limit: 50 km/h; length

Fig. 1. Driving simulators at the Transportation Laboratory of University of Padua.

2 km), and extra-urban (limit: 90 km/h; length 6 km). Moderate traffic conditions were simulated in the opposite direction (300 vehicles/h/lane). The environment in which the experiment is performed had a temperature kept constant, of 20–22° and illumination of 4lx. This scenario had previously been used for the PT experiment by Biondi et al. [5] discussed in Sect. 1, but also for other studies investigating the effect of mental models on ADAS systems [26] and the left-digit effect to nudge drivers to reduce speed [27].

2.4 Feedback System

The feedback system monitored vehicle position (centerline) every 10 m, identifying two conditions: a negative one, when the vehicle was outside the allowed area, and a positive one, when it was inside. The admitted area was defined (see Fig. 2a) considering the following criteria: (i) the driving rule requires the driver to maintain a position reasonably close to the right border of the lane; therefore, the axis of the admitted area was placed 0.25 m right from the lane axis; (ii) in previous experiments on the same simulator [28], the standard deviation of lateral position (SDLP) of unimpaired drivers was about 0.25 m; therefore, the admitted area had a width of 0.50 m.

The feedback system included an auditory cue and a visual one. The auditory consisted of two tones, high when the vehicle entered the positive feedback zone and low when it entered the negative feedback zone. Visual feedback consisted of a circle, placed at the top of the screen, with its color changing from white to black depending on the lateral position (Fig. 3). The choice of black and white contrast was motivated by the fact that human near-peripheral vision is more sensitive to changes in luminance than to changes in color tonality [29]. In addition to this, positive and negative feedback zones of the system were divided into three subzones each, with the colored circle changing its luminance depending on the subzone in which the vehicle was located. For the definition of subzones see Fig. 2b and Table 1.

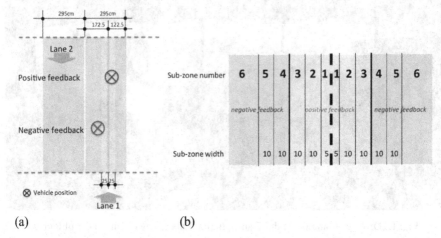

(a)   (b)

Fig. 2. (a) Positive and negative feedback zones [5]; (b) Definition of sub-zones (subzone with expressed in centimeters)

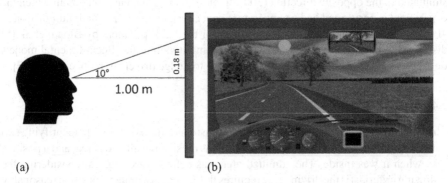

(a)   (b)

Fig. 3. (a) Circle position in feedback system (b) Visual feedback

2.5 Variables

The sampling frequency of the variables during each trial of the experiment was 50 Hz. Several variables were recorded by the driving simulator, including:

- x_j, the lateral position of the vehicle, relative to the axis of the admitted area, at time instant j; with $x_j = 0$ when the centerline of the vehicle is exactly on the axis of the admitted area, $x_j > 0$ when it is on the left and $x_j < 0$ when it is on the right;
- w_j, the lateral speed of the vehicle, at time instant j;
- α_j, the steering angle of the vehicle, at time instant j; with $\alpha_j = 0$ corresponding to no steering, $\alpha_j < 0$ steering to the left, $\alpha_j > 0$ steering to the right;

Table 1. Circle color in feedback system

Feedback zone	Sub-zone	Circle color
Positive	1	White
	2	20% Grey
	3	40% Grey
Negative	4	60% Grey
	5	80% Grey
	6	Black

j ranges in the interval 1...T, where T is the total number of records sampled during the experiment, and the time difference between two successive time instants j and $j + 1$ is 0.02 s. For each trial, these raw variables were aggregated into several indicators, which were used for the analyses.

SDLP is the standard deviation of lateral position, in meters:

$$\text{SDLP} = \sqrt{\frac{1}{T-1} \sum_{j=1}^{T} (x_j - \bar{x})^2} \tag{1}$$

ABSLP, the mean absolute lateral position, in meters:

$$\text{ABSLP} = \frac{1}{T} \sum_{j=1}^{T} |x_j| \tag{2}$$

LS, the mean lateral speed, in m/s:

$$\text{LS} = \frac{1}{T} \sum_{j=1}^{T} w_j \tag{3}$$

ABSSTEER, the mean absolute steering angle, in degrees:

$$ABSSTEER = \frac{1}{T} \sum_{j=1}^{T} |\alpha_j| \tag{4}$$

SDSTEER is the standard deviation of steering angle, in degrees:

$$SDSTEER = \sqrt{\frac{1}{T-1} \sum_{j=1}^{T} (\alpha_j - \bar{\alpha})^2} \tag{5}$$

SDABSSTEER is the standard deviation of absolute steering angle, in degrees:

$$SDABSSTEER = \sqrt{\frac{1}{T-1} \sum_{j=1}^{T} (|\alpha_j| - |\bar{\alpha}|)^2} \tag{6}$$

3   Analysis and Results

SData were analyzed using JASP Software [30].

3.1   Precision Teaching Effectiveness

In order to evaluate the feedback effect on lateral control, repeated measure ANOVAs were carried out. The response variables were: SDLP, ABSLP, LS, ABSTEER, SDSTEER and SDABSSTEER (all defined in Sect. 2.5), the within-factor was the trial (four levels), and no between-factor was considered.

Significant effect was found for all six variables: SDLP $F(3,48) = 75.86$, $p < .001$, ABSLP $F(3,48) = 66.77$, $p < .001$, LS $F(3,48) = 22.67$, $p < .001$, ABSTEER $(3,48) = 7.85$, $p < .001$, SDSTEER $(3,48) = 9.12$, $p < .001$, SDABSSTEER $(3,48) = 7.76$, $p < .001$. Average of variables across trials are presented in Table 2.

Post hoc comparisons with Bonferroni correction for the six variables are presented in Table 3.

Table 2. Average of variables across trials 1–4.

Variable	Trial1	Trial2	Trial3	Trial4
SDLP	0.256	0.173	0.165	0.153
ABSLP	0.271	0.155	0.146	0.131
LS	0.149	0.113	0.112	0.105
ABSTEER	8.118	7.359	7.332	7.219
SDSTEER	9.334	7.975	7.984	7.831
SDABSSTEER	4.393	3.038	3.102	2.982

3.2   Comparison with an Auditory-Only Feedback System

A mixed-factor ANOVA was carried out in order to compare the effectiveness of this feedback system with an auditory system analyzed in the previous study by Biondi et al. [5]; "feedback system" as between-factor (two levels) and "trial" as within-factor (four levels) were considered. A significant effect for ABSLP was found on trial ($F(3,132) = 65.80$, $p < .001$, on feedback system ($F(1,44) = 4.14$, $p = 0.048$, and interaction ($F(3,132) = 3.30$, $p = 0.025$. No other variables were significant on feedback system and interaction. Trend of ABSLP can be observed in Fig. 4.

Table 3. Post hoc comparisons with Bonferroni correction. Values in cells are t statistics and p-Values in parenthesis. Cells in italics have a p-value lower than 0.05.

Variable	Trial1 vs Trial2	Trial1 vs Trial3	Trial1 vs Trial4	Trial2 vs Trial3	Trial 3 vs Trial4
SDLP	*10.93* *(<.001)*	*11.91* *(<.001)*	*13.54* *(<.001)*	0.98 (1.000)	1.627 (0.661)
ABSLP	*10.43* *(<.001)*	*11.26* *(<.001)*	*12.57* *(<.001)*	0.837 (1.000)	1.307 (1.000)
LS	*6.086* *(<.001)*	*6.209* *(<.001)*	*7.525* *(<.001)*	0.123 (1.000)	1.316 (1.000)
ABSTEER	*3.651* *(0.004)*	*3.780* *(0.003)*	*4.328* *(<.001)*	0.129 (1.000)	0.547 (1.000)
SDSTEER	*4.112* *(<.001)*	*4.087* *(<.001)*	*4.550* *(<.001)*	−0.025 (1.000)	0.464 (1.000)
SDABSSTEER	*3.937* *(0.002)*	*3.752* *(0.003)*	*4.100* *(<.001)*	−0.185 (1.000)	3.348 (1.000)

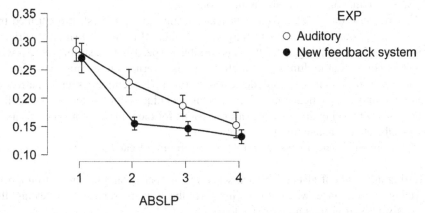

Fig. 4. ABSLP in meters across trials 1–4 for the new feedback system and the auditory one previously tested. Error bars show 95% confidence intervals, computed as in [31].

4 Discussion and Conclusion

The results presented in Sect. 3.1 showed that thanks to the precision teaching technique proposed in the present paper, participants improved their lateral control during the experiment. The decrease in SDLP, lateral speed, and the steering-related variables indicates an increasingly smoother lateral control of the vehicle, with fewer corrections on the steering wheel and an overall more flowing trajectory. The decrease in the absolute value of the lateral position (calculated with reference to the axis of the admitted area) indicates that participants were able to keep themselves closer to the ideal lateral position. Note that these improvements were not a byproduct of participants' increased familiarity with the simulated scenario, since in a previous study on the same scenario it was demonstrated that lateral control does not improve significantly with familiarity [5].

The effectiveness of the PT was already significant after the first trial with the feedback (see Table 3), while in the following trials there was a slight additional, albeit nonsignificant, improvement in lateral control (Tables 2 and 3). Previous studies suggest that this effect can be maintained over time [32].

In Sect. 3.2 the new feedback system was compared to the auditory-only feedback system of Biondi et al. [5]. Unlike the auditory-only system, in which participants progressively improved their performance throughout the trials, the new system was able to obtain similar results faster, after just one trial. This is consistent with the literature on redundancy gain, suggesting that the concurrent presentation of stimuli with different modalities can speed up processing and detection [14, 15], enhancing driver performance [33, 34]. It is important to note that this result was not observed in the study of Biondi et al. [5], and therefore the choice of designing the visual feedback in the present study was crucial, with the luminance of the stimulus significantly improving its detection.

In addition, the results shown in Fig. 4 seem to identify some sort of ceiling effect, which limits further improvements in lateral control: this may explain the fact that other lateral control variables (such as SDLP) could no further improve with the redundant feedback system, compared to the auditory-only one.

Nevertheless, the results of this study are of high interest. First, it confirmed the findings of previous studies, showing the potential of the PT technique to improve driving performance. Second, it suggested that it is possible to speed up the learning process with the use of concurrent multimodal stimuli, but it also warned on the importance of the feedback system design, as stimuli detection is crucial. These findings are of particular importance under a practical point of view, as this technique could potentially be applied in the real world, using driving simulation sessions for the training of novice drivers or drivers subjected to mandatory retraining.

There are still some interesting directions for future research:

- Testing the effect of visual feedback separately, to understand its ability to improve driving performance when no auditory feedback is presented, and testing the effectiveness of visual unimodal feedback
- Evaluating the effect of feedback on driver performance over time, with different time horizons (e.g., immediately after the treatment, after one week, three months, etc.)

Acknowledgment. The authors would like to thank Prof. Massimiliano Gastaldi, Alberto Sarto, Domenico Pizzorni and Alberto Tosolin for their support in designing the experiment, and Elisabetta Genovese, Caterina Buonocunto and the students from the course "Human Factors in Transport Systems Safety" of the Master Degree in Safety Engineering for their support during experiment execution and data collection.

Author Contributions. Conceptualization: RR, GDC, FO; methodology: GDC, FO; software: GDC, FO; formal analysis: GDC; investigation: GDC, FO; data curation: GDC, FO; writing – original draft: GDC, FO; writing – review & editing: RR, GDC, FO; visualization: GDC, FO; supervision: RR.

References

1. Lindsley, O.R.: Precision teaching's unique legacy from B. F. Skinner. J. Behav. Educ. **1**, 253–266 (1991). https://doi.org/10.1007/BF00957007
2. Binder, C.: Behavioral fluency: evolution of a new paradigm. Behav. Anal. **19**, 163–197 (1996)
3. Gallagher, E., Bones, R., Lombe, J.: Precision teaching and education: Is fluency the missing link between success and failure? Irish Educ. Stud. **25**, 93–105 (2006). https://doi.org/10.1080/03323310600597642
4. Marr, J., et al.: Precision teaching of an introductory physics E&M course for engineers. In: Proceedings - Frontiers in Education Conference, FIE, pp. 174–178 (1993). https://doi.org/10.1109/FIE.1993.405541
5. Biondi, F.N., Rossi, R., Gastaldi, M., Orsini, F., Mulatti, C.: Precision teaching to improve drivers' lane maintenance. J. Saf. Res. **72**, 225–229 (2020). https://doi.org/10.1016/j.jsr.2019.12.020
6. Hibberd, D.L., Jamson, A.H., Jamson, S.L.: The design of an in-vehicle assistance system to support eco-driving. Transp. Res. Part C Emerg. Technol. **58**, 732–748 (2015). https://doi.org/10.1016/j.trc.2015.04.013
7. Barbé, J., Boy, G., Sans, M.: GERICO: a human centred eco-driving system. IFAC Proc. **40**, 292–297 (2007). https://doi.org/10.3182/20070904-3-KR-2922.00051
8. Azzi, S., Reymond, G., Mérienne, F., Kemeny, A.: Eco-driving performance assessment with in-car visual and haptic feedback assistance. J. Comput. Inf. Sci. Eng. **11**, 041005 (2011). https://doi.org/10.1115/1.3622753
9. De Groot, S., De Winter, J.C.F., García, J.M.L., Mulder, M., Wieringa, P.A.: The effect of concurrent bandwidth feedback on learning the lane-keeping task in a driving simulator. Hum. Factors. **53**, 50–62 (2011). https://doi.org/10.1177/0018720810393241
10. Zhou, J., Peng, H., Gordon, T.J.: Characterization of the lateral control performance by human drivers on highways. SAE Int. J. Pass. Cars Mech. Syst. **1** (2008)
11. Navarro, J., Mars, F., Young, M.S.: Lateral control assistance in car driving: classification, review and future prospects. IET Intell. Transp. Syst. **5**, 207–220 (2011). https://doi.org/10.1049/iet-its.2010.0087
12. Okamoto, K., Tsiotras, P.: Data-driven human driver lateral control models for developing haptic-shared control advanced driver assist systems. Rob. Auton. Syst. **114**, 155–171 (2019). https://doi.org/10.1016/j.robot.2019.01.020
13. de Winter, J.C.F., van Leeuwen, P.M., Happee, R.: Advantages and disadvantages of driving simulators: a discussion. In: Proceedings of the Measuring Behavior Conference, pp. 47–50 (2012)
14. Diederich, A., Colonius, H.: Bimodal and trimodal multisensory enhancement: effects of stimulus onset and intensity on reaction time. Percept. Psychophys. **66**, 1388–1404 (2004). https://doi.org/10.3758/BF03195006
15. Forster, B., Cavina-Pratesi, C., Aglioti, S.M., Berlucchi, G.: Redundant target effect and intersensory facilitation from visual-tactile interactions in simple reaction time. Exp. Brain Res. **143**, 480–487 (2002). https://doi.org/10.1007/S00221-002-1017-9
16. Hansen, T., Pracejus, L., Gegenfurtner, K.R.: Color perception in the intermediate periphery of the visual field. J. Vis. **9**, 1–12 (2009). https://doi.org/10.1167/9.4.26

17. Kennedy, R.S., Lane, N.E., Berbaum, K.S., Lilienthal, M.G.: Simulator sickness question-naire: an enhanced method for quantifying simulator sickness (questions only). Int. J. Aviat. Psychol. **3**, 203–220 (1993). https://doi.org/10.1207/s15327108ijap0303_3

18. Rossi, R., Meneguzzer, C., Orsini, F., Gastaldi, M.: Gap-acceptance behavior at roundabouts: validation of a driving simulator environment using field observations. Transp. Res. Procedia. **47**, 27–34 (2020). https://doi.org/10.1016/j.trpro.2020.03.069

19. Rossi, R., Gastaldi, M., Gecchele, G., Biondi, F., Mulatti, C.: Traffic-calming measures affecting perceived speed in approaching bends: on-field validated virtual environment. Transp. Res. Rec. **2434**, 35–43 (2014). https://doi.org/10.3141/2434-05

20. Gastaldi, M., Orsini, F., Gecchele, G., Rossi, R.: Safety analysis of unsignalized intersections: a bivariate extreme value approach. Transp. Lett. **13**, 209–218 (2021). https://doi.org/10.1080/19427867.2020.1861503

21. Orsini, F., Gecchele, G., Gastaldi, M., Rossi, R.: Collision prediction in roundabouts: a comparative study of extreme value theory approaches. Transp. A Transp. Sci. **15**, 556–572 (2019). https://doi.org/10.1080/23249935.2018.1515271

22. Rossi, R., Orsini, F., Tagliabue, M., Di Stasi, L.L., De Cet, G., Gastaldi, M.: Evaluating the impact of real-time coaching programs on drivers overtaking cyclists. Transp. Res. Part F Traffic Psychol. Behav. **78**, 74–90 (2021). https://doi.org/10.1016/j.trf.2021.01.014

23. Rossi, R., et al.: Reducing elevated gravitational-force events through visual feedback: a simulator study. Transp. Res. Procedia. **52**, 115–122 (2021). https://doi.org/10.1016/j.trpro.2021.01.013

24. Rossi, R., Gastaldi, M., Orsini, F., De Cet, G., Meneguzzer, C.: A comparative simulator study of reaction times to yellow traffic light under manual and automated driving. Transp. Res. Procedia. **52**, 276–283 (2021). https://doi.org/10.1016/J.TRPRO.2021.01.032

25. Orsini, F., Tagliabue, M., De Cet, G., Gastaldi, M., Rossi, R.: Highway deceleration lane safety: effects of real-time coaching programs on driving behavior. Sustain. **13**, 9089 (2021). https://doi.org/10.3390/su13169089

26. Rossi, R., Gastaldi, M., Biondi, F., Orsini, F., De Cet, G., Mulatti, C.: A driving simulator study exploring the effect of different mental models on ADAS system effectiveness. In: De Paolis, L.T., Bourdot, P. (eds.) AVR 2020. LNCS, vol. 12242, pp. 102–113. Springer, Cham (2020). https://doi.org/10.1007/978-3-030-58465-8_7

27. Rubaltelli, E., Manicardi, D., Orsini, F., Mulatti, C., Rossi, R., Lotto, L.: How to nudge drivers to reduce speed: the case of the left-digit effect. Transp. Res. Part F Traffic Psychol. Behav. **78**, 259–266 (2021). https://doi.org/10.1016/j.trf.2021.02.018

28. Gastaldi, M., Rossi, R., Hadas, Y., Fasan, D., Keren, N., Mulatti, C.: Caffeinated chewing gum as countermeasure to drivers' passive task-related fatigue caused by monotonous roadway. J. Transp. Res. Board **2602**, 26–34 (2016). https://doi.org/10.3141/2602-04

29. Hansen, T., Pracejus, L., Gegenfurtner, K.R.: Color perception in the intermediate periphery of the visual field. J. Vis. **9** (2009). https://doi.org/10.1167/9.4.26

30. Love, J., et al.: JASP: graphical statistical software for common statistical designs. J. Stat. Softw. Artic. **88**, 1–17 (2019). https://doi.org/10.18637/jss.v088.i02

31. Morey, R.D.: Confidence intervals from normalized data: a correction to Cousineau (2005). Tutor. Quant. Methods Psychol. **4**, 61–64 (2008)

32. Rossi, R., De Cet, G., Gianfranchi, E., Orsini, F., Gastaldi, M.: How precision teaching can shape drivers' lateral control over time. Transp. Res. Procedia. **62**, 565–572 (2022). https://doi.org/10.1016/j.trpro.2022.02.070

33. Mohebbi, R., Gray, R., Tan, H.Z.: Driver reaction time to tactile and auditory rear-end collision warnings while talking on a cell phone. Hum. Factors. **51**, 102–110 (2009). https://doi.org/10.1177/0018720809333517

34. Spence, C., Ho, C.: Multisensory interface design for drivers: past, present and future. Ergonomics **51**, 65–70 (2008). https://doi.org/10.1080/00140130701802759

Extended Reality Technologies and Social Inclusion: The Role of Virtual Reality in Includiamoci Project

Carola Gatto[1]([✉]), Silvia Liaci[2], Laura Corchia[1], Sofia Chiarello[3], Federica Faggiano[3], Giada Sumerano[3], and Lucio Tommaso De Paolis[3]

[1] Department of Cultural Heritage, University of Salento, Lecce, Italy
{carola.gatto,laura.corchia1}@unisalento.it
[2] Department of European and Mediterranean Cultures, University of Basilicata, Potenza, Italy
silvia.liaci@unibas.it
[3] Department of Engineering for Innovation, University of Salento, Lecce, Italy
{sofia.chiarello,federica.faggiano,giada.sumerano,
lucio.depaolis}@unisalento.it

Abstract. In recent years we have witnessed a great change in the school and education system, that shifted from a culture of integration to a culture of inclusion, aimed at creating a condition of equal opportunity and making the uniqueness of individual, strength, and enrichment for all. Digital technologies are important to support the social inclusion of people with physical and mental disabilities because they enable the overcoming of some real-world barriers, and among these technologies, Virtual Reality plays an important role. The purpose of this paper is to examine the partial outputs of the activities carried out by the Augmented and Virtual Reality Laboratory (AVR Lab) as part of the "Includiamoci" project and to discuss the first results. In particular, the contribution concerns the implementation of a virtual museum aimed at ho using the works of art created by participants as part of Art Therapy sessions: within this, participants are active subjects, prosumers of the experience, as they generate it, narrate it and enjoy it, by means of a Virtual Reality (VR) headset.

Keywords: Social inclusion · Extended reality · Well-being · Virtual museum

1 Introduction

In recent years we have witnessed a great change in the school and education system: a shift from a culture of integration to a culture of inclusion. Integration can be read as the goal of an educational strategy for the participation and involvement of people with disabilities. Instead, the term "inclusion" refers to a strategy aimed at the participation and involvement of all students, with the goal of making the most of the learning potential of the entire class group. Thus, with the shift from integration to inclusion, the scope of education is moved further, thus fitting into an educational context of increasing complexity [1].

© Springer Nature Switzerland AG 2022
L. T. De Paolis et al. (Eds.): XR Salento 2022, LNCS 13445, pp. 335–346, 2022.
https://doi.org/10.1007/978-3-031-15546-8_28

This paper aims to illustrate the activities carried out by the Augmented and Virtual Reality Lab (AVR Lab) of the Department of Innovation Engineering (University of Salento) for the "Includiamoci" project and to partially discuss its results. The project, promoted by Nova Vita Elena Fattizzo Association (Casarano, Lecce), is aimed at creating "workshops of inclusion" for people with intellectual and/or relational disabilities. The project is carried out thanks to a strategic partnership that involves, in addition to the aforementioned, the Augmented and Virtual Reality Lab (AVR Lab) of the Department of Innovation Engineering (University of Salento), and the Astragali Teatro theater company of Lecce. It involves 21 participants, 10 of whom have completed the first phase of experimentation. The specific outputs of the project are:

- the creation of social inclusion workshops aimed at creating drawings and small sculptures with modeling dough;
- the implementation of a virtual museum designed to house the works of art created by the participants, in which they can navigate and enjoy their works, by means of a Virtual Reality (VR) headset;
- a theatrical performance realized entirely by the working group, both in the performance part and in the realization of the virtual sets, through the use of Spatial Augmented Reality (SAR) techniques.

The methodology adopted by the project is based on Art Therapy methodology, designed to stimulate participants and engage them in a creative self-expression process. The decision to use Art Therapy was dictated by the countless benefits of the art-making process, allowing each person to use nonverbal language to express feelings and emotions and to be able to communicate their state of mind even in the presence of obvious difficulties [2].

The use of technologies, such as VR for the virtual museum and SAR for the digital sets, made it possible to remove physical and mental barriers, immersing participants in a walkable and visitable space in which they themselves are protagonists as creators and visitors, thus responding to the user-generated content paradigm.

2 Digital Technologies for Social Inclusion: The Role of Virtual Reality

Digital technologies are important to support the social inclusion of people with physical and mental disabilities because they enable the overcoming of barriers that the real world imposes [3]. Virtual Reality understood as a computer-generated environment, allows users to really immerse themselves in natural, fantastic, and cultural settings, establishing contact with places that would otherwise be impossible. Thanks to the headset, the user is dropped into an environment that allows having new sensory experiences, moving in a space that simulates reality but is free of physical obstacles. In the museum field, in particular, recent years have seen a shift in the audience paradigm from places intended for elites to meeting spaces for the community in its broadest sense. Full enjoyment of the spaces and collections, however, required the search for new practices and tools that would enable effective participation of people with disabilities, starting with the design of paths customized to the different learning needs of visitors. Museums today are no longer understood as exhibition spaces but as places of exchange and encounter and, by extension, also for acting on people's mental and physical well-being [4, 5]. According to the most recent studies, in fact, these places, traditionally devoted to the dissemination of culture, can produce significant psychophysical benefits, helping to increase people's self-esteem and acting on each person's sense of identity. Many institutions have, in this regard, promoted various initiatives, targeting both art therapy and tactile and immersive experiences to offer their visitors.

Among the most significant experiences in recent years is that of the "The State Tactile Museo Omero", an exhibition space that allows visitors with visual impairments to touch the works on display, some 150 plaster and resin reproductions of classical masterpieces. A similar experience was also proposed at the Uffizi in Florence, which, on the occasion of the International Day for the Rights of Persons with Disabilities, offered a tactile reproduction of Sandro Botticelli's famous *Spring*. In the Virtual Reality field, "Il Museo delle pure forme" was proposed by the Scuola Superiore Sant'Anna in Pisa in 2001. The virtual exhibition path allowed visitors to interact with the digital models of some of the works preserved in the museums that joined the project [6].

In addition to tactile paths, "Virtual Museums," can be understood as immersive presentations of collections, usable through VR headset, or as an online tour of the 360 photos of the museum halls, for remote fruition [7]. An example of the second category is offered by the "Museo della Scienza e della Tecnica" in Milan, which, in addition to making its environments almost totally accessible to visitors, has put online a virtual tour that allows everyone to walk through the story of Leonardo da Vinci, discovering his life as artist and engineer. In this sense, virtual museums simulate and present tangible and intangible heritage in digital museum form to the public [8].

In general, we can assert that by means of VR we can enhance one's presence in a virtual environment, which is a cumulative effect of immersion and interaction, it does not necessarily imply that the digital environment is a representation of a fictitious world, indeed, techniques such as photogrammetry and laser scanning are used in order to build applications that are used for the virtual reconstruction of cultural heritage places, such as a virtual museum, for improving the accessibility to some difficult places [9–11].

3   Project Methodology: From Art Therapy to the Virtual Museum

The "Includiamoci" project was designed around the idea of active involvement of participants with intellectual and/or relational disabilities having an age between 28 and 50 years.

The first phase, which started in December 2021, involved a weekly workshop, which in turn was divided into several sub-phases:

- phase 1: group knowledge and ice-breaking;
- phase 2: introduction to augmented and virtual reality technologies;
- phase 3: Art Therapy workshops (drawings and figurines);
- phase 4: implementation of the virtual museum;
- phase 5: the creation of the video interviews;
- phase 6: VR test.

During all phases, the work team consisted of one or more educators and AVR Lab team members who are experts in technology, arts, and cultural heritage. We now pass to describe these phases more in detail.

Phase 1 was dedicated to ice-breaking in order to establish a horizontal trust relationship between the participants and the working group. By means of a careful selection of images and audio and video content, participants were stimulated and accompanied in a self-presentation, about themselves and their passions. Interaction with educators made it possible to draw up personal profiles for each participant and to be able to build a safe environment for all.

During phase 2, Virtual and Augmented Reality technologies were illustrated through a variety of examples of applications that the participants themselves could experience. The simple language was used at this stage to enable understanding of complex concepts and to gain gradual knowledge of the tools. The group assimilated basic notions for the continuation of the project and subsequent content creation.

During phase 3, through colors and modeling pastes, works of art have been created to be placed within the virtual space. The working environment allowed free expression and made each user feel like an active part of the creative process.

During phase 4, we passed on to the implementation of the virtual reality application. In the beginning, we chose a museum setting from a library, and we customized the model in Blender, by creating the spotlight and the frames and the shelves for the works of art. We proceeded to create the 3D models of the sculptures by means of photogrammetry, using Agisoft Metashape. The virtual environment has four halls, aimed at housing the works, and a cinema room for viewing a narrative video made by the interview participants. The VR application has been developed in Unity, more details are going to be provided in Sect. 4.

Phase 5 involved conducting the micro-interviews in which all of the participants tell about their experiences in the laboratory. These videos have been worked in postproduction, in order to get a short trailer that summarizes all of the activities of the project. The final video has been included inside the VR application, in particular inside the cinema room. More details are going to be provided in Sect. 4.

In Phase 6, users were able to navigate the VR application and discover their artworks. After the experience, we conducted two tests in order to evaluate the User Experience on one hand, in terms of perception, interaction, and visual consistency, and the improvement of well-being on the other. We are going to analyze these data and to provide the results in a next work.

4   User Experience Design

After creating all the artistic contents, we passed to design the features of the virtual experience, in order to create a virtual museum that had all the technical and aesthetic features to make participants feel comfortable during the experience, taking into account all of the aspects of user experience (UX), and calibrating the choices on the characteristics of our target audience. In fact, UX refers to all those choices that can influence user perception and interaction, and that involve both software and hardware [12].

In the present case, these are individuals with some motor difficulties and limited ability to interact with higher-ups. These considerations, of course, influence the model of interaction achievable in the virtual environment. However, immersiveness and a sense of presence must be ensured in every way, as well as realism and visual consistency.

The goals underlying the design can be broken down as follows:

- participants must recognize that they are inside a museum;
- participants must identify their works;
- participants must move either independently or through the assistance of a tutor, while maintaining the perception of moving around;
- participants need to feel immersed in another place but, at the same time, safe;
- participants must be enticed to complete the visiting experience.

UX and gamification aspects such as mechanics, dynamics, and aesthetics were all designed in order to meet these characteristics.

For instance, of relevant importance was the choice of device for Virtual Reality: each headset on the market has different processing characteristics, computing power and quality of visual representation. Another important aspect to consider is the interaction of degrees of freedom (DoF). After a series of evaluations, the Oculus Quest device was chosen because of its visual quality, the presence of the two integrated controllers, and because of its 6 DoF (rotational and translational motion tracking), which increases spatial consistency for the user in the virtual and physical environment.

The VR application has been developed with the first-person point of view, as it makes the personal and emotional experience and interaction with virtual elements more realistic. The main configurations with respect to the user's body position that can be applied are sitting or standing. The application is designed for a seated user, keeping his or her gaze in the virtual environment at mid-height, in order to facilitate the fruition of the works.

Application features were defined based on aspects regarding gamification in order to increase user engagement and create richer and more enjoyable experiences. So the application is described according to the characteristics of game mechanics, dynamics, and aesthetics. By mechanics we mean the virtual objects and actions that the user can perform; by dynamics, we mean the responses caused by the actions; by aesthetics, we mean the audiovisual representations that evoke emotions in the user. From these levels, we can define the elements of the VR experience, for the realization of our museum:

- virtual elements that are immediately recognizable;
- setting an end goal to be achieved and gratification in achieving it;
- responses to the user's positive actions to encourage them to continue;
- audio and visual effects in the virtual environment that evoke positive feelings.

Following careful analysis and evaluation carried out between the development team and the Association's educators, two modes of walking in VR were identified, both via teleportation but with different characteristics based on the different needs and faculties of users: on the one hand, the ability to visit the museum freely and independently, on the other hand, a guided tour that simplifies user interactions with the controllers.

The design of the museum environment is intended to welcome the user into environments characterized by low and soft lighting, simple, realistic, and immersive rooms that are easy to explore (Fig. 1). The path is divided into four halls that house the hand-crafted works created by participants during the art therapy workshop. Inside the virtual museum, the drawings have been framed and hung on the walls, while the statues have been placed on display cases.

The dynamics of the game involve each user interacting with the exhibited works through a pointer that activates some 2D animation. In this way, users get visual and audio feedback on their actions, which gratifies and amazes them at the same time.

The game ends in a room of the museum, called the "cinema room", inside which the user becomes a viewer of a video projected on the big screen that summarizes the entire workshop experience.

Fig. 1. Virtual museum hall

5   Implementation

In the following paragraphs, all the steps of realization of the application will be explained in detail, and in particular, the acquisition of the sculptures by resorting to photogrammetry techniques, the animation of the drawings, the realization and editing of the video projected in the cinema hall, and, finally, the implementation of the virtual environment by means of the Unity graphics engine.

5.1   Photogrammetry of Sculptures

Once the sculptures were created and given the participants a chance to paint them, we proceeded to create the 3D models, by means of photogrammetry. This technique makes it possible to create three-dimensional models of objects of different sizes through photos taken from different angles [13]. The association of commonalities between the photos-detected in the gait and color variations of the object was carried out using Agisoft Metashape software, which is capable of returning mesh details and texture shadings with extreme precision.

The first step performed was the photo set, conducted in an enclosed environment with neutral light. Taking care to place the objects against a background that created contrast with their colors, numerous photos were taken for each sculpture through manual mode and fixed values for ISO, aperture, and shutter speed; this step is extremely important for photo processing by photogrammetry software, which will be able, with photos having the same parameters, to recognize more accurately the commonalities between different shots. For the best result, we also chose to shoot with RAW extension, so as not to lose any data from the photo.

Once the shots were taken at different angles to cover the entire surface of the object, they were imported into Adobe Photoshop 2022's Camera Raw plug-in so that each parameter (e.g., exposure, contrast, temperature, and hue) could be adjusted manually and the photos were exported in.TIF format with 16-bit color depth per channel. This choice was always motivated by the need for high-resolution photos to allow the Agisoft Metashape software to recognize with extreme accuracy every point of overlap between different photos.

The TIF files were imported to Metashape and were scanned to eliminate all those that had a quality below 0.5, so as to prevent the software from generating overlapping errors. At this point, it was possible to proceed with the alignment of the photos (called Cameras) and the creation of the Dense Cloud from the High quality and with a depth set to the Mild parameter. Once the point cloud was generated, it was cleaned of all those points that, in creating the 3D mesh, might have generated aberrations; in addition to these, the points belonging to the background were removed.

Once finished the process of creating the mesh with high quality, processing was completed with the creation of the texture (Fig. 2). This process was performed for ten sculptures selected from those made during the workshop.

Finally, to allow the created 3D models to be properly imported and read on Unity, we exported each of them with the FBX extension with the corresponding texture in.jpg format (a choice motivated by the need to minimize the file size for the memory requirements of the Oculus Quest 2).

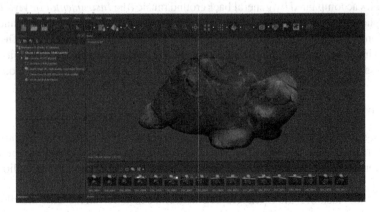

Fig. 2. Mesh 3D with texture

5.2 Drawings Animation

The activities carried out within Art Therapy workshops gave the participants the opportunity to express their creativity, working on some drawings. Each one of the participants drew and colored different subjects on papers in order to create content to be digitized and animated in post-production, through the use of Adobe Photoshop and Adobe After Effects software. The drawings were digitized by taking a photographic shot from above and then importing them into Photoshop. To carry out the animation, it was necessary to subdivide and save as separate images the different elements of each drawn figure: the main tools used were the quick selection tool and the clone stamp. The first tool served to contour the elements that would be animated in the next step, going on to create the two separate layers of the background and the cropped element.

Following the separation operation between the two layers, the next step was to fill the gap created by the contoured element, through the second tool: the clone stamp. This allows you to copy a pixelated portion of the design and duplicate it exactly in the desired area that you need to occlude. The images with their respective contoured elements were imported into Adobe After Effects to be animated: the animations were handled, within compositions, from the Timeline panel using Keyframe, and the parameters that can generally be animated are scale, position, rotation, and opacity. Considering their subsequent import into Unity, it was necessary to obtain simple, short animations (some of which had audio for the purpose of better user engagement) so as not to overburden the final virtual model.

5.3 Creating and Editing the Final Video

In order to create a heterogeneity of content within the virtual museum, in addition to the animated drawings, a video was developed that encompasses a montage of photographs taken during the drawing-making activity and video content on some of the interviews conducted. Again, it was necessary to develop a video that was not too long so as not to weigh down the model in Unity, so work was done on cropping and editing individual interviews accompanied by general background music (the *Instrumental* of *Viva la Vida* - Coldplay). In this case, Adobe Premiere Pro software was used to best handle the transitions of the individual clipped fragments of video with attached audio. The video opens with a film-style countdown that kicks off the interviews, which end with a collage of photographs of the participants surrounding the "Includiamoci" project logo.

5.4 Environment on Unity: Teleport and Triggers

The design of the Virtual Museum application "Includiamoci" consists of several stages, starting from those concerning the user's movement in the virtual world to the implementation of the experience through the inclusion of animated pictures and audio-visual content.

In the first instance, the Open XR plug-in must be installed on the Unity development platform in order to recognize and associate motion, rotation, and hand gesture inputs to each controller connected to the Oculus Quest 2 headset. The new "Action-Based" input system, through installation of the "XR Interaction Toolkit" package, contains a set of preset actions connected to individual buttons on the Oculus controllers, which can be customized if necessary. This procedure will be adopted when defining and implementing user movement in the virtual world. Twelve teleport locations were identified with equal spatial coordinates for both teleportation modes, based on the location of the displayed contents (both paintings and sculptures). In the first case, it will be possible to take advantage of the "anchor" teleport system present by default in the "Locomotion System," which handles all kinds of movement and rotation in the virtual environment. This type of teleportation allows the user to move only to a specific teleportation point, with coordinates set upstream by the developer, leaving, however, to the freedom of the user to choose on the spot which of the predetermined points to move to.

Fig. 3. Anchor teleport system

Therefore, it will be sufficient to intercept with the beam of the controllers each teleportation point marked by circular icons set up on the floor in order to make navigation faster and more intuitive (Fig. 3). Once the point is located, the XR Ray Controller will change color and you will need to press the controller's grip button (default for teleport) and then release it to make the move happen.

The second type of movement is more useful when simpler storytelling is to be proposed at the expense of a less autonomous game perspective.

In this case, customization of the preset "Input Actions" is envisaged, through the creation of new actions in the list, by selecting from the "Bindings" (literally "bindings") the button and the controller that you want to associate. Specifically, a new "Action Map" that can be renamed as "teleport" will have to be generated to which a new "Action" of type "button" will be connected, subsequently specifying from the Bindings drop-down menu the "primary Button" corresponding to the "A" button of the right Oculus controller. The choice of a button was weighted on the increased usability of the experience from a User Experience perspective, as the movement is managed by the educator with the right thumb during the game session enjoyed by the user wearing the visor.

The implementation of the command will be done through a special script that, after instantiating the 12 teleportation locations by declaring the spatial coordinates, for each "On click" on the button will vary the position of the camera, through the trick of increasing the "count" variable associated with each coordinate. The two modes of teleportation are complementary to each other: the first allows for a more autonomous and interactive use; the second adapts the virtual experience to users with disabilities, while at the same time ensuring that operators can monitor actions by mirroring the application in real time on any screen and device (smartphones, tablets, PCs and TVs).

The main functions within the game scene are designed to ensure the interaction is as simple and intuitive as possible and they are triggered by specific scripts. In particular, the user can view the 2D animations of the paintings by pointing the controller at the work itself. Under each painting, a Unity button has been placed connected to a script that allows the animation to be activated when the action is triggered, i.e., when the button is clicked. In this way, the click is triggered when the controller beam points at the painting. This is to simplify the activation of the animation and avoid the intermediate step of looking for the dedicated button and pointing at it. On the other hand, as far as the video content in the movie theater is concerned, it is activated either by guided teleport, or as an event that happens when you reach the theater, and in this case, it is placed as "Set Active" in the teleport script. Or it can be activated and deactivated in the same way as the picture animations, with a click on a transparent button that coincides with the video panel.

6   Conclusions and Future Developments

The present work aimed to illustrate an experience of social inclusiveness through the combination of art therapy activities and the use of new technologies and, in particular, Virtual Reality.

The approaches adopted during all phases of the work and extensively described here demonstrated that, for the purpose of achieving integration of all participants, the creation of a serene and confidential environment, in which everyone could feel welcome and comfortable, the inclusion of the other, understood as the recognition and enhancement of each person's differences, and teamwork, i.e., collaboration and continuous confrontation between educators and experts in *Information Communication Technology*, proved to be fundamental.

The fruitful exchange that, from the outset, has been the basis of interaction between all those involved has made it possible to pursue inclusive education, having the primary goal of guaranteeing people living in disadvantaged conditions full freedom of expression and equal educational opportunities.

The decision to introduce participants to new technologies by favoring gamification-driven didactics and simple, clear language, and to implement a virtual environment that adapted to specific physical and mental needs, was favorably received by all participants, demonstrating that, when experience is well designed and calibrated to each person's needs, new technologies can greatly reduce the limitations that the real world imposes. Although synthetic, these spaces allow each user to experience new and stimulating emotions and, by extension, freedom of thought and movement.

In conclusion, it can be argued that ICT can play a key role in social inclusion and enhancing the qualities of life enhancement, for each one, regardless of his or her physical and/or mental condition. To enjoy a virtual experience, it is not necessary to adapt to the hardware or software, rather, it must be the technology enough customizable to the characteristics of the users and allow them to fully enjoy the experience. It can, therefore, be reasonably argued that new technologies tend toward inclusiveness if the target we aimed to, or its representative organization, play an important role in the decision-making process, as we did with Nova Vita association staff when we planned the activities for the Includiamoci project.

Upcoming work will involve completing the testing of all participants and analyzing the data from the User Experience tests. Finally, more detailed information will be produced about the second technological output of the project, which is Video Mapping for the digital set design for the theatrical performance. Again, the creative, technological, and return process of the product will be described, analyzing critical issues and overall strengths of the entire project.

Acknowledgment. The project "Includiamoci" is promoted by the association NovaVita - Elena Fattizzo (Casarano) in partnership with AVRLab, of the Department of Innovation Engineering of the University of Salento and the Italian Center of the International Theatre Institute - Unesco, in collaboration with Istituto d'Istruzione Superiore Filippo Bottazzi (Casarano). The project has been co-funded by the Department of Universal Civil Service of the Presidency of the Council of Ministers under the Action and Cohesion Plan - Notice "Giovani per il Sociale – 2018".

We, therefore, thank all the operators who took part in the project, especially Cristian Fattizzo of Associazione NovaVita, who coordinated the entire project.

We thank all the participants because with their smiles they gave meaning to our work.

References

1. Resico, D.: Diversabilità e integrazione. Orizzonti educativi e progettualità. In: Pedagogia e educazione speciale, Franco Angeli (2005)
2. Gatto, C., D'Errico, G., Nuccetelli, F., DeLuca, V., Paladini, G.I., DePaolis, L.T.: XR-based mindfulness and art therapy: facing the psychological impact of Covid-19 emergency. In: DePaolis, L.T., Bourdot, P. (eds.) Augmented Reality, Virtual Reality, and Computer Graphics. LNCS, vol. 12243, pp. 147–155. Springer, Cham (2020). https://doi.org/10.1007/978-3-030-58468-9_11
3. Manzoor, M., Vimarlund, V.: Digital technologies for social inclusion of individuals with disabilities. Health Technol. **8**(5), 377–390 (2018). https://doi.org/10.1007/s12553-018-0239-1
4. Dodd, J., Jones, C.: Mind, Body, Spirit: How Museums Impact Health and Wellbeing. University of Leicester. Report (2014). https://hdl.handle.net/2381/31690
5. Silverman, L.H.: The Social Work of Museums, 208p. Routledge, New York (2010). 978-0-415-77521-2
6. Bergamasco, M., Avizzano, C., Di Pietro, G., Barbagli, F., Frisoli, A.: The museum of pure form: system architecture. In: Proceedings 10th IEEE International Workshop on Robot and Human Interactive Communication. ROMAN 2001 (Cat. No. 01TH8591), pp. 112–117 (2001). https://doi.org/10.1109/ROMAN.2001.981887
7. Gatto, C., D'Errico, G., Paladini, G.I., De Paolis, L.T.: Virtual reality in Italian museums: a brief discussion. In: DePaolis, L.T., Arpaia, P., Bourdot, P. (eds.) AVR 2021. LNCS, vol. 12980, pp. 306–314. Springer, Cham (2021). https://doi.org/10.1007/978-3-030-87595-4_22

8. Bekele, M., Pierdicca, R., Frontoni, E., Malinverni, E., Gain, J.: A survey of augmented, virtual, and mixed reality for cultural heritage. J. Comput. Cult. Herit. **11**(2), 7 (2018)

9. Katsouri, I., Tzanavari, A., Herakleous, K., Poullis, C.: Visualizing and assessing hypotheses for marine archaeology in a VR CAVE environment. J. Comput. Cultur. Herit. **8**(2), 10 (2015)

10. De Paolis, L.T., Chiarello, S., D'Errico, G., Gatto, C., Nuzzo, B. L., Sumerano, G.: Mobile extended reality for the enhancement of an underground oil mill: a preliminary discussion. In: DePaolis, L.T., Arpaia, P., Bourdot, P. (eds.) AVR 2021. LNCS, vol. 12980, pp. 326–335. Springer, Cham (2021). https://doi.org/10.1007/978-3-030-87595-4_24

11. Cisternino, D., et al.: Virtual portals for a smart fruition of historical and archaeological contexts. In: DePaolis, L.T., Bourdot, P. (eds.) Augmented Reality, Virtual Reality, and Computer Graphics. LNCS, vol. 11614, pp. 264–273. Springer, Cham (2019). https://doi.org/10.1007/978-3-030-25999-0_23

12. Ferrara, J.: Playful Design: Creating Game Experiences in Everyday Interfaces. Rosenfeld Media, New York (2012)

13. DePaolis, L.T., De Luca, V., Gatto, C., D'Errico, G., Paladini, G.I.: Photogrammetric 3D reconstruction of small objects for a real-time fruition. In: DePaolis, L.T., Bourdot, P. (eds.) AVR 2020. LNCS, vol. 12242, pp. 375–394. Springer, Cham (2020). https://doi.org/10.1007/978-3-030-58465-8_28

Author Index

Printed in the United States
by Baker & Taylor Publisher Services